Center for Modern Oriental Stucies

■ Jan-Georg Deutsch

Educating the Middlemen:
A Political and Economic History
of Statutory Cocoa Marketing
in Nigeria, 1936–1947

Studien 3

 Verlag Das Arabische Buch

Die Deutsche Bibliothek - CIP-Einheitsaufnahme

Jan-Georg Deutsch:
Educating the Middlemen: A Political and Economic History
of Statutory Cocoa Marketing in Nigeria, 1936-1947
Jan-Georg Deutsch: Das Arabische Buch, 1995
    (Studien / Forschungsschwerpunkt Moderner Orient,
    Förderungsgesellschaft Wissenschaftliche Neuvorhaben mbH; Nr. 3)
    ISBN 3-86093-095-8
NE: Förderungsgesellschaft Wissenschaftliche Neuvorhaben <München> /
Forschungsschwerpunkt Moderner Orient: Studien

Forschungsschwerpunkt Moderner Orient
Förderungsgesellschaft Wissenschaftliche Neuvorhaben mbH

Kommissarischer Leiter:
Prof. Dr. Peter Heine

Prenzlauer Promenade 149-152
13189 Berlin
Tel. 030 / 4797366

ISBN 3-86093-095-8
STUDIEN

Bestellungen:
Das Arabische Buch
Horstweg 2
14059 Berlin
Tel. 030 / 3228523

Redaktion und Satz: Margret Liepach, Helga Reher

Druck: Druckerei Weinert, Berlin
Printed in Germany 1995

Contents

List of Tables

List of Abbreviations:

A. & E.T.C.	: African and Eastern Trade Corporation
ADO	: Assistant District Officer
A.G.	: Action Group
A.W.A.M	: Association of West African Merchants
B.W.A.	: British West Africa
C.F.A.O.	: Compagnie Française de l'Afrique Occidentale
Cmd.	: Command Papers
CO	: Colonial Office
CS	: Chief Secretary
CSO	: Chief Secretary's Office
DA	: District Agent
DCI	: Department of Commerce and Industry
F.A.Q.	: Fair Average Quality
FCBWA	: Farmers' Committee of British West Africa
ICCMU	: Ibadan Co-operative Cocoa Marketing Union
Ib MinAgric	: Ibadan Ministry of Agriculture Records
Iba Prof	: Ibadan Divisional Records
NAAIE	: Nigerian Association of African Importers and Exporters
NAI	: National Archive Ibadan
NBN	: National Bank of Nigeria
NCBWA	: National Congress of British West Africa
NMTU	: Nigerian Motor Transport Union
NNDP	: Nigerian National Democratic Party
NPTU	: Nigerian Produce Traders Union
NYM	: Nigerian Youth Movement
OAG	: Officer Administering the Government of Nigeria
Ondo Prof	: Ondo Provincial Records
Oyo Prof	: Oyo Provincial Records
PRO	: Public Record Office, London
RCS	: Registrar of Co-operative Societies
S.C.O.A.	: Société Commerciale de l'Ouest Africain
SDO	: Senior District Officer
Secr.	: Secretary
SEP	: Secretary Eastern Provinces
SSP	: Secretary Southern Provinces
SWP	: Secretary Western Provinces
U.A.C.	: United Africa Company Ltd.
UNRRA	: United Nations Relief and Rehabilitation Administration

Acknowledgements

This book is based on a Ph.D. thesis, which was successfully defended at the School of Oriental and African Studies in London in November 1990. Field research in Nigeria, as well as in Britain, became feasible because of the generous financial help I received from the German Historical Institute (London), the German Academic Exchange Service, the University of London Central Research Fund and the School of Oriental and African Studies Travel Fund. I would like to thank those people who decided positively on my research funding for the trust they extended to me.

Whilst in Nigeria, I was offered ready advice from Prof. Wale Oyemakinde. I was also supported by the staff of the National Archive in Ibadan, especially by the Archivist Benjamin Evborokhap and the Assistant Archivist Olusegun Faleye, who under very difficult circumstances performed miracles in locating and producing files. I am indebted to them.

I am also grateful to the Centre for Modern Oriental Studies in Berlin, which in 1994 allowed me to undertake some further archival research in Britain and, moreover, financed the publication of this book.

Many ideas expressed in this book have been tried out in discussions I have had with Axel Harneit-Sievers, Philip Zachernuk, Paul Nugent, and Gavin Williams. Of course, all error of judgement in this study remains my responsibility, but I wish to thank them for the criticism they had freely offered.

During the time in which I wrote this book I shared accommodation with a number of friends in Hannover, London, Oxford, and Düsseldorf, who very likely learnt more about the Nigerian cocoa trade than they ever wanted to know. I would like to offer my apologies to Katja, Jenny, Regine, Axel, Oliver, Cord, Stephan, Douglas, Tom and H. Bush.

In the long period of preparing this book for publication I received invaluable assistance from Pip Austin (St. Albans), Dea Birkett (Folkstone/London) and from Margret Liepach (Berlin). They frequently had to deal with unreadable manuscripts, poor English and impossible deadlines. I am especially thankful to them.

Finally, I would like to express my sincere gratefulness to my academic teacher Prof. Richard Rathbone of the School of Oriental and African Studies in London for his unfailing enthusiasm, detailed criticism and moral support. I dedicate, however, this book to Heike Schmidt.

CHAPTER 1

Introduction

The study of the origins and history of statutory cocoa marketing in Nigeria in the period from 1936 to 1947 is justified on three grounds: the war-time West African cocoa control board was a model institution for the parastatals which mushroomed all over colonial West Africa, and especially in Nigeria, in the immidiate post-war period. In the late 1940s, for example, all major Nigerian agricultural export commodities were marketed by statutory government agencies. Furthermore, statutory cocoa marketing institutions, like the cocoa marketing boards, were used to raise large amounts of government revenue in the post-war period. Finally, the establishment of the post-war Nigerian Cocoa Marketing Board was a cornerstone in the political development of Nigeria leading to increased participation of Africans in the management of their own affairs which resulted in the formal attainment of independence in 1960.

There is a comparatively large body of source material in British and Nigerian official archives available for such a study.[1] In the relevant period, the Colonial Office published two major reports: *Report of the Commission of Inquiry on the Marketing of West African Cocoa* of September 1938 and *Report on Cocoa Control in West Africa, 1939-1943, and Statement of Future Policy* of September 1944, and a White Paper: *Statement on the Future Marketing of West African Cocoa* of November 1946 on the subject. A number of further reports were published by the Nigerian government.[2] In addition, valuable material can be found in private archives of European trading firms which were involved in the West African cocoa trade.[3]

The origins and history of statutory cocoa marketing in West Africa, and in particular Nigeria, has already attracted the attention of a number of historians and economists in the last 40 years.[4] The most influential single study was undertaken under the auspices of the Colonial Office in the early 1950s. Even today, P.T. Bauer's *West African Trade. A Study of Competition, Oligopoly and Monopoly in a Changing Economy*, published in 1954, is required reading for anyone interested in the subject. The most recent contribution to the debate is an extensive study of the history of the United Africa Company by D.K. Fieldhouse.[5]

The secondary literature offers an array of explanations as to why statutory cocoa marketing boards came into being in West Africa. Nigerian historians like W. Oyemakinde and G.O. Olusanya have maintained that statutory marketing boards were, by and large, an instrument for the exploitation of Nigerian farmers by European mercantile companies and the colonial state.[6] Other historians, in particular A.G. Hopkins and R.W. Shenton, have asserted that statutory marketing was a product of the performance of the world economy in the inter-war years and its crises, and that consequently the introduction of statutory marketing and its continuance after the Second World War should be seen as an attempt to rescue imperial capitalism.[7] A similar, if somewhat narrower, interpretation was put forward by the political economists V.D. Wickizer and G. Williams, who have argued that the establishment of marketing boards was largely a result of the failure of the 1930s free trade regime and an attempt by the European trading firms to protect their dominant position in the trade.[8] The political scientist C.E.F. Beer, however, has stressed the point that statutory marketing was a means to control the commercial profits of peasant producers[9], while the political economist B. Beckman has argued that statutory marketing came into being because of the close interaction between the colonial administration with British commercial interests and the 'over-development' of the colonial state in relation to the 'under-development' of indigenous private capitalism[10]. Finally, the economist P.T. Bauer, and the economic historians D.K. Fieldhouse and D.J. Morgan have suggested that statutory marketing was a war-time measure, whose continuation after the Second World War was largely due to the existence of strong self-perpetuating forces within the colonial administration.[11]

Despite the impressive amount of research on the evolution of statutory marketing institutions, there is no full-length historical study of the subject, which combines the use of British and Nigerian archives, as well as tries to capture both the local and the imperial perspectives. This study attempts to fill this gap. The research on the topic of this study was guided by the assumption that by working through the economic source material some new answers could be found to the basically political question of why the Nigerian government took over the control of the cocoa trade after the war. This methodology could be loosely described as a political economy approach.

Because of the abundance of source material, the focus of this book was narrowed to the history of cocoa marketing institutions in the Lagos/Benin area of Nigeria in the period between 1936 and 1947. These reference points were chosen because the 1936/37 cocoa season was the last season before the outbreak of the Second World War in which African traders could freely participate in the trade. The cut-off date 1947 is significant because the Nigerian Cocoa Marketing Board was established in that year.

This study consists of eight chapters each of which, apart from the introduction and the conclusion, highlights one particular theme in the history of statutory marketing in Nigeria. After the introductory chapter one, chapters two and three focus on the economic and then political, background of statutory marketing. They describe the evolution of the Nigerian cocoa industry and politics of the Nigerian cocoa trade. Chapter four analyses in some detail the origins of the 1937/38 conflict between African traders and European trading firms in Nigeria, its course and its political aftermath. The introduction of statutory marketing in Nigeria and the initial reaction of African traders and cocoa farmers form the subjects of chapter five. The subsequent chapter examines the impact of the war effort on the administration of cocoa control in Nigeria and its consequences for the cocoa industry. Finally, chapter seven evaluates the political and economic factors which led to the establishment of the Nigerian Cocoa Marketing Board in 1947. The book ends with a short concluding chapter.

One major problem in this study was determining the precise impact of the Second World War on the history of statutory marketing. It can be safely assumed that without the impetus of the war, the establishment of produce control boards would have been, for political reasons, exceedingly difficult. This, however, does not mean that the introduction of statutory marketing can be explained solely by war-time events. A review of the previous interpretations of the history of statutory marketing suggests that war-time changes were as much caused by developments which happened in the immediately preceding years as they were caused by the pressures and demands of the war itself. The judgement to what extent this book succeeds in disentangling in a satisfactory manner the multiplicity of these causal factors is left to the, it is to be hoped, benevolent reader.

Notes

1   See the very large number of files dealing exclusively with the marketing of cocoa in PRO: 6CO 852 (Economic Department) and NAI: CSO 26 (Chief Secretary's Office).

2   See, for example, Report of a Committee Appointed in Nigeria to Examine Recommendations Made by the Commission on the Marketing of West African Cocoa, (Chairman: E.J.C. Kelly), Nigerian Sessional Paper No. 20 of 1939, Lagos 1939.

3   See, for instance, the collection of the private papers of one of the trading firms, John Holt & Co. (Liverpool) Ltd., at Rhodes House Library, Oxford, Mss. Afr. s825.

4   Recent contributions to the subject include, for example, the articles by A. Harneit-Sievers, African Business, 'Economic Nationalism', and British Colonial Policy: Southern Nigeria, 1935-1954, paper presented to the African Studies Association Meeting, Toronto 3-6 November, 1994; D. K. Fieldhouse, War and the Origins of the Gold Coast Marketing Board, 1939-40, in: M. Twaddle (ed.), Imperialism, the State and the Third World, London 1992, pp. 153-182. R. Alence, The 1937-38 Gold Coast Cocoa Crises: The Political Economy of Commercial Stalemate, in: African Economic History, XIX (1990-91), pp. 77-104; D. Meredith, The Colonial Office, British Business Interests and the Reform of Cocoa Marketing in West Africa, 1937-1945, in: Journal of African History, XXIX (1988) 2, pp. 285-300; G. Austin, Capitalists and Chiefs in the Cocoa Hold-Ups in South Asante, 1927-1938, in: International Journal of African Historical Studies, XXI (1988) 1, pp. 63-95; G. Williams, Marketing without and with

Marketing Boards: The Origins of State Marketing Boards in Nigeria, in: Review of the African Political Economy, XXXIV (1985) 2, pp. 4-15.

5   D.K. Fieldhouse, Merchant Capital and Economic Decolonization: The United Africa Company, 1929-1989, Oxford 1994.

6   See W. Ojemakinde/R.J. Gavin, Economic Development in Nigeria since 1800, in: O. Ikime, Groundworks of Nigerian History, Ibadan 1980, p. 512; G.O. Olusanya, The Nationalist Movement in Nigeria, in: ibid., p. 549; A. Olorunfemi, Background to the Establishment of the Nigerian Cocoa Marketing Board 1947/48, in: ODU: A Journal of West African Studies, (Jan./July 1979) 19, p. 65.

7   See Shenton, The Development of Capitalism, p. 114, and A.G. Hopkins, An Economic History of West Africa, London 1973, p. 264.

8   See V.D. Wickizer, Coffee, Tea and Cocoa: An Economic and Political Analysis, Stanford 1951, p. 277, and Williams, Marketing without and with Marketing Boards, p. 7.

9   C.E.F. Beer, The Politics of Peasant Groups in Western Nigeria, Ibadan 1976, p. 238.

10   See B. Beckman, Organizing the Farmers. Cocoa Politics and National Development in Ghana, Uppsala 1976, p. 235.

11   Bauer, West African Trade, p. 267; D.J. Morgan, The Official History of Colonial Development, London 1980, Vol.III, p. 145; Fieldhouse, War and the Origins of the Gold Coast Cocoa Marketing Board, p. 176.

CHAPTER 2

The History of the Cocoa Industry, c. 1920-1940: An Overview

Cocoa farming like any other agricultural activity, depends largely on natural conditions. In Nigeria that specific combination of rainfall, temperature and soil qualities which favours cocoa production can only be found in the south-western part of the country. The core area of cocoa farming can be visualised as kidneyshaped and lies about 100 miles north-east of the country's capital, Lagos. In the late 1930s this area belonged administratively to the Western Provinces of Nigeria. While most of the cocoa was produced in the Abeokuta, Oyo, Ondo and Ijebu Provinces, some cocoa was also produced in the northern parts of the Colony of Lagos.[1]

It is not known how many farm-households were engaged in cocoa farming at the end of the 1930s. According to a survey conducted in the early 1950s, their number probably did not exceed 200,000.[2] Compared to the number of the total population living in the cocoa producing area, which was estimated to be about 4.5 million at the time, this number looks rather small. Yet, the economic importance of cocoa farming for the regional economy was far larger than such a comparison suggests. To start with, even small cocoa farmers used substantial quantities of hired labour on their farms. Furthermore, the cash income of cocoa farmers was perhaps the most important source of demand for locally produced goods and services, and also for imported goods. In addition, cocoa farmers were taxed by local Native Administrations and the Nigerian government, and for both, the revenue thus raised formed an important, though unquantifiable, part of their total tax revenue.[3]

The Growth of Cocoa Exports

Cocoa had been exported from Nigeria from as early as the mid1880s, but it was not until after the First World War that cocoa gained a significant importance in the export statistics. After the war cocoa exports grew fairly rapidly, so that by the end of the 1920s about 50,000 tons and by the end of the 1930s almost 100,000 tons were being exported annually.

The growth of cocoa exports was accompanied by a similar growth in export earnings, albeit at a very different pace. World market prices fluctuated violently throughout the period, and in the early 1930s reached such unprecedented low levels (see table one), that in some years export earnings actually decreased, while export volumes increased.[4] Despite these fluctuations, the value of cocoa exports in relation to the value of other exports from Nigeria increased in the 1920s and 1930s, so that in 1937 the value of cocoa exports accounted for almost 19 per cent of the value of all exports from Nigeria. In the same period Nigeria became one of the major world suppliers of cocoa, taking second place only after the Gold Coast (Ghana) in Africa and third place after Brazil on world scale. Together the Gold Coast and Nigeria supplied over half of the world cocoa in the 1936/7 to 1938/9 period.[5]

Table 1: Nigerian Cocoa: Seasonal Purchase Prices and Export Volumes 1916/17 - 1947/48 (Lagos f.o.b. grade II)

Season	£	Tons	Season	£	Tons
1916/17	23	(1917) 15,442	1932/33	17	71,900
1917/18	18	(1918) 10,219	1933/34	13	72,000
1918/19	20	(1919) 25,711	1934/35	15	72,300
1919/20	71	(1920) 17,155	1935/36	17	93,400
1920/21	20	(1921) 17,944	1936/37	38	101,700
1921/22	22	(1922) 31,271	1937/38	17	98,700
1922/23	24	34,600	1938/39	14	113,900
1923/24	18	34,100	1939/40	16.5	81,900
1924/25	28	40,000	1940/41	13.5	100,600
1925/26	31	41,400	1941/42	14.5	90,400
1926/27	54	45,600	1942/43	12.5	111,200
1927/28	48	45,500	1943/44	12.5	70,900
1928/29	36	52,800	1944/45	21.5	85,500
1929/30	30	54,500	1945/46	26	102,900
1930/31	19	51,600	1946/47	47.5	106,400
1931/32	18	58,300	1947/48	59	74,400

Sources: Prices: S. Berry, Cocoa, p. 223 (1916-1922); Colonial Reports (1920-1932); PRO: CO 657/47, Report of the Department of Agriculture (1939/40), p. 7 (1932-1939); Nigerian Gazette (1939-1948).
Volumes: same as above, except 1939/40. For this season see NAI: CSO 26, file 36148 S30, Reply by the Chief Secretary to the Government to Question No. 44 of 4th March 1940.
Note: Figures for export volumes from 1916/17 to 1921/22 are referring to annual exports.

Map: The Nigerian Cocoa Belt

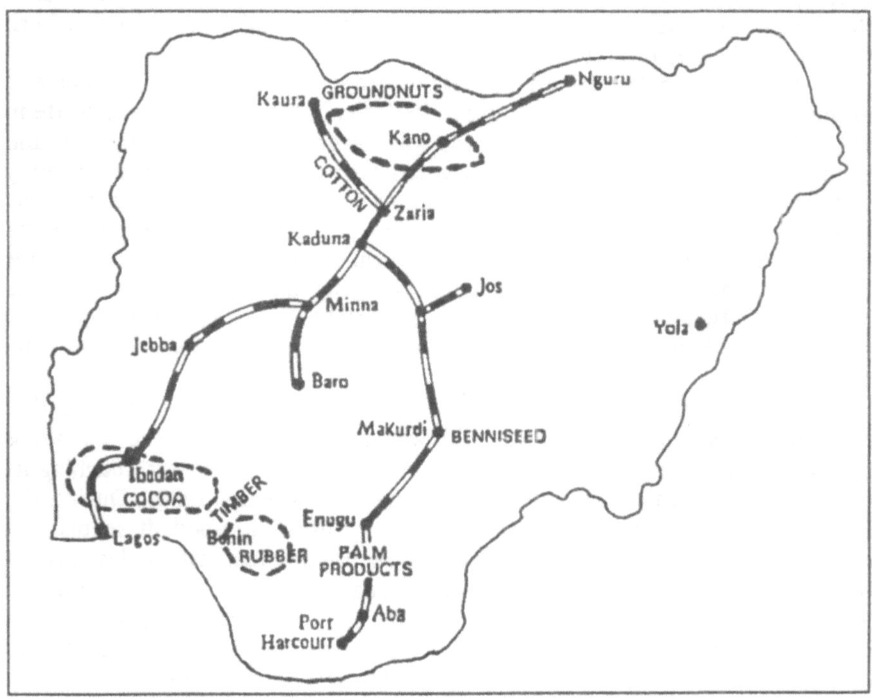

Adapted from M. Kwamena-Poh, *African History in Maps*, Harlow 1982, p. 61.

The Spread of Cocoa Farming in Western Nigeria

The history of the spread of cocoa farming in western Nigeria has been told elsewhere and it is sufficient here to summarise its major themes.[6]

Although cocoa had been known in Nigeria for some time, it was only in the 1880s that it became commercially viable. It is said that the first successful 'cocoa farmers' were Lagos traders who ventured from the palm oil trade into cocoa production as this particular trade had become unremunerative. Most of these early cocoa farms were established near Agege and Otta in the northern part of the Colony of Lagos.[7]

By the early 1890s farmers started to grow cocoa south of Ibadan and around Abeokuta. From there it spread to Ilesha in the late 1890s and to Ife in 1910. After the First World War cocoa was introduced in Ondo Province and in the Ekiti area. Most of these early cocoa farms were planted in the vicinity of towns, but as suitable land became more scarce, farmers had to move away from the towns into previously uncultivated forest areas. The expansion of cocoa farming was thus not only a geographical movement defined by its outer boundaries, but also a movement within the geographical area known as the 'cocoa belt'. By the 1920s cocoa farms were established in all the major areas of this cocoa belt, yet the spread of cocoa farming continued well into the 1960s.[8]

Before the First World War and during the war, cocoa acreage expanded at a comparatively modest rate. After the war and particularly in the late 1920s the acreage newly planted with cocoa increased rapidly each year, reaching its peak just before the onset of the Depression in the early 1930s. During the Depression and the late 1930s the rate of expansion dropped. It seems that during the Second World War cocoa farming became increasingly less attractive, and the acreage newly planted with cocoa further decreased accordingly. Though in some areas, and particularly in the Ife and Ondo areas, the acreage under cocoa grew in the late the 1940s and during the 1950s, the overall rate of expansion remained at a comparatively low level during that period.[9]

From the above it appears that between 1900 and 1960 cocoa farming was most attractive to farmers in the 1920s and 1930s. Cocoa farmers moved into previously uncultivated forest areas and as distances to the major towns increased, thousands of new settlements of a more permanent character were established. It was also during this period that cocoa production showed its most marked increases. This had important consequences for the process of cocoa marketing. As I will show later the increased distances between the cocoa farms and the market centres opened new opportunities to local entrepreneurs.

The spread of cocoa farming had been aided by a number of interrelated developments. The occupation of western Nigeria by British forces in the early 1890s ended the continuing civil war between the various factions of the dominant ethnic and sub-ethnic group of the area as well as the widespread exaction of extortionate road tolls, which had probably prevented an earlier spread of cocoa farming in the area. Once it was 'pacified', the colonial government embarked on infrastructural development. The initial expenditure involved in these undertakings was met partly by taxation, but the larger part of the expenditure was financed through loans, which the Nigerian government had raised on the London money market. The repayment of these loans later proved to be a very heavy burden on the Nigerian taxpayer. The most important project before the First World War was the building of a railway line, which reached Abeokuta in 1897 and Ibadan in 1901. After the war, the government in Lagos and the Native Administrations of the cocoa-producing areas concentrated most of their efforts on road building. In the beginning these were mostly feeder roads to the rail-way, but then roads which connected all the major towns in western Nigeria were increasingly built. By the end of the 1920s, Southern Nigeria possessed a comparatively well-developed road network.[10] This had important consequences for the development of cocoa farming in western Nigeria. The development of roads lowered transport costs and this made cocoa farming remunerative in areas in which the costs of moving produce by such means as for example head porterage, had made it previously unattractive.[11] In addition, road building and the advent of cars and particularly of light trucks gave birth to a new group of Nigerian entrepreneurs. They combined trade and transport, and it was from this group of traders that some of the most successful cocoa traders emerged.

The spread of cocoa farming was also directly supported by the Nigerian government, though only in a very limited way. The Botanical Gardens in Ebute Meta had distributed a number of cocoa seedlings and had given advice free of cost since the late 1880s. A small 'model' cocoa farm was also established in Ibadan in 1899.[12] The government was not, however, the main source of information about cocoa cultivation in western Nigeria. One source was the network of Christian teachers and missionaries, who according to one observer preached '...the gospel of coffee, cocoa, cotton and work as well as the scripture...'[13] and consequently some of the early cocoa farmers were members of Christian circles and societies. Another source were labourers, who had worked on the cocoa plantations in Agege and on cocoa farms elsewhere. When they returned to their home towns they brought with them the necessary basic knowledge about cocoa farming and perhaps cocoa seeds. A third source were traders, who saw the advantages cocoa farming could bring to farmers, and brought this knowledge back to their home towns.[14]

Yet, all this does not explain why farmers were able to move so quickly into cocoa farming and why, in particular, the late 1920s and early 1930s were the periods of its most rapid expansion. Here one has to turn to the micro-level of cocoa production. Generally speaking, as suitable land was relatively freely available until after the Second World War, even in the older cocoa-growing areas, the mobilisation of labour, its availability and price were the decisive factors which accounted for the expansion of the cocoa industry, apart from the level of cocoa prices. The immediate family was the most important source of labour used in the maintenance and expansion of cocoa farms, but hired labour (local or migrant, on a semi-permanent or casual basis) were also widely used. The attractiveness of cocoa farming was thus not only determined by the cocoa price, or the opportunity costs of producing cocoa, but also by the 'production' - costs in cocoa farming which are, in the main, labour costs.

Before the First World War and in the late 1920s high cocoa prices may have induced farmers to venture into cocoa farming, but in the 1930s the most important factor behind the expansion of cocoa farming was, according to S. Berry, not the cocoa price levels themselves, but the fact that price levels of other crops such as food crops and palm products had fallen at least as much as cocoa prices, and that labour costs had fallen as well.[15] While the first made cocoa particularly attractive to farmers who had previously farmed other crops, the latter might have generally induced farmers to expand their cocoa holdings. In the 1940s, particularly during the war, labour costs seemed to have risen substantially, while at the same time cocoa farmers received very low prices for their produce. This 'net profit squeeze' and the fact that gains from other income opportunities had increased during the war, are very likely the reason why farmers found cocoa far less attractive in the 1940s than in the 1930s.

Income and Social Stratification

There is very little statistical information available on the income and social stratification of cocoa farmers in the 1920s, 1930s and 1940s.[16] For the 1950s, however, much more detailed information is available through the research done by R. Galletti, K.D.S. Baldwin and I.O. Dina.[17] As there are no indications that cocoa farming had completely changed between the 1930s and 1950s, their research findings regarding income and social stratification are relevant to this study. There is no space to review the social structure of the cocoa economy in any detail, but three features of that economy appear to be of special importance. Galletti, Baldwin and Dina found that land, income and economic opportunities were very unequally distributed, that cocoa farmers possessed a high degree of occupational mobility, and finally, that after cocoa farming, trade was the most important source of income to the cocoa-farming households.[18]

They reported that small farmers cultivating less than one and a quarter acres, were most numerous, held little of the total land under cocoa and produced only a small part of the cocoa exported, while the large farmers with farms of more than six acres produced more than half of the cocoa exported. In the sample survey which they undertook, just 5 per cent of the families had nearly 29 per cent of the total income of the sample group. They also reported that cocoa farmers combined different types of occupation and had thus different sources of income at the same time.[19] Other income than that from cocoa sales included sales of other crops, such as kola nuts and sales of services, such as working as artisans or as labourers. The most important source of income other than sales of cocoa was trade and in particular the produce trade. Here they found two different types of farmers - those who were comparatively poor and who had made very little gains from their trading activities and those farmers who were rich and whose individual gains from trade exceeded the individual gains from other economic activities, including cocoa farming, of all farmers in the sample survey. This group of wealthy farmers are best described as farmer-traders. Together with other wealthy farmers, whose main sources of income were cocoa sales, they formed a distinct social sub-group within the rural communities, which one might loosely call nascent 'rural bourgeoisie'.[20]

The issue, to what extent these larger farmers formed a 'class' in the Marxian sense, has been discussed extensively in the secondary literature.[21] This is not a purely theoretical question, as some of the biggest farmers were also landowners with hundreds of tenants, employers of a substantial number of farm workers and finally money-lenders, who are said to have advanced substantial amounts of money to smaller farmers in the lean period of the cocoa season. Particularly at the upper levels of this rural society the categories of rich farmers, wealthy produce traders and here one should include the local political elite - the chiefs - '... merge imperceptibly into one another'[22]. If one looks at the biographies of some of the leading 'politicians' at the time, one finds that nearly all of them at one time had been produce traders and transport entrepreneurs, had tried at another time cocoa farming, and became in the end, for example, in the case of O. Awolowo, Premier of the Western Region or in the case of Sir Adesoji Aderemi I, Oni of Ife, the highest sacral/political authority in Yorubaland.[23] These are not, of course, representative examples, but they show the relative homogeneity of the group of people which I have mentioned earlier as nascent bourgeoisie. This nascent bourgeoisie was the reservoir from which the nationalistic movement, as I will show later, drew its main support and to which nationalist policies were directed.[24]

The Cocoa Consumers

Although cocoa has been known in Europe from the sixteenth century, it was only in the nineteenth century that cocoa products ceased to be a luxury and became a household item. Since then, population growth and rising per capita income has assured an ever-increasing demand for cocoa products. While world demand had amounted to only about 100,000 tons in 1900, world production rose to almost 700,000 tons in 1939, of which 39 per cent were consumed in the US, about 16 per cent in the UK and about 40 per cent in continental Europe. Germany and Austria together accounted for about 21.5 per cent of world consumption.[25]

Just before the Second World War per capita consumption of chocolate and confectionery in the UK had reached about 7 1/2 oz per week (!), and a thriving industry had developed to satisfy that demand.[26] The market leaders in the United Kingdom were Cadbury & Fry, followed by Rowntree, and British Cocoa Mills. The degree of dominance of Cadbury & Fry in the UK chocolate market can be gathered from the fact that, for example, in 1941 out of a total of 100,997 tons of West African cocoa to be distributed between the eighty-odd chocolate and confectionery manufacturers, Cadbury & Fry alone had a quota of 47,535 tons.[27] These quotas were based on pre-war consumption figures. A similar degree of concentration was prevalent in the US. The Nowell Commission reported that in 1937 the Hershey Chocolate Corporation consumed over '100.000 tons' of cocoa. In that year the total import of cocoa into the US amounted to 232.000 tons.[28]

The prices for raw cocoa which the manufacturers were prepared to pay varied enormously in the inter-war years.[29] As these prices were the basis on which 'producer prices' were calculated, it appears worthwhile to look into the reasons why these fluctuations occurred. Above all, it seems that cocoa prices are linked to the world trade cycle with its boom and gloom periods, e.g. in expectation of high chocolate sales or rising chocolate prices, manufacturers would increase their demand for raw cocoa, which in turn would drive up world cocoa prices.[30] Yet, this does not explain the short term, even daily, fluctuations of the world cocoa prices.[31] Some of these fluctuations in the 1920s and 1930s were certainly the result of speculative buying and selling operations by brokers and manufacturers, whose dealings were greatly assisted by the establishment of cocoa futures exchanges in New York and London in 1925 and in 1928, though these futures exchanges were originally designed to limit the risks of buyers and sellers in a market with particularly violent market fluctuations. At a more basic level, the fluctuations in the price were the result of a market situation in which a comparatively small over-supply or over-demand led to comparatively large price changes and in which supply and demand could not be forecast with any degree of reliability. Cocoa manufacturers relied on a continuous supply of raw cocoa, as the time cocoa could be kept in warehouses was limited to about six months. When stocks were running low and in particular in strong boom periods, manufacturers were prepared to pay nearly any price for raw cocoa as long as they could get in possession of that cocoa to keep production going.[32]

Yet, the cocoa manufacturers were not as dependent on the world cocoa market and its fluctuations as it appears at first sight. Larger manufacturers signed long-term contracts with the trading firms for future deliveries of cocoa, thereby becoming less dependent on the spot market. Moreover, as manufacturers bought only part of their cocoa requirements at a time, their average purchase price in a given period would change far less than the prices between each transaction.

Wide fluctuations of cocoa prices in the international markets as well as in the local markets of the producing countries was one of the constituent features of the cocoa trade in the inter-war years. These fluctuations had important consequences for the marketing process and were very much at the heart of the political controversies which cocoa marketing sparked off in the 1930s.

The Nigerian Cocoa Trade

The cocoa trade in Nigeria was shared out between four distinct types of traders. The first type was represented by the European trading firm. The second type was the African trader, who, although not a shipper of cocoa, controlled much of the trade in the interior. The third type were the Lebanese and Syrian traders who, by competing with the European trading firms, as well as with African traders, had found a niche for themselves in the cocoa trade. Finally, there were the Co-operative Cocoa Sales Societies and Unions. Though they were not privately owned trading firms, they should be included in the listing because the other traders or trading firms looked upon them as commercial competitors.

The European Trading Firms

The degree to which the European trading firms dominated the import and export trade of Nigeria is well documented and needs not to be reiterated in detail here.[33] Twenty firms accounted for about 90 per cent of all Nigerian non-mineral exports, and for about 58 per cent of all commercial merchandise imports in the late 1940s. They were also large employers, substantial contributors to government revenue and the capital they owned in Nigeria was estimated to amount to nearly a quarter of the total capital invested in Nigeria at the end of the 1930s.[34]

With some notable exceptions, most of the firms were "merchants", selling goods and buying produce for resale at the same time. Selling goods and buying produce were not separate activities of the firms, but rather one operation, since '...their business as buyers ... is largely carried on in order to assist them indirectly as importers'[35]. Being a seller of goods and a buyer of produce at the same time offered considerable advantages to the firms. Firstly, it made operations cheaper, as a number of fixed overhead costs could be spread over a large turnover. Secondly, savings were achieved on money transfer charges. Merchants could 'pay' for produce with goods, while acquiring their merchandise from the manufacturers with the proceeds of the produce sales.[36] Finally, a two-way trade reinforces ties with customers, as the middlemen, who sold the produce to the firms were also the firms' biggest merchandise customers. In general, the level of merchandise sales was dependent on the level of produce prices and in this respect merchants were interested in high produce prices, but as the Nowell Commission argued:

> If, for example, the alternative lay between paying £20 and £21 for cocoa, the merchant firms would clearly not choose the higher price for the sake of creating an additional £1 of purchasing power, for at best only a part of this sum could be returned to them in the shape of profits on merchandise.[37]

It appears, therefore, that these trading firms tried to conduct their business as profitably as they could on their merchandise selling side, as well as on their produce buying side, though temporary losses on one side of the trade could be made good through profits on the other side of the trade and this strengthened their competitive position vis-à-vis sole importers or exporters.[38]

During the 1920s and 1930s the number of firms in the cocoa trade had steadily decreased. Some firms went out of business completely while others were taken over by their competitors, so that by the end of the 1930s four firms accounted for over three quarters of the total cocoa export trade (see table 2).[39]

On the whole there were three reasons for this high degree of concentration. Firstly, in order to capture a sizeable proportion of the trade a firm needed considerable capital resources to conduct that trade. Secondly, cocoa was a risky business in the 1920s and 1930s. While in some years profits had been high, in other years, particularly after the First World War, during the Depression and in 1936/37, some firms had suffered great losses, and only firms with sufficient capital resources could survive this period. Finally, the fierce competition for tonnage between the European firms meant that profit margins in some years were quite low and that, moreover, even these modest profits were often only realised by successfully anticipating future trends of price movements in the world cocoa market, which of course also entailed the danger of suffering great financial losses.[40]

Table 2: Shipment of Cocoa by European Firms, 1936/37 - 1938/39, in Tons and as Percentage Shares of Total Cocoa Exports

	1936/37		1937/38		1938/39	
Shipper	Tons	%	Tons	%	Tons	%
United Africa Company Ltd.	35,202	37.35	27,734	31.75	37,842	33.23
G.B. Ollivant Ltd.	9,167	9.73	8,266	9.46	9,649	8.48
[UAL Group)	44,369	47.08	36,000	41.21	47,491	41.71
G.L. Gaiser	11,565	12.27	11,880	13.60	12,399	10.89
Cocoa Manufacturers Ltd.	11,248	11.94	8,530	9.77	12,284	10.79
John Holt & Co. (Liverpool) Ltd.	10.970	11.64	7,901	9.05	12,996	11.41
Paterson, Zochonis and Co.	5,673	6.02	6,825	7.81	6,270	5.51
Comp. Française de l'Afrique Occidentale	3,519	3.73	3,902	4.47	4,216	3.70
C. Zard & Co. Ltd.	2,310	2.45	3,538	4.05	4,878	4.28
Union Trading Comp. Ltd.	2,128	2.26	2,089	2.39	3,140	2.76
Witt & Busch Ltd.	1,192	1.26	1,714	1.96	3,039	2.67
London, Africa and Overseas Ltd.	-	-	1,413	1.62	2,367	2.08
Société Commerciale del'Ouest Africain	179	0.19	1,375	1.57	2,086	1.83
The English and Scottish Joint Cooperative Wholesale Society	742	0.79	998	1.14	383	0.34
		99.63		98.64		97.97

Note: The United Africa Company and G.B.Ollivant were both owned by Unilever (Mars, Extra-territorial Enterprises, p. 57).
Source: CSO 26, file 36148, file S 30, Nigerian Legislative Council. Reply by the Chief Secretary to Question No.44 of 4/3/1940.

The firms adopted a number of strategies to increase their profits. These were basically expansionist strategies as only an increased market share would promise higher profits. If a firm could increase its tonnage or turnover by offering, for example, slightly higher produce buying-prices, firms' profits tended to increase as more than compensatory savings were effected by decreasing unit overhead costs. As Hancock has shown, unit buying costs tended to decrease dramatically with increasing tonnage, because overhead costs of the produce trade were so abnormally high in West Africa in relation to the volume of sales. The costs of the employment of European supervisory staff contributed to these high overheads.[41]

It also appears that the desire to increase tonnage was also one of the reasons for the establishment of up-country buying stations.[42] The move from the ports to the towns in the interior had been made possible by improvements in the means of transport and communications, but had there not been consistently very low trade margins in Lagos and the desire to reduce purchasing costs by cutting out the Lagos-based middlemen and to increase tonnage, it seems very unlikely that the firms would have burdened themselves with large buying organisations with their built-in financial risks and high costs. Finally, firms could expand their market share by the acquisition of competitors, and then integrating them into their existing buying network.[43] The growth of the United Africa Company, which emerged at the end of the 1920s as the dominant firm in the import and export trade, is an example of this type of strategy.[44]

The expansionist strategy had its distinct disadvantages. In a limited market, the gains of one firm are the losses of another, and market shares were thus fiercely defended. In such a situation trade margins tend to be very small. There was, however, one principal alternative available to the firms. Firms concluded agreements with each other, which would give each firm a fixed share of the trade. In addition, the participants in such a 'pool' would agree upon a specific trade margin and produce buying and merchandise selling prices. As these buying and selling agreements will be analysed in some depth in chapters three and four, it is sufficient here to point out that these agreements rarely worked over a period of time. By restricting competition these firms tried to raise the profit margins of the participating firms, but at the same time they necessarily raised the profitability of the whole trade, and that attracted newcomers. After some time these new competitors would then force the 'Pool'-firms to abandon their price agreements as they were losing customers and trade to the newcomers, and consequently a new period of competitive buying and selling would ensue. Thus a peculiar cycle of competition and restriction developed in the 1920s and 1930s which ultimately came to an end when government control was instituted over the import and export trade at the outbreak of war in 1939.[45]

It is very difficult to come to any conclusions concerning the profitability of the trade. Above all there is a dearth of reliable data on all the major trading firms. There are, however, some data available for the United Africa Company. Between 1930 and 1937 this firm supposedly incurred losses on their cocoa trading account of £1,338,000, much of it in the 1936/37 season.[46] On the other hand, the company declared net profits on their total operations, including cocoa buying, between April 1930 and September 1937 of £4,459,950 and it also appears that in the period from September 1935 to September 1937 overall profits had been particularly high.[47] Yet, these data are somewhat misleading, as it is not known what costs had been incurred, starting with general expenses, taxes and depreciation allowances and ending with directors' fees and emoluments for the provident fund. It is also unknown where in a huge conglomerate such as the United Africa Company profits where actually made. For instance, while produce buying was rather unremunerative in the early 1930s, large profits were made on the transport side of the business.[48]

If the United Africa Company is taken as being representative of the bigger European firms, some tentative conclusions seem, however, to be valid. Firstly, the merchandise side of the firms was more profitable than the produce-buying side. Secondly, the produce trade in other commodities was probably more profitable than the cocoa trade in the 1930s as all the other major export crops were already covered by market-sharing agreements before the famous 1937/38 cocoa buying agreements were concluded. Finally, it seems that it was this imbalance which reinforced the firm's determination to work for a lasting market-sharing agreement in the cocoa trade at the end of the 1930s.

The African Cocoa Traders

It is known that most of the cocoa which the European firms exported before the Second World War was purchased from African traders (sometimes also called "brokers" or "middlemen") and not from cocoa farmers.[49] Yet, what constitutes a cocoa trader is rather difficult to define. For the majority of cocoa traders, buying and selling of cocoa was probably just one economic activity amongst others and thus the distinction between cocoa traders and other professions tended to get blurred. As I have mentioned earlier, there were large- and small-scale farmer-traders, traders who combined cocoa trading with transport businesses, and traders, whose main business was to purchase palm kernels and to sell imported merchandise, rather than to purchase cocoa.

Bearing these difficulties in mind, the internal cocoa trade system consisted of the following types of cocoa traders.[50] Most numerous were the small itinerant traders (also called pan or basket buyers). They bought small parcels of cocoa from the farmers and brought them to the next village or town markets.

Often these small traders were women and well known to the farmers, being either a relative or a member of the same community. In general, small traders had very little capital of their own and to carry out their trade they had to rely on advances given to them by bigger traders.

Next in the hierarchy of traders were the "scalemen". These traders were in charge of weighing machines, which because of their own heavy weight could not be carried around to the farms. They were mostly located in the bigger villages or at roadsides in the vicinity of major towns. They received cocoa from farmers and small traders and packed it into standardised units, usually a cocoa bag, weighing about 60 kg to 65 kg. Like the small traders, their trading capital resources were extremely limited.[51]

Before the cocoa ultimately reached the European trading firms, in most cases it passed through another layer of cocoa traders. These were either independent produce traders, commission buyers or the firms' depot clerks, who bought cocoa on their own account and sold it afterwards to the trading firms. Depot clerks (also called factors or depot agents) received a small salary and also a commission on the tonnage they handled. They were often also sellers of merchandise and were required by the firms to provide security for the merchandise which they had in stock and for the cash which was entrusted to them to buy produce. The position of the smaller commission buyers (also called agreemented buyers) was very much akin to that of the depot clerks and indeed the firms looked upon them as such, though they considered themselves more as independent traders. These commission buyers often worked from stores which were either rented or leased by their firms and were also supplied with the goods necessary to conduct their trade, such as scales, bags, twine and tarpaulin. The trading capital these commission buyers worked with was largely, though not completely, owned by the trading firms and thus they also had to provide security for the money entrusted to them. They too were paid according to the tonnage they handled, though their commission rates were usually higher than the rates depot clerks received. In addition, they were paid a retaining fee during the off season. Finally, at the top of the hierarchy of cocoa traders were the more independent produce brokers. The smaller independent cocoa traders were almost indistinguishable from the larger commission buyers, because a large part of their working capital was in fact provided by the firms, but the wealthy and most successful ones owned their own stores and in some cases their own transport businesses. Some of them also had substantial cocoa farms. They employed their own commission buyers and some of them maintained buying organisations very similar to those owned by the European trading firms. They partly operated with their own capital and received commission rates, which increased with the amount of cocoa they sold to the firms. These 'overriding' commissions far exceeded the commission rates other cocoa buyers received.

The commission rates were, however, only part of the income or profit cocoa traders gained. Cocoa traders could pocket the difference between the prices which they paid farmers or smaller traders for their produce and the prices which they received from the trading firms or, in the case of smaller traders, from cocoa buyers higher up in the hierarchy. This difference varied considerably between different areas of the cocoa belt and depended to a large extent on the degree of competition between cocoa buyers in these areas. There were, however, some other devices to increase price differences. Apart from outright abuses, such as using false weights, cocoa traders sometimes combined money-lending with produce trading. By borrowing money during the off-season, some farmers became tied to specific traders who were thus, in some cases, able to depress purchase prices artificially. As I will show later the evidence on the incidence of the combined activity of money-lending and produce trading is rather limited and in contrast, for example, to cocoa trading in the Gold Coast, has probably played no major role in the cocoa trade in Nigeria.

Finally, some of the biggest independent traders also exported cocoa. Though there had been numerous attempts by Africans to venture into that trade before the First World War and in the inter-war years, nearly all of them had been shortlived. This was mainly due to the crash after the First World War and to the Depression, but also as a result of fierce competition which they faced from the European trading firms and their business practices. At the end of the 1930s just a handful of traders maintained business links with mainly British brokers and for example their total cocoa exports in 1938/39 amounted to just 873 tons, but as I will show in chapter three, this is not an adequate measure of their strength vis-à-vis the European trading firms. A produce trader such as T.A. Odutola exported only 250 tons of cocoa in the 1938/39 season, yet, his total seasonal turnover amounted to 4,000 to 5,000 tons.[52] In the late 1930s he had built up his own buying organisation and largely financed his own trade, though he also received advances from one of the bigger European trading firms (John Holt & Co.).

The main local competitors to the African traders were not just the European trading firms, but also a relatively small number of traders of Greek and Lebanese (Syrian) origin who had come to Nigeria after the First World War.[53] Yet most of them lived in Northern Nigeria, where they had captured a substantial share in the groundnut trade, though they could also be found in any part of Nigeria, trading primarily in imported merchandise. There were also some Greek and Lebanese traders who in the 1920s and 1930s had ventured in the palm produce and cocoa trade, such as S. Thomopulos, C.S. Mandrides, A. Flionis and C. Zard. Most of these traders were tied to specific trading firms, like, for example, S. Thomopulos to the United Africa Company, but at the end of the 1930s they had started to export cocoa on their own account. These exports amounted to about 900 tons in 1938/39, though their turnover was, as in the case of the African traders, far bigger than this number suggests.[54] Like their African competitors, they combined produce trading with transport businesses.

African traders had mounted repeated campaigns against what they perceived as the 'Syrian threat', especially against their incursions into the business areas, such as the small merchandise and produce trade, which African traders regarded as their 'natural' domain.[55] These campaigns did not meet with much success before the Second World War. However, after the war, the colonial government became increasingly amenable to demands by African traders to restrict 'Syrian' business activities.[56]

From the point of view of the European trading firms, there was not much difference between the African and the Syrian traders. At least in the 1920s and 1930s the hostility shown towards African traders was equally matched by a marked hostility towards Syrian traders. They both appeared to challenge the hegemony of the European trading firms in the export trade and even more so in the internal trade. Trade practices, such as the elimination of competition between the participants of the Buying Agreement of 1937/38, were thus directed against both the Syrian and African traders alike.

The Co-operative Societies

Farmers' associations for the marketing of cocoa had been founded even before the First World War,[57] but probably because of the little cocoa which was exported at the time, these societies did not receive much attention from the government. This changed after 1918, when the government, and in particular the Agricultural Department, became involved in schemes to improve the quality of cocoa exported from Nigeria. It was, however, not until 1932 that the support of co-operative cocoa marketing societies was declared to be the official policy of the Agricultural Department. This was to some extent a reaction to the spectacular bankruptcy of the Ibadan Cooperative Planters' Association, a cocoa marketing society which consisted largely of wealthy farmer-traders.[58] In 1933 the Agricultural Department reorganised the cocoa marketing societies in the Ibadan area and in 1934 the Ibadan Co-operative Marketing Union was founded, which marketed cocoa centrally for its member societies. The supervision of the co-operative societies was strengthened by the promulgation of the Co-operative Societies Ordinance of 1935, which stipulated that marketing and thrift societies had to register with the Agricultural Department and that detailed accounts of the societies' transactions had to be kept. The Agricultural Department would then examine these accounts at least once a year. As the number of societies increased, it became necessary to create a special post of a Registrar of Co-operative Societies and in 1936 E.F.G.Haig was appointed.[59] Haig was a staunch supporter of the 'co-operative movement' and it is partly due to his efforts that co-operatives achieved the importance they did in subsequent years.[60]

At the end of the 1930s about 9,000 cocoa farmers were individual members of over 100 cocoa marketing societies which seasonally marketed about 5,000 tons of cocoa.[61] Until the 1937/38 cocoa season, most of the societies' cocoa was sold to the European firms by tender and the societies were usually able to secure for their members a premium over the price paid to other farmers of at least £1 per ton. After paying a levy of 10s per ton to the society, the member still had a net premium of at least 10s over the non-member. The European firms paid this premium as they were able to economise on their own marketing expenses by buying large parcels of cocoa. Another reason was probably the desire to show the government that the firms supported its policies.[62]

Both the European firms and the African traders regarded the co-operative societies as their potential competitors. Though the actual turnover of the societies was comparatively small, the African traders, and to some extent the European firms, feared that the government would introduce measures which would enable the societies to capture an increasingly larger share of the seasonal crop. This seems to be one of the reasons why African traders showed such remarkable hostility towards the co-operative societies.[63] The position of the European firms was more subtle. They publicly supported government policy towards the co-operative societies[64], but behind 'closed doors' their attitude was different[65] and rather similar to the position of the African traders.

The Cocoa Trade System

The cocoa marketing process can be visualised as a tributary system of a large river. Cocoa flows in small quantities from the widely dispersed farms to a smaller number of villages. From there it proceeds in increasing volume to the towns, and finally to the ports.[66] Like a tributary system this is a seasonal process as most of the cocoa is usually sold in the four months between November and February.

As mentioned earlier, cocoa passes through various hands in this process.[67] In the 1930s most of the farmers' cocoa was sold to itinerant traders, who bought small quantities of cocoa and sold small amounts of merchandise. Some cocoa was also bought by wealthier farmers and farmer-traders or sold directly to the firms. The price which itinerant traders and farmer-traders paid for cocoa was fixed in relation to a given volume of cocoa, such as a basket or a tin can. According to the quantity purchased, the cocoa was then either sold to scalemen, who operated weighing machines in the bigger villages or at the roadside in the vicinity of larger towns, or to commission buyers and produce traders, who also operated weighing machines, but were located in the bigger towns and who mostly purchased larger quantities of cocoa. After being weighed, the cocoa would be packed into bags and stored. Transport was delayed until enough produce had been collected because traders wanted only fully-loaded lorries to leave their stores, thereby economising on freight costs. That was the reason why even at the up-stream end of the flow cocoa was stored in sizeable amounts. The cocoa purchased by scalemen was immediately resold to larger traders or to the firms' depot clerks as normally they did not own storage or transport facilities. The commission buyers and produce traders then transported the cocoa to the produce-buying stores of the European firms, which were located in the bigger towns of western Nigeria such as Abeokuta, Ife, Ibadan, Ilesha and Ijebu-Ode or brought directly to the firms' stores in Lagos. Most produce-buying stores were also merchandise-selling stores and thus on their return journeys the lorries often carried consumer goods back to the cocoa-producing areas.[68] Finally, in Lagos the cocoa was again stored until shipment to the UK and other destinations in Europe.

At each stage in the marketing process a different price was paid for the produce. The difference between the price at which cocoa changed hands on the farms and the world market price consisted essentially of marketing costs such as, for example, transport and general overhead costs, of the remuneration for the intermediaries involved, and also of duties which the Nigerian government levied on the export trade and the British government on the import trade.

The way in which cocoa was marketed by the European trading firms in the 1930s almost always followed the same pattern.[69] Before the season started, the firms had to assess the current state of the world cocoa market and had to make a judgement about its likely future development.

The firms deducted a more or less fixed schedule of marketing expenses and a profit margin from the price they thought they would get for a given quantity of cocoa in the UK or elsewhere. This price was then cabled to the branch offices of the firms in Lagos and represented the maximum price local agents were allowed to pay.[70] The marketing schedule consisted of a variety of different items, such as freight and shipping charges, the overhead costs of the firms on the coast as well as office expenses in the UK, interest on the capital used during the transactions, and residual costs, for example the costs of twill bags and twine.[71] The schedule also contained an allowance for the payment of commission to produce traders and smaller buyers. When the firms bought cocoa up-country another schedule was subtracted which mainly covered the transport costs between the up-country buying stores and the firms' main stores in Lagos.

Table 3: Average Monthly Cocoa Prices, Paid in Lagos, 1924/25-1939/40 (ex scale, grade II, £ per ton)

	1924/25			1925/26			1926/27			1927/28		
	£	s	d	£	s	d	£	s	d	£	s	d
Oct.										51	5	0
Nov.	[October 1924 - December 1926:									50	10	0
Dec.										46	0	0
Jan.	no figures available]						60	0	0	47	0	0
Feb.							57	10	0	49	10	0
Mar							61	14	4	49	0	0

	1928/29			1929/30			1930/31			1931/32		
	£	s	d	£	s	d	£	s	d	£	s	d
Oct.	38	11	7	32	10	0	25	15	0	17	1	11
Nov.	36	0	8	30	0	0	20	13	2	19	13	4
Dec.	35	7	5	32	0	0	18	15	8	18	8	1
Jan.	33	6	8	33	2	6	18	2	6	16	15	0
Feb.	37	8	4	32	5	0	17	0	0	15	15	0
Mar	37	10	0	29	17	6	16	10	0	16	9	4

	1932/33			1933/34			1934/35			1935/36		
	£	s	d	£	s	d	£	s	d	£	s	d
Oct.	17	17	6	12	6	10	12	9	1	16	9	10
Nov.	17	16	0	12	1	7	13	6	11	16	6	1
Dec.	17	15	0	10	12	3	14	13	8	16	18	8
Jan.	16	9	9	12	9	9	16	14	4	17	13	2
Feb.	15	18	0	16	9	1	16	14	1	16	5	0
Mar	15	18	0	16	17	11	16	1	11	18	5	0

Table 3 continued

	1936/37			1937/38			1938/39			1939/40		
	£	s	d	£	s	d	£	s	d	£	s	d
Oct.	30	10	2	19	16	6	15	0	11	15	6	5
Nov.	34	8	2	18	4	0	14	7	3	15	12	1
Dec.	42	5	2	15	5	6	13	12	6	16	2	6
Jan.	45	1	9	16	8	9	13	10	11	16	2	6
Feb.	38	2	2	16	10	6	13	8	6	16	2	6
Mar	38	14	5	16	9	2	13	15	5	16	2	6

Source: PRO: CO 657/47, Administrative Reports 1939/40, Department of Agriculture, p. 7.
Rhodes House Library (Oxford), J.R. Mackie Papers, Vol.III, pp. 39-42
Note: Price fixed by Ministry of Food since December 1939.

In the 1930s, cocoa world market prices were particularly volatile and fluctuated during and between the seasons. The firms therefore had continuously to adjust local purchase prices to the changing world market prices.[72] The firms' headquarters in Europe thus daily and sometimes even more than once a day cabled new price limits to the branch offices in Lagos, which then relayed these price changes to the up-country buying stores. The local offices were always allowed to pay less than the cabled price limits, but as stated earlier competition between the firms kept purchase prices relatively close to the price limits set by the head office in Europe. In the season in which no market sharing agreement was in force, the price limits and thus local prices varied considerably between the firms and, in order to capture a sizeable proportion of the crop, firms had to watch carefully the prices offered by the other firms. Sometimes firms themselves did not set price limits but advised their local managers 'to follow competition'.

The price African traders received varied thus from day to day and between firms, which in turn made cocoa trading at the local level a highly speculative business. Though less formalised, African traders too had to budget for marketing costs, such as transport and, in the case of the larger buyers, commission for scalemen and basketbuyers. They also had to make a judgement about future price movements. As it took days or even weeks to move produce from the farms to the next cocoa buying station, and between the purchase and the sale, cocoa prices at the produce-buying store could have changed greatly. Though produce buying might have been less competitive for African produce buyers than for their European counterparts, it appears that African traders on the whole could not substantially depress the purchase price. Village prices, particularly in the cocoa-producing areas in the vicinity of large towns, such as the cocoa-producing areas south and east of Ibadan, followed produce store prices. In areas further away from towns, however, it seems likely that a lesser degree of competition allowed produce traders to pay prices which lay much below the prices offered at the firms' produce-buying stores.[73]

The Flow of Credit

The flow of produce from the farms to the ports was matched by an equal and opposite flow of money, credit and goods. Money and goods were primarily used for the payment of produce. Credit, however, made the movement of produce feasible.

Most produce traders did not have sufficient capital resources to buy produce in sizeable amounts. The firms thus gave advances to traders against the promise of future deliveries. Basically the firms offered credit because they could not get produce otherwise and an extension of the firms' buying organisations into every village in the cocoa-producing areas was not considered commercially viable.[74] In the 1930s the United Africa Company, for example, thus purchased about 85 per cent of its cocoa by means of advances.[75] The bulk of the advances were made interest free during the crop season. Most traders received relatively small advances in August, just before the beginning of the crop season; advances then increased and reached their height during December; then advances decreased so that by March most traders no longer had any debt outstanding with the firms.[76] The time for which advances were given was variable, ranging from days to months and averaged about three weeks. A trader therefore could renew his advance a number of times and as often as he returned cocoa to the firms' buying stores. On the average produce traders turned over their advances three to five times during a season.[77] The total of all advances did not equal the value of the crop purchased during a season as traders used their own resources alongside the firms' money, the amounts of which are unfortunately unknown. The sum which was necessary to move the crop from the farms to the port should not, however, be over-estimated. In the Gold Coast, for example, in which trading conditions were very similar to those of western Nigeria, it was thought that a capital outlay of £300,000 would be sufficient in the late 1930s to move a crop more than twice the size of the Nigerian crop from the farms to the produce-buying stations of the European firms.[78] The firms demanded some form of security for their advances, which was provided by the deposit of either cash and valuables or by deposits of deeds of buildings and in some cases of land if the trader had property in the Colony of Lagos, where British property law was applicable. Most common, however, were guarantees of sureties of standing, though it was usually very difficult to make sureties pay when a trader defaulted on his advances. The size of the advance depended not only on the security provided: performance in previous seasons as much as the personal relationship between the branch manager of the firm and the larger African traders determined the amount of money advanced. The terms on which advances were handed out to traders were usually fixed in written agreements. These agreements specified the amount of money advanced, the remuneration which traders would receive, and sometimes certain items which traders needed to conduct their businesses such as bags and twine. The agreement usually also specified the price at which cocoa would be bought. Yet, apparently the European trading firms were not able to force their buyers to accept agreements which would also specify when produce had to be delivered after the advance had been handed out, nor a clause that cocoa buyers had to declare their stocks, when a price change occurred. This gave even the traders who were tied to specific firms and received a monthly salary a large measure of de facto independence, of which they made increasing use in the second half of the 1930s, as will be shown further down.

The way in which cocoa traders worked in the Gold Coast was very similar to that in Nigeria. Therefore, in the absence of any direct evidence from Nigeria, it is justified to give one example from Nsawam in the Gold Coast to illustrate how the trade worked.[79] The broker in question had a cash deposit with John Holt & Co. On 1st September, 1936 his security amounted to £23. He then received an advance from John Holt & Co. and started buying. Until 31st March, 1937 he had bought 217 tons of cocoa on the firm's account and in addition 50 tons on his own account, thus selling all in all 267 tons to the firm. He bought cocoa at an average price of £36 18s 3d and resold at £38 13s 3d. He thus made a gross profit of about £467 on the difference between the buying and selling price. In addition, he received a commission of 15s per ton, which gave him another £200. Thus his gross profit amounted to £667 at the end of the season on a turnover of £10,322.[80] This might have been an exceptional season and an exceptional case, it shows however, that a relatively small security with a firm did not prevent traders from achieving quite a substantial turnover; that at least this particular trader apparently had considerable resources of his own and finally, that produce buying in some cases was a very profitable undertaking.

As stated above, most of the larger traders did not buy produce from the farmers themselves but purchased cocoa from smaller buyers. As most of these smaller buyers too did not have sufficient resources, they received advances from the larger buyers. Most of the advances were made during the season, but also a sizeable part during off season. Most of these advances were probably made from the larger traders' own capital resources as the firms usually did not hand out substantial advances before the season had started. Advances from larger to smaller buyers were guaranteed by some form of security, which could be the usufruct of the smaller buyers' own cocoa farms or sureties of local standing.[81] The relationship between larger traders and smaller buyers was probably not just an economic one. By accepting advances from a trader, who was usually also an important member of the local community and more often than not also a traditional titleholder (Chief), the smaller buyer became a client, who owed his patron some form of political allegiance. This probably gave the relationship between the bigger traders and smaller buyers a coherence which was absent in the relationship between the larger traders and the European trading firms. This in turn probably provided an additional security for the advances made to smaller buyers. Sometimes these advances were interest-bearing and in these cases produce buying became indistinguishable from money-lending.

Advances received from larger traders were either used by smaller buyers to purchase cocoa directly from farmers or were re-lent to the smallest category of traders, the itinerant basket-buyers. In the 1930s most of the cocoa was bought during the season, but a substantial, if unknown, part was bought in advance of the cocoa season.[82] Smaller traders and basket-buyers advanced money to farmers in the off-season mainly in order to secure the farmers' crop, thereby increasing their volume of trade and commission. The larger farmers particularly needed money to pay wages to labourers engaged in the maintenance of the cocoa farms during the off-season, but some money was also borrowed in order to establish new cocoa farms. In addition, farmers borrowed money, when extraordinary expenses had to be paid. Most of these advances were repaid either in cash or in kind after the cocoa had been harvested. Only some of these advances and particularly the ones which were repaid in kind were "interest" bearing, insofar as in the latter case the value of the cocoa received by traders in order to redeem the loan far exceeded the value of the loan. Again, in these cases there was no clear distinction between produce-buying and money-lending.

The evidence on the degree of indebtedness of cocoa farmers in the 1930s and 1940s is inconclusive.[83] It is known, however, that farmers received loans not only from traders, but also from wealthy farmers and from money-lenders. Interest rates and repayment periods were variable, ranging from zero interest to over 500 per cent, and from 40 days to indefinite.[84] Sometimes neither interest rates nor repayment periods were fixed in the loan agreements. Instead a farmer would promise to repay 1cwt of cocoa for each £1 borrowed some time in the future. Sureties for advances were given in various forms. Most common was probably the pledge of the usufruct of a cocoa farm, but sometimes the cocoa trees themselves were offered as a guarantee for the advance. In some cases the advance and the interest on it was paid in labour as sons of the debtor had to work on the farms of the creditor to redeem the loan. Yet, it is not known how many farmers were indebted and, in particular, how many farmers were indebted to produce traders in Nigeria in the 1930s and 1940s and that makes any judgment on the degree of indebtedness of cocoa farmers to produce buyers exceedingly difficult, if not impossible.[85] Research in the early 1950s, however, suggests that the degree of indebtedness had probably been over-estimated by officials in the 1930s.[86]

It has been repeatedly suggested in the secondary literature that the firms ultimately financed the advances which farmers received.[87] On the basis of the available evidence this statement has to be qualified. Most farmers borrowed against the future delivery of cocoa a considerable time before the actual buying by the firms started. Yet, the firms handed out most of their advances during the season after buying had started and tried to close the accounts with cocoa traders when actual cocoa buying had subsided.[88] It appears therefore that a large part of the off-season advances to cocoa farmers were financed from the cocoa traders' own capital resources. Moreover, there is some evidence which shows that the largest portion of the debt held by cocoa farmers was long-term loans, borrowed by wealthier farmers from money-lenders at high interest rates.[89] For these reasons it seems very unlikely that the trading firms' advance system had caused the long-term indebtedness of cocoa farmers.

Notes

1   R. Galletti/K.D.S. Baldwin/I.O.Dina, Nigerian Cocoa Farmers, Oxford 1956, p. 25; S.S. Berry, Cocoa, Custom and Socio-Economic Change in Rural Western Nigeria, Oxford 1975, p. 41. For an administrative history of the area see Lord Hailey, Native Administration in the British African Territories, London 1951, part. III, p. 9.
2   Galletti et al., Nigerian Cocoa Farmers, pp. 10-12.
3   See Galletti et al., Nigerian Cocoa Farmers, pp. 10-12 and pp. 94-107; G.O. Orewa, Taxation in Western and Mid-Western Nigeria, Ibadan 1979, pp. 1-14. For an estimate of import duties paid by cocoa farmers between 1936 and 1947, see appendix, table IV.
4   For the growth of export earnings see G.K. Helleiner, Peasant Agriculture, Government and Economic Growth in Nigeria, Homewood/Illinois 1966, tables 4-A-7 and 4-A-8. There are some unexplained inconsistencies between the cocoa prices given by different authors for certain years. For example, Berry, Cocoa, p. 223, table 3, gives different figures for 1933 and 1936 from Helleiner, Peasant Agriculture, table II-8-1.
5   M. Perham (ed.), Economics of a Tropical Dependency, Vol. I, pp. 8-9. For historical data on world production and consumption of cocoa, see Gill & Duffus Ltd., Cocoa Statistics, London, April 1981, p. 4.
6   This account of early cocoa farming draws heavily on research by Berry, Cocoa, chap. 2, pp. 37-53, and chap. 3, pp. 54-89.

7 The first successful cocoa farm in Nigeria was apparently established by a Lagos-based merchant named J.P.L. Davies near a small village called Ijan, in the vicinity of Lagos. See A.G. Hopkins, Innovation in a Colonial Context: African Origins of the Nigerian Cocoa-Farming Industry. In: C. Dewey and A.G. Hopkins (eds.), The Imperial Impact: Studies in the Economic History of Africa and India, London 1978, p. 88. See also J.B. Webster, The Bible and the Plough, Journal of the Historical Society of Nigeria, (1960-1963) 2, p. 425.

8 Berry, Cocoa, pp. 41-45, 57 and 163.

9 Galletti et al., Nigerian Cocoa Farmers, appendix, table IV, pp. 614 and 626, and O. Oni, An Economic Analysis of the Provincial and Aggregate Supply Response among Western Nigerian Cocoa Farmers, University of Ibadan Ph.D. thesis, Ibadan 1971, pp. 135-136; cf. Berry, Cocoa, p. 86.

10 J.A. Atanda, The New Oyo Empire: Indirect Rule and Change in Western Nigeria, 1894-1934, London 1973, pp. 217-219; see also W.I. Ofonagoro, Trade and Imperialism in Southern Nigeria, 1881-1929, New York 1979, pp. 201-207 and p. 403.

11 A. MacPhee, The Economic Revolution in British West Africa, London 1926, p. 118; W.I. Ofonagoro, Trade and Imperialism in Southern Nigeria, 1881-1929, New York 1979, p. 203.

12 Ibid., p. 224; see also NAI: CSO 26, file 39313. Letter from the Director of Agriculture to the CS, 20 April 1942.

13 Webster, The Bible and the Plough, p. 426.

14 Berry, Cocoa, pp. 40-45.

15 Ibid., p. 85; see also J.D.Y. Peel, Ijeshas and Nigerians: The Incorporation of a Yoruba Kingdom, 1890s-1970s, Cambridge 1983, pp. 119-120 and appendix, table III.

16 Though one should mention Forde's study of the late 1930s as a notable exception. See D. Forde, The Rural Economy of the Western Provinces. In: M. Perham, Economics of a Tropical Dependency, Vol.I, London 1946, pp. 78-101. For a descriptive account see Peel, Ijeshas and Nigerians, pp. 114-145.

17 Galletti et al., Nigerian Cocoa Farmers, p. 614.

18 Ibid., pp. 227, 274-286, 551-559, 592-593.

19 Ibid., pp. 149 and 227.

20 Many Yoruba farmers spent some part of the year in towns, despite the fact they obtained their incomes from agriculture. Therefore a clear-cut sociological division between urban and rural polities is somewhat problematic. The term 'rural bourgeoisie' is here only used to describe the main source of their income.

21 See, for example, the discussion in Berry, Cocoa, pp. 181-182; A.G. Hopkins, An Economic History of West Africa, London 1973, p. 239; G. Williams, The Social Stratification of a Neo-Colonial Economy: Western Nigeria. In: C. Allen/R.W. Johnson (eds.), African Perspectives. Papers in the History, Politics and Economics of Africa, Presented to T. Hodgkin, Cambridge, 1970, pp. 225. See also G. Austin, Capitalists and Chiefs in the Cocoa Hold-Ups in South Asante, 1927-1938. In: International Journal of African Historical Studies, XXI (1988) 1, pp. 67-69. It is noteworthy that the historiographical debate about the appropriate use of the term 'peasantry' has largely avoided to discuss the case of West African cocoa farmers. See F. Cooper, Peasants, Capitalists and Historians. A Review Article. In: Journal of Southern African Studies, VII (1980) 2, pp. 284-314.

22 This phrase is borrowed from R.J. Southall, Farmers, Traders and Brokers in the Gold Coast Economy. In: Canadian Journal of African Studies, XII (1978) 2, p. 187.

23   P. Ogunshakin, The End of an Epoch: Sir Adesoji Aderemi I, KBE., KCMG., Oni of Ife, (1930-1980), Lagos 1981, p. 4.

24   For a more descriptive account of the emergence of the 'Yoruba Middle Class', see P.C. Lloyd, Cocoa, Politics and the Yoruba Middle Class, West Africa, (17 Jan. 1953), p. 39. See also J.D.Y. Peel, Ijeshas and Nigerians: The Incorporation of a Yoruba Kingdom, 1890s-1970s, Cambridge 1983, pp. 136-145.

25   V.D. Wickizer, Coffee, Tea and Cocoa. An Economic and Political Analysis, Stanford 1951, pp. 303-306 and 320, table 17. These figures are related to the 1936-1939 period.

26   For the per capita consumption of chocolate and confectionery in the UK before, during and after the Second World War, see Cocoa, Chocolate and Confectionery Alliance (ed.), International Cocoa Conference 1948, Proceedings, Speech by P.S. Cadbury, p. 85.

27   PRO: MAF 75, File 31. Official History of the Ministry of Food during the War, p. 93.

28   Report of Commission of Inquiry on the Marketing of West African Cocoa (Chairman: W. Nowell), Cmd. 5845 of Sept. 1938, para. 397. (Thereafter cited as Nowell Report).

29   For a price series, which is based on actual purchases, see Cadbury Ltd. (Birmingham), Minutes and Reports 1934-1939, Report for the Year ending 30 September 1938 by A.V. Iredale, 1 February 1939. This report shows that between 1930 and 1938 prices for high quality cocoa varied in the Agege area between £ 12 2s per ton in 1934 and £ 44 9s per ton in 1937! For a price series, based on customs records, see table 3.

30   Galletti et al., Nigerian Cocoa Farmers, pp. 4-6.

31   For a series of daily prices offered for cocoa in Ibadan between 1st Jan., 1937 and 1st Feb., 1937, see John Holt Papers, Rhodes House Library Oxford (thereafter Holt Papers), Mss. Afr. s825 file 535(I). Statement of Purchases at Labipon No. 1 Store, Ibadan (1938); see also Nowell Report, table IVb, p.126. For a similar price series, see Cadbury Papers, University of Birmingham (thereafter Cadbury Papers), file 352, Nigerian Cocoa Purchases, 10 October 1936 - 20 February 1937.

32   Wickizer, Coffee, Tea and Cocoa, pp. 271, 274 and 365-366.

33   P.T. Bauer, West African Trade. A Study of Competition, Oligopoly and Monopoly in a Changing Economy, Cambridge 1954, pp. 71 and 220.

34   J. Mars, Extra - Territorial Enterprises. In: M. Perham, Economics of a Tropical Dependency, Vol.II, London 1948, p. 57.

35   Nowell Report, para. 325 and W.K. Hancock, Survey of British Commonwealth Affairs, Vol.II, Problems of Economic Policy, 1918-1939, London 1940, p. 209.

36   NAI: CSO 26, file 36148 S73 Vol. I. West African Cocoa Control Board Memorandum No. 38, Control of West African Cocoa, 12 June 1941, p. 5.

37   Nowell Report, para. 424.

38   Hancock, Survey, p. 209. See also Holt Papers, Mss. Afr. s825 file 535(I). Evidence submitted to the cocoa commission by Mr. J.F. Winter, District Agent, Lagos, April 1938.

39   Mars, Extra-Territorial Enterprises, pp. 47-50.

40   Bauer, West African Trade, pp. 104-119 and Hopkins, An Economic History, p. 202. For the firms' view see United Africa Company, Some Financial Aspects of Trading in West Africa. In: Statistical and Economic Review, IV (1949), p. 55. See also Cadbury Papers, file 289/403. Letter from F. Samuel and J. Cadbury to Sir Cecil Bottomly (Colonial Office), 27 September 1937.

41   Hancock, Survey, p. 204. See also Hopkins, An Economic History of West Africa, p. 201 and Holt Papers, Mss. Afr. s825 421 B(VII). Memorandum Price Agreements, 20 Feb. 1942.

42   L. Van der Laan, Modern Inland Transport and the European Trading Firms in Colonial West Africa. In: Cahiers d'Etude Africaines, XXI (1984) 4, pp. 549-556. See also Mars, Extra-Territorial Enterprises, p. 119. It is noteworthy that in the eastern part of the cocoa belt and in areas around Ibadan, some firms extended their buying networks as late as 1936. For a different view, see Hopkins, An Economic History of West Africa, p. 259.

43   Mars, Extra-Territorial Enterprises, p. 48. See also J.J. Milewski, The Great Depression of the Early 1930's in a Colonial Country: A Case Study of Nigeria. In: African Bulletin, (1975) 23, p. 12.

44   See D.K. Fieldhouse, Merchant Capital and Economic Decolonization: The United Africa Company, 1929-1989, Oxford 1994, pp. 3-41; Bauer, West African Trade, p. 77; Mars, Extra-Territorial Enterprises, p. 72. A good measure of the importance of the United Africa Company in the West African trade provide the quota allocations, which the company received during the Second World War. They were based on pre-war exports. By 1943, the United Africa Company controlled 47.53 per cent of the Nigerian and 35.76 per cent of the Gold Coast cocoa trade; 73.82 per cent of the Nigerian palm oil trade, 62.89 per cent of the Nigerian palm kernel trade and 47.37 per cent of the Kano (Nigerian) groundnut trade. For these figures see Holt Papers, Mss. Afr. s825 535(II). West African Produce Control Board Circulars C.L.B.12, C.GC.21, P.O.N.3, P.K.N.12, G.N.K.8 of 1943/44.

45   Bauer, West African Trade, pp. 224-225.

46   Nowell Report, para. 318.

47   Fieldhouse, Merchant Capital, pp. 84-85. See also P.A. Jones, The United Africa Company in the Gold Coast/Ghana, 1920-1965, School of Oriental and African Studies Ph.D. thesis, London 1983, p. 171. In the period from 1932 to 1938 the average yearly dividend, received by shareholders of the company, was about 5 per cent, while return to capital employed amounted to about 7 per cent. Judged from these figures alone, it appears that the United Africa Company was not an exceptionally profitable enterprise in the period concerned.

48   Fieldhouse, Merchant Capital, pp. 84-85, 117.

49   United Africa Company, Some Financial Aspects, pp. 51-53. See also K.D.S. Baldwin, The Marketing of Cocoa in Western Nigeria, London 1954, p.28.

50   For a description of the internal cocoa trade system in Nigeria before the Second World War see NAI: Oyo Prof 1, file 1441 Vol. I., Inquiry Regarding Cocoa Marketing in the Ibadan Division, by R.L.V. Wilkes (A.D.O. Ibadan Division) of September 1937. Incidentally, this report formed the basis for the Nowell Commission Report so far as Nigeria was concerned; see Nowell Report, para. 249. Some information can also be found in: Report of a Committee appointed in Nigeria to Examine Recommendations Made by the Commission on the Marketing of West African Cocoa (Chairman: E.J.C. Kelly), Nigerian Sessional Paper No. 20 of 1939 (thereafter Kelly Report) and in the Nowell Report itself. For the most recent overview see A. Harneit-Sievers, African Business, 'Economic Nationalism', and British Colonial Policy: Southern Nigeria, 1935-1954, paper presented to the African Studies Association Meeting, Toronto 3-6 November, 1994.

51 Figures on the number of scalemen and itinerant traders are extremely difficult to find, but it was reported that 130 'middlemen' with scales and 420 itinerant traders were working in Ibadan town and its environs in 1932. See Report on Land Tenure in the Yoruba Provinces (H.L. Ward-Price), Lagos 1933, p. 46.

52 NAI: CSO 26, file 36148 S30. Nigerian Legislative Council. Reply by the CS to Question No. 44 of 4 March 1940.

53 There is no full length published study which describes in any detail the history of the Syrian and Lebanese communities in Nigeria. For a treatment of the subject see T. Falola, Lebanese Traders in Southwestern Nigeria. In: African Affairs, LXXXIX (1990) 357, pp. 523-553, and R.B. Winder, The Lebanese in West Africa. In: Comparative Studies in Society and History, IV (1961), pp. 296-333, and D.M. Misra, The Lebanese in Nigeria, 1890-1960, University of Calabar Ph.D. thesis, Calabar 1985. See also A. Hinds, British Imperial Policy and the Development of the Nigerian Economy 1939-1951, University of Dalhousie Ph.D. thesis, Dalhousie 1985, pp. 234-286.

54 NAI: CSO 26, file 36148 S26. Letter from S. Thomopulos to Cocoa Controller, 16 Nov. 1939.

55 Thus the Syrian 'threat' was specifically mentioned in the 'Youth Charter' of 1938 of the Nigerian Youth Movement. See NAI: CSO 26, file 30055 Vol.I., Youth Charter, (n.d.), p. 7.

56 M. Crowder, West Africa under Colonial Rule, London 1968, pp. 294-298. For such a successful campaign see NAI: DCI 1/1, file 5159. Letter from SWP to the CS, 16 June 1947.

57 C.E.F. Beer, The Politics of Peasant Groups in Western Nigeria, Ibadan 1976, p. 19.

58 Beer, Peasant Groups, pp. 19-22, and D. Scott, Production for Trade. In: M. Perham (ed.), Economics of a Tropical Dependency, Vol. I, London 1946, p. 262.

59 Initially, the Registrar of Co-operative Societies was an officer of a sub-department of the Provincial Administration of Southern Nigeria. In 1943, the former sub-department was reorganised into a full government department under the direct control of the Nigerian Secretariat. It was then called Co-operative Department.

60 Beer, Peasant Groups, p. 19.

61 See NAI: Ib MinAgric 1, file 17980 Vol. I. Report of the Committee on Co-operative Societies, n.d. (1943), p. 2, and PRO: CO 852, file 272/1. Memorandum Cocoa Co-operative Societies, 8 June 1940. The growth of volume of cocoa marketed trough co-operative societies in the 1930s was quite astounding. For figures, see NAI: Ib MinAgric 1, file 17980 Vol.IV. Memorandum Recommendations in Connection with Continuance of Cocoa Control Scheme, 30 July 1940.

62 Kelly Report, para. 26.

63 Nowell Report, para. 267.

64 Kelly Report, para. 26.

65 See, for example, PRO: CO 852, file 256/3. Colonial Empire Cocoa Control, Minutes of Meeting, 15 Nov. 1939. One of the firm's representatives said in this meeting that '...the Co-operative Societies were merely a collection of middlemen....'

66 L. Van der Laan, Marketing West Africa's Export Crops: Modern Boards and Colonial Trade Companies. In: Journal of Modern African Studies, XXV (1987) 1, p. 12.

67 This section of the chapter is mainly based on NAI: Oyo Prof 1 file 1441 Vol.I., Inquiry Regarding Cocoa Marketing in the Ibadan Division, by ADO R.L.V. Wilkes of September 1937, and Holt Papers, Mss. Afr. s825, file 535(I), Evidence to Be Submitted to the Cocoa Inquiry Commission, by C. Foskett (District Agent, Ibadan), 27 April 1937; see also Bauer, West African Trade, pp. 202-204.

68   Galletti et al., Nigerian Cocoa Farmers, p. 53.
69   Nowell Report, paras. 105-108. For information on the firm's trading methods see also Holt Papers, Mss. Afr. s825, file 421B (VII), Memorandum Price Agreements, by D.L. Rawlings, Head of the Administrative Department of John Holt & Co., 20 Feb. 1942.
70   West Africa had been connected to Europe by telegraph since the late 1880s, which made direct communications possible between the Directors of the firms in Europe and local managers in West Africa. This had a profound impact on trading methods since it enabled firms to sell, for forward delivery in Europe and America, their West African stocks before shipment. Apart from improvements in shipping and the building of roads and railways, this was perhaps the most important means by which West Africa was integrated into the world market. See Van der Laan, Marketing West Africa's Export Crops, pp. 16-18.
71   For the 'Standard Marketing Expenses' of the United Africa Company, see Cadbury Papers, file 289/380, United Africa Company, Produce Accounts Department, Marketing Expenses 1937/38, 28 August 1937. It is noteworthy that these marketing expenses were considerably lower than the expenses specified in the later 'Pool Agreement'.
72   See table 3.
73   This is at least the impression one gets from the data supplied by Galletti et al., Nigerian Cocoa Farmers, p. 413; see also PRO: CO 657/17, Administrative Reports, Report of the Department of Agriculture for the year 1926, p. 8.
74   NAI: Oyo Prof 1, file 1441 Vol. I, Inquiry Regarding Cocoa Marketing in the Ibadan Division, by ADO R.L.V. Wilkes of September 1939, p. 9.
75   See United Africa Company, Some Financial Aspects of Trading in West Africa, p. 51. This is at best an estimate. The share of cocoa bought with advances as opposed to cash very likely varied considerably between seasons, since it depended on the degree of competition between firms. Unfortunately, no further information is available on this aspect of cocoa trading.
76   Ibid.; see also Nowell Report, para. 99.
77   Bauer, West African Trade, p. 210; see also Harneit-Sievers, Dependent Cocoa Buying, p. 16.
78   Nowell Report, para. 528.
79   Holt Papers, Mss. Afr. s825, file 536(II), Letter from the District Agent Nsawam to District Agent Accra, 'Brokers Buying Book', 4 April 1938
80   Ibid.
81   NAI: Oyo Prof 1, file 1441 Vol. 1, Inquiry Regarding Cocoa Marketing in the Ibadan Division, by ADO R.L.V. Wilkes of September 1937.
82   Nowell Report, para. 122. According to this report 1/4th of the crop was sold forward in the 1932/33 cocoa season in the Gold Coast.
83   Compare Nowell Report, para. 260; Hancock, Survey, pp. 275-282; Forde, Rural Economies, p. 98; Galletti et al., Nigerian Cocoa Farmers, p. 600.
84   NAI: Oyo Prof 1, file 1441 Vol. I, Inquiry Regarding Cocoa Marketing in the Ibadan Division, by ADO R.L.V. Wilkes of September 1937.
85   Information regarding the 1930s is particularly inconclusive. The Senior Resident of Ibadan, H.L. Ward-Price, reported in 1932 that '...indebtedness to traders has not yet developed sufficiently to cause any anxiety...', whereas the Assistant District Officer R.L.V. Wilkes stated in 1937 that 'During the years of depression practically every producer in the division was hopelessly indebted, but evidence has been forthcoming, that the higher prices obtained last season [1936/37] have relieved the majority from debt....' See Report on Land Tenure in the Yoruba Provinces (H.L. Ward-Price),

Lagos 1933, p. 77, and NAI: Oyo Prof I, file 1441 Vol. I, Inquiry Regarding Cocoa Marketing in the Ibadan Division, by R.L.V. Wilkes (A.D.O. Ibadan Division) of September 1937.

86   Galletti et al., Nigerian Cocoa Farmers, p. 503.

87   See, for example, R.J. Southall, Farmers, Traders and Brokers in the Gold Coast Economy, in: Canadian Journal of African Studies, XII (1978) 2, p. 188.

88   See Holt Papers, Mss. Afr. s825 535(I), Cocoa Commission: Question asked Mr C.A.V. Wood of John Holt & Co. (Ijebu-Ode) at Ibadan, 4 May 1938.

89   This was at least the situation in 1951/52, when Galletti et al. conducted their research. See Nigerian Cocoa Farmers, p. 505. There is no reason to suppose that the situation concerning the distribution of debt in the early 1950s was in this respect radically different from the situation in the late 1930s and 1940s.

CHAPTER 3

The Politics of the Cocoa Trade, c. 1920-1940

The establishment of statutory produce control at the outbreak of the war in 1939 and its continuation after the war cannot properly be explained without touching on the events of 1937/38. Yet, events were in themselves the result of earlier events. These were the recurrent trade depressions, the commercial policies of the trading firms, and the reaction of African traders and, to a much lesser extent, of the colonial government to these events.

The Impact of Trade Depressions

The first depression in the produce trade, including the cocoa trade, after the First World War occurred in 1920/21. During the war, trading conditions had been very unfavourable to African traders. Shipping was restricted and the European firms were largely able to exclude Africans from the trade by skillfully manipulating available shipping space. Thus the African traders were prevented from gaining any benefit from the demise of German trading firms at the beginning of the war and of the development of high price differentials between local and world market prices at the end of the war. For this reason, however, trade was on the whole exceptionally profitable for the European firms during this period.[1]

The shipping situation changed in 1918 when, in the aftermath of the entry of the U.S.A. into the war, shipping space became more freely available to African traders. Owing to the rapidly increasing world cocoa prices, trade differentials seemed to have remained very high and trade prospects in general looked very promising.

In the 1920/21 season, the post-war boom reached its peak and cocoa changed hands for more than £82 per ton in Ibadan in mid-season. In the previous season only a quarter of this price had been paid.[2] Most African traders and indeed the European trading firms expected that cocoa prices would stay at this level. Consequently, for some time, large amounts of money were invested in the forward purchase of cocoa or stocks of merchandise. Yet, at the end of the season cocoa prices tumbled to £28 per ton in Ibadan, and decreased even further in the next season. Other commodity prices fell too and traders generally found themselves in a situation of being either in possession of produce for which they had paid a much higher price than the current price or in possession of merchandise for which there was no effective demand, so that merchandise prices had to be substantially reduced in order to clear stock. This involved heavy losses and most traders had to write off a significant part of their trading capital or went bankrupt. Even relatively successful traders, for instance the Ibadan merchant S. Agbaje, experienced severe difficulties in keeping their businesses afloat.[3] Some of the larger European trading firms also suffered during the slump. On the whole, however, their ability to sustain losses was much stronger than that of their African counterparts. By contrast, many African firms (and a number of smaller European firms) went out of business or were sold to the surviving firms. This was a drastic setback for the African firms and traders and it took them years to rebuild their businesses. Meanwhile 'the confident independent businessmen of 1919/20 were back at their desks and canteens in 1921 working as clerks and agents for the now completely dominating European survivors'[4].

The second slump in the inter-war years occurred in 1929. This was the starting point of a depression which lasted in effect until 1935. The most prominent victim of the slump was the African and Eastern Trade Corporation, which was effectively taken over by Lever Brothers Ltd. which merged its subsidiary, the Niger Company Ltd., with the A. & E.T.C. into the United Africa Company Ltd. Another victim of the depression was G.B. Ollivants which went quietly into liquidation in 1933. The firm continued to trade under its own name, but was now owned by Unilever Ltd., a company which was jointly owned by the Union Margarine N.V. and Lever Brothers Ltd.[5] The African traders suffered perhaps less during this depression than their European rivals. It appears that they had become more cautious after the slump of 1920/21.[6] Another possible reason for the apparent lack of distress for African traders was that by the early 1930s there were no large Lagos-based traders left in the cocoa trade. Traders were located elsewhere, exported only very little cocoa on their own account and were thus less exposed to sudden price falls.

The slump of 1920/21 and the depression of 1929/1935 hastened the process of concentration in the export trade. This process is exemplified by the growth of the United Africa Company, which by the mid-1930s controlled about half of the Nigerian import and export trade, including the cocoa trade.[7] The African traders deeply resented the emergence of such large 'combines'. For them it symbolised a development in which they became increasingly restricted in their own business activities. Yet, this was not so much the result of the concentration process in the export trade, but rather the result of the firms' commercial policies towards their African competitors in the internal trade.

The Commercial Strategies of the European Trading Firms

It appears that the firms adopted three main strategies to increase the profitability of their produce-trading operations. These were the expansion of their buying networks up-country, the replacement of independent traders by commission buyers, and finally the collusion of buying agreements. There were also some other minor strategies such as the internal reorganisation which firms effected during the depression, but none of these had such an important impact on the African traders.

The Up-country Advance

The first European stores were opened in the interior of western Nigeria in the 1870s. It was not, however, until the 1890s that the up-country advance of the European firms really got under way.[8] This move was the result of a number of inter-related events and interests. The most important event was that the colonial government assumed political control of the interior in the 1890s. This was a necessary pre-condition for the up-country advance, at least in the case of south-western Nigeria. At the time, the firms were seeking new trade opportuni-ties. As in the previous two decades, competition in the trade, as well as a depression in produce prices, had cut profit margins. They reckoned that the increase in turnover, which an up-country advance would bring, would make trade more profitable. By advancing up-country, the firms also hoped to circumvent the coastal African traders, who until then had controlled much of the trade with the interior, to the firms' disadvantage.[9]

The up-country move of the firms was facilitated by the development of the infrastructure in southern Nigeria and by the emergence of new means of transport. In the 1870s stern-wheeled steamboats started to travel up the Niger on a regular basis[10], while the building of the railway in the 1890s, and a later the building of roads and the use of motor cars and lorries, particularly after the First World War, opened up most towns in western Nigeria to the firms[11].

The first store opened in Ibadan in 1899. Just seven years later their number had increased to twenty-four.[12] This was followed by the establishment of stores in other western Nigerian towns, for example in Oyo in 1907 and Oshogbo in 1909. In addition, the European banks set up branches in the interior, for instance, the Bank of British West Africa opened its first branch office in Ibadan in 1910. Thus at the outbreak of war in 1914, merchandise-retail stores and produce-buying stations were firmly established in most towns of western Nigeria. In addition, produce-buying stations had been set up by the cocoa-manufacturing firm Rowntree in a number of villages in the vicinity of Ibadan.[13] Rowntree built these 'pioneer curing stations' in order to spread information about the proper fermentation of cocoa more effectively than they thought they could do from their produce stores in Ibadan. Cocoa manufacturers generally had a special interest in particularly well-prepared cocoa as only this type of cocoa could be used in the production of high-quality chocolate. In 1922 these buying stations were taken over by a firm with the name Cocoa Manufacturers Ltd., whose three equal shareholders were Cadbury Brothers Ltd. (the leading cocoa-manufacturing firm at the time), Rowntree

Ltd. and Fry Ltd. In contrast to those buying stations owned by other European firms, these stations did not stock any merchandise and bought only high quality cocoa, but insofar as Cocoa Manufacturers Ltd. purchased cocoa from farmers who had not participated in the fermentation improvement scheme and also resold considerable quantities of cocoa to other cocoa manufacturers, there was not much difference between these buying stores and those owned by other European firms.

One result of the up-country move of the European trading firms was the demise of the coastal-based African traders as trade increasingly by-passed them. Traders who before 1900 had built up substantial firms in Lagos and in other coastal towns, found that they were no longer able to continue their middlemen role and were thus slowly driven out of the trade. Though they also tried to open stores in up-country towns, they could not compete successfully with the European firms and had to close them down after a relatively short time.[14]

It seems that during the 1920s and early 1930s the firms consolidated their position in the towns, though the actual number of buying stations in some towns may have decreased as a result of internal economies in the wake of the amalgamation of firms in response to the stringencies imposed by the depression. In the mid-1930s, however, the firms started to move into the villages.[15] Earlier attempts in 1930 and 1934 had been abortive, but by 1936 six firms had set up about twenty buying stations in outlying markets and villages in the Ibadan Division alone, and a further advance was planned.[16] At this point the Ibadan Native Authority intervened by refusing to sanction the lease of land on which the firms intended to build produce-buying stores. Though conclusive evidence is missing on this point, it seems that many Ibadan Chiefs saw their trading interests threatened by the advance of European trading firms into outlying villages. Until then the firms had only built buying stations on land for which such a sanction was not necessary.

The advance of the firms into the villages was largely due to intense competition in the mid-1930s for a share in the crop. But there was another reason for this advance. By moving buying stations to outlying markets and villages, the firms would be able to drive the larger independent produce traders out of the market. This they would achieve by manipulating the cocoa purchase prices in the villages relative to those in the towns. If they paid higher prices in the outlying markets than in the towns, the operations of the independent produce traders would become less profitable and they would ultimately be forced to leave the trade.[17]

In a report on cocoa marketing in the Ibadan Division, the Assistant District Officer, R.L.V. Wilkes, stated that 'the exporting firms deny that they habitually give higher prices in outlying markets than in Ibadan, ... evidence on this point is not entirely conclusive and it is possible that the exporting firms are encouraging in this way the small commission man against the independent middlemen with whom they have no wish to deal'[18]. Given that sort of evidence is always very difficult to get and that the report had been very carefully worded, this statement seems to suggest that there was indeed a very strong possibility that the firms indulged in such business practices. Moving buying stations into villages and outlying markets would also prevent traders from under-paying farmers in these markets, so it is not surprising that this provoked strong resistance from the African traders.

The Replacement of the Independent Produce Traders

The establishment of buying stations in villages and outlying markets was only one way in which the European firms tried to gain control over the larger independent produce traders. Since the early 1930s the number of commission buyers which the firms employed had increased.[19] This was partly due to the expansion of the cocoa industry itself but is also partly explained by the firms' commercial policy.

There was never any shortage of smaller traders who were anxious to enter the cocoa trade, as they usually had only to provide two suitable guarantors and a little capital to make the initial deposit in order to become a firm's commission buyer. In the 1930s the firms were taking on smaller traders in increasing numbers, offering them relatively liberal credit facilities and generous commission agreements.[20] This gave commission buyers a considerable advantage over larger independent traders, who had no access to such resources. Consequently, larger independent produce traders were increasingly replaced by smaller commission buyers as the main source of the firms' cocoa supplies.

This policy was not entirely successful. The larger traders survived, because the firms still purchased cocoa from them as it was ultimately more economical for the firms to buy cocoa in large parcels from produce traders than small amounts through their own buying organisations from their commission buyers.[21] The competition between the firms for such large parcels of cocoa enabled the produce traders in some years to extract higher commission rates from the firms. Moreover, as it seems very likely that some produce traders purchased cocoa in markets in which strong competition from commission buyers or other traders was absent, their position was at least not immediately threatened by the increase in the number of commission buyers.

It is also arguable that this policy was to some extent counter-productive. The replacement of independent produce traders by commission buyers and the increase in the number of the latter meant that the firms had to provide additional capital resources in order to finance the trading operations of their new commission buyers. This obviously increased the risks which the European firms were running by financing the trade because a number of commission buyers would default on the debt they owed to the firms or would speculate with the firms' advances against the firms.[22]

Finally, it is important to bear in mind that while the firms were pursuing such strategies, the cocoa industry itself expanded. Higher volumes of trade and in particular a wider catchment area meant that the dependency of the firms on intermediaries in the 1930s actually increased. Thus in the second half of the 1930s a situation developed in which African traders felt that their position was increasingly under threat, while at the same time their number and their strength vis-à-vis the European trading firms actually increased.

Agreements between European Trading Firms

'Understandings', 'pools' and 'agreements' were, at least since the 1870s, an integral part of the merchandise and produce trade in West Africa.[23] All these agreements aimed at reducing or eliminating the competition between firms. This suggests a certain degree of uniformity, and many writers on the subject have treated them as if they were very similar to each other.[24] A closer look at these agreements, however, reveals a bewildering array. Thus by treating them as uniform, the implicit historical dimension of these agreements tends to get lost. This is immediately evident if one compares informal agreements, which before the First World War were frequently concluded between the local representatives of firms covering only relatively small areas, and the highly sophisticated formal agreements of the 1930s, which managing directors of the leading firms worked out and often personally signed, covering whole crops or certain merchandise articles widely traded in West Africa at the time.[25]

Apart from the 1937/38 cocoa buying agreement, comparatively little is known about these agreements. For example the actual Merchandise Agreement of 1937 has never been published, though in terms of turnover it was certainly more important to the firms than the cocoa buying agreement of 1937/38.[26] For reason of brevity, I will concentrate in what follows on the 1933 cocoa and palm produce agreement and the 1936 merchandise agreement, which had the most profound impact on trade in southern Nigeria in the 1930s.[27] The 1937/38 buying agreement will be specifically reviewed in the next chapter.

The 1933 Cocoa Agreement

This agreement between the United Africa Company, G.B. Ollivant, John Holt & Co., Paterson Zochonis, and the Compagnie Française de l'Afrique Occiden-

tale covered cocoa, palm oil, and palm kernel exports from Nigeria, the Cameroons and Sierra Leone. It was effective from 3rd July 1933 for an unspecified
period.[28]

How, then, would the agreement operate? The participating firms formed an
Executive Committee in the U.K. which cabled maximum purchase price limits
to one of the firms in one of the so-called Pool Areas. In Nigeria there were six
areas, i.e. Lagos, Warri, New Calabar (Owerri Province), Port Harcourt, Opobo
and Calabar (Calabar and Ogoja Province). These firms were then supposed to
relay immediately these new prices to the up-country buying stations. In return
the firms cabled their weekly purchases back to the Committee in the U.K.
Every thirteen weeks in the case of palm kernels and palm oil and every four
weeks in the case of cocoa, the Committee would determine the amount of
produce which firms would hand over to one another in order to keep actual
purchases in line with the shares in the Pool purchases to which the firms had
agreed in advance.

The purpose of the Pool was, above all, to enhance the profitability of the
trade to the firms. In a memorandum sent to the local agents of John Holt &
Co. in Nigeria and the Cameroons, the director of the Administrative Department of John Holt & Co. stated:

> The Principals have come together in a spirit of helpful co-operation with
> one another to achieve the maximum of benefits for each of the Agree
> ments. This good-will is to be extended in Africa. The important objective
> of the Pool is to secure a collective trade of the Pool to the Pool, and that
> done, to make a reasonable profit for each and all of us from our produce
> business. There is to be no waste of effort and money in unnecessary
> bickering in Africa. What matters, and what alone matters, is that the
> Pool as a body shall do the collective maximum trade at a reasonable
> profit.[29]

The profit margins which the firms hoped to gain were not predetermined.
Local agents were encouraged to buy as cheaply as possible, the only limit
being competition from firms which operated outside the Pool. The memorandum reads on this point as follows:

> In non-competitive Areas, if the "Committee" is satisfied at any time that
> a reasonable margin can be safely made by buying under limit, they are
> authorised and encouraged to make that margin. This can most frequently
> and successfully be done by withholding the issue of limit changes up
> wards on a market rise when, in the opinion of the "Committee" trade
> would not be affected at all if the rise were not circulated.[30]

Thus, on a rising market, the local representative of the participating firms
were encouraged to withhold the price rise from producers as long as such a
policy would not effect the volume of purchases.

The principal outside competitor of the Pool was the Société Commerciale de l'Ouest Africain. They had refused to join the Pool as they did not consider the purchase in Nigeria large enough to make it worthwhile to them to agree to the share the other firms were offering to them. Thus the agreement specified that local agents might exceed price limits in the areas in which S.C.O.A. was active, if they were by competition forced to do so in order to prevent S.C.O.A. carrying out their stated intention of increasing their purchases at the expense of the other firms.[31]

In contrast to the 1937/38 Agreement, the 1933 Agreement had comparatively little to say on policy towards African traders. It merely mentioned that forward purchases should not be tolerated any longer. The memorandum states that,

> It is recognised that this is an evil which has grown considerably *in recent times* [my emphasis]. It is agreed that the Pool as at present constituted is strong enough to stop it altogether and it is an instruction of the Home Committee that you take steps at once, in co-operation, to arrange your business so that every customer of the pool is paid for his produce at the limit ruling on the day on which he sells and delivers it, and at no other rate. Clerks must not be allowed to declare as their buyings any produce which is not actually visible.[32]

This quotation suggests that in the early 1930s the firms were gradually losing control over their commission buyers and produce clerks: They received advances from the firms and used part of this money to purchase produce. Yet, they were not delivering it immediately to the firms' produce stores. Instead they speculated on a price rise which would allow them to pocket the difference and this gave them an extra profit over and above the commission they received from the firms. Alternatively, in the case of falling prices, they would claim that they had paid for all the produce in their possession the previously ruling higher price, but had not been able to deliver it. As the firms were not able to ascertain what prices their buyers had actually paid, some produce was bought at the current lower prices and the firms would be charged for expenses the buyers had not actually incurred. It was therefore of paramount interest to the firms to make sure that in the event of price drops, buyers were not allowed to '...declare as their buyings any produce which was not actually visible...' at that time.

The Agreement of 1933 lasted, as far as cocoa was concerned, until 1935 and in the buying season of 1935/36 competitive buying resumed.[33] As we will see in the discussion of the 1937/38 cocoa buying Agreement, the speculation by commission buyers with firms' advances against the firms resumed too. It might be sufficient here to point out that one of the most important aims of the 1937/38 buying agreement was to prevent this kind of speculation.

The 1936 Merchandise Agreement

Though this Agreement did not concern the produce trade in Nigeria, it is reviewed here because most of the African independent produce traders dealt in merchandise articles as well, and its impact on trading conditions in Nigeria was probably as profound as the produce buying agreements. There are also some hints that the protest movement which sprang up in 1938 in connection with the cocoa buying agreement, was to some extent fuelled by frustration about the restrictions which the Merchandise Agreement imposed upon the African traders.

The agreement was reached on 30th November 1936 between the following firms:

> The United Africa Company Limited
> John Holt & Co. (Liverpool) Limited
> Compagnie Française de l'Afrique Occidentale
> Société Commerciale de l'Ouest Africain
> G.B. Ollivant Limited
> Paterson, Zochonis & Company Limited
> Deutsche Westafrikanische Handelsgesellschaft
> Dekage, Handels-Aktiengesellschaft
> G.L. Gaiser
> Witt & Busch

It took effect from 1st December, 1936 and was supposed to last for four years.[34] Its purpose was to assure the participating firms a 'fixed and unalterable' share in the Pools' sales of a number of merchandise articles at agreed uniform minimum prices. These shares approximated very closely to the position which the participants had been in before the introduction of the Agreement in each of the commodities covered. These were beverages such as beer, gin and whisky; household articles like bread, flour, matches, salt, sugar, rice and tobacco; and building materials, like corrugated iron sheets and cement. It did not, however, cover cotton goods, which were among the most important merchandise articles in this period.[35] But the Agreement states that '...it is the wish of all concerned that the parties should take advantage of meetings to establish saner selling policies' for commodities other than those covered by the agreement,[36] and this is very likely to have influenced their prices.

The agreement was operated by local area committees in Lagos, Kano, Jos, Sapele, Port Harcourt, Onitsha, Calabar and Opobo. These area committees would then in turn be supervised by the 'London Committee', which was to be staffed by employees of the participating firms. The local area committees were supposed to furnish the London Committee regularly with a detailed list of the articles which the member firms sold in Nigeria, including the quantity of each item sold. These lists were then added up at the end of each financial year, multiplied with the agreed wholesale prices and the thus computed revenue distributed between the firms, according to the share to which the firms had agreed in advance. Eventual differences between sales and the share would then be equalised; that is to say, firms whose sales exceeded their share were obliged to pay over the difference to the firms whose sales figures showed a corresponding deficit.

The agreement did not specify any profit margin, but left it to the area committees to agree on the 'lowest price at which any company may sell wholesale'. This meant that firms were allowed to charge customers higher prices if the lack of competition from firms outside the Agreement warranted such higher prices. Such 'premiums' could be pocketed directly by the firms as they were not included in the final settlement.

The ultimate purpose was not, however, just '...to bring back selling prices to a more remunerative level...'[37], as the Agreement states. The participating firms also saw in the Agreement a medium through which the development of the colony would be stimulated, though it is debatable to what extent they really believed in this. Nevertheless, this quotation offers a rare glimpse of how the firms perceived their role in the colonies. The agreement reads as follows:

> In making this Agreement, the members have been influenced also by a desire to put the Nigerian business on a sound and satisfactory basis, believing that the colony cannot prosper unless it holds out some moderate reward for enterprise and the investment of capital, and without such reward the native population cannot expect to benefit by the continual expansion of European capital invested in the colony for his service. All the established trading companies recognise the responsibility which rests upon them in making certain that the requirements of the African in staple commodities are available at fair and reasonable prices.[38]

The Agreement only mentions African traders in passing. It states that the minimum wholesale prices would not be '...subject to any discount, rebate or allowance whatsoever'[39]. It seems that, as in the case of produce buying, competition for services of African traders meant that wholesale prices had sometimes been lowered considerably in order to induce traders to patronise a particular firm. Thus by playing off one firm against the other, African traders were able to obtain prices which would sometimes allow them to undercut the firms' retail store prices. They still made profits on these transactions as their costs were usually lower than those of the European firms and they were often satisfied with smaller profit margins.[40] The effect of the Agreement with regard to the African trader was thus that they would lose some of their profits. These would be transferred to the firms since the general price level and profit margins were then only determined by the competition between the firms operating inside and outside the Agreement.

The Politics of the European Trading Firms

In the U.K. and Nigeria the firms were usually represented either by individual firms or by trade organisations. The most powerful among the latter was the Association of West African Merchants. A.W.A.M., as it was known, was not a corporate body, and did not employ a secretary until 1941.[41] It was rather a loose association, founded in 1916 to assist the government in the prosecution of the war effort[42] and its membership consisted of a handful of large British firms. After 1938 other European firms were admitted as full members of the Association whose main function in the inter-war years was to provide a forum for the firms in which trade matters, such as prospective produce buying and merchandise agreements, were discussed. This is why the Association was frequently identified with pools and agreements, though its scope was much wider. In this period the Association consisted of a number of produce sub-committees in the U.K. and of area committees in West Africa. In Nigeria there were three local area committees (Kano, Calabar and Lagos) and in the 1930s their membership closely corresponded with that of the local Chambers of Commerce. This is of some importance as the Governor nominated the Commercial Members of the Legislative Council from these bodies.[43] This gave the Association of West African Merchants arguably a measure of influence on the decisions of the Legislative Council.[44]

There were, however, other channels of communication available to the firms than just their trade associations. Leading representatives of firms frequently had direct contact with high-ranking officials in the Colonial Office. It is important to recognize that these channels of communication existed, as they were not available in this form to other groups involved in the marketing of West African produce or in the import trade. However, the fact that such contacts frequently occurred is no direct proof for the suggestion that the Colonial Office was unduly influenced by the commercial firms.[45]

Politics, in the sense of party politics or participation in political movements, was generally very much left to the individual firms or their leading representatives[46] and it appears that even Commercial Members on the Legislative Council sat there in their personal capacity rather than as representatives of the Association of West African Merchants.[47] Though the firms restricted the active representation of their interests to the relatively narrow confines of trade matters, it cannot be concluded that they were apolitical. Above all, because of their dominant role in colonial economies, their actions and policies affected a large number of people, and thus were political issues as the crisis of 1937/38 has shown.

The Response of the African Traders

African traders were not just victims of developments outside their control. They tried to defend and, where possible, to enlarge their commercial interests as much as the European firms did. They were, however, in a very disadvantaged position. They had relatively few resources at their command and they were numerous, which made the organisation of their interests much more difficult.[48] This they made good to some extent by using political institutions such as Native Authorities and political movements like the National Congress of British West Africa, Nigerian National Democratic Party and Nigerian Youth Movement as a means of defending their interests, which enabled them to improved their position vis-à-vis the European trading firms. In the economic sphere they tried to advance their interests by collaborating in shipping and banking schemes, although these schemes met with limited success. In what follows I will look first into these schemes and then review major political disputes in which African traders played a prominent part. This is followed by an examination of the development of the nationalist movement in Nigeria and of the role which traders played in it.

Shipping Schemes

After the end of the First World War, some African traders tried on several occasions to circumvent the European trading firms by exporting cocoa directly to overseas markets. These schemes were generally short-lived and unsuccessful. Yet, they are important for two reasons. Firstly, if they had been successful, this would have meant that the European firms would no longer have been able to conclude comprehensive buying agreements and, probably, that they would have faced such strong local competition in the long run that they would have had to leave the export trade to local traders. This did not happen, as most of these schemes came to nothing because of internal division, petty corruption and perhaps the general inexperience of their protagonists. The firms, however, took them seriously and this strongly influenced their policies. Secondly, it is interesting to note that at one point or another a number of Nigerians who later became known as nationalist politicians were involved in these schemes.

The first scheme in Nigeria was probably initiated by Dusé Mohammed Ali. In 1920 he travelled to Nigeria, visiting Lagos, Abeokuta, Ibadan and Oyo. In

Ibadan he met A. Obisesan, who was then a cocoa trader[49], I.B. Akinyele, who later became the highest-ranking chief in Ibadan[50], and S. Agbaje, then probably the largest African trader and richest man in Ibadan[51]. Dusé Mohammed Ali succeeded in convincing Ibadan traders and some rich farmers to give sureties for him for some £30,000, though in the end the scheme was not realised for some unknown reason. This was not the first undertaking by Dusé Mohammed Ali. Before the First World War he had probably shipped cocoa from the Gold Coast. Dusé himself was an ardent 'Pan-Africanist' who had wide-ranging contacts in West Africa and in the U.S.[52] After most of his schemes had failed, in 1933 he founded a newspaper called *The Comet*, published in Lagos. He edited the paper until 1945, when it was taken over by N. Azikiwe's *West African Pilot*.[53] It also seems very likely that about 1920 an American scheme under the leadership of M. Garvey and his Universal Negro Improvement Society was discussed in Lagos. Garvey proposed to set up a shipping line, the Black Star Line, which would offer competition to the European lines by shipping produce directly from West Africa to the U.S. The Lagos branch of the Society was run by the young journalist E.S. Ikoli, who later became a leading figure in the Nigerian Youth Movement.[54] Though there is no firm evidence, it seems very likely that E.S. Ikoli was influenced by the Garveyite movement, and that the idea of establishing direct trade links between African traders and American black businessmen was current in Lagos at the time.

The next scheme was even more ambitious. In the second half of the 1920s and early 1930s, the Ghanaian businessman W. Tete-Ansa established a number of trading companies and also a bank in the Gold Coast and in Nigeria. The most important firm was the West African Co-operative Producers' Ltd., which had close links with Tete-Ansa's banking venture, the Industrial and Commercial Bank Ltd.[55] The West African Co-operative Producers' Ltd. was incorporated in the Gold Coast in 1925 and in Nigeria in 1928. Though the company had authorised capital of £250,000, only some £3,000 was subscribed and even less paid up. This did not prevent the company from making contracts over the delivery of produce with a number of Nigerian traders and 'Farmers' Associations'[56], and for some time the company seemed to have flourished. Its Board of Directors consisted of a number of Ghanaian and Nigerian businessmen, some of whom became prominent figures in the nationalist movement. The Nigerian directors were D.T. Sasegbon, C.C. Adeniyi-Jones, T.A. Doherty and J.C. Vaughan.[57] The company survived until 1930 or 1931, when, because of internal irregularities, it was forced to close down.[58] In subsequent years Tete-Ansa tried to set up similar companies, but none of them gained such importance as the West African Producers' Ltd.[59]

A prominent victim of the failure of the West African Producers' Ltd. was the Ibadan Co-operative Planters' Association, which lost some £11,000.[60] The

Association had shipped some 3,000 tons of cocoa directly to the U.S. through the West African Producers' Ltd., but it seems that it never received full payment.[61] Somewhat contrary to its title, the Association was actually run by produce traders. These were I.B. Akinyele, J.C. Aboderin, A. Obisesan and A.B. Akinloye.[62] The last-named was the secretary of the Association, who in 1931 had embezzled about £18,000 from the proceeds of sales and subsequently served a four year prison sentence for the misappropriation of money. The failure of the West African Co-operative Producers' Ltd. and the scandal surrounding A.B. Akinloye's activities cost the Association very dearly, not least because it lost its reputation amongst cocoa farmers, who quite understandably insisted thereafter on cash payments instead of handing over produce against a promise of future payment. The failure of the Association also prompted the government to intervene, and co-operative cocoa marketing societies were put under the supervision of Agricultural Officers. Three years after the failure of the Association, the Ibadan Co-operative Cocoa (later Produce) Marketing Union came into being. Its first President was A. Obisesan.[63]

During the second half of the 1930s, leading members of the Nigerian Youth Movement were frequently involved in produce-buying businesses and import and export companies. One such firm was the New Africa Company. It was set up in 1938 by the produce trader Peter Eket Inyang Udo, after his previous enterprises (such as the Ibibio Trading Company) had failed. The company had a very prominent Board of Directors, which included several leading nationalists of the time, such as N. Azikiwe, O.A. Alakija, J.Mbadiwe, and H.O. Davies. The General Manager of the company was S. Akinsanya.[64] Very little is known about this company, and it might have existed only for a very short time, but it is telling that precisely at the time when the Nigerian Youth Movement, to which all of the Companies' Directors belonged, was campaigning against the Agreement firms, leading members of that movement set up a company with the intention of breaking the firms' monopoly in the produce export trade.

Banking Schemes

The banking schemes were more successful. As stated above, the capital resources which African traders could command were much smaller than those of European firms. Africans generally believed that without equal capital resources, they would never be able to compete successfully with the European firms and so they turned to British-owned banks for credit. But they found that the banks' attitude towards them was less than helpful.[65] Complaints about the practices of British-owned banks were voiced as early as 1912,[66] but it was not until 1928 that an indigenous bank was established. This was the Industrial and

Commercial Bank Ltd., a company which Tete-Ansa had acquired in London in 1924 and which was registered in Nigeria in 1928.

After the bank experienced difficulties in the early 1930s, some Nigerian businessmen who had been active in Tete-Ansa's other companies established the Nigerian Mercantile Bank in 1931. Its Directors were Dr.A. Maya, T.A. Doherty and H.A. Subair; its Chairman was C.C. Adeniyi-Jones.[67] This bank only survived until 1936 and it seems that it did very little business. Three years earlier, however, in April, the Directors of the Mercantile Bank established another banking venture. This was the National Bank of Nigeria Ltd. Its directors were the aforementioned T.A. Doherty and Dr. A. Maja, and the traders A.L. Johnson and A. Adesigbin. H.A. Subair became General Manager of the bank, a post he occupied until 1951.[68] The bank's activities were initially rather limited, but by acquiring new depositors and, perhaps equally importantly, acquiring new shareholders like M. Bank-Anthony, a wealthy import merchant, and N. Azikiwe in 1938, its business slowly increased.[69]

The National Bank of Nigeria Ltd. was established explicitly to support African traders in their efforts to recapture some of the ground they had lost to the European trading firms. For example, Dr. A. Maja said in a speech to the shareholders of the bank at its first General Annual Meeting on 20th July 1934:

> Desperate disease, they say requires desperate cure; and is not our condition today desperate enough to stimulate desperate efforts? Time was when educated African traded side by side with European merchants on the Marina, and illiterate traders held sway along Balogun Street. Time was when Africans were heads of Government Departments ... Unless we mean to deceive ourselves, we must admit that we have lost ground and are losing daily. Ought we not to make some efforts to retrieve our position? And how best can we do that by co-operative and organised efforts? This, ladies and gentlemen, is the motive, the powerful motive, behind the momentous decision to open another native bank.[70]

Local Conflicts: The Ibadan Example

In the report which the Nowell Commission of Inquiry on the Marketing of West African Cocoa presented in 1938, the issue of local political conflicts with the firms was only mentioned in one sentence, perhaps because the Commission felt that these conflicts lay outside the Commission's terms of reference.[71] Local issues, however, were regarded by the African traders as equally important as buying agreements. For example, a memorandum written in late 1938 by the Secretary of the Nigerian Produce Traders Union, stated that '...the whole trouble at present could be removed if trading firms would honestly and truly withdraw the buying agreement effectively, ... confine their produce trading activities to important trading centers ... [and] leave the Districts and the producers alone'[72].

The view that local issues were as important as national issues is supported by the fact that African traders, and particularly the larger ones, were often themselves heavily involved in local politics. One might even argue that to some extent political power and economic success depended on each other. Political power seems to have been used, for example, in some cases in Ibadan to obtain cocoa from subordinate farmers at prices much below the current market prices, while payments in connection with the acquisition of titles were often derived from produce buying activities.[73] This does not mean that all Ibadan chiefs were produce traders or that all produce traders eventually crowned their careers with chieftaincy titles. Yet, there was a distinct overlap between these groups, which gave traders a particularly strong position in local politics, as the Ibadan example shows.

The conflict in question started in about 1930, when some European firms made representations to extend their produce-buying operations into the outlying markets of Ibadan. Yet, the firms were forced to withdraw when it became clear that local opposition was very strong. This opposition was lead by the Bale of Ibadan Okunola, who himself, respectively his family, had extensive trading interests. The opposition even gained support from the Senior Resident of Oyo Province, Ross. He was an particularly conservative administrative officer and thus probably resented the changes which the advance of the European firms into the villages inevitably would bring.[74]

The next attempt occurred in 1934, when the United Africa Company tried to set up some buying stations in outlying markets. The Bale and his Council sent a strongly-worded petition to the district officer in Ibadan, pointing out '...that the opening of new markets is another attempt to eliminate the middlemen from the market'[75]. Similarly, the African Commercial Union, which seems to have been the only existing trade association of the Ibadan traders, sent a petition to the Resident of Oyo Province. It was signed by S. Agbaje (President) and twenty-seven other Ibadan traders.[76] Apparently, these letters were not written in vain as the United Africa Company closed down their buying stations in the outlying markets soon after.

The issue came to the fore again in 1936 when the Ibadan Native Authority refused to grant approval for leases of land in outlying markets to the European firms. Prior to 1936 firms had set up a limited number of buying stations, either on land for which such approval was not necessary, or circumvented the provision that such approval was necessary by indirectly obtaining leases through the employment of an African trader on a salary or commission basis who would then own or hire such stores.[77]

In addition, the Ibadan Native Traders Union sent a petition to the Senior Resident of Oyo Province in October 1936, in which the Union protested '...against the move of the European firms to compete in the Native Traders "reserve" as their entry into the back places of trade would spell disaster and ... consequent ruin...'[78] In the petition the Union claimed to have over one thousand members and to employ a staff of seventy 'inspectors' who would look after its interests. The Petition itself was signed by S. Agbaje (President) and by another prominent Ibadan trader, A.O. Johnson (Honorary Secretary).

A further submission by the Union in January 1937 argued that their conflict with the firms was not only about economic opportunities, but also the question of what should be considered as 'just'.[79] The Union argued that

> In our ancient Customary Law, divisions of labour was at the root of the African idea of what the employment of men and women should be in the Community (sic). It is laid down as the first axiom of our philosophy on this question that women are fundamentally different from if not inferior to men in matters physical, emotional and intellectual; and in consideration of this the women's share in the output of aggregate labour in the community are (sic) regulated as regards quantity and quality in conformity with these differences.
>
> It was in this way that women happened to acquire monopoly over certain trades to the exclusion of any possible competition by men and vice versa. ... From economic point of view, the material results from this natural division of labour was that no un-employment was to be found in those days. In like manner there should be a division in produce trade between European Firms and African Middlemen.[80]

This argument impressed neither the District Officer, who conducted an inquiry into the whole issue, nor the firms. The latter demanded that they '...should be free to lease and rent land and/or stores wherever we desire or require'[81] and the District Officer recommended that Native Authority should grant approval for leases for short periods of time, albeit with a clause which would prohibit the firms from selling merchandise goods in these places.[82]

This was, however, not the end of the issue. In late 1937 the Olubadan and his Council wrote another petition to the Resident of Oyo Province, again protesting against the '...concerted move by the European firms to establish [buying stations] in all bush markets and eliminate the African middlemen...'[83] By then the political situation had greatly changed, as the European firms had earlier in the year concluded the 1937/38 Buying Agreement.[84] This political change is also reflected in the wording of the petition. The Olubadan states that,

> Apart from the planting, buying and reselling of cocoa, there is no other worthwhile industry in the country. The great bulk of the people are

produce buyers; these men will be ruined if the Capitalist (sic) firms are supported. There is no longer 'No man's Land' to which these men can go and farm.[85]

This quotation is of particular interest. Above all it shows the success of the nationalist campaign against the European firms which was at its height around the same time. It is telling that the Olubadan uses a phrase in the petition ('capitalist firms') which at that time could only be found in nationalist publications. Furthermore, it offers a glimpse into one of the wider issues behind the petition. Apparently land had become scarce in the vicinity of Ibadan and some people had difficulty in finding the means to support themselves. They had thus become 'unemployed' and the Olubadan was anxious that a further advance of the firms would close income opportunities in trade to these men.

Trade Associations

It was not until the late 1930s that associations developed in which larger cocoa traders organised themselves on a nationwide basis. Before this smaller traders organised themselves in trade guilds such as the Parakoyi associations in Egbaland, or in local associations like the Ibadan Native Produce Buyers Association.[86] In fact the Nigerian Producer Traders Union (NPTU), which later played such an important role in the conflict with the European firms in 1937 and 1938, was only set up in August or September of 1937, developing from an amalgamation of the Ijebu Ode Produce Traders Union and the Ibadan Native Traders Union.[87] Its first president was S. Akinsanya. It appears that the Union as such was only active for a relatively short period of time. During the very early part of the war, leading members of the Union were appointed to government committees. After that the Union seems not to have played any significant role in the public arena, but it is noteworthy that some of its functions were later taken over by the Ibadan Produce Traders Union (subsequently also called Nigerian Produce Buyers Union).

In 1941, however, an association was founded in order to represent the interests of larger traders vis-à-vis the government. This was the Nigerian Association of African Importers and Exporters (NAAIE). Its founding members, S.O. Gbadamosi and I. Williams, were engaged in the import rather than export trade[88], but later export merchants, such as T.A. Odutola, who had previously been active in the NPTU, became members of the Association[89]. The Association's organising secretary during the war and in the early post-war years was S. Daramola. Towards the end of the 1940s leading members of the Association also became members of the newly-established Lagos Chamber of Commerce, and by the early 1950s the Association was defunct.[90]

It was also during the war that another pressure group emerged in which traders had a large measure of influence. This was the Farmers Committee of British West Africa (FCBWA). In 1945 this group sent a delegation to London to demand higher produce prices and the deregulation of the cocoa market. Its history will be outlined in chapter seven of this book.

Trading Interests in Party Politics

The history of party politics in Nigeria before the Second World War has been well described by various authors[91] and needs only be outlined here very briefly. Party politics developed in Nigeria in response to the constitutional reforms introduced by Governor Clifford in the wake of the First World War. This gave Nigerian interests a very limited measure of elective representation in the Lagos Town Council and the Legislative Council. The Clifford Constitution of 1922 remained in force in its essential form until 1947 when it was replaced by a constitution which granted a wider franchise and also made room for a more representative government, though this reform fell far short of the demands by the now mature nationalist movement. However, in the inter-war years the election for the Lagos Town Council and for the Legislative Council provided the framework in which party politics developed.

But there was much more to these parties than their immediate purpose - the contest of elections - suggests. They were the cradle of the nationalist movement in Nigeria and, more specifically, the parties were places in which most of the 'politicians', who later took over the government from the British, served their political apprenticeship.

In these parties, trading interests were strongly represented: not only were leading party members import or export merchants, but the parties themselves made demands or drew up programmes which directly represented or appealed to traders. Indeed, one might even argue that these parties looked upon traders as one of their main constituencies. This peculiar mixture of party politics, nationalism (even in its most rudimentary form) and trading interests, proved to be politically very potent.

'Grievances' and the Nationalist Movement

Shortly after the Second World War, Obafemi Awolowo - one of the leading nationalists at the time - wrote that '...the fire of nationalism cannot burn without fuel - and grievances (real or imaginary) are the readiest fuel'[92]. The connection between nationalism and grievances is not, however, immediately obvious and begs the question why grievances played such an important role.

I would argue that in the context of the colonial economy[93] of the 1920s and 1930s the word 'grievances' did not just describe a feeling of having experienced injustice, but had a far wider meaning. First, it entailed that the place which individuals or groups of people actually occupied in the colonial economy was far below the expectations which they had; and secondly, and perhaps even more importantly, a recognition that the obstacles in the way towards the desired advancement were themselves a result of the concrete order of the colonial economy. Examples of these obstacles have already been given, the demise of the Lagos-based merchants, the replacement of the more independent produce traders by smaller produce buyers and the frequent market-sharing agreements between the leading European trading firms. To this one should add the numerous other restrictions which Africans had to face, for example, in government employment and in employment with the firms where they were usually barred from higher-level posts.

Movements developed in which members of those professions which were most significantly affected by these restrictions came together with the intention of achieving reform of the colonial economy and of the political system by which it was maintained. When, however, it subsequently became clear that demands for moderate reform had no chance of success and restrictions would remain in place or would even intensify, the aim of the nationalist movement changed from demands for greater participation in the colonial government to demands for the replacement of this government. In this perspective, the aim of the attainment of self-government was thus to some extent a means to better the situation of the individuals and the groups of people whose aspirations had largely remained unfulfilled under early colonial rule.

The Nigerian National Democratic Party (NNDP)

The NNDP was established in 1923. It emerged in response to constitutional reforms in the previous year which gave a small number of Lagosians and Calabaris limited elective representation on the Nigerian Legislative Council. The roots of the NNDP, however, lay in the Lagos branch of a pan-West-African movement, the National Congress of British West Africa, which had been most active in Lagos between 1919 and 1922. Not only were there many personal continuities - J.E. Shyngle, for example, who was the co-founder of the NNDP and had accompanied the FCBWA delegation to London in 1920 - but also the programmatic ideas of both associations were almost identical. These were mainly demands for constitutional reforms, the extension of educational facilities and changes in the career structure in the civil service, although some room was also given to economic concerns. This was very likely to have been due to the influence of a number of African entrepreneurs, such as J.H. Doherty, S.H. Pearce, D. Taylor and W. Tete-Ansa, who were members or associates of both organisations. Certain proposals which later became much more widespread were first seen here, such as the demand for the tightening of immigration laws, particularly in regard to the immigration of 'Syrians' or 'Lebanese' who started to emerge as competitors in the Lagos retail trade; a recommendation to set up a 'British West African Co-operative Association', which would offer shipping and banking facilities to African traders; and finally, the strongly-expressed conviction that the African entrepreneur, and in particular the African trader, did not occupy the place within the economy which was rightfully due to him. There is, however, little evidence which suggests that African entrepreneurs at the time advocated large-scale intervention from the government. It seems that though they strongly resented the restrictions imposed upon African traders by the European trading and shipping firms, they only demanded a return to '...free and fair trade in Nigeria and equal treatment of native traders and producers'[94].

During the second half of the 1920s and early 1930s, the NNDP became increasingly parochial and conservative in its outlook. This was probably due to the fact that most of its leading members belonged to the established Lagos elite, which had very little interest in radical reform of the colonial economy. In addition, the NNDP responded neither to the hardship which the depression imposed upon the Nigerian populace, nor to restrictions which the European trading firms imposed upon the African produce traders and smaller middlemen. However, in the mid-1930s a new movement or party emerged which was able to challenge successfully the supremacy of the NNDP in the elections of 1938 and whose programme, at least at the close of the 1930s, was far more radical than that advocated by the NNDP.

The Nigerian Youth Movement (NYM)

The predecessor of the Nigerian Youth Movement appeared in public for the first time in 1934. The 'Lagos Youth Movement', as it was then called, was founded in the wake of conflict over the status of the Yaba Higher College of Education by Dr.J.C. Vaughan, E. Ikoli, H.O. Davies and S. Akinsanya. Two years later it changed its name into the Nigerian Youth Movement. The original founders were not new to politics. Dr. J.C. Vaughan and E. Ikoli had been members of the 'Union of Young Nigerians' in the 1920s, an association which had been founded to oppose H. Macaulay's authoritarian style of leadership within the NNDP, while S. Akinsanya had been a member of one of the many literary and debating societies in Lagos at that time.[95]

The original programme of the Lagos Youth Movement did not radically challenge colonial rule. For example, the 'Booklet on the Constitution and

Rules of the Lagos Youth Movement' of 1935 lists as one of the principal aims of the movement, '...to seek by constitutional means the bestowal of the rights of British citizenship in its full measure on the people'[96]. One should not make too much of this, as party programmes in this early stage of the development of the Movement were generally written for single occasions and probably did not reflect the true convictions and intentions of their authors. Nevertheless, it is significant that the attainment of self-government was not the original platform on which the NYM campaigned in order to win wider support.

Moreover, it seems that on occasion the Movement even stressed its loyalty to the British Crown. For instance, O. Alakija, a prominent member of the NYM, accused H. Macaulay (NNDP) in the *West African Pilot*, in September 1938, of '...promoting the ill-feelings between His Majesty's Youth Movement and His Majesty's European subjects in a most wicked and satanic manner'[97]. Yet, the Movement's main slogan during the 1938 Legislative Council election campaign was 'Nigeria for the Nigerians' and in the NYM newspapers articles appeared which stressed the Movement's devotion to the nationalist cause. In particular, the Movement stressed the role it had played in the anti-pool agitation in late 1937 and early 1938 and charged that the NNDP had done very little to defend farmers and traders from the machinations of the 'Pool'.[98]

Despite its considerable shortcomings in terms of ideological homogeneity and despite the fact that it had only relatively recently entered the Nigerian political scene as a fully-fledged organisation, the Movement was able to capture three out of four seats at the Lagos Town Council elections in June 1938 and the three Lagos seats in the Legislative Council elections in October 1938. The franchise in these elections was very limited, however, as only adult male Lagos residents whose property or income exceeded a certain minimum threshold were allowed to vote.[99] Thus, for example, only 908 voters were entered in the electoral list of the 1938 Lagos Town Council elections, though many eligible voters might have decided beforehand not to take part in this election for fear of having to pay taxes afterwards, and so did not register with the electoral office. Only about 5 per cent of the people living in the Lagos municipal area voted.[100]

The low number of people who actually voted for the NYM in 1938 is not a good measure of public support enjoyed by the NYM in Lagos and elsewhere. In areas outside Lagos, this support was particularly noticeable in the towns in the cocoa-growing areas of western Nigeria, but it was also evident in other towns in southern Nigeria and in some towns in the northern part of the country.[101] One could even argue that the success of the NYM in 1938 was at least partly due to its early organisational efforts outside the Colony of Lagos, as it provided the NYM with the powerful argument that it, and not the NNDP, truly represented the national interest. The emergence of local branches of the NYM in western Nigeria was, however, also very important for a different reason. The existence of these local branches made it impossible for the government and trading firms to dismiss the intervention of the NYM into the conflict between the African traders and the European trading firms in late 1937 and early 1938 as completely insubstantial and unwarranted; and this fact to some extent explains why - as we shall see later - in the aftermath of this intervention, statutory marketing seems to have been such an attractive option for the colonial government.

The setting up of branches of the NYM in western Nigeria was probably largely due to the activities of S. Akinsanya, the 'Bulldog of the Movement' as one newspaper called him.[102] Not only was he the organising secretary of the Nigerian Produce Traders Union (NPTU) in 1937 and 1938, but he was also the president of another union: the Nigerian Motor Transport Union (NMTU) which he co-founded in 1932. If one compares the little that is known about the actual membership of the NYM in western Nigeria with what is known about the membership of these unions, one is struck by the apparent partial identity. Thus in *Ibadan* (O. Awolowo, S. Agbaje, D.A. Agbaje, A.O. Johnson), *Abeokuta* (D.F.G. Adekunle), *Ilesha* (J.O. Fadahunsi), and *Ijebu-Ode* (T.A. Odutola) leading local supporters or branch officers of the NYM were also the representatives or at least leading members of the NPTU[103] and in some cases (T.A. Odutola, O. Awolowo) also of the NMTU[104].

It therefore seems arguable that the NYM, as far as western Nigeria was concerned, did not develop from scratch. It built on an existing network of produce traders and transport entrepreneurs, which either in the case of the NMTU was already established and had been active in the national political arena[105] or, in the case of the NPTU, had been in existence for some time in the form of local produce traders' associations, such as the Ibadan Native Produce Traders Union or the Ijebu-Ode Produce Traders Union. Moreover, as many of the members of these Unions were the local 'Big Men', the influence of the NYM went far beyond the narrow confines of elitist Lagos politics. For example, one leading member of the Ibadan section of the NPTU was Bello Abasi, who was the son of Olubadan Okunola, while another leading member of the section, S. Agbaje, was not only a former nominated member of the Nigerian Legislative Council, but also a prominent member of the Ibadan Progressive Union, which played an important role in Ibadan politics at the time.[106]

The partial identity of the group of large produce traders and transporters with one section of the Nigerian Youth Movement was, however, important for the political development of Nigeria for two other reasons. First, it seems that the NYM anti-pool campaign in late 1937 and early 1938 was serious - as far as the trading firms and the government was concerned - precisely because of this identity. This is the impression one gets from reading reports on the political situation in Nigeria in 1938, which the local manager of one of the leading European trading firms wrote in that year.[107] It is thus, perhaps, this partial identity which gave the protest movement of 1938 its specific clout. Secondly, it is clear, that the traders' section together with other business sections such as the National Bank of Nigeria associates[108] within the NYM, were able to influence substantially the contents of the Nigerian Youth Charter, the party programme which the NYM published in April 1938, just after the campaign against the European firms and their trading practices had come to an end.[109]

One could argue that although party programmes mattered relatively little in this phase in the political development of political parties in Nigeria, it was nonetheless on this programme that the NYM won both the Lagos Town Council elections and the Legislative Council elections in June and October 1938. Furthermore, it seems that this programme enjoyed a remarkable longevity. Thus O. Awolowo wrote in 1946 that the Charter was at that time still 'unrevised'.[110]

The actual manifesto was probably written by H.O. Davies, the Secretary of the NYM in 1938.[111] Essentially it consisted of two parts: the first labelled 'Political Charter', while the second was named 'Economic Charter'. The Political Charter of the NYM stated that its main goal was to '...obtain complete autonomy within the British Empire...' and '...complete independence in the local management of our affairs.'[112]. In the Economic Charter, there are various elements of analysis, concrete demands and ideas, some of which were directly related to the situation of traders within the colonial economy.

In the Economic Charter the NYM described the '...original Nigerian economic system as being in the process of disintegration and the Nigerian as still adjusting to the new system'[113]. The most pressing problems at the time for Nigerian traders and businessmen in general were seen as insufficient capital, no access to bank credit, lack of opportunity to study modern business methods and organisation, and finally as having no recourse against the trading practices of the European firms.

Apart from pledging its support for African entrepreneurs in very general terms, the NYM declared its full support for indigenous banking institutions (i.e. the National Bank of Nigeria) and proposed the establishment of a Five Year Economic Plan. This plan was basically a recommendation to NYM members to set up thrift societies in order to raise capital for investment in privately-owned Nigerian firms.

With regard to the trading situation in Nigeria at the time, the NYM stated that

> We pledge ourselves to demand for our people opportunities equal to those enjoyed by foreigners... In fact we will urge on the Government to protect our people against unequal competition, *if necessary by legislation*

> [emphasis added]. The aim of ours is coterminous with the avowed prin-
> ciple of trusteeship that where our interests clash with those of foreigners
> in this country, it is the duty of government to see that our prevail.[114]

It also repeatedly re-affirmed its opposition to the 'ruinous practice by foreign firms of squeezing out the retail traders by invasion of their markets'; to 'unfair competition and a monopoly for big business interests'; and to 'all forms of privilege in business whether in the sale of foreign products or in the purchase of local commodities'[115].

The Charter also mentions the eventual establishment of marketing boards. After having declared its support for the development of co-operative societies[116] and agricultural banks, the NYM stated that

> until the co-operative systems are centralised into marketing boards
> functioning in a produce exchange, it is a duty for the movement to watch
> the interests of our farmers and to obtain a fair price for their efforts.[117]

As the meaning of the term 'marketing board functioning in a produce exchange' was not spelled out anywhere in the document, the significance of this is difficult to assess. It seems to mean that the NYM favoured the idea that co-operatives should form the basis of some sort of central marketing scheme or central selling organisation, but beyond such a statement any interpretation of the schemes seems to be rather speculative, especially as the role of produce traders in the scheme was not made clear, and thus perhaps not much weight should be given to it.

In comparison to the 1934 NYM party programme and the political and economic ideas earlier proto-nationalist movements expressed, the Youth Charter of 1938 indicated a fundamental change in political attitudes. In the Charter the NYM for the first time officially stated that its ultimate goal was the attainment of self-government, while in the economic sphere it demanded such large-scale government intervention that, had it been carried, it would have meant a partial restructuring of the colonial economy. Government intervention was thereby understood not as being a desirable aim in itself but rather as a means to support the emerging entrepreneurial classes in Nigeria in general and the produce traders in particular.

A.G. Hopkins has argued that this radicalisation occurred largely in response to the trade depression of the early 1930s and the subsequent hardship this depression imposed upon the Nigerian economy, and to the failure of government to react positively or adequately to this crisis.[118] It also seems arguable, however, that this radicalisation was moreover, at least to some extent, a result of the trading practices of the European firms in as much as they tried to undermine the economic position of African traders in the pre-Second World War marketing system.[119]

At this point it seems appropriate to review briefly the main result of the examination of the involvement of traders in politics. I have argued that traders went into politics in order to defend their economic interests and if possible better their economic position. It seems that at the local level this strategy was successful in some cases, as the Ibadan example has shown. Then I tried to demonstrate why and how traders became increasingly involved in nationalist politics. Here I have argued that while their initial participation in early nationalist politics may have been sporadic and inconsequential, by the mid-1930s traders and their representatives formed an integral part of the nationalist movement itself.

One purpose of the examination of the role of traders in politics was to illuminate the kind of leverage produce traders could use in their conflicts with the European trading firms and later in conflicts with the colonial government. As I will argue in subsequent parts of this study in more depth, it was this political leverage which was very much at the back of the minds of the managers of the European trading firms and government officials alike when decisions were made which directly affected the position of produce traders in the marketing system, as for example at the outbreak of war in 1939.

Government Policy

It seems that apart from the previously-mentioned policy of giving some support to the co-operative cocoa marketing societies, the introduction of a comprehensive system of produce inspection and produce grading was the government's main intervention into the cocoa trade. From 1911 any consignment of cocoa from Nigeria had to carry a government seal, which indicated that this consignment had been inspected by government officials and graded according to certain standards. It also indicated the firm which originally assembled that particular consignment of produce. Produce grading stations were subsequently established in all major towns and also in some bigger villages in the cocoa growing areas in western Nigeria.[120]

The main purpose of the scheme was to give American and British manufacturers some measure of certainty about the quality of Nigerian cocoa. It was hoped that this would increase the attractiveness of Nigerian cocoa in the international markets. It is difficult to come to any conclusion about the merits of this scheme. In the short term it seems that the main beneficiaries of the scheme were the European trading firms and some large African traders, in as much as part of their previous buying costs, such as the costs of employment of experienced personnel, were now paid for by the government.

The cautious support for co-operative marketing societies and the introduction of a produce inspection scheme were the major initiatives the government undertook in the inter-war years. As these initiatives did not change the relationship between the major participants in the cocoa trade, Margery Perham's famous description of the role which the government had played in the economy in the 1930s as one of a '...somewhat inattentive umpire...'[121], while the different economic interest groups played out their game, seems particularly accurate with regard to the cocoa trade.

It is open to question, however, if the government played the role of an 'umpire' willingly. In the 1930s there had been repeated discussions about reform of cocoa marketing in Nigeria, particularly after the events of 1937/38, but it seems that proposals in that direction failed, not least because the Nigerian government itself could not afford such a scheme, given the precarious state of its finances, and the Imperial Treasury refused to accept the financial liabilities such schemes would have involved.[122] It is thus arguable that if the resources had been available, the colonial government might have attempted to reform the cocoa marketing system. This is not just mere speculation. As will be shown in chapter five, it was the availability of resources which strongly influenced the colonial and imperial government decision to continue the war-time produce control scheme after the war itself had ended.

There was also one government scheme which, if it had succeeded, would have changed the pattern of trade in Nigeria. This does not invalidate the general notion of the government as a 'somewhat inattentive umpire' as this seems to be true for most of the 1930s. It only shows that the government was not completely inactive as far as the cocoa trade was concerned.

In late 1938, the Nigerian government, apparently without prior knowledge of the Colonial Office in London, approached American manufacturers through U.S. government channels, with an invitation to consider direct purchasing from West Africa, and in particular from Nigeria.[123] This invitation was accepted by a small, hitherto relatively unknown firm of Rockwood & Co., an agent of the leading American cocoa manufacturer at the time, the giant Hershey Chocolate Corporation.[124] Rockwood made it known to the government that it was particularly interested in high-quality cocoa and that it intended to buy up to 20,000 tons of cocoa in the approaching 1939/40 season. To this end the firm made the necessary banking arrangements and even printed leaflets in English and in Yoruba to make its intention known to farmers and traders alike. It also conducted negotiations with the Registrar of Co-operative Societies about the delivery of large parcels of co-operative cocoa, promising to pay £3 to £4 more per ton of cocoa than its competitors would offer.[125] This intention was also made known to co-operative leaders.[126]

In the end the scheme came to nothing. When war broke out in September 1939, all exports of cocoa were banned except under licence. Although the colonial government had issued one licence for the export of 1,000 tons to Rockwood for direct export to the U.S. and a second licence for 5,000 tons was already approved in principle in early September 1939, later these licenses were revoked as American firms purchasing cocoa directly from Nigeria did not fit into the design of the cocoa control scheme, whose details were finalised at the time.[127] This prompted the American embassy to write a strongly-worded memorandum to the Foreign Office, in which it objected to this decision, pointing out, among other things, that the effect of this decision would be only '...to strengthen the monopoly control of the entrenched interests and to close the West African trade to American participation...'[128] But this initiative did not meet with any success.

The reasons why the government thought it necessary to exclude Rockwood & Co. from buying cocoa in Nigeria will be examined in chapter five of this book; here it is sufficient to point out that apparently there was a division of interest between the colonial government and the European trading firms at the close of the 1930s. The government seems to have tried to keep a check on the activities of the European trading firms by inviting American firms. Thus, for example, the Assistant Financial Secretary in the Nigerian Secretariat minuted after the decision was made to revoke the export licenses of Rockwood & Co. that

> ... Government would, I think, welcome outside competition in the cocoa industry and if there was no control scheme we should be only too pleased to grant them export licenses to the United States of America.[129]

The 'Rockwood' episode shows that by the end of the 1930s the Nigerian government apparently was no longer following a strict non-interventionist policy with regard to the cocoa trade.

In this Chapter I reviewed the major policies and economic and political strategies of the main participants in the cocoa trade in the inter-war years. These were: the up-country advance of European trading firms, their attempts to restrict competition in trade as well as to replace the independent African trader; the response of the African traders to this strategy (politically and otherwise); and finally the 'laissez faire' policy of the colonial government. In this review the crucial conflict between the African traders and the European trading firms of 1937/38 was largely omitted. This conflict, its origins and its aftermath will be the topic of the next chapter.

Notes

1   A. Osuntokun, Nigeria in the First World War, London 1979, pp. 37-40.

2   J.A. Atanda, The New Oyo Empire: Indirect Rule and Change in Western Nigeria, 1894-1934, London 1973, p. 225.

3   G. Williams, Garveyism, Akinpelu Obisesan and his Contemporaries: Ibadan 1920-22, paper presented at St. Peter's College, Nigerian Research Seminar, Oxford, 10 Oct. 1988, p. 2.

4   W. Ojemakinde/R.J. Gavin, Economic Development in Nigeria. In: O. Ikime, Groundworks of Nigerian History, Ibadan 1980, p. 505.

5   D. K. Fieldhouse, Merchant Capital and Economic Decolonization: The United Africa Company, 1929-1989, Oxford 1994, pp. 1-41.

6   See J.D.Y. Peel, Ijeshas and Nigerians: The Incorporation of a Yoruba Kingdom, 1890s-1970s, Cambridge 1983, p. 135.

7   A.G. Hopkins, An Economic History of West Africa, London 1973, p. 199.

8   Ibid., p. 198.

9   Ibid., pp. 154-155. See also W.I. Ofonagoro, Trade and Imperialism in Southern Nigeria, 1881-1929, New York 1979, pp. 74-131.

10   M. Lynn, From Sail to Steam: The Impact of the Steamship Services on the British Palm Oil Trade with West Africa, 1850-1890. In: Journal of African History, XXX (1989) 2, pp. 227-245.

11   W.I. Ofonagoro, Trade and Imperialism, p. 192. See also A. MacPhee, The Economic Revolution in British West Africa, London 1926, p. 72 and pp. 106-129.

12   Atanda, The New Oyo Empire, p. 229.

13   NAI: Oyo Prof 1, file 1441 Vol.I., Enquiry Regarding Cocoa Marketing in the Ibadan Division by ADO R.L.V. Wilkes, September 1937, p. 7.

14   See MacPhee, The Economic Revolution in British West Africa, p. 100; Ofonagoro, Trade and Imperialism, pp. 105-106, and Atanda, The New Oyo Empire, p. 231. See also J.B. Webster, The Bible and the Plough, Journal of the Historical Society of Nigeria, (1960-63) 2, p. 431. Webster records that before the First World War, some cocoa was shipped by S. Thomas & Co., and perhaps also by J.H. Doherty. For a list of African Exporters in the early 1920s, see PRO: CO 657, file 7. Administrative Reports (1922), Department of Customs and Excise, p. 4; see also Hopkins, An Economic History of West Africa, pp. 153-156; Mars, Extra-territorial Enterprises, p. 119, and MacPhee, The Economic Revolution in British West Africa, p. 84.

15   Hopkins writes that in the 1930s most of the firms closed down some of their up-country branches. In the light of the "Wilkes Report" this view needs some revision. See Hopkins, An Economic History of West Africa, pp. 258-259.

16   NAI: Oyo Prof 1, file 1441 Vol.I., Enquiry Regarding Cocoa Marketing in the Ibadan Division by ADO R.L.V. Wilkes, September 1937, Appendix G.

17   This argument was forcefully made in a petition which the Ibadan Native Traders Union wrote to the Senior Resident of Oyo Province on 22nd October, 1936. See Appendix A of the Enquiry Regarding Cocoa in the Ibadan Division by ADO R.L.V. Wilkes, September 1937.

18   Ibid., p. 10.

19   Nowell Report, para. 253 and para. 345.

20   NAI: Oyo Prof 1, file 3909. Act. Resident Oyo province to Secretary Western Provinces, 18 April 1947. See also Peel, Ijeshas and Nigerians, p. 133.

21   Holt Papers, Mss. Afr. s825, file 353(II). District Agent Port Harcourt to District Agent Lagos, 25 Oct. 1943. See also Nowell Report, para. 345.

22   Holt Papers, Mss. Afr. s825, file 535(I), J.F. Winter (District Agent Lagos) to H.C.R. - Goddard (District Agent Accra) of John Holt & Co., 12 Feb. 1938.

23   MacPhee, The Economic Revolution in West Africa, pp. 73-74. See also Nowell Report, para. 390, and D. K. Fieldhouse, Merchant Capital, pp. 124-175.

24   See for example P.T. Bauer, West African Trade. A Study of Competition, Oligopoly and Monopoly in a Changing Economy, Cambridge 1954, pp. 224-225.

25   For shipping pools, see Hopkins, An Economic History of West Africa, pp. 200-201. There were also produce selling pools. An example of such agreements can be found in: Holt Papers, Mss. Afr. s825, file 535(I), Memorandum of Agreement for the Selling of Palm Oil and Palm Kernels ..., of June 1931.

26   For figures see Holt Papers, Mss. Afr. s825, file 516, Merchandise Pool Turnover at Selling Price, 21 March 1941, and G.K. Helleiner, Peasant Agriculture, Government and Economic Growth in Nigeria, Homewood/Illinois 1966, table 4-A-8.

27   There were other agreements in the 1930s which covered the groundnut, cotton and benniseed trade in Northern Nigeria. See NAI: CSO 26, file 25807 S9, Memorandum: Produce Buying and Merchandise Agreements in Nigeria by the Director of the Department of Agriculture, J.R. Mackie, 12 April 1938, and PRO: CO 852, file 133/4. Note on a discussion by C.G. Eastwood, 29 April 1938. See also A. Harneit-Sievers, Zwischen Depression und Dekolonization: Afrikanische Händler und Politik in Süd-Nigeria, 1935-1954, Saarbrücken/Fort Lauderdale 1991, pp. 47-56, und Bauer, West African Trade, pp. 228-229. For earlier agreements in the cocoa trade see Osuntokun, Nigeria in the First World War, London 1979, p. 37 and p. 61, note 59.

28   Holt Papers, Mss. Afr. s825, file 484(I), Memorandum Produce Pool by D.L. Rawlings, 5 July 1933, para. 1.

29   Ibid., para. 20.

30   Ibid., para. 30.

31   Ibid., para. 24.

32   Ibid., para. 32.

33   NAI: CSO 26, file 25807 S9. Memorandum: Produce Buying and Merchandise Agreements in Nigeria by the Director of the Department of Agriculture, J.R. Mackie, 12 April 1938. See also Nowell Report, para. 241.

34   Holt Papers, Mss. Afr. s825, file 516, Merchandise Agreement, 30 Nov. 1936, p. 1. See also D. K. Fieldhouse, Merchant Capital, pp. 124-175.

35   Bauer, West African Trade, p. 47.

36   Holt Papers, Mss. Afr. s825, file 516, Merchandise Agreement, p. 4.

37   Ibid., p. 2.

38   Ibid., p. 5.

39   Ibid., p. 3.

40   NAI: CSO 26, file 25807, Memorandum: Produce Buying and Merchandise Agreements in Nigeria by the Director of the Department of Agriculture, J.R. Mackie, 12 April 1938.

41   Holt Papers, Mss. Afr. s825, file 232, Minutes of a meeting of the A.W.A.M., Accra, 5 Nov. 1941.

42   Osuntokun, Nigeria in the First World War, p. 41.

43   For the history of the Lagos Chamber of Commerce, see A.G. Hopkins, The Lagos Chamber of Commerce 1888-1903. In: Journal of the Historical Society of Nigeria, III (1964-67), pp. 241-248.

44   T.N. Tamuno, Unofficial Representation on Nigeria's Executive Council, 1886-1943. In: ODU: A Journal of West African Studies, (1970) 4, pp. 46-66, and C.R. Nordman, The Decision to Admit Unofficials to the Executive Councils of British West Africa. In: Journal of Imperial and Commonwealth History, IV (1976) 2, pp. 194-205.

45   For an interpretation of the contacts between Colonial Office officials and representatives of the firms, see D. Meredith, The Colonial Office, British Business Interests and the Reform of Cocoa Marketing in West Africa, 1937-1945. In: Journal of African History, XXIX (1988) 2, p. 287.

46   The commitment to humanitarian causes by Cadbury Bros. ltd. is an example of the engagement of firms in extra-economic activities. See R.J. Southall, Cadbury on the Gold Coast, p. 6. He argues however that the political engagement of Cadbury Bros. Ltd. also offered them certain political and economic advantages.

47   Wheare, The Nigerian Legislative Council, p. 59.

48   For this argument see R.H. Bates, Markets and states in Tropical Africa. The political Basis of Agricultural Policies, Berkeley 1981, pp. 81-95.

49   Akinpelu Obisesan was heavily involved in Ibadan politics, and later became the President of the Ibadan Co-operative Cocoa Marketing Union (1934), the Member for Oyo Province in the Legislative Council (1943) and one of the first African Directors of the Nigerian Cocoa Marketing Board (1947). See also the numerous references to Obisesan in C.E.F. Beer, The Politics of Peasant Groups in Western Nigeria, Ibadan 1976, and in K.W.J. Post/G.D. Jenkins, The Price of Liberty. Personality and Politics in Colonial Nigeria, Cambridge 1973.

50   Sir Isaac Akinyele became Olubadan of Ibadan in 1955. He was also member of the Advisory Committee to the Nigerian Cocoa Marketing Board in 1947.

51   I. Duffield, The Business Activities of Dusé Mohammed Ali: An Example of the Economic Dimension of Pan-Africanism, 1912-1945. In: Journal of the Historical Society of Nigeria, IV (1969) 4, p. 581. In the 1930s, S. Agbaje's fortunes declined, because of his increasing involvement in Ibadan politics, which left little time for his business. His last shipment of cocoa ocurred in 1934/35 when he exported 450 tons of cocoa. See NAI: Ib MinAgric 1, file 17980 Vol.IV, Letter from S. Agbaje to Senior Resident Oyo Province, 5 Oct. 1940.

52   For example, Marcus Garvey is said to have been greatly influenced by Dusé Mohammed Ali. See Duffield, Business Activities, p. 585.

53   The Comet was a comparatively conservative paper and did not take part in the press campaigns against the Pool, conducted by the other more radical nationalist papers in 1937/38. This was probably due to the fact that the Comet was partly financed by the United Africa Company. See Duffield, Business Activities, p. 593.

54   M. Crowder, West Africa under Colonial Rule, London 1968, p. 412, and J.S. Coleman, Nigeria: Background to Nationalism, Berkeley 1958, p. 191.

55   Crowder, West Africa under Colonial Rule, p. 412, and Coleman, Nigeria: Background to Nationalism, p. 191. See also Harneit-Sievers, Depression und Dekolonization, pp. 187-190.

56   Beer, The Politics of Peasant Groups, p. 21.

57   D.T. Sasegbon was later appointed as the second African member of the Kelly Committee of 1939 in order to represent producers' interests. C.C. Adeniyi-Jones, T.A. Doherty and Tete-Ansa himself were prominent members of the Nigerian National

Democratic Party and, finally, J.C. Vaughan was a founding member of the Nigerian Youth Movement. See Harneit-Sievers, Depression und Dekolonization, pp. 182-187, und A.G. Hopkins, Economic Aspects of Political Movements in Nigeria and in the Gold Coast 1918-1939. In: Journal of African History, VII (1966) 2, p. 139.

58 See Hopkins, Economic Aspects, p. 142, and G.O. Olusanya, The Nationalist Movement in Nigeria. In: O. Ikime, Groundworks of Nigerian History, Ibadan 1980, p. 550.

59 Hopkins, Economic Aspects, p. 145.

60 Beer, The Politics of Peasant Groups, p. 21.

61 For export figures of the Association, see Hopkins, Economic Aspects, p. 141, and D. Scott, Production for Trade. In: M. Perham (ed.), Economics of a Tropical Dependency, Vol. I, London 1946, p. 262.

62 Post/Jenkins, The Price of Liberty, p. 20.

63 The Akinpelu Obisesan Papers, University of Ibadan Library, Ibadan (thereafter Obisesan Papers), Report by the Acting Registrar for Co-operative Societies on the Development and Progress of Cocoa Marketing Societies by A.G. Stainforth, April 1943, p. 1.

64 I. Duffield, Pan-Africanism, Rational and Irrational. Review Article. In: Journal of African History, XVIII (1977) 4, p. 613. See also PRO: CO 583, file 249, Internal Intelligence Report of the Royal West African Frontier Force, half-year ending 30th June, 1939, p. 2.

65 British-owned banks were very reluctant to gain African traders as credit customers. Their attitude has been described as either being 'extremely conservative' or even 'racist'. See International Bank of Reconstruction and Development, Report of a Mission Organized by the International Bank for Reconstruction and Development at the Request of the Governments of Nigeria and the United Kingdom, The Economic Development of Nigeria, Baltimore 1955, p. 156; Olusanya, The Nationalist Movement, p. 549, and Coleman, Nigeria: Background to Nationalism, pp. 85-86. Apart from their general attitude, banks were also unwilling to lend money to African traders because these traders very often could not provide the necessary security. This was usually property, and since land outside the Colony could not be alienated it was not accepted as collateral. See also W.T. Newlyn, Money and Banking in British Colonial Africa: A Study of the Monetary and Banking Systems of Eight British African Territories, London 1954, p. 121, and G.O. Olusanya, Fifty Years of National Bank of Nigeria Limited, Festschrift: A Golden Jubilee Souvenir, Lagos n.d. [1983], p. 6.

66 Newlyn, Money and Banking, p. 119.

67 Hopkins, Economic Aspects, p. 138 and p. 145.

68 Olusanya, Fifty Years, p. 5. and p. 28. Dr. A. Maja remained Chairman of the Bank until 1961.

69 For detailed statistics relating to the bank's activities, see Newlyn, Money and Banking, p. 100. For the shareholders of the bank, see Olusanya, Fifty Years, p. 6.

70 Minutes of the first General Meeting of the National Bank of Nigeria Ltd., held at Broad Street, Lagos on the 20th July, 1934, cited in: Olusanya, Fifty Years, p.5. The connection between nationalism and banking was also recognised by the colonial authorities as early as 1938. See PRO: CO 583, file 240, Internal Intelligence Report of the Royal West African Frontier Force, half-year ending 31st Dec. 1938, p. 2.

71 Nowell Commission, para. 254.

72 NAI: CSO 26, file 34883 Vol. I., Memorandum Produce Buying Agreement by the Secretary of the Nigerian Produce Traders' Union, S. Akinsanya, 30 Dec. 1938. - Akinsanya is sometimes misspelled in documents as Akisanya. In what follows the

name Akinsanya will always be used, apart from direct quotations, when it is clear from the context that the Secretary of the Produce Traders' Union and cofounder of the Nigerian Youth Movement is meant.

73 NAI: Oyo Prof 1, file 1441 Vol.I., Inquiry Regarding Cocoa in the Ibadan Division' by A.D.O. R.L.V. Wilkes of September 1937, p. 5, and ibid., Letter from Senior Resident, Oyo Province (Mr. Findlay) to Secr. Southern Provinces, 23 Jan. 1937. For Ilasha, see Peel, Ijeshas and Nigerians, p. 143.

74 Ibid. Appendix A, p. 3. See also H.L. Ward-Price, Report on Land Tenure in the Yoruba Provinces, Lagos 1939, pp. 59-60 and p. 153.

75 NAI: Oyo Prof 1, file 1441 Vol.I, Petition by the Bale and Council of Ibadan, 30 Aug. 1934.

76 Ibid. Petition by the African Commercial Union to the Resident of Oyo Province, 27 Aug. 1934.

77 This was at least the impression of the officer who conducted the 1936 inquiry. See NAI: Oyo Prof 1, file 1441 Vol.I, Enquiry Regarding Cocoa in the Ibadan Division' by A.D.O. R.L.V. Wilkes of September 1937, p. 13.

78 Ibid., Letter by the Ibadan Native Traders' Union to the Senior Resident Oyo Province, 22 Oct. 1936.

79 Cynics might argue that by stating what customary law allegedly had been, the Union was only disguising its rather narrow economic interests. This may be so, but there is no evidence that the Union members did not believe in it. Moreover, this quotation is only one example of many in which African traders basically used moral arguments as opposed to solely economic arguments in their disputes with the European trading firms. It would thus be very biased to deny completely that these disputes were at least to some extent fuelled by a certain sense of moral outrage.

80 NAI: Oyo Prof 1, file 1441 Vol.I, Submission by the Ibadan Native Traders' Union, 19 Jan. 1937.

81 Ibid. Letter from the District Agent (Lagos) of John Holt & Co. to 'Ibadan', 15 Feb. 1937.

82 Ibid., Inquiry Regarding Cocoa Marketing in the Ibadan Division by A.D.O. R.L.V. Wilkes of September 1937, p. 16.

83 Ibid., Petition by Olubadan Okunola and Council, 18 Nov. 1937, p. 1.

84 This was the opinion of the Acting Director of the Department of Agriculture. See NAI: Oyo Prof 1, file 1441, Letter by the Act. Director of the Department of Agriculture G. Bryce to the Secretary Southern Provinces, 8 Nov. 1937.

85 Ibid., Petition by Olubadan Okunola and Council, 18 Nov. 1937, p. 2.

86 A.G. Hopkins, The Lagos Chamber of Commerce 1888-1903. In: Journal of the Historical Society of Nigeria, III (1964-1967), p. 241.

87 West Africa, 11 Sept. 1937, p. 1230. The Ibadan Native Traders' Union itself came into being some time between August 1934 and October 1935. See NAI: Oyo Prof 1, file 1441, Letter from the African Commercial Union to the Resident Oyo Province, 17 Aug. 1934.

88 S.O. Gbadamosi was the owner of the Ikorodu Trading Company. He was also a shareholder of the National Bank of Nigeria, as well as involved in the Nigerian Youth Movement and later in the Action Group (AG). For the establishment of the NAAIE see NAI: CSO 26, file 41229, Letter from L. Odunsi (solicitor) on behalf of the NAAIE to the Registrar of Companies, 24 Nov. 1941. See also Harneit-Sievers, Depression und Dekolonization, pp. 198-285.

89   T.A. Odutola was the local secretary of the NPTU in Ijebu-Ode in 1937. He later became the Life Vice-President of the Lagos Chamber of Commerce, whose member he had been from about 1948. See O. Longe, A Rare Breed: The Story of Chief Timothy Adeola Odutola, Ogbeni Oja Ijebu-Ode, Lagos 1981, p. 40.

90   During the war the NAAIE nominated representatives to a number of government committees, which inter alia allocated import licenses to smaller African traders. In 1946 the Association had a meeting with officers of the Supply Branch and the Controller of Imports to discuss export restrictions for cocoa to the United States. It was represented by T.A. Doherty, J.A. Williams, Dr. A Maja, C. de Medeiros, A.V. Sunmola, O.A. Alakija, J.B. Daramola, S.O. Gbadamosi and F.A. Doherty, all of whom were one way or the other involved in political activities (Nigerian Youth Movement) or in nationalist business enterprises (National Bank of Nigeria). For this meeting see NAI: CSO 26, file 38300 S112, Minutes of Meeting held on the 6th of June, 1946 at the Import Control Office.

91   The 'classic' accounts of the history of the nationalist movement in Nigeria are Coleman, Background to Nationalism; Sklar, Nigerian Political Parties; Tamuno, Nigeria and Elective Representation and J.A. Langley, Pan-Africanism and Nationalism in West Africa, 1900-1945. A Study in Ideology and Social Classes, Oxford 1973.

92   O. Awolowo, Path to Nigerian Freedom, London 1947, p. 31.

93   The term 'Colonial Economy' is used here to describe an economy of which a substantial part - in the Nigerian context the import and export trade, and wage and salaried employment - is controlled by expatriate interests and in which this structure was largely the result of the imposition of colonial rule.

94   Coleman, Background to Nationalism, p. 198.

95   Coleman, Background to Nationalism, pp. 217-218. T.N. Tamuno states that the Lagos Youth Movement was actually founded in 1933 and that the decision to change the name of the Movement was made in 1935. See Tamuno, Nigeria and Elective Representation, p. 51.

96   NAI: CSO 26, file 30055 Vol.I., Extract from the Booklet on the Constitution and Rules of the Lagos Youth Movement, 2 April 1935.

97   West African Pilot, 26 Sept. 1938, cited in: Tamuno, Nigeria and Elective Representation, p. 56. A.O. Alakija was one of the successful NYM candidates in the 1938 Legislative Council elections.

98   Ibid., p. 76 and 88.

99   In the 1938 Lagos Town Council elections the threshold was the payment of a property tax of £15 per annum on residential homes in Lagos. In the case of the Legislative Council elections the prospective voter had to prove that his annual income exceeded £100. See T. Schärer, Das Nigerian Youth Movement, Bern 1986, pp. 194-203.

100   Ibid., p. 193. It was estimated that Lagos had a population of 126,108 in 1931. See Tamuno, Nigeria and Elective Representation, p. 2, note 3, and p. 126, appendix 8. Incidentally, Ibadan was estimated to have a population of 387.133 at the time!

101   Tamuno, Nigeria and Elective Representation, pp. 51-54.

102   West African Pilot, 20 Oct. 1938, cited in: Tamuno, Nigeria and Elective Representation, p. 2. S. Akinsanya resigned from his post as Vice-President of the NYM in 1941. He subsequently became the highest ranking chief in his home town and officially called 'Oba Akinsanya, the Odemo of Ishara'. In that capacity he became a member of the Western House of Chiefs in 1952. He was also a Minister without portfolio in

the Action Group government from 1952 to 1955. For the development of the NYM elsewhere see Coleman, Background to Nationalism, p. 225.

103 For individual membership of the NPTU and NYM, see Kelly Report, appendix A, and NAI: Ondo Prof 1/1, file 638, Notes on a Discussion, Presided over by His Excellency Sir Bernard Bourdillon, 29 Dec. 1937, and Beer, Peasant Groups, p. 231, note 36.

104 For the membership of the NMTU see G.O. Ogunremi, The Nigerian Motor Transport Union Strike of 1937. In: Journal of the Historical Society of Nigeria, IX (1977-1979), pp. 127-144.

105 The NMTU organised a strike in 1938, which lasted from 7th to 13th January 1937, in order to protest against the higher levies which the government had imposed on lorries plying those routes which were also served by the railway. The Assistant Secretary of the Union was O. Awolowo. See O. Awolowo, Awo: The Autobiography of Chief Obafemi Awolowo, Cambridge 1960, pp. 126-128; Ogunremi, The Nigerian Motor Transport Union, p. 140, and P.H. Drummond Thompson, The Development of Motor-Transport in South-Western and Northern Nigeria, 1907-1937, School of Oriental and African Studies Ph.D. thesis, London 1987, pp. 275-324. The NMTU was one of the largest unions in Nigeria at the time. According to a list of some 85 unions which were registered between 1940 and 1944, the NMTU was the biggest in terms of the number of its members at the time of registration. See Anonymous, Two Nigerian Lists, in: African Affairs, XXXXIV (1945) 174, pp. 164-165.

106 Jenkins, Politics in Ibadan, North-Western University Ph.D. thesis (Wisconsin 1965), pp. 93-95.

107 Holt Papers, Mss. Afr. s825, file 535(I), Letter from J.F. Winter to D.L. Rawlings, 7 Jan. 1938, and J.F. Winter to H.C.R. Goddard, 12 Feb. 1938.

108 The General Manager of the National Bank of Nigeria (NBN), H.A. Subair, was the Treasurer of the NYM in 1938 and the NYM's successful candidate in the Lagos Town Council elections of the same year, while the Director of the NBN, Dr. A. Maja, was a member of the Executive Committee of the NYM. See Sklar, Nigerian Political Parties, p. 52, note 28.

109 NAI: CSO 26, file 30055 Vol.I, Letter from H.O. Davies to the Governor of Nigeria, 4 May 1938. This letter contains a copy of the Youth Charter. Another copy of the Charter can be found in PRO: CO 583, file 234.

110 Awolowo, Path to Nigerian Freedom, p. 57.

111 H.O. Davies rejoined the NYM after his return from Britain where he had studied Economics at the London School of Economics from 1934 to 1937. For his authorship of the Charter, see Awolowo, p. 155.

112 NAI: CSO 26, file 30055 Vol.I, Nigerian Youth Charter: The Official Programme of the Nigerian Youth Movement (thereafter Youth Charter), p. 2. Apparently the original draught of the Charter was even more explicit. There it is stated that the principal aim of the NYM was '...a complete taking over of the Government of Nigeria into the hands of the indigenous people of our country'. See Tamuno, Nigeria and Elective Representation, p. 52.

113 Youth Charter, p. 7.

114 Ibid., p. 4.

115 Ibid., p. 7.

116 The support for the co-operative movement was probably overstated in the Charter, not least because the NPTU strongly opposed any proposals to increase the assistance which co-operative societies already received from the government. See Kelly Report, para. 12.

117   Ibid., p. 6.

118   Hopkins, An Economic History of West Africa, p. 267.

119   It could be argued that the buying agreements between the European firms were themselves a result of the 1930s trade depression. Yet, I would argue that the main purpose of the 1930s trade agreements was to restrain the growth of African and Syrian competitors and very likely would have been concluded even in a period of trade prosperity, though admittedly the pressure to form buying pools was probably most strongly felt by the firms in periods when they incurred losses on their trading operations.

120   Njoku, Evolution of Produce Inspection, pp. 43-57.

121   M. Perham (ed.), The Native Economies of Nigeria, being Vol.I of Economics of a Tropical Dependency, London 1946, p. 16.

122   See PRO: CO 852, file 66/13, West Africa, 22 Jan. 1938, p. 49, and Ehler, Handelskonflikte, p. 96, on the origins of the scheme in the aftermath of the cocoa hold-up in the Gold Coast in 1930/31.

123   Manchester Guardian, Letter to the Editor by A. Singer, 15 April 1940; see also Kelly Report, para. 67.

124   PRO: CO 852, file 318/5, Letter from G.L.M. Clauson (C.O.) to N.B. Ronald (F.O.), 17 Dec. 1939.

125   NAI: CSO 26, file 36148 S73 Vol.I, Letter from the Acting Registrar of the Co-operative Societies to the CS, 21 Nov. 1941; see also NAI: CSO 26, file 36148 S116, Letter from the RCS to the CS, 21 Oct. 1943. According to the Registrar, the Ibadan Co-operative Cocoa Marketing Union had already made firm arrangements for the shipment of cocoa to the United States.

126   NAI: CSO 26, file 36148 S73 Vol.I, Letter from the Act. Registrar of Co-operative Societies to the CS, 21 Nov. 1941.

127   NAI: CSO 26, file 36148 S1 Vol.I, Letter from C.C. Wooley to A. Singer, 14 Sept. 1939. At the same time the Colonial Office in London had already decided not to issue export licenses to Rockwood & Co. See PRO: CO 852, file 256/1, Minute by E. Melville, 14 Sept. 1939.

128   PRO: CO 852, file 318/5, Memorandum by A. Schoenfeld (U.S. Embassy, London), 29 Nov. 1939.

129   NAI: CSO 26, file 36148 S1 Vol.I, Minute by G.F.T. Colby, 18 Oct. 1939.

CHAPTER 4

The 1937/38 Conflict and Its Aftermath

The immediate cause of the conflict was an agreement concluded by European trading firms in November 1937 in order to eliminate 'harmful competition and the abuses hitherto associated with cocoabuying in Nigeria'[1]. In what follows I will first examine the reasons why the firms came to such an agreement and then review the ensuing conflict. The last part of the chapter will be devoted to the aftermath of the conflict.

The Background to the 1937 Cocoa Buying Agreement

The 1930s were a difficult time for trade. The severe trade depression in the first half of the decade had badly hit the merchandise and produce trade and it was only in the second half of the 1930s that produce prices and the value of imports and exports slowly recovered to previous levels. Apart from the general state of depression, it seems that increased intensity of competition between firms reduced the firm's profit margins, particularly those from their cocoa-buying operations, in Nigeria. The precise profit margins of the firms on their cocoa buying operations are unknown.[2] However, it is possible to show that profit margins in the 1930s must have been much smaller than profit margins in the 1920s, since the difference between the Lagos purchase price and the Liverpool selling price was considerably lower in the later period.[3] The same argument can be applied to the firms' cocoa trading operations in the Gold Coast.

It seems that this development was largely due to the expansion of the cocoa industry. This expansion had two dimensions: one was a sharp increase in the volume of exports, while the other dimension concerned the extension of the cocoa producing area. During the 1930s, cocoa trees which had been planted further afield from the firms' buying stores and railway stations became productive. In order to get as near the source as possible, the firms followed this movement by gradually extending their buying network, which led to a marked increase in their overhead costs. The answer to this development was a general increase in the level of competition between the firms, since, as one local agent of John Holt & Co. put it:

> As our buying stations went further afield, nearer to the producer, the increased overhead expenses had to be covered by increased tonnage.[4]

'Increased tonnage' could, however, only be secured by paying higher commission rates or higher produce prices, and thus it seems that in the 1930s there was some kind of self-perpetuating process at work, where higher overhead costs induced a higher level of competition, while a higher level of competition led, via the extension of the buying network and the increase in buying costs, to generally higher overhead costs.

The expansion of the cocoa industry also gave rise to a new type of intermediary. These were produce traders who were able to combine their produce buying businesses with transport enterprises.[5] Though this development was already noticeable in the early 1920s, when the first produce traders bought lorries to transport their purchases to the firms' buying stations, it was only in the 1930s that this development made itself felt in the produce trade, probably because of the improvement and extension of the road network. Thus during the 1930s the tonnage that was taken to Lagos, for example by road, steadily increased. This increase was partly due to the increase in the volume of trade itself, but it seems it was also due to the geographical extension of the cocoa-producing areas. Thus in towns like Ilesha and Ijebu-Ode, which were located further away from the railway and whose importance as cocoa-buying centres had increased in the 1930s, a large proportion of the crop was transported directly to Lagos instead of being brought to the nearest railway station.[6]

The size of African transport businesses in aggregate is not known but there is evidence which suggests that the 1930s saw the emergence of a new type of African entrepreneur. When, for example, the Assistant District Officer of the Ibadan Division made an inquiry into cocoa marketing in that division, he remarked, *inter alia*, that the larger local middlemen '...in almost all cases own motor transport'[7]. Moreover, almost all of the leading produce traders in south-western Nigeria had owned transport businesses. Thus in the 1930s, in Ibadan for example, transport and produce-buying businesses were owned by S. Agbaje, A.O. Makanjuola, and the Syrian A.K. Zard, while in Ilesha J.O. Fadahunsi and in Ijebu-Ode T.A. Odutola maintained their own lorry parks.[8]

The fact that these businesses survived the difficult times of the 1930s, despite the depression and competition from European trading firms, was largely a result of the way they operated and their better knowledge of local conditions. They were generally more flexible and worked on profit margins substantially lower than those of the European firms. They were also low cost operators, in that they did not have to pay relatively high wages to European supervisory staff.[9] Moreover, European employees were also more expensive, inasmuch as a substantial number of them were always on leave or ill. For example, the firm of John Holt & Co. held a 'reserve for relief' in 1937 of twenty-nine (!) employees to enable only some ninety-six European supervisory staff to conduct its business in Nigeria.[10]

The emergence of independent produce buying and transport entrepreneurs had a number of effects on the trading operations of the European firms. They lost their former control over evacuation routes, and produce traders were now able to offer parcels of produce to different firms. This in turn led to an increase in commission rates as produce traders could now play off the firms against each other. But even more importantly, it seems that produce traders were increasingly able to compete successfully with the firms' own buying organisations. Despite their dislike of larger, independent produce traders, the firms regularly bought substantial amounts of cocoa from larger produce traders. They found bulk purchasing quite attractive because it lowered their overall buying costs. This was, it seems, the reason why they occasionally offered substantial 'overriding' commissions to certain produce traders, since they knew that they could save an equal amount or even more on their own buying costs. At the same time, these produce traders were able to compete successfully with the firms' agents in local markets by offering higher produce prices as their cost of operation was lower than those of the firms' network maintained in the cocoa producing areas. This again, it seems, raised the overall level of competition.

This raises the question why these produce traders did not venture into the export market, if they were such relatively successful entrepreneurs. The usual explanation is that they lacked capital, skills and could not compete with the big European firms which, by their volume of trade, were able to effect considerable economies of scale.[11] It seems, however, that there were other reasons. First, the differences between the world market and the local purchase price of cocoa in the 1930s were much lower than in the 1920s and thus export cocoa did not offer particularly high rewards. Secondly, it is arguable that dependent cocoa buying, i.e. cocoa buying with advances from the firms, was more profitable than independent cocoa buying. Some of these produce traders owned substantial amounts of capital but they did not choose to employ it in the produce trade as probably other, more profitable, income-generating investment opportunities were available to them, such as money-lending. Finally, there is some evidence that suggests that the intermediary role itself was more profitable than exporting ventures. For example, T.A. Odutola was the biggest supplier of cocoa to the firm of John Holt & Co. and his deliveries to this firm alone exceeded 1,200 tons in each of the 1937/38 and 1938/39 cocoa seasons.[12] At the same time he exported only 250 tons of cocoa on his own behalf in the 1938/39 cocoa season.[13]

Even if T.A. Odutola had lacked capital of his own, there were facilities, albeit costly, available in Nigeria at the time which would have enabled him to export his total seasonal purchases. These facilities included London brokers who were willing to arrange credit in Nigeria.[14] There was also the possibility to 'hypothecate' cocoa. This was a device which allowed produce traders to borrow money from the banks on the production of a receipt from a shipping agent for cocoa already delivered to the shipping agent's warehouses. In such cases no additional collateral was necessary, although the sum of money lent by the banks was considerably lower than the value of the cocoa in the shipping agent's warehouse.

It is very likely that such facilities were open to traders like T.A. Odutola and they chose not to export but rather to sell most of their seasonal purchases to the European trading firms. Despite the fact that commission rates for intermediaries had declined in consequence of the 1937 Buying Agreement in the late 1930s, it appears that, at least for some produce traders, internal marketing was at least as financially rewarding as 'breaking' into the export trade. In addition, produce traders were at the time probably also not prepared to risk the little capital they had in the export trade, even if it perhaps sometimes offered high rewards when sure return could be obtained in the internal trade.

Incidentally, the existence of these larger produce traders made it impossible for the firms to lower purchase prices in Nigeria substantially below world market prices for a long time. It seems that they had tried this in the groundnut trade, but it had prompted local competitors to take over a substantial portion of the export trade.[15]

However, it seems that the emergence of a new type of intermediary, as well as the expansion of the cocoa industry and the extension of the road network in south-western Nigeria, generally raised the level of competition. One outward sign of this development was the steady rise in monetary and non-monetary inducements to sell cocoa to particular firms. In a memorandum written by one of the trading firms in defence of the Buying Agreement of 1937, it is stated that,

> Intense competition between the merchants for cocoa tonnage has, in the past, resulted in competitive bidding for the services of middlemen with connexions in wide areas, and who were thereby in a position to offer attractive tonnage. Inducements to secure the tonnage offered by brokers have taken many forms among which may be enumerated here cash advances, commissions, allowances for the loss in weight...[16]

Though it is impossible to pinpoint precisely what kind of inducement cost the firms incurred in their buying operations, but it seems that in general non-monetary inducements were financially more harmful to the firms than monetary ones. As already mentioned in the previous chapter, competition induced the firms to extend larger and larger amounts of credit in the form of advances to their commission buyers. This was, apart from the increase in the credit risk, financially not too injurious to the firms. Yet, competition forced the firms to allow their buying agents extending periods between the declaration of purchases and the actual delivery of these purchases to the firms' produce stores.[17] Though this practice seems to have not been completely new to the trade,[18] it appears that it became more widespread in the 1930s. This opened up new income opportunities to commission buyers which far exceeded the income derived from commission rates since they could now speculate successfully against the trading firms without any risk.

If the market looked bullish, produce buyers would purchase cocoa with the firms' advances and hold it until a price rise occurred, thus pocketing the difference. The firms naturally tried to insist on the terms of the previously-concluded buying contract, but commission buyers could, for example, evade the firms' claim by pretending not to have bought any cocoa and transferring the actual stock bought to other buying agents who would then sell this at the current higher price to their principals. As one firm's local representative put it: 'We as a company were forced to accept ... [these] declarations or lose the tonnage to competitors who would accept large declarations.'[19]

In cases where the market looked more bearish, commission agents would not buy cocoa immediately but would wait for a price fall. The whole system was described by a District Agent of John Holt & Co. in Ibadan as follows:

> The pernicious practice of declarations which has grown up through the competition between the firms to obtain tonnage, allowed buyers to 'declare' tonnage bought at the higher price on a fall price, the purchases so declared not actually being delivered at the price change but being delivered at various periods afterwards.[20]

This opened the door to the practice which was considered by firms as one of the prime 'abuses' of the trade. Because commission buyers could deliver produce a considerable time after they had 'declared' the amount in their possession, commission buyers were induced habitually to over-declare their purchases and actually buy the difference at the current lower price, which of course gave them an extra profit. The commission buyers were, in effect, operating a highly sophisticated futures cocoa market, in which the inherent risk was shifted squarely onto the firms. This particularly incensed the firms which did not object to the practice where produce traders were doing it with their own capital, but were highly irritated when commission buyers used for this practice the firms' advances.[21]

The firms were to some extent forced to accept these declarations since, if they only paid the current lower price for cocoa delivered, they ran the risk of ruining their own 'honest' buying agents, for which the payment of the current lower prices would mean a clear loss. This in turn would endanger the credit which the firms had advanced to the buying agents. It was, in the words of the District Agent of John Holt & Co. in Lagos, the somewhat unpleasant choice 'between losing money on cocoa or losing money outstanding' and 'between overstepping Produce Department's [price] limits and losing credit'[22].

This raises the question why the firms extended their produce buying net-works and expanded the volume of credit to commission buyers in circum-stances which were clearly unfavourable to them. The Nowell Commission argued that this was largely due to the competition between the firms them-selves which forced them to adopt this policy and that the purpose of the Buying Agreement of 1937 was consequently an attempt to eliminate such competition.[23] Yet, one wonders if the firms really had no other policy options like, for example, the one which the Nigerian Director of Agriculture had suggested. He argued that instead of concluding a buying agreement, all that was needed was an agreement between the firms that '...no cash advances should be made and that the produce trade should be converted solely to one of cash on delivery'[24]. This, he argued, would make it impossible for commis-sion buyers to speculate against the firms. Regarding the extension of the firms' buying network, it seems equally sensible to argue that all that was needed was an agreement between the firms to preserve the *status quo* or even to reduce the existing network. Why then did the firms not choose this option? So far as a policy which would limit the firms' buying networks was concerned, it seems that they feared that under the circumstances prevalent at the end of the 1930s, control of outlying markets and especially of newly-developing markets in areas which had only fairly recently come into production would be placed into the hands of larger produce traders,[25] and this, from the firms' point of view, had to be avoided.

In the matter of the implementation of cash-delivery policy, the argument is somewhat more complicated. In a reply to a letter from the District Agent in Accra, which suggested such a course,[26] the Director of the Administrative Department of John Holt & Co. Ltd., argued that:

> If the native cocoa dealers of the Gold Coast can in fact finance the cocoa crop without credit facilities, how long do you think the exporting houses can remain in business without paying forever a higher price on the Gold Coast than the African shipper can get on the home market. A direct shipper can hypothecate his cocoa shipments through the Bank. In the long run does not it come down to this - that the exporting houses have got to choose between paying more on the Gold Coast than the average home market, ... or alternatively financing the marketing of the crop, in the hope of getting a substantial proportion of tied customers, and being able to buy at a rather lower price, than they would have to pay if all the cocoa were free cocoa.[27]

Though clearly this letter was written with the Gold Coast situation in mind, it seems that this argument is also valid for Nigeria, in that the marketing system in both countries in this respect was very similar. It seems, therefore, that it was not only 'competition' between the firms which induced them to embark on policies which were in the short run clearly to their detriment; long-term considerations, such as a certain amount of apprehension about the emergence of the new type of middleman, also guided the firms' policies. If this argument is valid, then the conventional interpretation of the advance system as it existed at the end of the 1930s and of the Buying Agreement of 1937, needs some amendment. Concerning the interpretation of the advance system, the view that it mainly existed because of the 'absence of a local capitalist class'[28] with sufficient capital resources has to be turned upside down: it existed because of the presence of a local capitalist class, even if this class existed at that time only in very small numbers. With regard to the 1937 Buying Agreement, it seems that it came about not only as a means to eliminate the competition between the firms, but also to limit the damaging effects of a financial system which the firms maintained in order to keep their dominant position in West African trade.

In the following two sections of this chapter we will see what prompted the firms to conclude a buying agreement in 1937. Then the Agreement itself will be examined.

The 1936/37 Debacle

In the early phase of the 1936/37 season, prospects looked quite bright. Prices had improved since the last season, and there was heavy demand for cocoa from European and, particularly, from American manufacturers, who expected a marked increase in chocolate consumption in 1937. There was, however, great uncertainty about the size of the forthcoming crop and some manufacturers, and also some speculators, started to invest heavily in cocoa stocks, expecting that in 1937 world demand would considerably outstrip world supply, thus speculating on a further price rise. This induced the trading firms in Nigeria and in the Gold Coast (Ghana) to embark on somewhat feverish competition for tonnage. While prices in the early part of the season were, according to the forecasts, still rising, the outward sign of strong competition, already mentioned in the previous chapter, began to appear. It seems that a previously-concluded 'gentleman's agreement' between the firms broke down and commission rates, advances, etc. began to rise. The United Africa Company and Cocoa Manufacturers Ltd. in particular were engaged in such fierce competition that smaller firms considered it unwise to follow their example. 'Obviously', the Director of John Holt & Co. commented, 'we cannot join in a fight between "giants"'[29].

By December 1936 the Lagos price of cocoa exceeded £42 per ton. Such prices had not been paid since 1928 and to contemporary observers they must have appeared as the end of the long depression in produce prices between these years; in the same month in the previous year, for example, prices had not even reached £17 per ton.[30] Equally, commission rates, advances and allowances of all sorts increased, and traders, as well as cocoa farmers, enjoyed a brisk and profitable season.

Apparently cocoa trading was so attractive that the activities of '...every farmer and trader in Ibadan and Ife [were diverted] to cocoa, to the exclusion of other crops'[31]. Moreover, high cocoa prices, according to one observer, 'relieved the majority of cocoa farmers from debt'[32]. As regards the profitability of the trade to produce traders, we have the evidence of O. Awolowo, who wrote in his autobiography:

> The 1936-7 season witnessed the best cocoa boom for many years... Business was brisk all around and it was all too easy to make money. As a matter of fact, I made enough profit during the season to pay my associates their capital and shares of profit in full, and to enable me with strict economy, to proceed to the United Kingdom to study law.[33]

Since there are no reasons to believe that Awolowo was a particularly gifted businessman, this quotation shows what size of income produce traders could derive from trading activities in exceptionally favourable circumstances.

The boom did not last. In early January 1937, it was realised that the crop would be far larger than expected and that the prospects for increased consumption had been seen in too rosy a light. Especially the larger American buyers, like the Hershey Corporation, consequently withdrew from the market and prices began to fall. Although selling prices for cocoa in the international markets stayed high for another two to three months, local prices tumbled.[34] Thus, for example, the price at which cocoa changed hands in Ibadan dropped from over £47 on 19th January, 1937 to £38 on 27th January, 1937, a fall of almost 20 per cent![35]

Local prices started to fall earlier than world market spot prices because at this point of the season, trading firms did not buy to fulfil already existing contracts, but bought substantial quantities of produce in order to be able to sell later in the year. It seems that the managers of the produce departments of leading European firms in January shared a very dim view of the prospects of the development of cocoa prices. This view was eventually proved to be accurate as cocoa prices in the international markets steadily and steeply declined from March 1937.[36]

The sudden decline in cocoa prices had two effects on the firms' profit margins. It seems that at the end of the main season in March 1937 they were in possession of considerable quantities of cocoa, some of which they knew could only be sold at a loss because of the future price prospects. This as such was not unusual in West African trade, as firms habitually held significant quantities of cocoa at the end of the main season, and in the particular season their gamble about future price movements had turned out to be rather disadvantageous to the firms, while apparently in others this kind of speculation had been quite rewarding. For example, at the end of the 1935/36 cocoa season, the firms had in their possession some 106,000 tons of cocoa for which they had not found a buyer, but as prices improved during 1936 they sold this quantity at a profit. But still, the 46,000 tons which they held at the end of the 1936/37 main season represented a substantial loss to the firms, and particularly to the United Africa Company which alone had some 29,000 tons for which they had paid more than it would eventually realise on the world market.[37]

However, part of this loss was not just the result of a misjudgment about future price movements. It seems that the firms tried to decrease local purchase prices in expectation of future lower prices. At this point the previously mentioned 'overdeclarations' came into play. When the firms announced continuously lower purchase prices during the course of January and February 1937, they were flooded with declarations.[38] Some of these declarations might have been genuine, but it is very likely that a substantial number of produce traders overdeclared their purchases. This led to a situation in which the firms were unable to buy cocoa at the ruling current price because they were outbid by their own commission buyers who bought cocoa at higher prices in order to fill the gap between their earlier actual purchases and the declared tonnage.[39] In this way the firms' agents sometimes paid purchase prices which in a given period were on average higher than they were allowed by the limits the firms' headquarters had cabled to them, and thus occasionally '...the average price paid locally by all the competing firms ... [had] been higher than the corresponding price in the American and European market'[40].

It is impossible to find out whether the firms would have made a profit on their produce-buying operations if they had been able significantly to depress local prices below those paid in January and February 1937, or if the loss of the firms in that season was mainly a result of a collective misjudgment about future price movements. In the event they made these losses and this led the firms to look for a remedy for what they regarded as abuses in the trade.

The 1937 Buying Agreement

Negotiations about a buying agreement between the major firms in the cocoa trade started in December 1936 or January 1937.[41] Though this early attempt to conclude an agreement did not meet with success, it seems that it prepared the ground for subsequent negotiations. Thus in June 1937 the major hurdle to an agreement was overcome, which was the desired participation of the manufacturing firm of Cadbury. This was achieved by a special arrangement between the United Africa Company and Cadbury regarding its supplies[42] and a special clause in the agreement that Cadbury, in contrast to the other participating firms, could withdraw from the Agreement after one year, if dissatisfied, while the other firms had no such facility and were legally bound to the Agreement for four years.[43] The negotiations between the firms were so successful that in the end only two firms with offices in London did not sign the Agreement. These were the English & Scottish Co-operative Wholesale Society and the Syrian firm of C. Zard, both whose share in the West African cocoa trade was rather small, so that it did not matter too much to the signatories.[44]

Though the legally binding agreement was not signed until 10th November, 1937, a Letter of Instruction was sent to the local agents of the participating firms in Nigeria and the Gold Coast on 18 September 1937.[45] It informed local agents that the firms had concluded a buying agreement, how it would work and what practical consequences it would have for buying operations in West Africa.

According to the Letter of Instruction, the firms agreed to eliminate competition by fixing the share in the crop which the participating firms were allowed to purchase in the forthcoming 1937/38 season. These shares were based on the relative performance of the firms in the previous two seasons (1935/36 and 1936/37). Table four shows how they were distributed between the members of the 'Pool':

Table 4: The 1937 Agreement Buying Quotas (in percent)

	Main Crop	Light Crop
Cocoa Manufacturers Ltd.	13.50	-
Compagnie Française de l'Afrique Occidentale	4.40	2.32
G.L. Gaiser	12.38	16.32
John Holt & Co. (Liverpool) Ltd.	12.05	12.39
G.B. Ollivant Ltd.	8.68	15.22
Paterson, Zochonis & Co. Ltd.	6.30	5.62
Société Commerciale de l'Ouest Africain	2.10	-
The United Africa Company Ltd.	34.53	44.10
Union Trading Company Ltd.	3.06	1.03
Witt & Busch	3.00	3.00

Source: Holt Papers, Mss. Afr. s825, file 535(1). Letter of Instruction, 18 Sept. 1937.

Thus depending on the relative size of the main crop, i.e. October to March purchases, and the intermediate or light crop, i.e. April to September purchases, the United Africa Company and the other subsidiary of the Unilever Group, G.B. Ollivant, accounted for about 45 per cent of the agreement firms' total purchases, as the light crop usually came to less than one-tenth of the main crop. Its nearest rival, Cocoa Manufacturers, had a share of some 13 per cent. This again highlights the dominant position the United Africa Company occupied in the Nigerian cocoa trade.[46]

These shares were '...fixed and immutable during the continuance of the scheme...'[47], which ran from 1st October, 1937 to 30th September, 1941. It was almost impossible for individual members to withdraw from the Agreement before its expiry in September 1941. The only exception was Cocoa Manufacturers Ltd., which was allowed to withdraw earlier in case the firm was dissatisfied with the working of the Agreement. This clause had been inserted in order to overcome to initial reluctance of Cocoa Manufacturers Ltd. to join the Agreement which could only be terminated when seven out of its ten members wished to do so. This, as it will be shown later, had some important consequences when the members of the Agreement were faced with the loss of European customers at the outbreak of war in 1939.

In order to keep actual purchases in line with the pre-fixed shares, the members of the Agreement consented to a somewhat cumbersome equalisation procedure which included weekly returns to a committee in London and a monthly settlement of accounts during the cocoa buying season. One feature of this procedure was that it made sure that members had no interest in overbuying their share. In the event that firms overbought, the Agreement stipulated that they had to hand over their excess tonnage to the firms which had underbought, but would receive a price for their excess tonnage which would not cover their buying costs.[48] This is the reason that this type of buying agreement was later called a 'penalty pool'.

The whole scheme was supervised by a General Committee in London, whose main tasks were administering the computation of handovers and determining the prices to be paid to traders and producers at the port of shipment. This price was usually cabled to Lagos once a day and was known as the 'Tansley/Iredale Price' in order 'to indicate that both merchants and manufacturers had studied the market and had arrived at a conclusion'[49]. It was based on either the actual market price of cocoa, i.e. the price at which cocoa changed hands on the spot or the next shipment from Lagos and Accra, or on terminal market price, i.e. for shipments three or six months ahead. In the event that in the terminal markets of London and New York, cocoa was sold at considerably lower or higher prices, this price determined buying prices in Nigeria; if, however, the differential between actual market prices and terminal market prices was rather narrow, the actual market price formed the base price. To arrive at the port of shipment price a schedule of marketing costs was deducted from this base. This schedule included Nigerian export taxes, genuine marketing costs, such as shipping and insurance, and a margin for profits. Local agents were thus only in a very limited way involved in the actual running of the scheme. This was quite deliberate for the agreement stated that: 'It is the intention to operate the agreement as much as possible from Europe.'[50]

The committee consisted of J.W. Knight, a director of the United Africa Company and J. Cadbury of Cadbury Bros. Ltd. Each of them nominated a representative. These were N. Edwards of Cadbury Bros. Ltd. and E.C. Tansley, head of the cocoa department of UAC. The latter was doing the day-to-day work of the scheme while Edwards probably had more of a controlling function.[51] Thus, through buying to predetermined shares and fixing a standard purchase price, competition between the firms was completely removed from the cocoa trade. ·

The removal of competition as such did not improve the balance sheets of the trading firms. This could only be achieved through a number of specific means. How then did the firms increase their profit margins? Basically there were three options open to them and probably each was used. First, they could take a 'pessimistic' view about the future movement of the cocoa price in the international markets. Even if the person with the responsibility of determining the base price was 'entirely scrupulous' and had 'absolute fairness of mind'[52], it seems unlikely that this person would err on the 'right' side, from the Nigerian point of view, for any prolonged period and pay higher prices locally than subsequently the state of the world market warranted, without incurring the wrath of his superiors; while if he were erring on the 'wrong' side and as long as no new entrants into the trade would appear as competitors to the firms, the person in charge could be sure of his superiors' gratitude.

There is, however, no evidence that prices were manipulated in this way, partly because after the introduction of the Agreement, they seem to have been largely based on spot market prices and not on terminal market prices, probably because in the context of the political aftermath, it would have been extremely foolish to manipulate buying prices in this way.

The second way in which the margin between the buying price in Nigeria and the selling price could be enlarged was to introduce a 'generous' marketing cost schedule. This schedule consisted of sixteen separate cost and profit items, like cost of ocean shipping, headoffice expenses in London and Liverpool, the cost of borrowing capital from the banks, as well as local costs, such as inspection fees and the cost, which the firms incurred in maintaining a produce buying network. This schedule was deducted from the ruling world market price to arrive at a standard ex-scale port of shipment purchase price. The difference between the European reference price (c.i.f. Hamburg) and the port of shipment price (Lagos) was fixed at £7 8s 7d per ton. The value of some cost items depended on the ruling world market price of cocoa, like, for example, the cost of financing the working capital which was required to move the crop. The schedule was thus based on a north European port of shipment selling price of £35 and for each £1 rise or fall, 16d was subtracted or added. The schedule also included one item which seems to represent pure profit. This was the item 'Head Office Commission' which was fixed at 1 per cent on the selling price.[53] Many authors on the subject have stated that the schedule was far too generous, and that the profit item was only part of the overall profits. It has been suggested that in particular the item 'cost establishment charges' of 15s per ton, which included, for example the cost of housing for the firms' local representatives and their salaries, was fixed on the high side.[54]

Yet, it seems that probably all items of the 1937/38 schedule were fixed at a premium since the schedule which the firm of John Holt & Co. had compiled 'for use against severe competition'[55] in the previous season of 1936/37 had amounted to only £5 5s per ton, despite the fact that world market prices were much higher in that season.[56] The difference between the 1936/37 and 1937/38 schedule comes to £2 2s 7d per ton. This suggests that the profits which the firms had made in the 1937/38 cocoa season were much larger than the Nowell Commission had assumed. It reported that in the 1937/38 cocoa season the profit margin had come to only about 5s per ton.[57]

Finally the firms agreed on a number of measures aimed at a reduction of buying costs. As the firms bought most of their cocoa from produce traders and buyers, these measures were necessarily designed in the first place to squeeze the profit margins of the intermediaries and, secondly, to a lesser extent, to reduce the prices cocoa farmers received. This was achieved by stipulating that commission payments should not exceed 10s per ton and that commissions should be *deducted* from the standard ex-scale buying price. This measure meant that the firms' produce clerks could offer a higher price in local markets than the commission buyers in the vicinity of buying stations and that payments of overriding commission or commission payments on a sliding scale, that is, a commission which increased *pro rata* with the volume delivered, were ruled out. Furthermore, the signatories agreed not to offer employment to buyers of another member without prior consultation of that member and also not to act as an agent for Nigerian produce traders. The local representatives of the firms were also instructed to eliminate practices such as 'forward contracts' and the 'acceptance of declarations on a fall in price of the quantity of a buyer's or broker's normal delivery capacity and at the expired price'[58]. In fact, the firms agreed to limit a declaration on a fall in price to one-sixth of the buyers' previous six-day reports,[59] thus making it almost impossible for produce traders and buyers to speculate with the firms' money against the firms. Finally, the agreement contained a clause which disallowed the members of the Agreement to pay a premium for co-operative cocoa.

Judged from its pre-history and from the text of the Agreement alone, the firms seem to have been trying to achieve several aims at the same time. The Agreement shifted a large part of the commercial risk involved in cocoa buying from the firms to their customers, i.e. the traders. The schedule of marketing costs and thus the margin of profit was increased, but not, apparently, to an excessive degree. Finally the agreement tried to limit the commercial opportunities of the Nigerian produce traders and buyers in the cocoa trade. In that sense one might call it a multi-purpose agreement, in which the short term interests to merely increase trade margins on the coast merged with the more radical long term interest to solve once for all the middlemen problem.[60]

The only safeguard for traders and producers was that, in case of blatant 'misuse' of the Agreement, outside competitors would emerge in the trade. The larger the difference between the local purchase price and the world market price, the more attractive the trade would become for American and British trading firms and specifically to Nigerian-owned trading firms, which had not been signatories to the Agreement. It seems that the firms themselves were quite aware that this possibility existed and that they reacted by adjusting their policy accordingly. From the firms' point of view, it did not make sense to restrict competition for commission buyers, while at the same time pursuing a policy which would attract outside competitors to the trade. In the words of one of the directors of a firm which participated in the Agreement, 'there would have been no advantage in insuring against one form of suicide by committing another'[61]. It seems, therefore, that the firms tried to increase the profitability of the cocoa trade only to an extent which ensured that no new competitors would be attracted to the trade or existing competitors, such as the Nigerian produce traders, would gain the impression that venturing into the export market would offer considerably higher reward than the internal market.

The Conflict

It is convenient to divide the course of the conflict into two separate periods, according to who was involved in the conflict. Nigeria was concerned with the discussions between September and November 1937 and these discussions were held largely within government circles. Only from December 1937 did the wider public take part in these discussions, which, as we will see, changed the course of the conflict.

The first reports about the Agreement appeared in the British press in early September 1937 and in journals which were widely available in West Africa in the second half of September 1937.[62] These reports seem to have prompted the firms to take the initiative. 'Rather than', wrote one of the directors of John Holt & Co., 'that false impressions of what the Cocoa Pool is should be gathered in official circles, it was thought wise to take the Government completely into the confidence of the Pool'[63]. This is a somewhat problematic statement, as neither was the government taken completely into confidence, nor could one argue that the action was directed only at informing the government about the Agreement, but it might be accurate insofar as the firms tried to head off the predictable criticism of the Agreement by informing the government.[64] However, the firms asked the Colonial Office for a meeting, held on 24th September, 1937. At this meeting, at which J. Cadbury and F. Samuel represented the firms, and the Under-Secretary of State, Sir Cecil Bottomly, G. Clauson and C.G. Eastwood from the CO were present, the firms' representatives informed the Colonial Office in broad terms about the Agreement and asked the Colonial Office to advise the governments of the Gold Coast and Nigeria to support the Agreement by making information available to District Officers who would then be able to answer eventual questions regarding the Agreement. Although the officials present at the meeting were aware that the Agreement could give rise to difficulties in the Gold Coast and in Nigeria, they apparently promised their support.[65] They also asked for a copy of the Agreement. Four days later the Colonial Office received a copy of the Gold Coast Letter of Instruction, though not a copy of the Agreement between the firms, nor the text of the Nigerian Letter of Instruction or the schedule of marketing costs.[66]

On the basis of this information the Secretary of State for the Colonies sent a despatch on 7th October, 1937 to the Governors of the Gold Coast and Nigeria, in which he outlined the Agreement (only the Governor of the Gold Coast received a copy of the Letter of Instruction at this time) and indicated that he favoured the scheme.[67] He also suggested that the Governors should send a circular to District Officers in order to inform them about the existence and the essential features of the Agreement.

It seems that the Governor of Nigeria did not think that the matter needed his immediate attention as it took him more than six weeks to reply to the despatch. When he did so on 25th November, 1937, Governor Bourdillon somewhat ambiguously stated his support for the scheme. Though he was apparently aware that the effect of the scheme might lead to a reduction of trader and producer incomes, he thought that long-term advantages would outweigh short-term disadvantages.[68] On the day he sent his reply to the Secretary of State, he directed the Chief Secretary to send a circular to District Officers in order to inform them about the existence of the Agreement.[69]

This circular makes interesting reading since it shows how the Nigerian government perceived the Agreement and its main objectives. Apart from giving a broad outline about how the scheme would work, the Governor wrote:

> To avoid misapprehensions as to the object of the agreement the firms have stated that the intensive competition between firms had in the past led to various practices which resulted in the remuneration of brokers and middlemen in excess of the value of the services rendered by them. The object of the agreement is to eliminate undue competition and the excessive remuneration of the middlemen caused thereby and to induce

healthier conditions into the market. There is no desire on their part to reduce the returns of the growers.[70]

Thus at the end of November 1937 the Governor of Nigeria supported the Agreement, albeit cautiously. Two months later however, in January 1937, the Governor changed his mind. He then strongly criticised the Agreement and also the firms themselves. What apparently made the Governor change his mind is the subject of the following section of this chapter. At the end of that section, Bourdillon's new position will be reviewed in some detail.

The Nigerian Protest Movement

The movement which emerged in Nigeria in order to force the firms to withdraw the Agreement consisted of three different groups. The first group opposed the Agreement on principle. They saw it either as a violation of the current doctrine of 'free trade' or the doctrine of 'trusteeship' which the colonial government allegedly abandoned by not protecting the Nigerian traders from the machinations of the 'combine'. The second group were the produce traders and buyers. The third group supported the protest movement, not so much because it was directly economically hit by the Agreement, but rather because of the circumstances in which the Agreement was introduced, i.e. the severe depression in the trade in 1938 for which the firms were - largely mistakenly - blamed.

In order to explain why these groups opposed the Agreement one has, however, not only to look at the Agreement and the Letter of Instruction, but also at how the Agreement worked in practice and at what precisely were the circumstances under which the Agreement was introduced.

The Agreement at Work

In as much as one can gather from the internal correspondence between firms' representatives in Nigeria and between representatives in Nigeria and the Gold Coast, the local agents of the firms executed the Agreement according to plan,[71] coupled with a certain amount of emotional satisfaction. Thus, for example, the District Agent of John Holt & Co. wrote to the 'Ondo Ventures':

> With regard to declarations you will have trouble with your buyer at first, so will other firms... We have now the opportunity of educating these buyers to get the cocoa in from the bush day by day, get it graded and shipped... Do not worry if your buying drop while you are educating the

> buyers, it is quite likely that some of the pool firms will not be so rigid as
> we intend to be, but if so they will soon see the error of their ways.[72]

The idea of the firms' managers to 'educate' the middlemen appears in retrospect to be rather odd. As has been argued at the beginning of this chapter, the development of the market had reached a point at which the position of the firms had become increasingly tenuous and the Agreement between the firms was ultimately an exercise to consolidate their position. To argue, as firms apparently did, that the Agreement had some 'educational' benefits, even if it just meant in the sense of 'corrective' seems to reveal a surprising amount of conceit.

One of the first measures the senior representatives of the firms undertook seems to have been to regain control of their outlying buying stations. In rather drastic words[73] the local 'ventures' were told that the main office in Lagos would not accept cocoa at prices higher than those cabled to them. The firms also stopped paying a premium for co-operative cocoa[74], reduced commission payments to the standard rate of 10s per ton[75], limited cash advances to the commission buyers' tangible security[76], and probably also dismissed a number of produce buyers[77].

Yet, the main thrust of the Agreement - as far as one can judge from the internal correspondence of one of the firms (John Holt & Co.) - was directed against the practice of traders and buyers to 'over'-declare their purchases on a falling market. This subject almost completely dominated their correspondence, as the following quotation from a letter from the District Agent, Lagos to the District Agent, Accra, shows:

> Now the trouble here is, we as a pool want to stamp out abuses... Today
> we refuse to accept declarations and price drops and refuse our buyers
> the right to store up cocoa against us, waiting for a price advance before
> reporting it as a purchase. Our buyers have no legitimate kick, they are
> employees paid to do a job, i.e. buy produce and report each day what
> they have bought at that day's price. To the middlemen and free sellers
> we have said "We will buy just what you can deliver each day at that day's
> 'price'", which means they can no longer make 'forward contracts',
> 'declarations'... They have to take the loss if they buy 'high' and the price
> drops before they can deliver it. For the first time in produce history they
> are called upon to take their own risk in buying and marketing... THEY
> DO NOT LIKE IT [*sic*].[78]

The implementation of the Agreement was, however, only one of the reasons the protest movement in Nigeria gained comparatively widespread popular support. There were clearly other factors at work, including a severe trade depression which occurred at the same time.

Since the end of the previous season, produce prices had steadily declined and when, at the opening of the 1937/38 season, the first cocoa reached the market in October 1937, it changed hands in Lagos for only about half the price it had in the previous season. Produce prices declined even further during the season and in December 1937 reached a seasonal low of about £15 per ton, while just two months earlier over £20 per ton was paid for grade II cocoa.[79] Despite an improvement in prices during the course of January and February 1938, it is unlikely that many farmers could take advantage of this improvement since usually 60 per cent of the crop was sold by December.

The decline in prices had different effects on traders, farmers and the firms. There are some hints that the firms themselves did not expect such a decline in prices. At least John Holt & Co. had, in expectation of higher produce prices, stocked considerable amounts of merchandise which they now feared could only be sold at a loss.[80]

The situation for the traders was even more uncomfortable. They had advanced money to their sub-buyers or had already bought cocoa with the firms' advances at the beginning of the season and were now unable to recoup their outlay. Previously part of that loss was borne by the firms but, owing to the implementation of the Agreement, only one-sixth of the previous six days' purchases could be declared as having been bought at the former higher prices. Thus many traders were faced with a partial loss of their own trading capital in cases where they used their own money, or they were faced with the loss of the deposits they had with the firms in cases where they used the firms' advances.

The loss suffered by Nigerian traders in the 1937/38 season is well documented in Awolowo's biography. After he had made substantial profits in the previous season, he decided not to proceed to study law in Britain but,

> decided to stay in business until the 1937/38 cocoa season... Many produce buyers including myself speculated heavily and in very high spirits in preparation of the 1937/38 season. The forecasts for the season proved all wrong; there was a big slump, and I not only lost everything but became also indebted to the firms for whom I bought produce.[81]

Finally, cocoa farmers, and in particular the larger farmers, experienced severe difficulties. It seems that they were not only hit by low produce prices but by an even more severe decline in 'net profits' since production costs, mainly the cost of employing wage labour, which had shown a rapid advance in the previous season, remained high.[82] The Resident (Ondo) reported in April 1938, for example, that: 'A certain amount of hardship has been caused in Ondo Division to the producer in a fairly large way of business. He finds himself unable to pay his labourers.' The Resident also remarked that in his opinion opposition to the Pool had been shown 'only by the large producer who is usually 50 per cent a middleman as well'[83]. Moreover, real incomes seem to have declined even more, owing to the fact that the cost of living was considerably higher in 1938 than in 1936, though slightly lower than in 1937. Lastly, there were some attempts in the late 1930s by Native Authorities to re-impose some form of income tax on cocoa farmers in Oyo Province. These taxes had not been collected for some time, but in the 1936/37 season the Ibadan Native Administration, for example, instructed cocoa farmers to pay 1s per 100 cocoa trees in bearing. Though this levy was reported to have been halved in the following season, the fact that they collected it presented an additional loss of net income for the cocoa farmers.[84]

Thus in the 1937/38 season the standard of living of cocoa farmers greatly declined. This is demonstrated in a petition from the Ibadan Co-operative Cocoa Marketing Union to the Governor of Nigeria in February 1938:

> At present he [the cocoa farmer] cannot send his children to school and pay their fees early, ... [and] his tax ... is a burden upon him. The upkeep of the very farm which is the source of his living is very difficult.[85]

This, of course, is circumstantial evidence for the reasons why in late 1937 a movement sprang up in Nigeria which found support in parts of the population which hitherto had been largely outside the realms of 'politics'. In the absence of any other evidence to the contrary, however, it seems not unreasonable to conclude that the coincidence of the depression in the cocoa trade with the implementation of the Buying Agreement, to some extent explains why the latter drew so much criticism and also to some extent why the sectional interests of produce traders became the focus of a national campaign. How and by whom that campaign was conducted and how widespread its support was will be seen in the next part of this chapter.

The Campaign (December 1937 - January 1938)

While reports in the British press prompted the firms to take the initiative and inform the Government about the Agreement, the same press reports, and also probably some deliberate leaks from one of the agreement firms[86], inspired leaders of public opinion in West Africa, including the infant nationalist press, and leaders of farmers' and traders' unions, to organise opposition against the implementation of the Agreement. During the course of the conflict this developed into more fundamental opposition to colonial governments in the Gold Coast and in Nigeria.

At this point in the narrative, it is no longer possible to separate developments in Nigeria from those which occurred in the Gold Coast as they influenced and reinforced each other.[87] Since in Nigeria not much happened until early December 1937, events in the Gold Coast in October and November 1937 require mentioning. It is very likely that certain aspects of the movement which developed in the Gold Coast, served as a model for the movement which the leaders of the traders' union and the Nigerian Youth Movement hoped to organise in Nigeria.

The first articles which informed cocoa farmers about the existence of the Agreement and suggested, as a response, a general refusal to sell cocoa to the European trading firms until the Agreement was withdrawn, appeared in the Gold Coast press in October 1937. At the end of that month and in the beginning of the next month, mass meetings were held in towns in the centre of the cocoa producing areas, in which the participants agreed to boycott the European trading firms, i.e. to not sell cocoa to the firms and not to purchase merchandise goods which were not vital from the companies' stores. This boycott was almost completely effective from mid-November 1937. Despite many attempts by the firms and also by the Secretary of State for the Colonies to convince farmers and traders to sell cocoa to the firms, the boycott lasted almost six months, until in April 1938 a 'truce' was negotiated by a Royal Commission which the Secretary of State for the Colonies had appointed as a means to dissolve the crisis.[88]

In contrast to the Gold Coast, it took much longer in Nigeria for a reaction to the implementation of the Agreement to emerge. Although the Nigerian press carried a number of articles on the Agreement in October and November 1937, it was not until about mid-December that the opposition began to marshall their forces.

On 11 December, the Nigerian Produce Traders' Union wrote a letter to the Gold Coast Farmers' Association in which they expressed their intention of visiting the Gold Coast in January 1938 and the hope that both organisations would co-operate in their fight against the agreement. Three days later the Union wrote a second letter to the Chief Secretary to the Government and asked for the opportunity to discuss the matter of trade policies of the firms with the Governor of Nigeria, Bourdillon.[89]

The Governor of Nigeria invited all the groups he thought were involved in the conflict to a 'round table discussion' on 29th December, 1937. The list of people at the meeting is almost a 'who's who' of the cocoa trade in Nigeria at the time. Thus for the NPTU S. Akinsanya appeared as its spokesman while D.F.G. Adekunle (Abeokuta), A.O. Johnson (Ibadan), Alhaji A.R.A. Smith (Ilesha and Ife), T.A. Odutola (Ijebu-Ode and Epe), and A. Odunsi (Lagos) represented the Union's local branches. For the agreement firms, the most senior agents of the United Africa Company (R.M. Williams), John Holt & Co. (J.F. Winter), Cocoa Manufacturers Ltd. (P.H. Soper), and the Compagnie Française de l'Afrique Occidentale (A. Esnee) took part in the discussion. On the government side, apart from Governor Bourdillon, no less than five officials were present. These were the Chief Secretary to the Government

(J.A. Maybin), the Financial Secretary (H.L. Bayles), the Director of Agriculture (Captain J.R. Mackie), the Assistant Director of Agriculture, Southern Provinces (Dr. G. Bryce) and the Superintending Inspector of Produce, Lagos, (E. McL. Watson). In addition a number of observers were invited. These were F.W. Jones from the Co-operative Wholesale Society, E.O. Moore (First Lagos Member of the Legislative Council), N.D. Oyerinde (Member for Oyo Division of the Legislative Council) and the leading journalists at the time, H. Macaulay (*Lagos Daily News*), C.A. Titcombe (*Nigerian Daily Times*) and N. Azikiwe (*West African Pilot*).[90]

The list of people who were invited to the meeting is almost as interesting as the list of people who were not invited. Thus there were no farmers' representatives nor members of that class of people who were usually supposed to speak for farmers in the cocoa-producing areas, such as, for example, the Oni of Ife or the Olubadan of Ibadan. This is in striking contrast to the situation in the Gold Coast, where discussions were largely held with the representatives of the farmers' union and with local Chiefs, such as Sir Nana Ofori Atta or the Ashanti king, the Asantehene Prempeh II.[91]

The meeting itself was largely unsuccessful. The firms merely reiterated what they had said before in public, pointing to the statement published in the Gold Coast press on 14th December, i.e. that the sole purpose of the Agreement was to eliminate 'abuses' in the trade. They even tried to convince the other participants in the discussion that the Agreement was not a 'Pool' and that there was 'no limitation of the tonnage which any firm was permitted to buy'[92]. This was - to say the least - a misrepresentation of facts, since the Agreements' 'handing-over' procedure precisely limited the tonnage each firm could buy.

The Governor of Nigeria seems to have confined himself to a number of introductory remarks in which he strongly emphasised the neutrality of the colonial governments in the Gold Coast and Nigeria and of the Colonial Office in London in the matter. He made the point that the Nigerian government had not been asked to approve the Agreement and that 'it had merely been told of something which had already been decided...'[93] He justified his decision to approve the suggestion of the firms that a Colonial Office representative should attend the meetings of the London Committee of the agreement firms by saying that in his view such a representative would not be a participant in the Agreement but merely an observer.

To this argument the spokesman of the NPTU, S. Akinsanya replied that acceptance of the firms' suggestion would mean that the Government gave the Agreement moral support. He then stated why the NPTU opposed the Agreement: it would limit the tonnage of cocoa the firms bought in Nigeria, and it would also limit the price farmers and traders would receive for the cocoa beans. He argued that the agreement would create a monopoly, which would drive produce traders out of the market. As regards 'abuses' he said that a buying agreement was not necessary to check dishonest practices of produce traders because the law could see to that.[94]

There was a heated exchange between S. Akinsanya and the UAC representative, R.M. Williams about the existence of the clause which permitted Cadbury Ltd. to withdraw from the Agreement earlier than other participants. The firms categorically denied the existence of this clause, while the NPTU, knowledgeable of at least part of the text of the Agreement, insisted that this clause was part of it, as indeed it was. This part of the discussion was very embarrassing to the firms as they felt they had been caught 'lying'. One wonders what the government made of this, since the NPTU was obviously better informed than the Nigerian government which only later - on the 20th January, 1938 - received a full copy of the Agreement.[95]

Even if the meeting on 29th December, 1937 had no practical results, there are some indications that the NPTU and S. Akinsanya in particular were very much impressed by the way in which the Governor had handled it. Though it is easy to overstate the argument, S. Akinsanya later wrote that,

> ... if his Excellency the Governor had failed to give the ready and willing hearing which he gave to the people's complaints and the sympathetic attitude shown at the meeting we had with him on the 29th December 1937 ... perhaps there would have been greater panic in Nigeria than there was in the Gold Coast.[96]

It looks, therefore, as if opposition to the Agreement in Nigeria in 1937 was rather weak and was largely upheld by produce traders and their organisations, the Nigerian Youth Movement and the Nigerian press. This changed to some extent in January 1938, when a delegation of the NPTU (S. Akinsanya, N.P. Fale and A.O. Johnson) and, most significantly, the President of the Ibadan Co-operative Marketing Union, A. Obisesan, visited the Gold Coast. They arrived in Accra to take part in the 'Joint Economic Conference by Paramount Chiefs of the Gold Coast, British Mandated Togoland and Nigerian Delegation' on 17th January.[97] At the conference the Nigerian delegation and its Gold Coast counterparts seem to have had some disagreement about the central purpose of the conference. While speakers like Sir Nana Ofori Atta and Kwame Ayew, both very much central figures in the Gold Coast anti-pool movement, mainly complained about Lagosian produce traders selling cocoa despite the hold-up of the European trading firms, which must have been embarrassing to the NPTU representatives, the Nigerian delegation stressed the political dimension of the meeting.[98] S. Akinsanya even referred to the at the time largely defunct National Congress of British West Africa. He argued that the Congress had fought for political goals while now would be the time to fight for economic goals on a West African basis. He also expressed his profound regret about the fact that Nigerian traders were apparently breaking the hold-up in the Gold Coast.

The outcome of the second public meeting of the conference on the 18th January, 1938 was a resolution which reaffirmed the determination by Gold Coast and Nigerian farmers and traders to work together for the withdrawal of the Agreement.[99] The assembly resolved that a 'Joint Central Board of Control' under the direction of farmers' and produce traders' representatives should be set up in the Gold Coast and in Nigeria.[100]

Before leaving Accra, the Nigerian delegation had a further number of private meetings with leaders of the Gold Coast hold-up movement. It also met influential Lagosian traders, probably in response to demands from the leaders of the Gold Cost and Ashanti Farmers' Union. The Nigerian delegation returned to Lagos on 19th January, 1938.

Three days later a reception was held in Glover Hall, Lagos, to welcome the delegation which according to one newspaper report was attended by over 3,000 people.[101] The Chairman was Dr. K.A. Abayomi, who had just become President of the Nigerian Youth Movement after the death of its co-founder, J.C. Vaughan. Almost all 'officers' of the Movement were present at the meeting. According to a belated report in the weekly journal *West Africa* of 5th March, 1938, the main speakers at the meeting were, apart from Dr. Abayomi, E. Ikoli, N. Azikiwe, H.O. Davies and Dr.A. Maja. The Assembly carried a resolution, proposed by Maja, which expressed its '...determination to oppose the buying agreement by all peaceful means...' and called upon 'the Imperial and Colonial Governments to seek the dissolution of the pool and the cancellation of the agreement'[102].

At this point in the narrative it is perhaps appropriate to return briefly to the discussion between the Governor of Nigeria and the Colonial Office in London about the situation in Nigeria as regards the political 'fall-out' of the Agreement, since it was precisely at the end of January 1938 that the Governor of Nigeria, B. Bourdillon, revised his position towards the agreement and the policies of the Colonial Office.

The Immediate Political Effects of the Protest Movement

In early 1938 the Nigerian Government significantly changed its position towards the Agreement and this move, together with a similar move by the Gold Coast government, forced the Colonial Office in London to rethink its policies. Since this episode is well researched,[103] it is sufficient to outline the causes which led to this development.

During January 1938 the Secretary of State for the Colonies tried repeatedly to convince the Governors of Nigeria and the Gold Coast to come out in support of the Agreement. This for various reasons they refused to do, not least because they feared that such action would endanger the position of 'neutrality' which they were anxious to preserve. They argued that any action which would appear to take sides with the firms would do nothing to alleviate the crisis but would draw the government into the conflict. Criticism which had hitherto been directed towards the firms would then be directed towards the government.

They in turn suggested that the firms should publish the text of the Agreement as a means of defusing any misapprehension which cocoa farmers and traders might have. This the firms refused, arguing that the publication of the Agreement, and in particular the publication of the schedule of marketing costs, would give competitors an unfair advantage.[104]

Since the farmers and traders in the Gold Coast showed no inclination to resume the sale of cocoa to the firms until the agreement was withdrawn, a deadlock developed, which increasingly threatened to impair the Gold Coast economy.[105] Simultaneously opposition towards the Agreement developed into opposition to the government and, on 28th January, 1938, the Gold Coast government suggested to the Secretary of State for the Colonies to appoint a Royal Commission to look into the marketing structure of West African cocoa.[106]

In Nigeria no such deadlock developed, because no hold-up occurred. In this aspect, the situation in Nigeria was far less grave than in the Gold Coast. Nevertheless it seems that the change in the Nigerian Government's views ultimately convinced the Colonial Office, including the Secretary of State, that more was required than the publication of articles in the Gold Coast press to resolve the problem.

On 29th January, 1938 the Governor of Nigeria sent a telegram to the Secretary of State for the Colonies in which he categorically stated that he would under no circumstances advise farmers to sell cocoa in the event of a hold-up in Nigeria. Most significantly, he also wrote that he would withdraw his previous decision to agree to the presence of a Colonial Office representative at meetings of the London Committee of the agreement firms, thus signalling that he himself no longer believed in the benefits of the Buying Agreement to Nigerian farmers. The Governor of Nigeria now also demanded the appointment of a Royal Commission.[107] Two days later, on 1st February, 1938, the Secretary of State gave in and his decision was officially announced in Parliament on 14th February.[108]

In a despatch to the Secretary of State, the Governor of Nigeria later explained why he had changed his mind. His main argument was that when he had agreed to the presence of a Colonial Office representative on the London Committee, he had seen the problem solely from a Nigerian point of view. Since then, however, events in the Gold Coast which he had not foreseen, had not gone unnoticed in Nigeria. The repercussions of the events in the Gold

Coast, in particular on the politically more aware part of the Nigerian population, now forced him to change his position.[109] This is clearly a reference to the fact that - as we have seen - in early January 1938 the protest movement in Nigeria began to broaden its base, involving not only produce traders, but also co-operative leaders and the most active political group at the time, the Nigerian Youth Movement.

The Campaign (February - March 1938)

At the beginning of February, leaders of the Nigerian Youth Movement[110] had another meeting with the Governor of Nigeria and a number of high-ranking officials. According to a report in *West Africa*, the initiative to discuss the Agreement had come from the Nigerian Youth Movement which wanted to convey to the government its demand that the Colonial Office representative should be withdrawn from the London Committee and that a commission of enquiry should be appointed. The Governor seems to have responded to these demands by saying that he had already advised the Colonial Office to withdraw its representative. He is also reported to have said that he thought that a commission of enquiry was hardly necessary at that moment.[111]

It appears that this meeting again had no practical results. Yet, it shows that a polarisation between the government and main protagonists of the protest movement as had happened in the Gold Coast did not occur in Nigeria. This was certainly partly due to the relative weakness of the Nigerian protest movement, but also reflected different styles in the management of the crisis by the Governors of the Gold Coast and Nigeria. It seems that Governor Bourdillon engaged the leaders of the protest movement in continuous dialogue, with the effect that a radicalisation of the protest movement in Nigeria was successfully preempted.[112]

After the announcement of the appointment of a Royal Commission in mid-February 1938, the Nigerian Produce Traders' Union and the Nigerian Youth Movement changed their policies. While until February 1938 the main demand of these groups was simply the withdrawal of the Buying Agreement, after February 1938 they became more ambitious in their aims.

In March 1938, S. Akinsanya (NPTU/NYM), E. Ikoli (NYM) and M. Bank-Anthony (Lagos retail merchant, associated with the NYM) travelled through the cocoa producing areas of southern Nigeria on what the Nigerian Youth Movement called a 'Special Mission Tour'.[113] According to an advance notice sent to all the District Offices of the areas concerned, the mission intended to leave Lagos on 3rd March and then visit Abeokuta, Ibadan, Ilesha, Ife, Akure, Ondo, Ijebu-Ode, and Shagamu.[114] Its official purpose was 'to study conditions in the Cocoa producing areas in view of appointment of Commission to enquire Cocoa marketing'[115].

The purpose of this tour was, however, much wider than the study of cocoa marketing. It seems that the special mission called on local notables, such as D.T. Sasegbon (Agege) and the farmers' union in order to get their support for the protest movement in general, and for the Nigerian Youth Movement in particular.[116] Thus, for example, after their visit to Ondo the Ado-Ekiti Farmers' Associations submitted a petition to the Resident (Ondo Division) protesting against the firms' Buying Agreement[117], while after their visit to Shagamu a local branch of the Nigerian Youth Movement was set up[118].

There were two other aims which the members of the mission hoped to achieve: the foundation of a 'Central Farmers' Organisation' and the establishment of a 'Million Shillings Fund'.[119] Though both undertakings seem to have come to nothing, at the time they attracted a certain amount of attention. Thus the Registrar of Co-operative Societies wrote a long letter to the Chief Secretary in which he emphasised that he considered the establishment of a 'Central Farmers' Organisation' a 'most undesirable development'. As regards the 'Million Shillings Fund', he proposed that 'farmers should be warned not to subscribe money' to the fund.[120] Further, at least one of the European trading firms was quite alarmed about the 'Million Shillings Fund' since the purpose of such a fund was in his opinion to finance, in the event of a hold-up, the purchase of cocoa from farmers who were forced to sell cocoa for want of cash.[121]

The essential features of the protest movement in Nigeria in 1937/38 were a press campaign, a trip to the Gold Coast, a number of meetings with the Governor, and a 'mission tour' through the main cocoa-producing areas in south-western Nigeria. This does not seem to be very much. But one is tempted to ask why the conflict in Nigeria had such importance, and whether the Nigerian movement was just an off-shoot of the movement in the Gold Coast?

In order to answer this question the differences between the Gold Coast movement and the Nigerian movement must be examined, which largely reflected differences in the economy and society. Thus, for example, in the Gold Coast the chiefs widely supported the protest movement or were even part of the movement[122], while in Nigeria such support was negligible[123]. Moreover, due to a higher degree of specialisation, household incomes from the sale of cocoa were higher in the Gold Coast than in Nigeria. These higher incomes probably made it easier to embark on a more radical course in the fight against the Agreement, since they enabled farmers to sustain a hold-up economically.[124] Conversely, the higher degree of diversification in Nigeria probably mitigated the impact of rapidly falling cocoa prices on household incomes, probably one of the reasons there was not such widespread dissatisfaction among cocoa farmers. Finally, there was no historical tradition of hold-ups in Nigeria which could have served as a precedent to the events of 1937/38.[125] These are only examples, since an in-depth comparison lies outside the focus of this study, but they illuminate the argument that the Nigerian protest movement has to be seen in its own light and not just as an off-shoot of the Gold Coast movement.

The reasons the firms and the government took the Nigerian movement seriously was most likely because of its dynamic and considerable potential. To start with, the firms and the colonial government were completely surprised by the strength of the movement in Nigeria and its apparent radicalisation and politicisation during the course of the conflict[126], which also revealed to them that their knowledge of the Nigerian cocoa industry and political scene was rather limited[127]. The firms and the government apprehensively noted the apparent overlap between the leadership of the Nigerian Produce Traders' Union, the Nigerian Motor Transport Union and the Nigerian Youth Movement.[128] Both feared that S. Akinsanya would be able to convince the members of the Motor Transport Union to come out in support of the Traders' Union and organise a strike like the one the Union had organised in early 1937.[129] This, it was argued, would open up the possibility of some sort of 'General Strike'. Thus for example the District Agent (Lagos) of John Holt & Co. wrote in February 1938:

> I am convinced that there will be no general cocoa hold-up in this country to which the farmers would acquiesce. The real danger lies in this, Akinsanya may call a strike of the Nigerian Transport Union and even have the following to call out other unions which will involve a Railway stoppage and a Customs Labour stoppage - he will secure the support of the Nigerian Youth Movement which may act as the entire Movements Police (sic) and intimidate people desirous of trading with firms in one way or another.[130]

Even if the local agent of John Holt & Co. sometimes was inclined to over-estimate the capabilities of the Nigerian Youth Movement, he was on other occasions an astute observer of political developments. He repeatedly stressed the point, for example, that the Nigerian Youth Movement was different from previous political movements in Nigeria and that this fact would have unforeseeable consequences. He argued that

> ... hitherto one of the weaknesses of political organisations in Nigeria has been the tribal and racial and religious dislike in existence and consequently agitation of any sort has been local and easily suppressed. The introduction of the Nigerian Youth Movement has helped to eliminate all these difficulties to a large degree... The movement is helped considerably when it can find a common enemy which leaves race and tribe outside the issue and it is for this reason that I now say we cannot

predict how far the agitation may go and how effectively it can organise a boycott of any kind.[131]

With regard to the role of the Nigerian press, and the *West African Pilot* in particular, the District Agent wrote that

> Akinsanya ... is backed by a news journal which is gaining a following because of its agitatory tone, which to the ignorant (sic) appears to be authoritative, the West African Pilot. Had the movement not got this press, the whole thing would have collapsed and been forgotten in Nigeria by now.[132]

and

> Behind them all is the Editor of the West African Pilot - Mr Mnamdi (sic) Azikiwe, M.A., M.Sc. etc. - who was turfed out of the Gold Coast. He is another "Ghandi" (sic), he is giving courage to people like Akinsanya (the Nigerian Motor Union and the Produce Traders Union) and now has roped in the Nigerian Youth Movement which is really a powerful organisation numerically.[133]

This quotation shows that contemporaries were not only aware of the links between produce traders, the nationalist movement and the press, but also how strongly the firms reacted to the appearance of these links.

There was also a number of other factors which probably contributed to the sense of uncertainty which emerged after 1938. One was the participation of farmers' associations and other groups in the conflict, which signalled that the protest movement was not solely a produce traders' affair. There was at least one petition from an Ondo Farmers' Representative Union[134], while other associations such as the Agege Planters' Union and the Egba Farmers' Association publicly declared their opposition to the 'Pool'[135].

The Ibadan Co-operative Marketing Union, the biggest farmers' association at the time, also seems to have played an active part in the protest movement. Not only was its president, A. Obisesan, one of the four official delegates who went to Accra in January 1938, but he also wrote a strongly-worded petition to the Governor of Nigeria. Though A. Obisesan was initially very reluctant to do so, since he would run the risk of falling out with the Registrar of Co-operative Societies, E.F.G. Haig who had strongly advised him against such action,[136] demands from local farmers seem to have prevailed at last.

Obisesan argued quite convincingly that he saw no reason why farmers should suffer from an agreement which allegedly was designed to curb the activities of 'dishonest' middlemen.[137] He also expressed the apparently widely-held view that current low produce prices were a result of the amalgamation of the firms into 'combines' and mentions this specifically in connection with the United Africa Company, which he argued was able to dictate produce prices, as well as merchandise sales prices. Finally, he made the point that since wages and merchandise prices had stayed high in 1938 after their rise in the previous season, the real standard of living in the current season had declined even more than the low produce prices would indicate. These arguments were not taken seriously however, and the Ibadan Co-operative Marketing Union received only a rather patronising letter from the Chief Secretary to the Government.[138]

Another factor was the spread of the protest movement into other trades, particularly into the palm produce trade. It seems that in early 1938 farmers and traders in the south eastern part of Nigeria began to organise opposition to the palm produce agreement. In March 1938 the Resident Owerri Province reported that local farmers had demanded that the terms of reference of the Cocoa Commission should be extended to palm produce and expressed the opinion that this demand was 'inspired by the events in the Gold Coast'[139].

The agitation for an inquiry into the palm produce trade was followed by a partial hold-up of produce in Warri, Benin and Ondo between August and November 1938[140] and in December 1938 farmers in Owerri Province even ceased to pay taxes. Demonstrations were also held, since the Secretary Southern Provinces reported that at one point it became 'necessary to disperse an armed mob of 3,000 men'. Explaining the reason for the development of this protest, he wrote that in his view the underlying cause of these demonstrations was that farmers and traders opposed the system of fixed prices and believed that the government was in league with the firms.[141] Thus in the palm produce industry, a similar movement to that in the cocoa industry was about to develop.

This protest movement seems to have lasted for a relatively short time and its longer-term impact was probably very limited. Its emergence, however, in a sense vindicated the firms' stubbornly-pursued policy of not yielding to pressures to withdraw the agreement or publish its contents. There are numerous references in the internal correspondence of at least one member of the 'Pool' to the danger of a further spread of the protest if the Agreement was withdrawn. For example the District Agent (Lagos) of John Holt & Co. urged his superiors in Liverpool that

> The Pool must not be broken up - if it is, attacks will be made on every other Pool and agreement until these "red organisations" control the entire situation, dictating policy to merchants and Government alike, threatening trouble at every refusal of their terms...
>
> I cannot too strongly emphasise that the Pool must not go ... it must fight on. I am convinced that if we lose this fight ... then it will be the end of all Pools, all genuine co-operation out here; it will destroy the morale of the Europeans responsible for co-operation and operating Pools.[142]

When this letter was written (January 1938), farmers and traders in the palm oil industry had probably already started to organise opposition to the Agreement. Their protest would certainly have received a great boost if the firms had withdrawn the Agreement under the pressure from cocoa traders and farmers alone. In the conflict of 1937/38 there was more at stake than the position of the European trading firms and their profits in the cocoa trade. A complete victory of the Nigerian cocoa traders would have created a precedent for other trades in which European trading firms had a similar position and employed the same business strategies, such as the palm produce, groundnut and merchandise trade. From this point of view, the tactics which the firms adopted were not so much stubborn obstinacy as a skewed calculation about the likely consequences of any other course of action.

In short, the significance of the Nigerian protest movement was not that it posed a threat to the economic interests of the European trading firms or a political threat to the colonial government, since there was no hold-up nor large-scale riots, but that the protest movement contained the potential for such a threat. The protest movement of 1937/38 created an atmosphere of uncertainty about the political consequences of the firm's business strategies, as well as about the effects economic hardship would have in political terms on farmers in southern Nigeria. In particular the firms, and indeed the government, could no longer assume that opposition to their policies would only be sporadic and localised; they had now to reckon with a wide-ranging alliance of various opposition groups, whose real strength they were unable to fathom.[143] This was arguably the most important effect of the crisis of 1937/38 in Nigeria and it strongly influenced the policies the colonial government embarked on in subsequent years.

The Termination of the Conflict and its Aftermath

The Royal Commission, which the Secretary of State had appointed in late February 1938, arrived in Accra on 23rd March, 1938. It was headed by W. Nowell, a former Director of the East African Research Station and consisted of two further members (R.S. Thompson and L.M. Irving) and a Secretary (E. Melville).[144]

The Commission essentially had two assignments: to inquire into the marketing of West African cocoa in order to find the causes which had led to the conflict in the cocoa industry; the other, more immediate, assignment was to negotiate a solution to the ongoing conflict, a task which proved to be exceedingly difficult.[145]

The main problem was how to overcome the deadlock, because when the Commission arrived in the Gold Coast, farmers and traders were still by and large refusing to sell cocoa to the trading firms or to buy merchandise goods from the firms' retail shops, while the agreement firms were still determined not to yield to the demands for a dissolution of the 'Pool'.

The Nowell Commission became convinced, after hearing their first witnesses, that the hold-up would not be terminated without a formal undertaking by the firms to withdraw the Agreement and that there was no prospect that the farmers and traders would change their minds on this issue in the immediate future. They therefore urged the firms to reconsider their position and to agree to a proposal for a compromise by which the firms would temporarily suspend the Agreement in order to end the hold-up in the Gold Coast and to give the Commission time to make its inquiries. This proposal was flatly refused. Instead the firms came up with a counter-proposal. They would only agree to a temporary suspension of the 'Pool' on condition that the 'orderly marketing' of the 1937/38 crop would be guaranteed by statutory export control which would prevent the resumption of competitive buying between the firms in the Gold Coast.[146]

Though the Commission itself did not favour such a solution, pressure from the Colonial Office, which seems to have been interested in a speedy end to the crisis on whatever conditions, prompted the Commission to have informal discussions with the leaders of the hold-up movement, who informally gave their consent to the proposal.[147] Accordingly, on 13th April, 1938, the Gold Coast Legislative Council, after some discussion, passed a Cocoa (Control of Exportation) Ordinance. The Ordinance prohibited the export of cocoa except under licence until 31st October, 1938. These licences covered a fixed amount of cocoa in a given period, 94 per cent of which was distributed between existing shippers according to their export performance in the previous two seasons. The remaining 6 per cent (or 2,000 tons, whichever was higher) was left to the Governor for distribution at his discretion to newcomers, and African shippers in particular.

The passing of this ordinance, however, did not immediately lead to the end of the conflict, since the firms had not yet formally agreed to suspend the Agreement. Negotiations so far had only been conducted by the United Africa Company and Cadbury Brothers Ltd. and, in order to make the arrangement effective, the consent of the other agreement firms was needed. They met on 24th April, 1938 and passed a resolution to that effect. Four days later, on 28th April, the Gold Cost government publicly announced that a 'truce' had been concluded between the parties, and farmers and traders should resume selling cocoa to the trading firms. However, when farmers, traders and certain firms found out how the 'truce' actually operated, it became the object of fierce criticism,[148] which included a petition from 'Twenty Paramount Chiefs' of the Gold Coast on 13th May, 1938. In this petition the Chiefs deplored, among other things, that competition in the cocoa trade had become extinct.[149]

The obviously one-sided solution of the conflict in favour of the firms was also recognised by the Nowell Commission, which later stated in its Report that

> We are not convinced that this [the export licence system] was technically the only practicable basis of export control. It was open to the grave objection that, in effect, it not only continued with statutory sanction the sharing of purchases among the Agreement firms, which was the essential feature of the Buying Agreement, but also precluded any development of independent competition.[150]

In the negotiations over a solution to the conflict, Nigerian interests or the Nigerian government, for obvious reasons played only a very minor role. One effect, however, was that on the same day that the truce was announced in the Gold Coast, the Governor of Nigeria disclosed that he had received a declaration from the agreement firms. It read:

> In consequence of the suspension of the Gold Coast Cocoa Agreement from the 28 April till 30 September 1938 we the undersigned have decided to suspend the Nigerian Cocoa Agreement for a similar period.[151]

There is no direct reason which would explain why the firms made this declaration, but one could speculate that they felt that without such a declaration the protest movement in Nigeria would argue that Nigerian farmers and traders would be treated unfairly in comparison to the Gold Coast farmers and traders, and that a new debate about the Agreement would resuscitate protest in Nigeria, which at the time was already dying down. Moreover, one could argue that since most of the main cocoa crop was already marketed in February 1938, this declaration did not materially effect the firms' cocoa-buying operations, and could in these circumstances only improve the firms' public standing.[152]

The news of the suspension of the 'Pool' was strongly welcomed by produce traders and farmers in Nigeria and was attributed, at least partly, to the activities of the Nigerian Produce Traders' Union and the Nigerian Youth Movement. This, as I have argued earlier, greatly enhanced the Movement's public standing and provided the NYM with the argument that they and not their political rivals in the forthcoming Lagos Town Council and Legislative Council elections, the Nigerian National Democratic Party, would 'truly' represent Nigerian interests.

However, as far as the cocoa trade was concerned, opposition to the firms calmed down after the announcement of the suspension of the Agreement, though this was probably also due to the fact that the cocoa season was almost over and problems in the cocoa trade were attracting increasingly less attention. It appears as if the Nigerian Produce Traders' Union and the Nigerian Youth Movement adjourned their campaign until the beginning of the next cocoa season a couple of months ahead. They now concentrated their efforts on organising their evidence to the Nowell Commission.

The Nowell Commission, its Investigation and Report

The Commission stayed in Nigeria for less than a fortnight, returning to London on 7th May, 1938. It collected evidence from the colonial government officials, representatives of agreement firms and from a number of farmers' associations and traders' organisations. It also heard witnesses from the Nigerian Youth Movement, but, in contrast to the Gold Coast where the Commission had meetings with Asante and other chiefs, there was no formal session with the chiefs in Yorubaland.

The Nowell Commission heard evidence from traders and firms in Nigeria, the Gold Coast and the United Kingdom. While the traders maintained that the 'Pool is nothing short of a monopoly designed to control prices for the benefit of the interested firms and the disadvantage of the producers and others interested in the cocoa trade'[153] and therefore 'oppression of the gravest kind'[154], the firms repeated their view that the purpose of the Agreement was to rid the trade of 'abuses' and bring 'sanity' to it[155].

Whatever the weight of the evidence from each side, there were two factors that guaranteed that the firms' evidence, and thus their view, would to some extent prevail. Being an interest group of only a handful of firms they could, and did, effectively orchestrate their evidence. 'All evidence is vetted ...' wrote, for example, one of the directors of John Holt & Co. to the local Agent in Lagos.[156] This co-ordination of evidence was organised by a sub-committee of the General Committee of the agreement firms in London,[157] while in Nigeria and in the Gold Coast two representatives of the Committee oversaw the evidence which was to be submitted to the Commission.

It is difficult to measure with any precision the effect this orchestration of evidence had on the Commission, but together with the second advantage the firms had over produce traders - the fact that the Commission relied for much of its information on the firms themselves - it is possible that the firms were able at least to some extent to manipulate the Commission and thus the outcome of the investigation. There was, for example, the question if and to what extent the schedule of marketing costs which the firms used after the introduction of the Agreement, and in particular the item 'coast establishment charges' in the schedule, was different from the schedule the firms had used in the previous season under the conditions of free competition. Since the marketing schedule represented the difference between the world market price of cocoa and the price farmers and traders received in the Gold Coast and Nigeria, the answer to this question was crucial in the Commission's verdict on the merits of the Agreement. The Commission reported that it was informed by the firms that

> the lowest figures for establishment charges which were actively charged against cocoa purchases in the books of any of the firms concerned for the 1936/37 season were adopted for inclusion in the schedule.[158]

In the light of the evidence presented earlier in this chapter about the difference in the marketing schedule the firm of John Holt & Co. used in the 1936/37 season and the schedule the same firm used in the following season as part of the Pool, the contention by the firms that 'only the lowest figures' were used in the Agreement schedule, appears to be a deliberate misrepresentation.[159]

Despite the efforts of the agreement firms to influence the outcome of the investigation, they could not prevent the Commission from reaching the conclusion that a continuation of the Agreement was 'undesirable' and that the Agreement itself should be 'in any circumstances ... ultimately withdrawn'[160]. The Commission considered the Agreement unfair to produce traders and farmers inasmuch as it suppressed competitive buying. Moreover, the Commission criticised the method of price fixing which the Agreement contained. It argued that, since the firms' selling operations would influence - 'whether they desire to do so or not' - the price of cocoa in the world markets, to base the fixing of the local purchase price on the world market price was in principle unsatisfactory. It also objected to the provision in the Agreement that profit margins were to be fixed by the firms themselves.[161]

However, the Commission exonerated the firms from having caused the conflict. Instead the Commission argued that it was primarily the condition of West African trade which had compelled the firms to try to seek redress in the formation of a buying pool, and however inappropriate the Agreement might have been, the blame should be squarely put on these conditions. The Commission accepted the firms' contention that trade had been unremunerative to them in the 1930s and argued that this had been caused by the firms' intensive competition for tonnage and the services of produce traders and buyers, which had frequently increased purchase and marketing costs of cocoa in West Africa beyond the value the cocoa would generate on immediate sale in the international market.[162] In short, the Commission agreed with the firms' assertion that there was a need for reform of cocoa marketing in West Africa, but it rejected the type of reform the firms had tried to bring about through the implementation of the Agreement.

The Commission also addressed the question of what type of reform should be undertaken. Matters, the Commission argued, could not be left as they were, since there was a danger the firms would just re-implement the Agreement, if nothing were changed in the condition which had prompted the firms to form a Pool in the first place, and that might easily cause a new hold-up and another 'dislocation of economic life'[163].

As regards the Gold Coast, the Commission recommended that all cocoa farmers should be organised in a statutory marketing association, whose activities would be supervised by a Board of Directors consisting of farmers' representatives, official representatives and one or two co-opted members. This association was supposed to sell cocoa on behalf of the farmers either to firms established in the Gold Coast, including newcomers, or directly to manufacturers through brokers in London and New York.[164]

It is interesting to note with respect to arguments advanced later, what the Commission did *not* recommend. The proposed scheme neither contained the idea that purchase prices should be fixed for a longer period than two or three weeks nor that the firms should receive fixed export quotas. There was, in particular, no proposition to 'break the direct link between the producers' price and world market prices'[165], since the Commission recommended that the proposed association 'should be free ... to ship directly to world markets'[166].

However, the Commission estimated how much the proposed scheme would cost. It calculated that an initial capital outlay of £300,000 would be necessary, while annual costs of the scheme would amount to about £250,000, which should be financed by grants or loans from the Government or from the Colonial Development Fund.[167]

With regard to Nigeria, the recommendations of the Commission were less far reaching, in that it considered marketing reform in Nigeria 'not so urgent as to require the adoption of compulsory measures...'[168] Instead it proposed to expand the already existing co-operative cocoa marketing societies voluntarily, which should be supported by the government.[169] The Commission also recommended a number of accompanying measures, such as the setting up of agricultural credit schemes, the regular inspection of weights and measures of produce traders, the licensing of produce buyers and buying stations and the regular publication of world market prices locally on noticeboards fixed to produce stores, post offices and administrative buildings.[170]

Like the Gold Coast recommendations, the Nigerian proposals did not contain any clause which favoured seasonally-fixed produce prices or export quotas. On the contrary, the Commission said that the government should set up a special export agency for co-operative cocoa marketing societies to enable them to sell their produce directly on the world market without any statutory restrictions as regards quantity or price.[171]

The Reception of the Report

The Report of the Commission was published simultaneously in the Gold Coast, Nigeria and the United Kingdom on 24th October, 1938. The Nigerian Government even took care to make the essential conclusions of the Report known to a wider audience, issuing a special number of the *Nigerian Gazette* the following day which summarised the Commission's findings.[172]

The Commission's recommendation that the firms should withdraw the Agreement was received in Nigeria, according to one observer, with a 'feeling of pleasure amongst all'[173]. This satisfaction was apparently shared by cocoa farmers, who expected that after the publication of the Report, produce prices would start to rise.[174]

As regards the other main recommendation of the Commission, the voluntary expansion of co-operative marketing societies, the reactions by the farmers seem to have been largely indifferent.[175] This was certainly not the attitude of produce traders and their organisations. While they naturally particularly welcomed the demand of the Commission for the abolition of the Pool, they seem to have equally strongly resented any plans for large-scale government support for co-operative marketing societies. This attitude was particularly noticeable in Abeokuta where traders were said to have 'oppose[d] to the utmost the establishment of a cocoa export agency and buying through co-operative societies'[176]. There were similar reports from Ilesha and Ijebu-Ode, but not from Ibadan, where the local branch of the NPTU had chosen not to make any comment on the recommendations of the Commission.[177]

The report from the Acting Resident of Ijebu Province is in this respect especially revealing, since it mentions some of the reasons behind the opposition to the recommendation to adopt a co-operative marketing system. The Acting Resident stated that

> The local middlemen, although glad that the commission recommends the withdrawal of the Agreement, resent the criticism levelled against them as a class and would be very definitely hostile to any attempt, however gradual it may be, to dislodge them from their position in the marketing process...[178]

The Nigerian Produce Traders' Union appears to have held a very similar view. In a memorandum, entitled 'Produce Buying Agreements', the Union's President, S. Akinsanya, at first argued, after having expressed his profound satisfaction with the Commission's recommendation as regards the Buying Agreement, that it would now be up to the government to act upon it. He also asked the government to investigate other agreements, and in particular the Merchandise Agreement. Concerning the proposal to develop co-operative societies, he did not directly state his opposition, but pointed out that 'a simpler method rather than a complicated one can be adopted and peace in trade be restored' and argued that

> ... the whole trouble at present could be removed if trading firms would honestly and truly withdraw the buying agreements effectively and leave the produce market void of unsavoury manipulation, confine their produce trading activities to important trading centres, such as Lagos, Abeokuta, Ibadan, Ilesha and Ijebuode (sic) etc. and leave the districts and producers alone...[179]

This quotation suggests that produce traders regarded the Buying Agreement not as a single incident, but rather as an element in the whole range of activities or policies in which the firms were seen to be engaged in order to limit produce traders' commercial advance. This supports one of the central arguments in this book that the protest movement of 1937/38 was not a single-issue movement.

The Nigerian Youth Movement's protest against plans to strengthen the co-operative movement in Nigeria was probably more explicit than the protest from any other group. This is somewhat surprising, since it was likely to offend the leaders of the co-operative movement and A. Obisesan in particular, with whom the movement had previously worked.

When giving evidence to the Committee which the Governor had appointed to examine the recommendations of the Commission, the representative of the Nigerian Youth Movement, E. Ikoli, was reported to have said

> ... that the farmer did not benefit in any way by selling through the co-operative marketing societies which ... [the Nigerian Youth Movement] feared were created with the sole object of facilitating the buying of cocoa by European firms and suppressing competition by eliminating the African brokers.[180]

The only genuine support for the recommendations of the Commission appears to have come from the Ondo Farmers' Representative Union and from the Ibadan Co-operative Cocoa Marketing Union (ICCMU).[181] Interestingly the ICCMU also suggested that 'Chiefs must be educated to realise the benefits of the Co-operative Movement, because if the latter is to become an institution of the people the support of the natural rulers is indispensable'[182]. This was probably an allusion to the fact that a number of Ibadan Chiefs had a strong interest in the cocoa trade and were thus inclined to use their position to obstruct the development of co-operative marketing societies.[183]

The reaction of the firms to the Commission's recommendation was divided. Officially the firms took the position that they would welcome the plan to develop co-operative marketing societies on the basis that their development was gradual and voluntary. With respect to the recommendation to set up an export agency for co-operative cocoa, they argued that this was disadvantageous to the co-operative movement, since it would cost money and the firms were anyway paying the highest possible price![184] Unofficially, however, they opposed both recommendations, but chose to keep quiet about it, because they were anxious not to run the risk of incurring even more political opposition than they were already facing after having lost the argument about the Buying Agreement. They trusted that the opposition of produce traders would be sufficient to deter the government from implementing any major scheme, whom they would, if possible, encourage and support.[185]

The reception of the Report in government circles ranged from half-hearted acceptance to outright hostility. The Nigerian government, though agreeing in principle to the main recommendations of the Nowell Commission, seems to have been most concerned about the speed with which these recommendations should be implemented. Regarding, for example, the recommendation to develop co-operative societies, the Governor, as well as the Director of Agriculture and the Registrar of Co-operative Societies, argued strongly that such a development should be gradual, voluntary and, above all, not too rapid.[186]

The reception of the Report in the Colonial Office was even less positive. Apart from a general belief that most of the Commission's recommendations were 'impractical'[187], in particular the proposals to organise farmers in the Gold Coast into a marketing co-operative on a statutory basis and to set up an export agency for co-operative cocoa marketing societies in Nigeria, there was apparently no political will to provide the necessary finance for the schemes[188]. Moreover, there were grave doubts as to whether co-operative principles would offer a solution to the problems of the West African cocoa industry. As regards the Commission's idea that co-operative marketing societies could help to relieve the indebtedness of farmers, one official in a rare display of frankness minuted

> ... in the conditions which exist in most of the backward colonies, where the native inhabitants by instinct and breeding are incapable of drawing the distinction between mine and thine and were in a long tradition of indebtedness, it has been found to be impossible to provide credit ... with any success.[189]

This might not be representative, but since the official who wrote this minute (E. Melville) later played an important role in the administration of the war-time cocoa control schemes and in the framing of the post-war marketing policy, his manifest attitude towards Africans in general and his view about their ability to organise themselves in particular have a wider significance.

Given the hostile reception to the recommendations of the Nowell Commission, there was very little prospect in 1938 that these recommendations would ever be realised. This argument is also supported by a number of press articles which appeared at the time. Thus, for example, a letter was published in *West Africa*, in which the author ('a Trader') stated, with obvious satisfaction, that 'it is [now] confidently asserted that the report is as dead as the proverbial mutton'[190].

This was not, however, the end of the *Nowell Report*, since in both the Gold Coast and Nigeria local committees were appointed specifically to examine the recommendations of the Commission, which will be reviewed briefly in the next section of this chapter.

The Kelly Committee

The appointment of the Kelly Committee in March 1939 was largely a consequence of the previous appointment of a similar committee in December 1938 in the Gold Coast, where the government had thought it advisable to regain the initiative after the publication of the Report of the Nowell Commission.[191] The Nigerian government saw the situation differently, and it was only after it received a letter from the Secretary of State for the Colonies in February 1939 in which he suggested the appointment of such a commission that the government decided to follow the Gold Coast example.[192]

Initially, the Nigerian Committee consisted of only three governmental members, the Resident (Oyo Province) E.J.G. Kelly, the Director of Agriculture J.R. Mackie and the local Senior Manager of the Bank of British West Africa D.D. Gibb. Their appointment was officially announced in a Legislative Council meeting on 15th March, 1939.[193] Contrary to the government's expectation, these appointments were not well received by the African members of the Legislative Council. Three days after the announcement O. Alakija, who had been a member of the Legislative Council since 1933 and had been re-elected to the Council in 1938 as a candidate for the Nigerian Youth Movement, saw the Chief Secretary in order to express the Movement's dissatisfaction with the composition of the Committee, because it would not include any African representatives. He also suggested that S. Akinsanya should be appointed as a full Committee member.[194] The latter demand was refused, and instead the government appointed the barrister E.O. Moore to the Committee. The Nigerian Youth Movement considered this solution inadequate and made further representations to the government, pointing out that E.O. Moore had very little understanding of business matters and of the cocoa industry in particular,[195] though it was probably also the fact that E.O. Moore was a prominent member of the Nigerian National Democratic Party and, moreover, known for his conservative views which prompted the Nigerian Youth Movement to oppose his appointment. However, in a meeting with the Governor, the representatives of the Movement, H.S.A. Thomas, S. Akinsanya and E. Ikoli, came up with the proposal to appoint in addition to E.O. Moore the Chairman of the Agege Farmers' Union and 'prominent cocoa farmer', D.T. Sasegbon.[196] The Governor agreed to this demand and thus finally in April 1939 the Committee could begin its work.[197]

The dispute about the composition of the Committee would be insignificant were it not for the fact that its outcome was regarded as a political victory for the Nigerian Youth Movement. The episode reveals how the Nigerian Government responded to demands from the nationalists. This was also noticed by a number of Nigerian newspapers, one of which, for example, wrote that

> These new appointments to supplement the original unpopular personnel are proofs positive that the Nigerian government is amenable to public opinion in the true spirit of democracy.[198]

This episode indicates that there was a slight shift in government policy or attitude in 1938/39. The Nigerian government began to take the nationalist movement seriously, at least inasmuch as economic policy was concerned, and this was arguably the result of both the campaign of 1937/38 and the success of the Nigerian Youth Movement in the 1938 Legislative Council elections.

The task of the Kelly Committee was to find out what 'action should be taken to give effect to such of the Commission's proposals as appear to be practical and advisable'[199]. During its investigations, the Committee thus heard a substantial number of witnesses, including colonial officials, representatives from the trading firms and from farmers' associations, and delegates from the Nigerian Youth Movement and from the Nigerian Produce Traders' Union.[200] The evidence which the Committee collected, however, was not very different from the public statement which the various groups had made after the publication of the *Nowell Report*, and need not, therefore, be examined here in detail.

The Kelly Committee finished its work on 30th May, 1939 and largely endorsed the recommendations of the Nowell Commission. Yet, at the same time it had strong reservations about the extent and the speed with which these recommendations should be implemented. While the Nowell Commission had recommended the wholesale adoption of a co-operating marketing system, the Committee doubted that a rapid development of co-operatives would be possible and that co-operative marketing societies would 'ever handle the bulk of the cocoa crop'[201]. They concluded that the development of the co-operatives was desirable, but it should be gradual and strictly voluntary, and for this reason produce traders and buyers would have to perform a useful role in the marketing of cocoa for many years to come. In practical terms, the Committee suggested the establishment of a separate Co-operative Department since the administrative officers hitherto concerned with co-operative matters, such as the Registrar of Co-operative Societies, had been part of the Chief Secretary's office. The Committee also recommended that the staff of this new department should be enlarged.

With respect to the recommendation to set up an export agency, the Committee took the view that such an agency would be expensive and cumbersome to administer, and that there was insufficient need for such an agency. Instead, the Committee proposed that the government should employ a special Marketing Officer, whose duties would be to advise co-operative societies and African traders over direct export possibilities. In addition, the Marketing Officer would be charged with the task of distributing information about marketing costs, produce prices and market prospects for cocoa and other crops.[202]

There was one recommendation of the Kelly Committee which went further than the corresponding recommendation of the Nowell Commission. While the latter had suggested that the government should generally support credit and thrift societies, the Committee came to the conclusion that a Co-operative Bank was needed, which under the direction of the Registrar of Co-operative Societies should provide loans to farmers in order to alleviate their inter-harvest cash flow problems and relieve them of indebtedness.[203] The Committee also strongly supported the recommendation of the Nowell Commission that the government should spend more money on research and suggested in this respect that a detailed land survey of cocoa-producing areas should receive highest priority. These were the four recommendations of the Committee which, if realised, would have involved increased government expenditure. In addition, the Committee produced a list of recommendations which would have only required new legislation, such as statutory control of weights and measures, the licensing of produce traders and buying stations, and the compulsory display of prices outside produce stores.[204]

The Nigerian government strongly endorsed the recommendations of the Kelly Committee in principle,[205] but when it came to the point of transferring recommendations into reality, the initial support faded away. Thus, none of the legislative actions which the Committee had proposed were actually undertaken, and as regards the other recommendations, there was no political will to overcome the perennial argument of colonial Finance Secretaries that there was no money available for such projects.[206]

The Nigerian Government instead asked the Secretary of State for the Colonies for permission to apply for a grant of some £44,000 from the Colonial Development Fund. Almost a month later, on 23rd August, 1939, the Nigerian government received an answer from the Secretary of State, in which he explained that it was not possible to make a decision on the matter since he had not yet consulted the trading firms on the Committee's Report, but expressed his hope that a decision would soon be made, probably in early October 1939.[207]

The outbreak of war in September 1939 necessarily changed the situation and caused some further delay. In December 1939 the Secretary of State gave his consent to the recommendation to employ a Marketing Officer, whose responsibilities were enlarged to assist in the development of Nigeria's self-sufficiency in essential foodstuffs, which at the time was one of the major policies the Nigerian government had been advised to pursue by the United Kingdom government in order to support the British war effort.[208]

Concerning the other central recommendation of the Committee to further the development of co-operative marketing societies and to establish a Co-operative Bank, the Secretary of State seven months later came to the conclusion that under the prevailing circumstances no positive decision could be made. In a letter to the Governor of Nigeria of 31st July, 1940, he argued that:

> Expenditure of Imperial funds on Colonial Development can now only be justified on projects of first importance and urgency, and I feel sure that you will agree with me that in the present circumstances in the cocoa trade in Nigeria financial assistance for the co-operative movement cannot be regarded as coming into that category.[209]

The phrase 'present circumstances in the cocoa trade in Nigeria' was probably an allusion to the fact that the United Kingdom government had to provide some extra money to make good the losses which the government cocoa control scheme had incurred in its first year of operation,[210] and the argument was perhaps that it was in these circumstances too much to ask the United Kingdom government for further assistance. At least this was the position of an Assistant Secretary in the Colonial Office, E. Melville, who maintained in a Minute that

> The cocoa industry in Nigeria is now a definite liability to His Majesty's Government and the policy henceforth must be to arrange the purchase and sale of Nigerian crops with least possible loss to His Majesty's Government. In determining "least possible loss" one must, of course, bear in mind the political importance of maintaining a certain level of cash income to cocoa producers, but the present is clearly not the time to expand the organisation of the cocoa industry in such a way as to increase rather than diminish the expense of handling the crop.[211]

Thus the outbreak of war seems largely to have wrecked, for the time being, the plans to achieve even the few reforms the Kelly Committee had proposed: all that was obtained was the appointment of a Marketing Officer and even his time was not completely devoted to the co-operative societies or African exporters and was instead taken up by other matters, such as the marketing of foodstuffs and distribution of imported goods.[212]

In this respect one cannot but conclude that the protest movement of 1937/38 and the ensuing investigation of the Nowell Commission and the Kelly

Committee were largely unsuccessful and had almost no immediate practical consequences.[213] As I have argued earlier, this does not, however, mean that the protest of 1937/38 had no political consequences, one of which will be discussed in the next chapter.

There remains the question whether the protest movement of 1937/38 and the Nowell Commission were successful in compelling the trading firms to completely *abandon* the 1937 Buying Agreement. The firms had declared publicly in April 1938 that they would merely *suspend* the Buying Agreement until 30th September, 1938. Hence the last section of this chapter will address the question of what was most likely to be the policy of the firms in the 1938/39 cocoa season.

'Unofficial' Arrangements between the European Trading Firms

On the 1st September, 1938 Colonial Office officials and representatives of the trading firms met to discuss future marketing arrangements.[214] The background to these discussions was that the *Nowell Commission Report* was not ready for publication before the beginning of the 1938/39 cocoa season. The question was therefore how cocoa should be marketed in the forthcoming season. The Governor of the Gold Coast had urged the Secretary of State for the Colonies not to agree to the continuation of export legislation on the grounds that such a policy would probably provoke political turmoil in the Gold Coast, while the Governor of Nigeria had emphatically argued for a continuation of the suspension of the Agreement.[215] The purpose of the meeting with the firms on the 1st September, 1938 was to ascertain how they approached the question.

In the discussion, one of the Directors of the United Africa Company, F. Samuel, told officials that a clandestine arrangement between the firms had been in operation for several months and that the firms would under no circumstances return to the condition of free competition. However, he asked

> whether it would help if the agreement continued in force but the overt signs of it were removed; for instance the share out of cocoa could take place on this side rather than in Africa and even, if necessary, the firms could arrange that the prices offered by the representatives of the various firms in Africa should nor always be identical. They could give all the appearance of competition ... although they were not prepared to give the agreement up altogether, they were quite prepared to camouflage it in any way.[216]

In the subsequent discussion on this proposal

> ... it was suggested that it would help a good deal if the offending legal document could be removed even though there were some temporary arrangement between the firms, provided that the natives were not given any grounds for thinking that they had been in any way deceived.[217]

The outcome of the discussion was that the firms agreed that the 1937 Buying Agreement should be further suspended until the firms had time to consider the *Nowell Commission Report* and that in the meantime the firms would co-operate with each other in the purchase of the West African cocoa crop. The Colonial Office was also told by the firms that 'in the event of the Agreement becoming again operative, its provisions shall be retroactive as from 30th September, 1938'[218]. Consequently, local agents of one of the participating firms (John Holt & Co.) was told in mid-September 1938 that 'Your policy should ... be to organise as though there were a Pool...'[219]

The *Nowell Commission Report* was published on the 24th October, 1938, and in retrospect one should have expected a declaration of the firms some time later about their intentions as regards the Buying Agreement. Yet, there was no such declaration and the question remains what the most likely policy of the trading firms after the publication of the *Nowell Commission Report* was.

There are a number of reports from Nigeria, including one from the Nigerian Produce Traders' Union, which allege that the firms were operating an arrangement of one sort or another at the *end* of 1938, but apparently the mere suspicion that the firms were operating a pool was not enough to prompt either the government or the produce traders to formally protest against 'unofficial' arrangements or to campaign for the realisation of the Nowell Commission's recommendation to withdraw the Buying Agreement.[220]

Yet, there is indeed some evidence from the firms' internal correspondence that suggests that at least a clandestine arrangement was in force in 1938/39. Thus, for example, the District Agent (Accra) of John Holt & Co. was informed by his principals

> ... that there is a substantial measure of co-operation in cocoa and, that, though the Pool Arrangement is suspended it is, in fact, suspended so far as the Coast alone is concerned. For your strictly private information ... Members experimented last season with a modified form of co-operation. Each Member undertook to control, by means of limits, his buying to share and there was a frequent and regular exchange of information as to everybody's limits, buying, and the coast of his cocoa... It was an experiment to see if a Pool could be operated entirely at this end, under which each firm on the cost had a very large measure of liberty of action and under which there was a semblance of competition in Africa so as not to

exacerbate local feeling. It was an astonishingly successful experiment...[221]

From the above it is evident that in the 1938/39 cocoa season, a 'modified form of co-operation' existed between the firms. It is, however, less clear what was meant by 'co-operation'. There are only two possibilities: either the firms had continued to suspend the 1937 Buying Agreement and instead co-operated with each other as if they had not suspended the Agreement[222] or they had re-introduced the Buying Agreement and were operating it clandestinely from the London end. If the latter is true, the firms would have accomplished the remarkable feat of deceiving not only colonial governments, farmers and produce traders, but also their own local agents in West Africa.

There is some incidental evidence which suggests that the firms had indeed chosen the latter course, i.e. that there existed a legally binding document, in which the firms committed themselves only to purchase a predetermined share of the seasonal cocoa crop. The difference between 'co-operation' and a full agreement is that participants in an agreement could be charged with a breach of the agreement in the courts, which provided the necessary cohesion to the Pool, while in the case of an 'unofficial arrangement', such action was not open to aggrieved parties.

The first piece of evidence is a letter from John Holt to the Directors of the United Africa Company from May 1938 in which he agreed to a suggestion to extend the 'Cadbury-Clause' in the 1937 Agreement for another year.[223] The original clause had allowed Cadbury to quit the Pool, if the firm wished to do so on 30th September, 1938. The option to terminate the 1937 Agreement was now extended to 30th September, 1939.

The second piece of evidence is the way the firms reacted to the introduction of statutory control in November 1939. Local agents of John Holt & Co. were informed that statutory control would not alter existing arrangements. 'In practice', they were told, 'at all events, the cocoa agreement will remain...'[224]

Thirdly, there are the minutes of a meeting of the British and French firms which signed the 1937 Buying Agreement, held in Liverpool in July 1944:

> The Chairman [F. Samuel] said that the purchasing, shipping and disposal of all Nigerian Cocoa had been assumed by the Ministry of Food in 1939 and subsequently by the West African Produce Control Board, and that consequently it was desired to record that the Agreement for the dividing of cocoa purchased in Nigeria, including all the Cocoa normally shipped through Calabar emanating from the British Mandated Territory of the Cameroons, by all the signatories to the Agreement dated 10th November 1937 terminated on the date in 1939 on which the Ministry of Food assumed control. The Chairman's proposal was duly seconded and carried unanimously.[225]

Leaving the question aside for the time being why the firms desired to record this motion in July 1944, this document indicates that at least in the early part of the 1939/40 cocoa season the 1937 Agreement was in force, since it makes no sense to convene a special meeting in 1944 in order to carry a motion that in retrospect the 1937 Agreement terminated in November 1939, if it was not in operation at the time.

Lastly, there are the minutes of a meeting of the directors of Cocoa Manufacturers Ltd, which was held on 12 August 1938. There one reads, that

> The United Africa Company Ltd. have written reminding us that the suspended Lagos Agreement becomes again effective on the 1st October 1938.[226]

Taking all the evidence together, the most likely course of events is that the firms revived the 1937 Agreement in the autumn of 1938 and that they kept this fact secret from the public and even from their own buying agents in West Africa. This policy seemed to have worked quite well until the outbreak of the Second World War, which necessitated a change in that policy.

As regards the question to what extent the protest movement of 1937/38 and the ensuing investigations of the Nowell Commission and the Kelly Committee had any concrete effect, the answer must be that in the short term it was marginal and of little consequence. Politically, however, the effect of the 1937/38 protest movement was far greater. It contributed, as we have seen, to the development of a distinct nationalist programme or 'ideology'. This development seems also to have been noticed by the Nigerian government which reacted to it, though in a very small way, by trying to accommodate some demands from nationalist leaders. The main conflict between the firms and the African traders, however, remained unsolved for the time being.

The account of the pre-history of the introduction of statutory marketing in Nigeria so far largely is a history of the conflict between Nigerian produce traders and buyers and the European trading firms. Government necessarily did not loom large in this account since it did not intervene directly into the marketing process, at least as far as Nigeria was concerned, and was only involved in the conflict to the extent that it had to cope with its political fall-out. However, the role of government changed dramatically with the introduction of statutory control in 1939. Thus in the succeeding chapters of this study, much more attention will be paid to government policy and its motives.

Notes

1   Holt Papers, Mss. Afr. s825, file 535, Scheme for the Division of Cocoa Purchased in the Colony and Protectorate of Nigeria, 18 Sept. 1937. For the Gold Coast version of the Letter of Instruction see Nowell Report, appendix j, pp. 209-216.

2   Yet, see the profit and loss account of Cocoa Manufacturers Ltd between 1921 and 1938, in: Cadbury Ltd. (Birmingham), Minutes and Reports 1934-1939, Report for the Year ending 30. September 1938 by A.V. Iredale, 1 February 1939, which seems to sustain the argument in general.

3   The margin between Liverpool and Lagos prices in the second half of the 1920s was about £16 per ton, while in the 1930s this margin declined to about £7. For seasonal averages of cocoa prices see Rhodes House Library Oxford, Mss. Afr. s913, Cocoa in West Africa, 1930-1945, Memorandum for the Transmission to the Commission of Enquiry, prepared by W.K. Beckett of the Department of Agriculture/Gold Coast, 22 March 1938, p. 14, table 4 (Accra cocoa, ex-quay Liverpool). For the profit and loss account of the United Africa Company, see D. K. Fieldhouse, Merchant Capital and Economic Decolonization: The United Africa Company, 1929-1989, Oxford 1994, pp. 84-85.

4   Holt Papers, Mss. Afr. s825, file 535(I), Evidence submitted to the Cocoa Commission by J.F. Winter, District Agent (Lagos), April 1938. See also Cadbury Ltd. (Birmingham), Minutes and Reports 1934-1939, Report 'Visit to Nigeria' by N. Edwards, 2 March 1936.

5   See L. Van der Laan, Modern Inland Transport and the European Trading Firms in Colonial West Africa. In: Cahiers d'Etudes Africaines, XXI (1984) 4, p. 567.

6   G.O. Ogunremi, The Nigerian Motor Transport Union Strike of 1937. In: Journal of the Historical Society of Nigeria, IX (1977-79), p. 129.

7   NAI: Oyo Prof I, file 1441 Vol.I, Inquiry Regarding Cocoa in the Ibadan Division by ADO R.L.V. Wilkes of September 1937. It is noteworthy that import figures for lories and motor cars show a dramatic increase in the second half of the 1930s. See A. Harneit-Sievers, Zwischen Depression und Dekolonisation: Afrikanische Händler und Politik in Süd-Nigeria, 1935-1954, Universität Hannover Ph.D. thesis, Hannover 1989, p. 94.

8   For a list of Lagos based motor transport business, see Drummond Thompson, The Development of Motor Transport, p. 151.

9   W.K. Hancock, Survey of British Commonwealth Affairs, Vol. II, Problems of Economic Policy, 1918-1939, London 1940, pp. 193-204.

10   Holt Papers, Mss. Afr. s825, file 536(II), Memorandum 'Means of Capital Employed During Financial Year Ending 30th September, 1937', undated.

11   P.T. Bauer, West African Trade. A Study of Competition, Oligopoly and Monopoly in a Changing Economy, Cambridge 1954, pp. 115-118.

12   Holt Papers, Mss. Afr. s825, file 535(II), Letter from the District Agent Port Harcourt to District Agent Lagos, 25 Oct. 1943.

13   NAI: CSO 26, file 36148 S30, Reply by the CS to Question No.44, 4 March 1940.

14   Kelly Report, p. 15.

15   Bauer, West African Trade, p. 225.

16   Holt Papers, Mss Afr. s825, file 536(II), Memorandum to be submitted to the Cocoa Inquiry Commission, 'Justification of a Cocoa Buying Agreement from the Merchant's Standpoint', n.d. (April 1938).

17   Nowell Report, para. 347. See also N. Edwards, Cadbury on the Gold Coast, Cadbury Ltd. company archive, ms. 1955, pp. 29-30.

18   See University of Ibadan Library, Obisesan Diary, entry 10 Oct. 1929, cited in G. Williams, J. Akinpelu Obisesan: A Biographical Essay, paper presented at St. Peter's College seminar, Oxford, Nov. 1988, p. 9.

19   Holt Papers, Mss. Afr. s825, file 535(I), Evidence to be submitted to the Cocoa Commission by C.A.V. Woods, DA Ijebu Ode, n.d. (April 1938).

20   Ibid., Evidence to be submitted to the Cocoa Commission by C. Foskett, DA Ibadan, 27 April 1938.

21   Ibid.; see also in the same file the letter from the DA Lagos to the DA Accra, 12 Feb. 1938.

22   Holt Papers, Mss. Afr. s825, file 92(V), Letter from the Administrative Department of John Holt & Co., Liverpool, to DA Lagos, 8 Dec. 1936.

23   Nowell Report, para. 473.

24   NAI: CSO 26, file 25807, Memorandum 'Produce Buying and Merchandise Agreements in Nigeria' by the Director of the Department of Agriculture, J.R. Mackie, 12 April 1938.

25   Kelly Report, p. 25.

26   Holt Papers, Mss. Afr. s825, file 92(V), Letter from the DA Accra to Administrative Department of John Holt & Co., 11 Feb. 1937.

27   Ibid., Letter from Administrative Department of John Holt & Co. to DA Accra, 17 March 1937.

28   Bauer, West African Trade, p. 16.

29   Holt Papers, Mss. Afr. s825, file 92(V), Letter from the Administrative Department of John Holt & Co. to the DA Lagos, 8 Dec. 1936. For the break down of the previous 'gentlemen agreement, see Cadbury Ltd. (Birmingham), Minutes and Reports 1934-1939, Report 'Visit to Nigeria' by N. Edwards, 2 March 1936.

30   PRO: CO 657/47, Administrative Report 1939/40, Department of Agriculture, p. 7.

31   Oyo Province, Annual Report 1936, cited in S.S. Berry, Cocoa, Custom and Socio-Economic Change in Rural Western Nigeria, Oxford 1975, p. 55, note 3.

32   NAI: Oyo Prof 1, file 1441 Vol.I, Inquiry regarding cocoa marketing in the Ibadan Division by ADO R.L.V. Wilkes of September 1937, p. 18.

33   O. Awolowo, Awo: The Autobiography of Chief Obafemi Awolowo, Cambridge 1960, p. 93.

34   Rhodes House Library Oxford, Mss. Afr. s913, Memorandum for Transmission to the Commission of Inquiry, prepared by W.K. Beckett (Department of Agriculture, Accra), p. 16, table 4, 22 March 1938.

35   Holt Papers, Mss. Afr. s825, file 536(II), Statement of Purchases at Labipon No. 1 store, Ibadan, 1 Jan. - 1 Feb. 1937.

36   Holt Papers, Mss. Afr. s825, file 421 B(VII), Memorandum 'Price Agreements', prepared by D.L. Rawlings (?), 20 Feb. 1942.

37   Nowell Report, para. 414.

38   Holt Papers, Mss. Afr. s825, file 536(II), Statement of purchases at Labipon No. 1 store, Ibadan, 1 Jan. - 1 Feb. 1937.

39   Ibid., Memorandum 'Justification of a Cocoa Buying Agreement as Seen from a Merchants's Standpoint', n.d. [April 1938].

40　　Ibid.; see also Nowell Report, para. 473.
41　　See D. K. Fieldhouse, Merchant Capital, pp. 124-175, and Southall, Cadbury on the Gold Coast, pp. 403-5. For a discussions of the details of the proposed agreement between F. Samuel (UAC) and J. Cadbury, see Cadbury Papers, file 289/289. Notes on a Meeting held at Cadbury Hall, 24 August 1937. According to the Cadbury Ltd. papers, J. Cadbury was approached by the United Africa Company with the proposal to form a buying pool already in December 1936. See Cadbury Ltd. (Birmingham), Minutes and Reports 1934-1939, Minutes of Meeting held at the Queen's Hotel, 23 Mai 1937.
42　　Ibid., p. 407.
43　　Holt Papers, Mss. Afr. s825, file 535(I), Memorandum of an Agreement, n.d. (August 1937), p. 2.
44　　The Co-operative Wholesale Society exported only 742 tons in 1936/37 and 998 tons in 1937/38. See NAI: CSO 26, file 36148 S 30, Reply by the CS to Question No.44, 4 March 1940.
45　　Holt Papers, Mss. Afr. s825, file 525(I); see also Nowell Report, para. 160. It is interesting to note that the document which committed the firms to the Agreement was signed at a time when opposition to the Agreement in the Gold Coast and Nigeria was almost at its peak. One should also note that the Agreement did not specify a particular schedule of marketing expenses nor indeed a specific rate of profit on turnover. Thus the participating firms agreed in legal terms only to keep their actual purchases in line with pre-determined shares or quotas and only in the case of disagreement could these be enforced in the law courts.
46　　The agreement firms accounted for about 92 per cent of the export of cocoa in the 1937/38 season. It has been argued that Unilever was running the United Africa Company and G.B. Ollivant as separate entities. See P.A. Jones, The United Africa Company in the Gold Coast/Ghana, 1920-1965, School of Oriental and African Studies Ph.D. thesis, London 1983, p. 137. Yet, there is evidence that in crucial areas like finance all three firms were directed as one corporate body. See for example PRO: CO 852, file 319/7, Letter from F. Samuel to E.C. Tansley, 14 Nov. 1940.
47　　Holt Papers, Mss. Afr. s825, file 535(I), Letter of Instruction, 18 Sept. 1937, p. 3.
48　　Firms which overbought received only the average weekly ex-scale port of shipment (Lagos) price for excess tonnage. This price represented the price the local members of the Agreement were advised by the London Committee to pay traders or producers for cocoa delivered to the firms' warehouses in Lagos. The port of shipment price in contrast to the f.o.b. price did not include buying costs, export duty, commission charges and a margin for profit, and thus the firms which received such a price for their excess tonnage would make a clear loss in this tonnage.
49　　Iredale was a representative of Rowntree&Co. and Cocoa Manudactueres Ltd. Tansley was employed by the United Africa Company. For the citation see W.M. Hood, Cocoa in West Africa. In: Bournville Works Magazine, XLIII (1946) 2, p. 25.
50　　Holt Papers, Mss. Afr. s825, file 535(I), Letter of Instruction, 18 Sept. 1937, p. 2.
51　　Nowell Report, para. 438.
52　　Ibid., para. 441.
53　　Holt Papers, Mss. Afr. s825, file 535(I), Letter from Produce Department of John Holt & Co. to DA Lagos, 2 Nov. 1937. This letter to some extent contradicts the later findings of the Nowell Commission. The Commission stated that the determination of the profit margin was left to the discretion of the General Committee in London (Nowell Report, para. 450). In the above letter, however, it was made clear that the

schedule represented the whole margin between north European ports of shipment and Lagos prices. According to the Nowell Report (vide para. 451) the actual profit margin in 1937/38 came to 5s per ton.

54   See for example Bauer, West African Trade, p. 207.

55   Holt Papers, Mss. Afr. s825, file 535(I), Letter from Produce Department of John Holt & Co. to DA Lagos, 2 Nov. 1937.

56   Ibid., Letter from the DA Lagos to Produce Department of John Holt & Co., 12 Nov. 1937.

57   Nowell Report, para. 451.

58   Holt Papers, Mss. Afr. s825, file 535(I), Letter of Instruction, 18 Sept. 1937, p. 5.

59   Ibid., Questions and Answers by Cocoa Commission: C.A.V. Wood of John Holt & Co. (Ijebu-Ode), 4 May 1938.

60   For a discussion of this problem, see Fieldhouse, Merchant Capital, p. 174.

61   Holt Papers, Mss. Afr. s825, file 421(VII), Memorandum 'Price Agreements' by D.L. Rawlings of John Holt & Co., 20 Feb. 1942. See also ibid., file 535(I), Letter from DA Lagos to Produce Department, 12 Nov. 1937.

62   West Africa, 18 Sept. 1937, p. 1283.

63   Holt Papers, Mss. Afr. s825 535(I), Letter from Administrative Department of John Holt & Co. to DAs Accra and Lagos, 13 Oct. 1937.

64   It is noteworthy that it was J. Cadbury who insisted that the government should be informed about the Agreement. See Cadbury Papers, file 289/289, Notes on a Meeting held at Cadbury Hall, 24 August 1937.

65   D. Meredith, The Colonial Office, British Business Interests and the Reform of Cocoa Marketing in West Africa, 1937-1945. In: Journal of African History, XXIX (1988) 2, pp. 286-288.

66   Nowell Report, para. 166.

67   Ibid., para. 243. The Governor of Nigeria received a copy of the Nigerian Letter of Instruction and a copy of the Agreement only in January 1938 (!). See ibid., para. 245.

68   Ibid., para. 243.

69   NAI: Ondo Prof 1/1, file 638, Letter from the CS to the SSP, 25 Nov. 1937.

70   Ibid.

71   Nowell Report, para. 301.

72   Holt Papers, Mss. Afr. s825, file 535(I), Extract from DA's 'Notes to Ondo', 16 Oct. 1937.

73   Holt Papers, Mss. Afr. s825, file 92(V), Letter from District Agent, Lagos, to all 'Ventures', Lagos District, [November] 1937. The senior agent of John Holt & Co. wrote that in the event local agents bought cocoa at higher prices than the cabled prices, this cocoa *will be thrown back to you to do whatever you like with but the company will not buy it'* (sic).

74   Ibid., file 535(I), Letter from DA Lagos to DA Accra, 12 Feb. 1938.

75   Nowell Report, paras. 207, 298 and 303.

76   Holt Papers, Mss. Afr. s825, file 535(I), Evidence to be submitted to the Cocoa Commission by C.A.V. Woods, DA Ijebu-Ode (April 1938).

77   Ibid. Extract from DA's notes to Ondo, 16 Oct. 1937. This point was also made by J.R. Mackie. See NAI: Oyo Prof 1, file 1441 Vol.I, Letter from the Director of Agriculture to the SSP, 8 Nov. 1937. For a discussion on the possibility to reduce advances, see Cadbury Papers, file 289/289. Notes on a Meeting held at Cadbury Hall, 24 August 1937. See also Cadbury Ltd., Minutes and Reports, Agent's Report 1937/38 by P.H. Soper, 30 June 1938, and Report for the Year ending 30 September 1938 by

A.V. Iredale, 1 February 1939. Both reports contain a comprehensive survey on the actual working of the agreement.

78   Holt Papers, Mss. Afr. s825, file 535(I), Letter from DA Lagos to DA Accra, 12 Feb. 1938.

79   For figures see chapter six, table 8.

80   Holt Papers, Mss. Afr. s825, file 535(I), Letter from Administrative Department of John Holt & Co. to DA Lagos, 29 Dec. 1937.

81   Awolowo, Awo, pp. 94, 98-99.

82   NAI: CSO 26, file 25807 S8, Letter from the RCS to the CS, 5 March 1937. According to the Registrar of Cooperative Societies, rural wages increased between 1936 and 1937 by about 25 per cent to 50 per cent.

83   NAI: Ondo Prof 1/1, file 638, Letter from the Resident Ondo Province to the SSP, 21 Jan. 1938.

84   NAI: CSO 26, file 25807 S8. Letter from the RCS to the CS, 5 March 1938. See also ibid., file 25807 S6. Memorandum 'Cocoa Tax' by SSP, 22 April 1938.

85   NAI: CSO 26, file 25807 S8, Petition from the ICCMU addressed to the Governor of Nigeria, 16 Feb. 1938. The petition was signed by A. Obisesan.

86   Thus, for example, S. Akinsanya was at one point better informed about certain clauses in the Agreement than the Governor of Nigeria. See Holt Papers, Mss. Afr. s825, file 535(I), DA Lagos to Administrative Department of John Holt & Co., 25 Jan. 1938. See also Beer, Politics of Peasant Groups, p. 225.

87   For the most recent analysis of the 1937/38 conflict in the Gold Coast, see R. Alence, The 1937-38 Gold Coast Cocoa Crises: The Political Economy of Commercial Stalemate. In: African Economic History, XIX (1990-91), pp. 77-104.

88   Books, thesis and articles which have been written on the conflict in the Gold Coast would merit a bibliography on their own. This account here is largely based on the Nowell Report, para. 1 and paras. 175-189; F. Ehler, Handelskonflikte zwischen europäischen Firmen und einheimischen Produzenten in British West Afrika - Die Cocoa "Hold-ups" in der Zwischenkriegszeit, Zürich 1977, pp. 140-237; G. Austin, Capitalists and Chiefs in the Cocoa Hold-Ups in South Asante, 1927-1938. In: International Journal of African Historical Studies, XXI (1988) 1, pp. 63-95; R. Alence, The 1937-38 Gold Coast Cocoa Crises: The Political Economy of Commercial Stalemate. In: African Economic History, XIX (1990-91), pp. 77-104; D. K. Fieldhouse, War and the Origins of the Gold Coast Marketing Board, 1939-40. In: M. Twaddle, (ed.), Imperialism, the State and the Third World, London 1992, pp. 153-182, and Meredith, The Colonial Office, pp. 285-300.

89   Ehler, Handelskonflikte, pp. 202-204.

90   NAI: Ondo Prof 1/1, file 638, Notes of a Discussion at a Meeting Presided over by his Excellency Sir Bernhard Bourdillon, 19 Dec. 1937, p. 1.

91   Austin, Capitalists and Chiefs, p. 82.

92   NAI: Ondo Prof 1/1, file 638, Notes of the Discussion at a Meeting Presided over by His Excellency Sir Bernard Bourdillon, 19 Dec. 1937, p. 6.

93   Ibid., p. 3.

94   Ibid., p. 4.

95   Holt Papers, Mss. Afr. s826, file 535(I), Letter from DA Lagos to Administrative Department of John Holt & Co., 25 Jan. 1938. See also PRO: CO 852, file 133/2. Telegram from the Governor of Nigeria to the Secr. of State for the Colonies, 30 Jan. 1938.

96   NAI: CSO 26, file 34883 Vol.I, Memorandum 'Produce Buying Agreement' by S. Akinsanya, 30 Dec. 1938. See also West African Pilot, 26 Oct. 1938 and PRO: CO 852, file 133/2, Enclosure II in Gold Coast Conf. B. of 21. Jan. 1938. Report by Captain O'Morchoe, Criminal Investigation Department on Meeting, 19 Jan. 1938.

97   West Africa, 26 Feb. 1938, p. 235.

98   PRO: CO 852, file 133/2, Enclosure III in Gold Coast Conf. B. of 24 Jan. 1938. Report by the Commissioner Eastern Province on Meeting of the Joint Economic Conference, Accra, 17 Jan. 1938.

99   PRO: CO 852, file 133/2, Resolution of the Joint Economic Conference of Producers of Nigeria and the Gold Coast, Adabraka, 18 Jan. 1938. The conference observed that the '...respective Governments of Nigeria and the Gold Coast ..[had failed]..to protect the economic interests of the producers of the two countries from the exploitation of capitalists who by combination of interest are determined to monopolise the produce markets of the two countries'.

100   Ibid. The meeting resolved, that '... an alliance is hereby made between the producers of Nigeria and the Gold Coast with an understanding to form a Joint Central Board of Control for the protection of the economic interests of the two countries and the establishment of a scientific system of co-operative marketing'.

101   The source for this figure is a report in the Nigerian Daily Times, 24 Jan. 1938, which probably overestimated the number of people who attended the meeting.

102   West Africa, 5 March 1938, p. 269.

103   Ehler, Handelskonflikte, pp. 126-137; see also Alence, The 1937-38 Gold Coast Cocoa Crises, pp. 83-99.

104   The request for the publication of the Agreement was probably also a response to the demands made by the NPTU in a meeting on 29th December, 1937. See Nowell Report, para. 244. However, the decision not to publish the Agreement despite pressures from colonial governments and even from local agents of the firms seems to have been most strongly advocated by J. Cadbury who feared the reputation of Cadbury in the Gold Coast and in Nigeria would be impaired if the special clauses regarding the position of Cadbury within the Pool became publicly known. For other reasons, see Nowell Report, para. 186.

105   Nowell Report, para. 11 and 488. In the words of the Report, the hold-up 'brought the trade of the Gold Coast almost to a standstill, and cut off the main sources of Government revenue. The question became then one of public policy'. On the importance of tax revenue derived from cocoa exports, see Alence, The 1937-38 Gold Coast Crises', p. 87; see also ibid. p. 81 note 11, his reference to D. C. North, Structure and Change in Economic History, New York 1981, pp. 20-33.

106   Austin, Capitalists and Chiefs, p. 91, note 155. See also Ehler, Handelskonflikte, p. 223.

107   See Ehler, Handelskonflikte, p. 207.

108   Nowell Report, para. 190; see Ehler, Handelskonflikte, pp. 197-202, 237-247 and also Meredith, The Colonial Office, p. 289.

109   PRO: CO 852, file 133/2, Despatch from the Governor of Nigeria to the Secr. of State for the Colonies, 30 Jan. 1938; see also Ehler, Handelskonflikte, pp. 207-208.

110   West Africa, 5 March 1938, p. 269.

111   Ibid. This statement by the Governor of Nigeria is somewhat surprising, since only three days earlier he had asked the Secretary of State for the appointment of such a commission.

112   See for example the high praise for the 'statesmanship' of B. Bourdillon which he was considered to have shown during the conflict in the West African Pilot, 26 Oct. 1938.

113 Nigerian Daily Times, 5 March 1938. Later E. Ikoli maintained that he was the head of the 'mission'. See NAI: CSO 26, file 36148 S73A Vol.I, Copy of a speech by E. Ikoli in the Nigerian Legislative Council, 8 March 1945.

114 The NYM had apparently informed the government of its tour in advance in early February 1938. See Minute by (?) on a letter in: NAI: CSO 26, file 25807 S8, Letter from the RCS to the CS, 9 March 1938.

115 NAI: Ondo Prof 1/1, file 638, Telegram from Resident Ondo to DO ADO-Ekiti, 2 March 1938.

116 This point is stressed by Awolowo in: id., Awo, pp. 123-124.

117 NAI: CSO 26, file 25807 S8, Letter from the RCS to the CS, 9 March 1938.

118 Schärer, Das Nigerian Youth Movement, p. 172. The fact that the NYM was canvassing for support outside the Colony was particularly emphasised by J.S. Coleman. See J.S. Coleman, Nigeria: Background to Nationalism, Berkeley 1958, p. 226 and 460, note 53.

119 Nigerian Daily Times, 5 March 1938.

120 NAI: CSO 26, file 25807 S8, Letter from the RCS to the CS from 9 March 1938.

121 Holt Papers, Mss. Afr. s825, file 535(I), Letter from DA Lagos to all Ventures (Lagos District), 18 March 1938; see also ibid., Letter from DA Lagos to DA Accra, 12 Feb. 1938.

122 Austin, Capitalists and Chiefs, pp. 78-79; see also Nowell Report, para. 138.

123 Holt Papers, Mss. Afr. s825, file 535(I), Letter from DA Lagos to Administrative Department John Holt & Co., 7 Jan. 1938, and ibid., DA Lagos to DA Accra, 12 Feb. 1938. In theoretical term, the events in Nigeria provide a very good example for the 'free rider' problem as discussed by R.H. Bates, The Commercialization of Agriculture and the Rise of Rural Protest, in: R.H. Bates, Essays on the Political Economy of Rural Africa, Cambridge 1983, pp. 92-104, and North, Structure and Change, pp. 45-59.

124 Ehler, Handelskonflikte, p. 210.

125 On the hold-ups in the Gold Coast in general see Austin, Capitalists and Chiefs, pp. 63-95, and the articles by R.J. Southall, Farmers, Traders and Brokers in the Gold Coast Economy, in: Canadian Journal of African Studies, XII (1978) 2, pp. 185-211, and J. Miles, Rural Protest in the Gold Coast: The Cocoa Hold-ups, 1908-1938, in: C. Dewey and A.G. Hopkins (eds.), The Imperial Impact: Studies in the Economic History of Africa and India, London 1978, pp. 152-170.

126 NAI: Ondo Prof 1/1, file 638, Letter from the Resident Ondo to the SSP, 21 Jan. 1938; see also Holt Papers, Mss. Afr. s825, file 535(I), DA Lagos to Administrative Department of John Holt & Co., 25 Jan. 1938.

127 For example, government officials apparently did not know that the firm G.B. Ollivant was part of the Unilever group. See the evidence which the Nigerian Director of Agriculture gave to the Nowell Commission in NAI: CSO 26, file 25807 S9, Memorandum 'Produce Buying and Merchandise Agreements' by J.R. Mackie, 12 April 1938.

128 Holt Papers, Mss. Afr. s825, file 535(I), Evidence Submitted to the Cocoa Commission by J.F. Winter, DA Lagos of John Holt & Co., April 1938; see also Ehler, Handelskonflikte, p. 206, and Drummond Thompson, The Development of Motor Transport, p. 305.

129 Drummond Thompson, The Development of Motor Transport, p. 276, and Ogunremi, The Nigerian Motor Transport Union Strike, pp. 138-139.

130 Holt Papers, Mss. Afr. s825, file 535(I), Letter from DA Lagos to the DA Accra, 12 Feb. 1938; see also Cadbury Papers, file 289/232, Letter from J. Holt to J. Cadbury, 20. January 1938.

131   Ibid., Letter from the DA Lagos to the Administrative Department of John Holt & Co., 25 Jan. 1938.

132   Holt Papers, Mss. Afr. s825, file 535(I), Letter from DA Lagos to the DA Accra, 12 Feb. 1938.

133   Ibid., Letter from the DA Lagos to the Administrative Department of John Holt & Co., 25 Jan. 1938.

134   NAI: Ondo Prof 1/1, file 638, Extracts from Residents Reports, Ondo Province, to SSP, 26 April 1938.

135   Beer, Politics of Peasant Groups, p. 228, note 19, and Nowell Report, para. 389. Conf. also NAI: Ondo Prof 1/1, file 638, Notes of a Discussion at a Meeting Presided over by His Excellency, the Governor of Nigeria, 29 Dec. 1937, and NAI: CSO 26, file 34883, Question No. 35 and No. 52, Nigerian Legislative Council, 28 Nov. 1938.

136   Williams, J. Akinpelu Obisesan, p. 6.

137   NAI: CSO 26, file 25807 S8, Petition to His Excellency, the Governor, Sir Bernard Bourdillon by the Ibadan Co-operative Cocoa Marketing Union, 16 Feb. 1938.

138   Ibid., Letter from the Acting Chief Secretary to the Government, G.C. Whitely to the President of the Ibadan Co-operative Marketing Union, 16 March 1938.

139   NAI: CSO 26, file 25807 S6, Letter from the SSP to CS, 25 March 1938, and NAI: CSO 26, file 34883 Vol.I, Letter from the SSP to CS, 14 Feb. 1938; see also PRO: CO 583, file 240, Internal Intelligence Report of the Royal West African Frontier Force for half year ending 31 Dec. 1938. See PRO: CO 583, file 249, Internal Intelligence Report of the Royal West African Frontier Force for half year ending 30th June 1939. According to these reports, there was a hold-up of palm produce in Ondo Province in late 1938 and early 1939, because traders felt that they were not getting '... a fair deal from the firms...' See also Harneit-Sievers, African Business, 'Economic Nationalism', and British Colonial Policy: Southern Nigeria, 1935-1954, paper presented to the African Studies Association Meeting, Toronto, 3-6 November 1994.

140   PRO: CO 583, file 240, Intelligence Report for half-year, ending 31 Dec. 1938; see also West African Pilot, 28 Oct. 1938.

141   PRO: CO 657, file 46, Administrative Reports 1938: Eastern Provinces, p. 16; see also Administrative Reports 1938: Western Provinces, p. 6.

142   Holt Papers, Mss. Afr. s825, file 535(I), Letter from the DA Lagos to the Administrative Department of John Holt & Co., 25 Jan. 1938.

143   See West Africa, 7 Jan. 1939, p. 1855. In a review article on main events of the year 1938, the author B. Randolphe came to the conclusion that '...the whole lesson of the hold-up is the register of progress, in the sense that African powers of combination and maintained resistance to conditions which they consider unfair have been demonstrated'.

144   West Africa, 26 Feb. 1938, p. 226. R.S. Thomson was a London cocoa broker, while L.M. Irving was employed by the Ministry of Agriculture. E. Melville was working in the Colonial Office. He subsequently became the Colonial Office 'expert' in cocoa matters.

145   Ehler, Handelskonflikte, pp. 264-274.

146   See PRO: CO 852, file 133/4, Letter from J. Knight, E.C. Tansley and J. Cadbury to the Secr. of State for the Colonies, 12 April 1938; see also PRO: CO 852, file 134/2, Minute by C.G. Eastwood on a meeting between the F. Samuel, J. Cadbury, A. Mellor, O.G.R Williams, Sir Henry Moore and C.G. Eastwood in the Colonial Office on the 1st September, 1938, 3 Sept. 1938, and Cadbury Papers, file 289/146, Letter from J. Cadbury to N. Edwards, 29 April 1938. The argument that the firms policy almost

amounted to blackmail was also made by Ehler, Handelskonflikte, p. 265, and Meredith, The Colonial Office, p. 289.

147   That was on 8th April, 1938. For details see Ehler, Handelskonflikte, pp. 265-267.

148   See for example the report on the complaints by the Scottish & English Wholesale Society in the 'Memorandum by the Committee Appointed by the Governor of the Gold Coast to Examine the Report and Recommendations of the Cocoa Inquiry Commission' in Rhodes House Library Oxford, Mss. Afr. s604.

149   Rhodes House Library Oxford, Mss. Afr. s604, The Humble Petition of the Paramount Chiefs, Cocoa Producers and other responsible Africans of the Gold Coast, 31 May 1938; also cited in Ehler, Handelskonflikte, p. 284.

150   Nowell Report, para. 195. The Chairman of the Commission, W. Nowell, later bitterly complained about the terms of the truce. See PRO: CO 852, file 133/4, Letter from W. Nowell to the Secr. of State for the Colonies, 15 April 1938.

151   Holt Papers, Mss. Afr. s825, file 535(I), Minutes of the Opening Session of the Cocoa Inquiry Commission, 28 April 1938. The Commission had arrived in Lagos on the previous day.

152   Holt Papers. Mss. Afr. s825, file 535(I), Letter from the DA Lagos to the DA Accra of John Holt & Co., 12 Feb. 1938.

153   Nowell Report, para.389, Evidence from the Nigerian Produce Traders Union.

154   Ibid.; Evidence from the Nigerian Youth Movement.

155   Holt Papers, Mss. Afr. s825, file 535(I), Evidence to be submitted to the Cocoa Commission by J.F. Winter, DA Lagos of John Holt & Co., April 1938.

156   Ibid., Letter from the Administrative Department to the DA Lagos of John Holt & Co., 2 April 1938; see a similar letter in Cadbury Papers, file 289/173, Letter from E.A. Ellis to J. Cadbury, 11 March 1938.

157   Ibid., Minutes of Meeting of the General Committee (Nigerian Cocoa Scheme) held at Unilever House, 23 Feb. 1938.

158   Nowell Report, para. 141.

159   The argument, that the Agreement schedule of marketing expenses was somewhat generously calculated by the firms, was made by several authors on the subject, for example by Bauer, West African Trade, p. 207. The argument here, however, is that the firms were able to hide this fact successfully from the Nowell Commission.

160   Nowell Report, para. 489.

161   Nigerian Gazette Extra-ordinary, Press Communique: Report of the Commission on the Marketing of West African Cocoa, 25 Oct. 1938.

162   Nowell Report, para. 473.

163   Here I follow Southall's interpretation of the Commission's report. See Southall, Cadbury on the Gold Coast, p. 447.

164   Nowell Report, para. 514.

165   This famous phrase can be found in the Report on Cocoa Control in West Africa, 1939-1943, and Statement of Future Policy, Cmd.6554 of Sept. 1944, London 1944, pp. 10-11.

166   Nowell Report, para. 515.

167   Ibid., para. 528.

168   Nowell Report, para. 545.

169   Ibid., para. 546.

170   Ibid., paras. 551-568.

171   Ibid., para. 555.

172   Nigerian Gazette Extra-ordinary, Press Communique: Report of the Commission on the Marketing of West African Cocoa, 25 Oct. 1938.

173   NAI: CSO 26, file 34883 Vol.I, Letter from the Director of Agriculture to CS, 15 Nov. 1938.

174   Ibid., Letter from the Governor Deputy C.C. Wooley to the Secr. of State for the Colonies, 15 Nov. 1938. These expectations, however, were strongly disappointed, since cocoa prices in the 1938/39 season even fell below the prices farmers had received in the previous season.

175   Ibid., Letter from the Resident Oyo Province to CS, 23 Nov. 1938.

176   Ibid., Letter from the Director of Agriculture to the CS, 15 Nov. 1938, see also ibid., Letter from the Resident Abeokuta Province to CS, 4 Nov. 1938, and Beer, Politics of Peasant Groups, p. 230.

177   NAI: CSO 26, file 34883 Vol.I, Letter from the Director of Agriculture to the CS, 15 Nov. 1938.

178   Ibid., Letter from the Acting Resident of Ijebu Province to the CS, 3 Nov. 1938.

179   NAI: CSO 26, file 34883 Vol.I, Memorandum 'Produce Buying Agreements' by S. Akinsanya, 30 Dec. 1938; see also Kelly Report, para. 109.

180   Kelly Report, para. 24.

181   NAI: CSO 26, file 34883 Vol.II, Comments from the Ibadan Co-operative Cocoa Marketing Union, 28 Feb. 1939. For the positive reaction of the Ondo Farmers Representative Union, see NAI: CSO 26, file 34883 Vol.I, Letter from the Resident Ondo Province to the CS, 11 Nov. 1938.

182   NAI: CSO 26, file 34883 Vol.II, Comments from the Ibadan Co-operative Marketing Union, 28 Feb. 1939.

183   See NAI: CSO 26, file 34883 Vol.I, Letter from the Director of Agriculture to the CS, 18 Nov. 1938.

184   There are a number of letters from the firms which contain this argument, see for example NAI: CSO 26, file 34883 Vol.I, Letter from the local agents (Lagos) of G.B. Ollivant and Cocoa Manufacturers Ltd. to the CS, 23 Feb. 1939.

185   Holt Papers, Mss. Afr. s825, file 535(I), Letter from Administrative Department of John Holt & Co. to the DA Accra, 15 Nov. 1938.

186   NAI: CSO 26. file 34883 Vol.I, Letter from the Director of Agriculture to the CS, 18 Nov. 1938, and ibid., Letter from the RCS to the CS, 15 Nov. 1938.

187   PRO: CO 852, file 134/6, Minute by O.G.R. Williams, 12 Nov. 1938.

188   E. Melville, The Marketing of West African Cocoa. In: Cocoa, Chocolate and Confectionery Alliance Ltd. (ed.), International Cocoa Conference 1948, London 1949, p. 72.

189   PRO: CO 852, file 193/3, Minute by E. Melville, 25 July 1939.

190   West Africa, 12 Nov. 1938, p. 1556.

191   NAI: CSO 26, file 34883 Vol.I, Copy of a letter from the Governor of the Gold Coast to the Secr. of State for the Colonies, 30 Dec. 1938.

192   Ibid., Letter from Secr. of State for the Colonies to the Governor of Nigeria, 11 Feb. 1938.

193   Government Notice No. 373, 15 March 1939.

194   NAI: CSO 26, file 34883 S4 Vol.I, Minute by Acting CS G.C. Whitely, 18 March 1939.

195   Ibid., Minute by Acting CS G.C. Whitely, 24 March 1939; see also West African Pilot, 25 March 1939.

196 Ibid., Minute by Acting CS G.C. Whitely, 28 March 1939. D.T. Sasegbon was a retired customs clerk who owned a large cocoa farm near Agege. He was also one of the local notables who the delegates ('mission') from the Nigerian Youth Movement visited in March 1938. For the phrase 'a prominent cocoa farmer' see NAI: CSO 26, file 36517, Letter from the CS to the Secr. of State for the Colonies, 27 June 1939.

197 Ibid., Letter from the CS to E.J.G. Kelly, 30 March 1939.

198 Nigerian Advertiser (June 1938?) cited in West Africa, 8 July 1939, p. 909; see also West African Pilot, 3 April 1939.

199 Government Report No.375, 15 March 1939.

200 Kelly Report, appendix I, 'Witnesses'.

201 Kelly Report, para. 34.

202 Kelly Report, paras. 62-68. The idea of the employment of a special Marketing Officer was not new. Previously it had been suggested by the Member for the Rivers Division in the Legislative Council meeting in March 1938. See NAI: CSO 26, file 34883, Letter from the Director of Agriculture to the CS, 18 Nov. 1939.

203 Ibid., para. 56.

204 Ibid., para. 129.

205 NAI: CSO 26, file 36517 Vol.I, Letter from the Governor's Deputy to the Secr. of State for the Colonies, 27 June 1939.

206 Ibid., Minute by Financial Secretary, 15 June 1939.

207 NAI: CSO 26, file 36517 Vol.I, Letter from the Secr. of State for the Colonies to Governor of Nigeria, 23 Aug. 1939.

208 PRO: CO 852, file 193/3, Telegram from the Secr. of State for the Colonies to the Governor of Nigeria, 20 Dec. 1939.

209 NAI: CSO, file 36517 Vol.II, Letter from the Secr. of State for the Colonies to the Governor of Nigeria, 31 July 1939.

210 Report on Cocoa Control in West Africa, 1939-1943, and Statement of Future Policy, Cmd.6554 of Sept. 1944, London 1944, p. 16.

211 PRO: CO 852, file 272/1, Minute by E.Melville, 2 June 1940.

212 W. Ojemakinde, The Pullen Marketing Scheme: A Trial in Food Price Control in Nigeria, 1941-1947. In: Journal of the Historical Society of Nigeria, VI (1973) 4, pp. 413-423; see also PRO: CO 852/47, Administrative Reports, Department of Agriculture, p. 3.

213 One of the first Marketing Officers which the Colonial Government employed was H.O. Davies, a prominent member of the Nigerian Youth Movement and presumably the author of its Youth Charter. See G.O. Olunsanya, The Second World War and Politics in Nigeria, 1935-1953, Lagos 1973, p. 38.

214 PRO: CO 852, file 134/2, Minute by C.G. Eastwood on a meeting between F. Samuel, J. Cadbury, A. Mellor, O.G.R. Williams, Sir Henry Moore and C.G. Eastwood in the Colonial Office on the 1st September, 1938, 3 Sept. 1938; see also Meredith, The Colonial Office, p. 290, and Ehler, Handelskonflikte, pp. 287-289.

215 PRO: CO 852, file 134/2, Letter from the Governor of the Gold Coast to the Secr. of State for the Colonies, 27 Aug. 1938, and ibid., Letter from the Governor of Nigeria to the Secr. of State for the Colonies, 26 Aug. 1938.

216 PRO: CO 852, file 134/2, Minute by C.G. Eastwood on a meeting between F. Samuel, J. Cadbury, A. Mellor, O.G.R Williams, Sir Henry Moore and C.G. Eastwood in the Colonial Office on the 1st September, 1938, 3 Sept. 1938.

217 Ibid.

218   Ibid., Letter from F. Samuel to Sir Henry Moore, 9th September, 1938; see also PRO: CO 852, file 134/2, Minute by Sir Henry Moore, 6 Sept. 1938.

219   Holt Papers, Mss. Afr. s825, file 535(I), Letter from Administrative Department of John Holt & Co. to DA Lagos, 13 Sept. 1938. About three weeks earlier, the DA Lagos wrote to John Holt's local buying agents: 'We have agreed with firms on the Coast, we shall co-operate with each other as fully as if the Pool existed...' See ibid., Letter from DA Lagos to all ventures Lagos District, 22 Aug. 1938.

220   NAI: CSO 26, file 34883 Vol.I, Memorandum 'Produce Buying Agreement' by S. Akinsanya, 30 Dec. 1938; see also ibid., Letter from the Director of Agriculture to the CS, 15 Nov. 1938.

221   Holt Papers, Mss. Afr. s825, file 536(II), Letter from Administrative Department of John Holt & Co. to DA Accra, 20 June 1939. It is revealing to cite the answer from the DA Accra in full since it shows how representatives of the firms outmanoeuvred colonial governments. He wrote: 'I am extremely obliged for the very clear guidance your letter contains. I did have an idea that there was, during the past season, some arrangement at home, but carefully avoided discussions with people who seemed to know all about it, so that when asked directly by Government officials if there was an Agreement of some description being run in England, I could truthfully answer that to the best of my knowledge there was not. I was asked this question on a number of occasions.' See ibid., Letter from DA Accra to Administrative Department of John Holt & Co., 29 June 1939.

222   This is the interpretation advanced by Ehler, Handelskonflikte, p. 308, and Shenton, The Development of Capitalism, p. 110.

223   Holt Papers, Mss. Afr. s825, file 535(I), Letter from John Holt Jr. to the Directors of the United Africa Company, 23 May 1938; see also Cadbury Papers, file 289/359, Letter from J. Cadbury to H. Giles (Rowntree), 27. May 1938. For the Cadbury-clause in the 1937 Buying Agreement, see ibid., Memorandum of an Agreement, (August) 1937, p. 2, para. 1.

224   Holt Papers, Mss. Afr. s825, file 535(II), Letter from Administrative Department of John Holt & Co. to DAs Lagos and Accra, 15 Nov. 1939.

225   Holt Papers, Mss. Afr. s825, file 535(II), Copy of the Minutes of a 'Meeting of Members who are Signatories to the Agreement for the Dividing of Cocoa Purchased in Nigeria...Held...on Thursday, the 20th July 1944'. The meeting was attended by representatives from Cocoa Manufacturers Ltd., Companie Française de l'Afrique Occidentale, John Holt & Co. (Liverpool) Ltd., G.B. Ollivant Ltd., Paterson Zochonis & Co. Ltd., and Overseas Buyers Ltd. (Union Trading Company). Of course, the German firms of G.L. Gaiser and Witt & Busch did not take part in the meeting. For a similar statement, see Cadbury Ltd. (Birmingham), Minutes and Reports 1934-1939, Minutes of the Meeting of Directors held at the Station Hotel, York, 18 August 1944.

226   Cadbury Ltd. (Birmingham), Minutes and Reports 1934-1939, Minutes of Meeting of Directors held at the Queen's Hotel, Birmingham, on Friday 12 August 1938.

CHAPTER 5

The Introduction of Statutory Cocoa Marketing

The introduction of produce control was part of the much wider transformation which the Nigerian economy experienced during the Second World War. However, since this transformation lies outside the focus of this study, many aspects of it will only receive a passing reference, though many of them merit studies of their own.[1]

The Arguments in Favour of Control

In reviewing the reasons why statutory control was introduced in the first months of the Second World War the interests of the European trading firms must be distinguished from those of the Nigerian and British government.

Both the European trading firms and the United Kingdom government faced to some extent the same problem. Apart from the actual hostilities which the outbreak of war eventually caused, the declaration of war between Germany and Britain meant that economic relations between the two powers were severed. Since Germany was a large importer of goods and raw materials which Britain and its Colonies produced, the outbreak of war caused considerable dislocation in economic life. The cocoa trade, and thus Nigeria and the Gold Coast, were particularly badly hit, since both countries supplied about half of the world's cocoa in the 1930s, while at the same time the German market consumed about one-fifth of the world's supply, a large part of which came from West Africa.[2]

The Firms' Point of View

The firms had not made any contingency plans for that event, so that when war broke out the sudden loss of the entire German market created dire problems. As has been mentioned in the previous chapter, the firms customarily bought substantial quantities of cocoa for which they had no immediate buyer. They usually also bought the entire West African cocoa crop. Since a large chunk of the market now became inaccessible, this policy entailed the danger of buying more cocoa than the firms would be able to sell and would have involved the likely risk of suffering substantial losses, which the firms were naturally reluctant to assume.[3] From this perspective, it is understandable that the firms' first reaction to the outbreak of war was to slow down their cocoa purchases in West Africa.[4]

The alternative was to buy only part of the crop and leave the rest in the hands of producers and indigenous traders. But this strategy was also fraught with risks. In the event, an oversupply of cocoa would drive local prices down. Though the cocoa trade itself might have been extremely profitable to the firms, since the margin between local purchase prices and selling prices would widen, a decline in local prices would reduce purchasing power and this would hit the merchandise trade, especially since a large amount of merchandise had already been shipped to the Gold Coast and Nigeria in anticipation of the approaching cocoa season.[5]

Finally, there was the problem of the 1937 Buying Agreement. By signing the Agreement the firms had committed themselves to buy not more nor less than a fixed percentage of the pool's overall purchases. In 1939 the larger firms, and in particular the United Africa Company, were forced by the Agreement to take on more cocoa than they thought they were able to sell. In a letter to the senior local agents of the firm, one manager of John Holt & Co. (D.L. Rawlings) describes the situation as follows:

> To give you an indication as to how serious the situation was, it was until recently, quite problematical whether the Imperial Treasury would approve of this Government transaction [i.e. the cocoa control scheme]. The U.A.C. were so alarmed at the prospect before the cocoa trade that they told the pool that, unless the Government Control scheme were launched quickly they, the U.A.C., would have to move the abandonment of the cocoa agreement because they could not face the liability of having to buy their pool share of cocoa at their own risk. We had arrived at the extraordinary position where the biggest shareholder in the cocoa pool was gravely disquieted because his pool share was too big.[6]

Given these prospects, it is not surprising that the United Africa Company was the first to approach the Colonial Office and suggest that government should purchase the entire West African cocoa crop, and relieve the firms from commercial risks relating to cocoa marketing which the war was likely to cause.

It can be argued that it was a letter of 8th September, 1939 from A.R.I. Mellor, a member of the Board of Directors of the United Africa Company, to G.L.M. Clauson, the Head of the Economic Department of the Colonial Office at the time, which started the discussion about the government assuming control of the cocoa trade. The memorandum attached to that letter raised for the first time the idea that it would be in the interest of government to purchase the entire West African cocoa crop. It also included several arguments as to why government should do so, many of which later became the official government position.[7] They will be discussed later in this chapter.

When government finally decided to assume control of cocoa in November 1939, this news was enthusiastically welcomed by the firms. One Director of

John Holt & Co. wrote that 'the hope ... has ... now been fulfilled'[8], while the weekly journal *West Africa*, usually very well informed on the opinion of the firms, though not always taking their side, ran headlines like 'West African Cocoa Crop Purchased by British Government: Great Benefit to Producers and Merchants'[9].

It is not suggested here that the decision by the government to purchase the West African cocoa crop in 1939 was just a response to the demands made by West African merchants. It is, however, significant that the decision was in accord with the short-term interests of the firms, for whom the scheme seems to have presented almost the only way to avert serious losses.

The Government's Point of View

The Colonial Office expected that two factors would cause a dramatic fall in cocoa purchase prices in West Africa. One was the loss of the German market, so that cocoa production in West Africa would far exceed the demand from mainly British and American manufacturers. The other was the limitation of shipping facilities which the war was likely to impose on West African trade. As regards the latter, the Colonial Office believed that a repetition of the World War One experience was imminent.[10] Then the lack of shipping had created a bottleneck. British manufacturers had strongly competed for the limited supply which was available, while part of the West African crop had rotted away in warehouses and on cocoa trees. The huge margin which consequently developed between the Lagos price and the Liverpool price of cocoa had assured some of the firms' excessively high profits.[11] At the same time, the low purchase price of cocoa and other export crops like palm produce, together with a general shortage of imported consumer goods, had created considerable political difficulties for the Nigerian government.[12]

It was thus thought that if nothing was done political discontent would re-emerge, especially since, as the Colonial Office argued

> In recent years the question of what is a fair price for cocoa has become the subject of bitter controversy, culminating in a wide-spread hold-up of the Gold Coast cocoa crop during the 1937/38 cocoa season... A slump in cocoa would produce serious discontent and might even lead to an outbreak of trouble which is of course essential to avoid at a time like this.[13]

Moreover, low produce prices would reduce government revenue from customs receipts, which again would have serious political consequences. The revenue derived from cocoa exports in Nigeria was estimated to be about £900,000[14] and the Nigerian government could not afford to lose even part of this sum without being subsequently forced to make cuts in vital services. Nigeria had at the time almost no reserves and its administration was run on a shoe-string budget. Thus if government revenue was reduced through the loss of customs revenue, the Governor would be forced to increase taxation, which was seen, in combination with substantially reduced incomes caused by a fall in produce prices for the lack of customers or the lack of shipping, as a recipe for political turmoil. Thus the British government had to step in and it was even argued that from the standpoint of the British taxpayer, there was not much difference between bailing out the Nigerian cocoa producer or bailing out the Nigerian government, since in both cases the Treasury had to foot the bill.[15]

Furthermore, it was argued that the establishment of a control scheme would be commercially advantageous to the United Kingdom. If government fixed purchase prices in West Africa at a higher level than they were expected to fall, neutral countries - in particular the United States - would have to pay these higher prices for their cocoa imports. Thus foreign exchange earnings would increase, if the same volume of sales was maintained. Since the United Kingdom and the countries whose trade was conducted in Sterling were likely to have a substantial balance of payments deficit during the war with those countries which conducted their trade in Dollars, this argument held some weight.[16]

The establishment of a comprehensive system of price control was relatively easy to achieve. All that was needed was to fix a maximum price for colonial imports in the United Kingdom and prohibit the export of such goods to other destinations. Local prices would then also be fixed, since the trading firms would only be allowed to subtract their normal purchase costs from the United Kingdom price to arrive at the port of shipment price in West Africa.[17]

Such a system was, for example, in operation for the palm produce trade. But it was not considered to be satisfactory for cocoa where fixed local export prices would not guarantee that the whole crop would be purchased. A large part of the crop was usually sold to neutral countries and to the United States in particular, on whose purchase prices the British government at least at this stage of the war had no influence. It was therefore argued,

> The apparent danger of a limited control...is that if the local pegged price were too high there would be no inducement for shippers to purchase cocoa for the United States market and producers would be left to discontinue producing or to carry large stocks. If on the other hand the New York price remained above the parity of the United Kingdom pegged price, shippers would obtain the full benefit of the Dollar premium.[18]

This argument has to be evaluated against the background of the most likely evolution of prices in the United Kingdom and in the United States. The premium which trading firms obtained in the U.S. market at the time[19] was likely to increase and become permanent, since the British government was determined to keep prices down in the United Kingdom, not least because it wanted to encourage cocoa consumption and to protect British consumers from high price rises. 'The fixed price' the Governor of Nigeria was informed, 'could clearly not be so high as that current in New York.'[20]

If, however, the United Kingdom price remained permanently below the New York price, trading firms with U.S. customers would obtain excessively large profits. Such profits, it was argued, belonged to the government and not to the trading firms, for they were not the result of the commercial acumen of the trading firms but of government pricing policy. Consequently a more elaborate system of control, as, for example, in the case of palm produce, was necessary.

The Colonial Office therefore proposed that government should purchase the entire West African cocoa crop and employ the trading firms as its agents. In that capacity the firms would only receive a commission and would have to surrender all eventual trading profits to the government.[21] Such a system would also ensure that no cocoa would remain unsold in West Africa, which in effect meant that government, instead of the trading firms, would shoulder the commercial risks of the West African cocoa trade during the war.

It could be argued that the question of who was rightfully entitled to the war-time profits in the U.S. market was only a minor aspect in the discussions about the control scheme. But it seems that the argument held some weight. There was, for example, the case of the American firm Rockwood & Co. which had come to Nigeria at the 'unofficial' invitation of the government in 1938 to purchase cocoa on behalf of American manufacturers and the Hershey Corporation in particular.[22] Rockwood was about to start buying cocoa in October 1939 when its export licenses, which the firm had received in the previous month, were revoked. This decision was probably welcomed by the European firms which dominated the Nigerian market at the time and who saw in Rockwood an unwelcome competitor. However, the decision to revoke these licenses seems not to have been a result of lobbying by the trading firms, but was taken because the Colonial Office feared that Rockwood would pay higher prices in Nigeria than it was thought desirable and still secure a large part of the New York premium.[23] This argument is supported by further evidence. There was a long discussion in a later state of the war about the question of whether the cocoa control scheme should be extended to other crops, such as palm kernels. In 1941 British trading firms began to export palm kernels to the United States, where much higher prices were paid than in the United Kingdom. Again, the argument about 'unjust profits' emerged and consequently produce control was extended to include palm kernels.[24]

The argument about "unjust profits" also raised the question as to who was ultimately entitled to them. The Colonial Office and the Ministry of Food argued that these profits should be shared between the United Kingdom government and the West African governments, the latter in the proportion of produce delivered.[25] It was not made clear what share the West African governments would receive, but in any case there was no discussion at this time[26] about returning such profits to cocoa producers, to whom - one should think - they rightfully belonged.

The reason why the Colonial Office thought it would be desirable for the United Kingdom government to purchase the West African cocoa crop can be summarised as follows: It was thought that some form of control was necessary, since in its absence political difficulties would arise in West Africa and certain commercial advantages would be lost. When it came to the question of what kind of control should be established, it was clear that a system like that established for the palm produce trade was not sufficient, because of the danger that part of the West African cocoa crop would not be bought by the trading firms. Moreover, there was the likelihood that some firms would obtain excessively large profits in the markets which were not controlled by the United Kingdom government. The system which was consequently proposed was designed to make good the disadvantages which would result from a limited form of control. The best solution was thought to be a government purchase scheme, whereby government would essentially assume the role of a statutory trading firm.[27]

There was thus a convergence of the arguments for an extended system of produce control between the trading firms and the government. It was obviously in both parties' interest to come to an arrangement, and in the next section of this chapter we will see how the details of the scheme worked out.

The Negotiations in London

In the discussions about the eventual purchase scheme, historical precedents were hardly mentioned. The export legislation which the Gold Coast government had enacted in the wake of the hold-up in 1938 had provided some experience, it was said, but it was not specified what precisely that experience was.[28] Without a "model" many details of the scheme were thus settled in various discussions between the trading firms and the British government. This makes it necessary to describe the kind of institutional framework in which these discussions were held.

The Institutional Role of the Firms

It was decided early on that the Ministry of Food would be responsible for the administration of the cocoa control scheme. It was claimed that since the Ministry of Food was charged with the bulk purchase of cocoa and its sale and allocation between British manufacturing companies, it would not make sense to have a separate West African cocoa purchase scheme run by a different government department. The Ministry of Food somewhat reluctantly accepted this argument.[29]

The Ministry of Food had no previous experience in the administration of cocoa purchase schemes and relied therefore on the firms for much of its technical advice. Thus, on the 12th September the 'U.K. Advisory Committee' was set up, whose main function was to work out the distribution of supplies between United Kingdom manufacturers.[30] It consisted of the various parties involved in the pre-war British domestic cocoa trade. J. Cadbury, for example, sat on the Committee to represent the interests of manufacturers, while E.C. Tansley from the United Africa Company appeared for the West African merchants. Other members were R.E. Hurlston (Elder Dempster Lines) and F.E. Williams (English and Scottish Co-operative Wholesale Society).

As regards the purchase of cocoa in West Africa, a somewhat different approach was chosen. Here the Ministry of Food did not constitute an advisory committee but seems to have contacted the Association of West African Merchants' Cocoa (Nigeria Section) Sub-committee[31], which had been formed in September 1939 to represent the interests of the firms engaged in the Nigerian cocoa trade at the time. It consisted of E. Deresse (Compagnie Française de l'Afrique Noire), A.V. Iredale (Cocoa Manufacturers Ltd.), John Holt jr. (John Holt & Co.), F. Samuel and E.C. Tansley (both United Africa Company), all of whom had been leading members of the 'London Committee' of the 1937 cocoa pool, which shows a remarkable degree of personal continuity.[32]

The Ministry of Food recognised the 'Cocoa (Nigeria Section) Sub-committee' as the legitimate representative of the interests of the British firms engaged in the Nigerian cocoa trade. This led to a number of complications since not all such firms were members of the Association of West African Merchants. Thus a number of smaller independent cocoa brokers were excluded from the discussions about the future arrangement in the marketing of Nigerian cocoa, while a special compromise had to be found for the small but influential English and Scottish Co-operative Wholesale Society, which was given extra representation in the meetings between the Ministry of Food, the Colonial Office and the Association of West African Merchants. These gatherings later became known as the meetings of the 'West Africa Committee'.[33]

The official status of the 'West Africa Committee' was of a somewhat dubious nature, since it had no statutory backing unlike, for example, the 'U.K. Advisory Committee'. There were no official appointments, press releases and such like, but it had a secretary and its minutes were meticulously kept.[34] It was arguably in this committee that the most important decisions were made about the future arrangements in the Nigerian war-time cocoa trade.

The 'West Africa Committee' met several times during October, November and December 1939, until it was merged with the 'U.K. Advisory Committee' in January 1940 to form the 'Advisory Committee on Raw Cocoa'[35]. This new committee had over 20 members, including representatives from trading firms, smaller brokers, cocoa manufacturers and unions, such as L.A. Pearmaine of the Transport and General Workers Union and W.W.T. Barnett of the National Union of Distributive and Allied Workers.[36] West African cocoa producers and cocoa traders had no direct representation on the committee, but it was assumed that the Colonial Office would look after their interests. In any case the new committee had only very little influence, since most of the more important structural details of the scheme had already been previously worked out in the negotiations between the Association of West African Merchants and the Ministry of Food.

J. Cadbury and E.C. Tansley were not members of the new 'Advisory Committee on Raw Cocoa'. Earlier, in November 1939, they had become Ministry of Food executives and occupied the posts of Cocoa Controller and Deputy Cocoa Controller respectively, where they were responsible for the supervision and administration of the government cocoa purchase scheme.[37] In that capacity they were also the official representatives of the Ministry of Food in negotiations and discussions with other government departments, such as the Board of Trade and the Ministry of Shipping, with the trading firms and the 'Advisory Committee on Raw Cocoa'.

Thus, insofar as their institutional role was concerned, the position of the Association of West African Merchants - in effect, the 1937 agreement firms - within the control machinery was extremely strong. They had managed to exclude other British interests, such as independent cocoa brokers, from participating in the early discussions about the West African cocoa purchase scheme, while two of its leading members, J. Cadbury and E.C. Tansley were employed, though not paid,[38] by the Ministry of Food to run the scheme itself.

Yet, this was not the only reason why the Ministry of Food and the Colonial Office were in a relatively weak position vis à vis the firms as I will argue in the next section of this chapter.

The 1939 'Deal'

It seems that the strong position of the firms in the negotiations with the Ministry of Food and Colonial Office officials was the result of the eagerness of the latter to secure the co-operation of the firms in the actual running of the control scheme. One aspect of this co-operation, as already mentioned, was of a technical nature, since neither the Ministry of Food nor the Colonial Office had any previous experience in the administration of large scale overseas purchase schemes. Arguably, the most important aspect of this co-operation, however, was financial.

In the previous section of this chapter it was explained why the Colonial Office favoured a scheme for the purchase of the entire West African cocoa crop. But such a scheme also had some distinct disadvantages, notably that complete government control would cost millions of pounds of Treasury money. Under the circumstances prevailing in September 1939 such an amount was not likely to be forthcoming and a different solution therefore had to be found. The Colonial Office argued that,

> Provided the co-operation of shippers could be obtained - and there is reason to believe that this would be readily given - the proposed scheme would not involve the purchase of the whole crop by the United Kingdom Government. Shippers would continue to finance cocoa purchases as previously and make sales in approved markets in co-operation with the United Kingdom Cocoa Controller. Government finance would be required only a) to make good any losses on sales to markets other than the United Kingdom, and b) to take over surplus stocks at the end of the season.[39]

The co-operation of the firms thus had its price. If the firms were to provide the necessary finance to run the scheme, government would purchase cocoa only through the Association of West African Merchants, which would be allowed to share out the crop amongst its member firms. As some sort of collateral, government would ensure, by statutory export regulations (export quotas), that member firms would not ship more cocoa from Nigeria during the season than their pre-determined share or quota allowed them to do and that non-member, mostly Nigerian, firms were unable to wreck that arrangement.

It seems that there was no formal agreement between the government and the firms about this aspect of the scheme, but there is some evidence which suggests that at least an understanding of this sort existed. Thus, for example, when the Governor of Nigeria complained about the rigidity of the scheme as regards the position of exporters who were not members of the Association of West African Merchants, he was told by the Secretary of State for the Colonies that,

> ...I appreciate that political difficulties may arise over allocation of the crop between buyers. In order to limit Government's financial obligations it is essential that existing trade organisations should be used to the full.[40]

The understanding between the firms and the government was, from the government's point of view, a compromise between the wish to control the cocoa trade and the need to accommodate the interests of the firms in order to execute such control.[41] This at least would explain why the structure of the eventual scheme contained such a curious mixture of private and governmental elements: while government was to purchase the cocoa crop, fix seasonal minimum prices and direct sales to United Kingdom and overseas customers, the firms were to effect actual purchases, provide the finance for the scheme and share out the bulk of the crop. As regards the financial results of the scheme, the firms would only receive remuneration for their services, while government would shoulder the commercial risks involved in the trade, which meant that it would be liable for any losses and entitled to any profits the scheme might produce.[42]

It is important to notice that this understanding was reached very early in September 1939 and that neither the Nigerian government nor the Nigerian exporters and produce traders (or commission buyers) had any say in it. Later, when they became involved in the negotiations about the fine details of the scheme, it seems that it was too late for their opposition to effect any significant changes in the basic structure, though - as we will see in the next section of this chapter - minor alterations were achieved.

The Finer Details of the Scheme

After the Colonial Office, the Ministry of Food and the firms had reached an agreement about how the scheme should be run in principle, prolonged negotiations started about the finer details. These concerned roughly four areas. There was the question of what export quotas should be allocated to the Nigerian, British, French and Dutch firms which had been involved in the prewar cocoa trade. Then the control authority had to decide what remuneration its various agents should receive for their services and what price producers would be paid for their produce. Finally, there was the question of what, if any, specific arrangements should be made for the purchase of cocoa from co-operative cocoa marketing societies.

The Quota Question

There is some evidence which suggests that so far as the determination of export quotas for the European firms was concerned, government left it to the Association of West African Merchants to share out their total seasonal shipments amongst themselves.[43] The firms just informed government about the actual distribution of the crop and that, it seems, was the end of the matter.[44]

Part of the government probably realised that its power to control the firms was, without a fully fledged government purchase scheme, rather limited. For example a Director of John Holt & Co. could write to the District Agent of the firm in Lagos when the scheme was still under discussion:

> For your own information, whatever may be the shipping quotas allotted to each individual exporter of cocoa, what will in fact happen is that as between members of the Cocoa Pool, the share will remain intact.[45]

It was perhaps felt that it was more practical to leave the determination of the export quotas to the Association of West African Merchants.

The fixing of the quotas was not an easy task. Not all firms which had previously participated in the West African cocoa trade were members of the Association of West African Merchants. These firms, the English and Scottish Co-operative Wholesale Society and the Greek firm of A.G. Leventis, could not be legitimately excluded from the scheme just for this reason. They were thus coaxed, if not forced, into becoming temporary members of the Association. They joined the war-time pool in late 1939.[46] Then there was the problem of what should be done with the 1937 pool share of enemy firms (the German firm G.L. Gaiser) or with the pool share of firms which were suspected of having German chocolate manufacturers (the Dutch firm Witt & Busch) as their main customers. The solution the Association came up with was rather simple: Their shares were eliminated and distributed between the remaining Pool members.[47]

The combined purchases of Witt & Busch and G.L. Gaiser amounted to about 14 per cent of the Nigerian cocoa exports[48] and it is perhaps not too far-fetched to suppose that the remaining firms were rather pleased to take over the German and Dutch quota, since that increased their business in Nigeria substantially. Thus, for example, the United Africa Company alone, which in 1937/38 and 1938/39 had shipped about 32 per cent of the Nigerian crop, could raise its market share to about 38 per cent in 1939/40.[49] A full listing of each share is reproduced below in table 5.[50]

The fact that the Association of African Merchants in effect determined their own purchase shares was later masked by the invention of an official formula for the division of the bulk of the crop between the European trading firms. It read:

> Each Group "A" Shipper [i.e. member firms of the Association] will during the period 1st September 1939 to 30th September 1940, buy an amount of cocoa available for purchase by Group "A" Shippers, which in relation to the purchases of all Group "A" Shippers during the same period bears the same proportion as his aggregate purchases of cocoa over the three crop years 1936/7 to 1938/9 bears to the aggregate purchases of all Group "A" Shippers over the same period.[51]

Table 5: Nigerian Cocoa Export Quotas for European Trading Firms in 1939/40 (as percentage of total European shipments)

United Africa Company Ltd.	38.07%
G.B. Ollivant Ltd.	9.94%
Compagnie Française de L'Afrique Occid ntale	4.55%
Société Commerciale de l'Quest Africai	2.08%
Union Trading Company Ltd.	3.12%
Cocoa Manufacturers Ltd.	13.35%
John Holt & Co.	13.02%
Paterson, Zochonis and Co. Ltd.	6.73%
C. Zard	5.70%
E. & S. Co-operative Wholesale Society	.93%
London, Africa and Overseas Ltd.	2.51%

Source: NAI: CSO 26, file 36148 S 28, Letter from E. Melville to C.C.
Wooley, 25 April 1940.
Note: The tonnage quotas (2,600 tons of less than 2.5% of the Nigerian crop as it turned out) of African exporter were listed separately.

This formula was supposed to express the principle that no firm or individual should illegitimately gain or suffer from government intervention. Thus the position of each participant in the cocoa and other markets would be 'frozen' for the duration of the war. This was called the 'standstill policy'.[52]

However, the formula, which appears to be a practical example of that principle, was in reality something rather different. Since 1937/38 the firms' purchases were controlled by the 1937 cocoa Agreement and the distribution of the crop which that Agreement specified was largely based on the purchases of the firms in the 1936/37 season. Thus the formula above was in effect an official recognition of the 1937 Buying Agreement. This explains why the Administrative Department of John Holt & Co. could inform its local Agent in Lagos in January 1940 that

> ...both in the Gold Coast and Nigeria, our Government quota percentage and our Pool percentage are the same thing. This simplifies matters enormously.[53]

Yet, the Association was not given a completely free rein. The Colonial Office argued that 'for political reasons, it would be necessary to allocate part of the purchases to non-European (chiefly African) buyers'[54]. As has been shown in the previous chapter, there existed a small but influential group of Nigerian produce traders (and a rather larger group in the Gold Coast) who - before the war - had exported cocoa on their own account, and it was thought that their elimination from the war-time cocoa trade would, especially in the light of the events of 1937/38, create trouble for the government.

Thus a second category of exporters was invented, who were called the "B" Shippers. The firms which fell into this category, were, unlike the "A" Shippers, not real exporters. It was argued that it would be almost impossible to properly supervise the business activities of such firms, not least, because their head-quarters lay outside the United Kingdom. These firms were therefore only employed as agents of the Ministry of Food up to the f.o.b. point (port of shipment), where their parcels of cocoa were taken over by either United Kingdom based brokers or by "A" Shippers, both of whom could be more easily controlled by the relevant government bodies.[55] Since Nigerian based firms had neither any influence over what happened to their parcels of cocoa beyond the f.o.b. point or any option to make any sales on their own except to U.K.-based brokers or to the "A" Shippers, they were not real exporters in the same sense as the "A" Shippers.

Discussions about the export quotas of such firms were long and at times rather acrimonious. Initially, the Colonial Office and the Ministry of Food had proposed that the 'standstill formula' should also be applied to the "B" Shippers, but it seems that they changed their mind when it was pointed out that this formula would produce rather unsatisfactory quotas for the "B" Shippers. Some of them, like S. Thomopulos had only recently entered the cocoa trade and a quota computed on the basis of average shipments in the three cocoa seasons between 1936/37 and 1938/39 would have yielded for some firms a quota which would have been far below their actual 1938/39 shipments. In the end a formula was found which took these considerations into account. It read:

> Each Group "B" Shipper will buy a fixed quantity of cocoa equal to the tonnage shipped by him during 1938/39 crop year plus his proportionate share of enemy purchases.[56]

In the 1938/39 cocoa season the total shipments of Nigerian-based exporters amounted to 2,091 tons.[57] To this figure the Ministry of Food and the Colonial Office added what they thought would be a proportionate share of enemy purchase and, after consultation with the Association of West African Merchants in December 1939 and the Nigerian government, authorised the latter to issue export licences for up to 2,500 tons, the distribution of which among individual 'exporters' is shown in table 5.

Table 6: Nigerian Cocoa Export Quotas for Nigerian Based Firms in 1939/40.
(name/proprietor/location of headquarter/tonnage)

Nigerian:

United Development Trading Company (A.O. Makanjuola/Ibadan)	596 tons
Anglo-Nigerian Trading Corporation (E. Dada/Lagos)	326 tons
Odutola Brothers (-dto-/Ijebu-Ode)	270 tons
African Industrial Shipping & Importing Company (Rev. D.Q. Arthur/Lagos)	54 tons
Nigerian Produce Farmers Association (J.A. Cole (manager)/Abeokuta)	28 tons

Lebanese/Greek:

S. Thomopulos (-dto-/Lagos)	776 tons
Flionis Brother (-dto-/Ondo)	408 tons
C.S. Mandrides (-dto-/Benin City)	28 tons

British:

W.E. Griffith & Co. (-dto-/Nwaniba via Uyo)	14 tons

Total	2,500 tons

Source: NAI:Ib MinAgric 1, file 17980 Vol.I. Letter from G.F.T. Colby (Cocoa Controller) to all Shippers, 13 Dec. 1939.

The consultations with the firms were largely held during November and early December 1939 in the 'West Africa Committee'. The minutes of the committee reveal that apart from minor changes, the Ministry of Food and the Colonial Office accepted almost every proposal the Association of West African Merchants put forward.[58] The only opposition seems to have come occasionally from J. Cadbury, who attended these meetings in his capacity as 'director-designate' of the future 'Colonial Empire Cocoa Control', as the scheme was later officially called. Yet, his opposition was not too vigorous and almost invariably faltered when the Colonial Office officials indicated that they would support the claims of the European trading firms as they repeatedly did.[59]

The second set of discussions was held between the governments of the Gold Coast and Nigeria, and the Colonial Office. Here again one finds that the Colonial Office almost always sided with the firms, which was particularly noticeable in the question of the treatment of the "B" Shippers. Thus, for example, the issue of the apportionment of the German quota between the member firms of the Association of West African Merchants and the Nigerian-based cocoa exporters particularly incensed the Nigerian government, which in the end had almost to be forced to abandon its opposition to this aspect of the scheme as will be shown later.

This somewhat hostile attitude towards the claims of Nigerian- based firms and more sympathetic attitude towards the claims the European trading firms was largely caused by the Colonial Office's anxiety that the firms would deny the scheme their technical and financial support if the Colonial Office thwarted their requests. There were, however, also other, less obvious, reasons for this attitude. As D. Meredith has recently shown, Colonial Office officials were excessively ideologically biased with respect to Nigerian exporters and to the role they played within their societies.[60] Thus, for example, the Assistant Secretary, G.L.M. Clauson put on record:

> I hope that the concessions to the "B" Shippers will be kept within the smallest possible dimension for two reasons. The first is a natural objection to being blackmailed. The second is that I am much opposed to the creation or rather strengthening of a small capitalist class of Africans with incomes out of all proportion to the income of their fellow countrymen. Capitalists are, in my view, essential to society, but we have found by experience in this country that capitalists ought not to be too few or individually rich. The position in West Africa is approaching that in pre-war Russia with a very small relatively rich class and a proletariat. We know what happened in Russia and we do not want history to repeat itself.[61]

This was an extreme but certainly not untypical view within the Colonial Office. There are other minutes in which Nigerian exporters are classified as being 'selfish rogues, only anxious to exploit the African farmers'[62] who were 'unfortunately ... literate and vocal and have the ears not only of the chiefs, but also of the press' (emphasis added)[63].

Finally, there was the argument that the establishment of a government purchase scheme would enable Nigerian exporters to increase their market share at the expense of the European trading firms, if their exports were not fixed at the pre-war level.[64] The Colonial Office assumed that if Nigerian and European firms received the same commission rates from government for their services, Nigerian firms would be placed in a more competitive position, since their businesses were run on much lower overheads. This would enable them to pay higher prices for produce than the European firms profitably could and thus their market share would be bound to increase over time. This had to be avoided and since it was obviously politically inopportune to pay different commission rates for the same services to Nigerian and European firms, the only way to stop the advance of the Nigerian firms would be to fix quotas for the volume of their exports.

The three reasons why the Colonial Office so strongly favoured the adoption of 'standstill policy' were thus, firstly and perhaps most importantly, a marked interest in obtaining the co-operation of the firms; secondly, a heavy ideological bias against Nigerian exporters, and thirdly, a more general regard for the position of European (British) firms vis-à-vis local competitors in colonial markets. These arguments were not readily accepted by the Nigerian government, and in the next section of this chapter its point of view will be more thoroughly investigated.

The Dispute over the Quota System

Initially, the Nigerian government had strongly welcomed the idea of setting up a cocoa purchase scheme but, when it subsequently became increasingly involved in the finer details of the scheme, its attitude became more and more critical. This was particularly noticeable in the discussion about the quota system.

The Governor of Nigeria argued that to fix seasonal export quotas would mean the elimination of any competition in the cocoa trade and he was very concerned what effects this would have on the position of independent produce traders vis-à-vis the European firms. He was, however, not so much concerned about the position of the "B" Shippers, since their numbers were small and their position secure, if limited, in scope. In a telegram to the Secretary of State for the Colonies the Governor also expressed his anxiety about what he thought would be the likely political consequences of the imposition of the quota system. He wrote on the 25th November, 1939 that

> In the cocoa industry there is a considerable body of small firms who in the past have not shipped. They are not middle men (*sic*) in direct touch with producers but are better described as commission men (sic). Their activities have consisted of purchasing cocoa from the middle men (*sic*) and bag it and sale to the highest bidder among the large firms in parcels ready for shipment. Firms maintain that such commission men are parasites and speculators but I cannot agree... You will appreciate readily that the scheme as drafted will eliminate such commission men from the trade ... and will deprive them of their means of livelihood in so far as cocoa is concerned... Such commission men (*sic*) are largely Syrian. There are also

a number of Africans in the same position and the Nigerian produce traders union (*sic*) a well organised and vocal African body which was prominent in the Cocoa Pool (*sic*) agitation writes in this connection "There will remain no doubt in our minds that advantage is being taken of present war conditions to impose unreasonable hardship on large section of our community". You will appreciate that if the control scheme is to put out of business the above important section of the industry ... there may be acute political difficulties. Indeed I can think of no greater potential cause of discontent.[65]

The Governor of Nigeria objected especially to the 'standstill policy', arguing that he saw no reason why under a government purchase scheme competitive buying should completely cease in Nigeria, since it was both in the interests of the producer and the efficiency of the industry as a whole that it should be continued. Against these interests, other interests, such as those of the European trading firms, had to take second place.[66] He was also not prepared to overlook the fact that the consequences of that policy (foremost, the likely elimination of the independent produce traders or "commission men") were - in his phrase - 'scarcely consistent' with the policy's avowed principle.[67]

The Governor of Nigeria had also tried to gain some influence in how the system would work eventually in practice. He had assumed that he would have the power to control the purchases of African and European shippers and in this capacity he would be able to allocate some part of the seasonal purchase at his discretion. He thus asked the Secretary of State for the Colonies to confer on him the right to fix export quotas for about 12 per cent of seasonal purchases. This he argued was a reasonable amount, since the quota for German and Cameroonian firms whose exports had ceased, had amounted to about 15 per cent in the 1938/39 cocoa season. In this connection, he proposed that cooperative marketing societies should receive a substantial part of that allocation and would thus become exporters in their own right.[68] This proposal was refused.

The Governor then even undertook a last-minute attempt to convince the Secretary of State for the Colonies to abolish the quota system. He stated that, as far as Nigeria was concerned, he believed 'that the interests of the producers, co-operative societies and all Africans concerned in the trade would be best served if this elaborate scheme were abandoned and if the Food Controller merely undertook to purchase all Nigerian cocoa at fixed prices with a premium for Grade I cocoa...'[69]. It was, however, already too late to stop the scheme.

The negotiations, including to what extent the Governor of Nigeria would be allowed to control purchases of all shippers and allocate export quotas at his discretion, dragged on for a considerable period.[70] This caused some confusion in the early months of control, for the Nigerian government assumed that it was to issue monthly export licenses to the "A" and "B" Shippers in Nigeria. The former, however, thought that they were to receive their instructions from their London headquarters and thus did little to comply with the directives from the Nigerian government. In the end, the view of the Colonial Office that the responsibility for the control of the purchases of the "A" and "B" Shippers should rest with the authorities in London prevailed.

While the dispute lasted, the Governor became more and more incensed by the treatment he received from the Colonial Office and by the policy it pursued, the ulterior motives of which he apparently deeply mistrusted. Thus, for example, he wrote to the Secretary of State for the Colonies in February 1940 that,

> I cannot see that this measure [the distribution of the ex-German quota] would have afforded any reasonable grounds for complaints to the exporting firms, and I cannot refrain from expressing the opinion that in this respect, as in others (notably in the excessive amount of guaranteed profit) His Majesty's Government have had altogether too tender a regard for the susceptibilities of the British firms. This opinion, which I fear that I have reiterated *ad nauseam* and almost to the point of insubordination, is fully shared by all my advisers.[71]

The standstill and quota policy of the Colonial Office was obviously unpopular with the Nigerian government. The question of how this had effected the long-term policy of the Colonial Office will be examined in chapter seven. At this point, however, it seems necessary to review in more detail what the Governor meant by his reference to the other controversial aspects of the purchase scheme.

The Dispute over the Expenses and Profits of the European Firms

Since the Ministry of Food was to employ Nigerian and European firms as its agents, it had to determine how much it would pay for their services. The Ministry of Food distinguished between paying for what it thought would be the actual expenses these firms would incur in their buying operations and paying an agreed amount of remuneration for their services. In addition, the Ministry of Food fixed the amount of money independent produce traders and commission buyers were to receive from those firms.

As regards the exporting firms, the Ministry of Food differentiated between European ("A" Shippers) and Nigerian-based firms ("B" Shippers). For each class of exporter the Ministry fixed a different schedule of marketing costs, including an amount of money which represented profits or remuneration.[72]

The Ministry of Food relied for the actual determination of the costs of the marketing of cocoa in Nigeria and between Nigerian and British ports almost entirely on information from the Association of West African Merchants.[73] The Association supplied the Ministry with a schedule of marketing costs for the two classes of exporters which the latter, after making some minute changes, accepted without much discussion. There were no consultations with representatives of the Nigerian-based firms, nor was it ever explained why it was necessary to set up two different schedules of marketing costs for European- and Nigerian-based firms for exactly the same kind of services rendered to the Ministry.

These schedules consisted of some fifteen odd different items. Most of the items in the two schedules were identical, since both "A" and "B" Shippers had to pay the same money for the same services and goods, like bags, harbour dues and government inspection fees, but five items were fixed at different rates according to the status of the exporter. These were the coast overheads, allowance for the costs of remittance, head office overheads, remuneration, and interest on the capital used during the buying operation.

It is impossible to compare the item 'interest' in the two schedules, since different interest rates were paid for different maximum periods of time. However, the other four items in the two schedules had specific values or were expressed as percentages of known figures, which allows us to estimate their value and makes a comparison possible.

With regard to the item 'coast establishment charges', "A" Shippers received 17s 9d per ton, while "B" Shippers were paid only 8s 9d per ton. The difference of 9s per ton between the two sums was supposed to represent the higher costs European firms incurred on their buying operations in Nigeria. A closer look at the composition of the item 'coast establishment charges' reveals that these higher costs almost entirely consisted of expenses which the firms incurred in order to attract and maintain a European work force, such as better housing ("bungalows"), passages to and from Nigeria, medical expenses, and, above all, European salaries and furlough pay.[74]

The item 'remuneration' was also differently fixed according to the status of the exporter. Thus European firms received 4.5 per cent on all sale proceeds credited to the Ministry of Food, while Nigerian- based firms received only 2.5 per cent on the local purchase price. "B" Shippers had to employ British brokers in order to effect overseas sales. The remuneration for the services of these brokers (1.5 per cent on sales credited to the Ministry of Food) has therefore to be added to compare the remuneration for "A" and "B" Shippers. Given the local Ministry of Food purchase price of £21 5s 5d per ton (producer price plus expenses of the "B" Shippers), and the expected British and overseas sales prices of £25 per ton, it is possible to work out the proxy difference in the remuneration of "A" and "B" Shippers. It amounted at least to 4s 4d per ton.[75]

There were two other items which the European firms were allowed to debit the Ministry of Food. There were no such items in the "B" Shipper schedule. These were an allowance for the costs of remittance of capital used in the buying operations (2s) per ton and an allowance for costs of maintaining a head office in Britain (5s) per ton.[76]

Taken together the differences in the values for these items add up to about £1 0s 4d per ton. There was - in as much it is known - no opposition against the introduction of two different schedules. Instead criticism concentrated on the percentage of the Ministry of Food sales European shippers received as remuneration and on the value of the item overhead charges. This criticism was repeatedly voiced by the Governor of Nigeria respectively by his chief advisers.[77] It was also later frequently stated by various authors on the subject, such as P.T. Bauer and J. Mars[78], that the schedule for remuneration and coast establishment charges was far too generous. Yet, these authors offer very little evidence for their contentions and one is left with the question to what extent their criticism was really justified.

One way to find an answer to that question seems to be to compare the schedule of marketing costs the firms had used in the 1937 Cocoa Agreement with the schedule of marketing costs the Ministry of Food used in the 1939/40 cocoa season. A comparison of certain items in the two schedules seems to suggest that indeed certain costs were inflated in order to increase the profits of the European firms. Thus the item 'coast overhead charges' which had been valued in the 1937 Agreement at 15s per ton was now in 1939/40 valued at 17s 9d.[79] Most pronounced was, however, the increase in the remuneration or profits of the firms. Whereas in 1937 the firms had been content with a profit margin of 5s 1d per ton[80] - or about 1 per cent of the expected sales prices, this margin was fixed by the Ministry of Food at 4.5 per cent of the sales prices. Thus under statutory control the profit margin of the European firms involved in the Nigerian cocoa trade at the time seems to have increased by at least 450 per cent since the sales prices in the 1939/40 season turned out to be higher than those current in the 1937/38 season.[81] As the volume of trade for both seasons is known, it also seems possible to estimate the approximate absolute value of this increase. In the 1937/38 season the participants in the Cocoa Agreement apparently allowed themselves a composite profit of about £25,000 on their cocoa buying operations. Two years later, the composite profits of the "A" Shippers seem to have increased to at least £85,000.[82]

The rate of remuneration and value for the various items in the marketing schedule were frequently changed in subsequent seasons, because the Ministry of Food and the Colonial Office later reorganised the scheme.[83] There is not enough space to analyse all these changes in detail but, on the strength of the evidence, it seems that when the scheme was introduced the firms had advanced their own material interests to an extent, that, in retrospect, the charge of 'war-time profiteering' appears to be justified.

The dispute between the Governor of Nigeria and the Colonial Office over the rate of remuneration which the Ministry of Food had set for the firms, was influenced moreover by the way the Ministry treated other participants in the Nigerian cocoa trade. As already mentioned the Ministry of Food determined the rate of remuneration which independent produce traders and commission buyers were to receive from the firms. The controversial point here was that remuneration or "brokerage" (5s) per ton and the allowance for marketing expenses (2s 6d) per ton, such as bagging, were included in the local ex-scale buying prices.[84] This provision created some considerable hardship for this class of traders and was seen by the Governor of Nigeria as a particularly unfair aspect of the purchase scheme.[85]

In Ibadan, for example, unbagged cocoa was purchased in 1939/40 at the local buying stations of the firms at £15 7s 6d per ton.[86] Since brokerage was included in the buying price, the firms were not required to pay any remuneration for the services independent produce traders and commission buyers rendered to them. Instead independent produce traders and commission buyers were credited in the books of the firms with a fictitious lower purchase price of £15 2s 6d per ton and the difference between these two prices of 5s per ton was supposed to represent remuneration for their services.[87] Consequently, produce traders and commission buyers found it very difficult to do any business in the vicinity of the Ibadan buying stations, since there were no economic reasons why farmers should sell their produce to them at the lower price, if they could get a higher price around the corner at the firms' buying stations.[88]

Thus, in the 1939/40 season many independent traders and commission buyers stopped buying cocoa altogether, while those who remained in business were forced to relocate their trading activities in areas outside the ambit of the official buying stations.[89] Yet, this move was not necessarily disadvantageous to all of these traders. Prices were fixed only at buying stations and no attempt was made by the government to control the transactions between produce traders, commission buyers and the farmers in outlying villages. Some traders, especially those who had access to transport facilities or even owned their own lorries, found their new position highly rewarding, since they could purchase cocoa in some, especially outlying, villages at a much lower price than the price they would receive at the nearest buying station.[90]

Nevertheless, the provision that brokerage should be included in the ex-scale buying prices led to the demise of a substantial number of independent produce traders and commission buyers, and it was for this reason that the Governor of Nigeria so vehemently opposed the way in which the Ministry of Food was treating the firms. He argued that it would be unfair, as well as politically dangerous, if the Ministry of Food set up a scheme which apparently safeguarded the interests of the European firms while the interests of other participants in the trade, especially those of the smaller independent produce traders and commission buyers were wilfully neglected.[91] This theme re-emerged, as we will see in the next section of this chapter, in the context of another dispute the Governor of Nigeria had with the Colonial Office, which concerned the way the Ministry of Food dealt with the problem of the role of co-operative marketing societies within the scheme.

The Dispute over the Marketing of Co-operative Cocoa

In discussions about the details of the scheme, the Association of West African Merchants proposed that cocoa sold to the firms by co-operative marketing societies should be treated in the same way as cocoa sold to the firms by independent produce traders and commission buyers, i.e. that they should only receive the gazetted minimum price less 5s brokerage.[92]

Before the imposition of control, co-operative marketing societies had usually sold cocoa to the firms in large parcels by tender which enabled them to obtain a premium of about 20s on the current price. This was partly a recognition of the fact that co-operative marketing societies produced exceptionally well-fermented and clean (Grade I) cocoa, but was also a result of competition between the firms for larger parcels of cocoa. The European firms achieved certain economies of scale on bulk purchases, and were prepared to pass on part of these savings to the co-operative marketing societies. These larger parcels of cocoa were moreover purchased on a cash and carry basis. This enabled the firms to avoid financial risks, for instance bad debts, which the more widespread advance system usually entailed.[93]

Under the control system, co-operative societies no longer received such a premium. This would have hit co-operative societies very hard for under the previous system the premium had both provided an incentive for farmers to join, as well as provided the means to maintain such societies.[94] Consequently the government of Nigeria came up with a plan which would have made the marketing of co-operative cocoa more profitable to the societies. The Governor argued that co-operative societies should be elevated to "B" Shipper status, which would ensure their financial survival and perhaps further growth. As a practical measure he proposed that the co-operative marketing societies should receive a substantial part of the ex-German (G.L. Gaiser) quota, the availability of which would provide a 'golden opportunity' to further develop the co-operative marketing movement in Nigeria. He pointed out that the established firms had no reason for complaint since their interests would not be prejudiced by such a policy.[95]

The firms saw that matter rather differently. In a meeting between the firms and the government a representative of the Association of West African Merchants confessed that he was 'shocked' by the proposal, while another maintained that co-operative societies did not merit special treatment, since they were anyway 'merely a collection of middlemen'[96].

These objections seem to have impressed the Colonial Office and Ministry of Food representatives, since it was decided not to proceed with the plan. The Colonial Office argued that although in principal it favoured the further development of co-operative marketing societies in Nigeria in peace-time, the outbreak of war had now completely changed the situation.[97] Moreover, the Colonial Office put forward the more practical argument that if co-operative societies were to receive a quota, how then could claims for a quota from other interested parties be convincingly repudiated, such as from the American firm Rockwood & Co. or from independent middlemen, who had not previously shipped cocoa? Finally, the Colonial Office indicated that in as far as the allocation to co-operative societies of a quota would involve increased government spending, the Imperial Treasury would strongly object to such plans.[98]

Nevertheless, the Colonial Office and the Ministry of Food seem to have accepted that the purchase scheme as it was would seriously impair the position of co-operative marketing societies. The firms were therefore pressed to make special arrangements for the purchase of cocoa from these societies.[99] After much haggling they agreed to pay out of their own pockets a premium of 12s 6d per ton for such cocoa. This sum was thought to be the minimum requirement to financially maintain the societies during the war.[100]

In the first three war-time cocoa seasons the firms financed co-operative marketing societies in Nigeria, until in 1942 they decided to discontinue the payment of this subsidy.[101] In this connection it is noteworthy that the Cocoa Controller later minuted that he

> never liked the premium mainly because the firms try to make out that the co-operative societies are living on their charity whereas in fact of course nothing is further from the truth. The co-operative premium is really a sop to keep the societies quiet and to prevent them from agitating to become exporters.[102]

The Nigerian government was moreover 'extremely disappointed'[103] about the decision not to allow the Governor to allocate an export quota to co-operative societies, for it ran contrary to the policy of the Nigerian government to support their development. In a letter to the Secretary of State for the Colonies, Governor Bourdillon argued that,

> For some years past we have been preaching to the cocoa farmers the doctrine that the co-operative movement provides his one hope of salvation, and that a steady increase of that movement is the best, if not the

> only method of ensuring that he gets the best possible price for his cocoa.
> If we are now compelled to tell him that as a result of a scheme for which
> His Majesty's Government are entirely responsible, we must discourage
> the formation of new societies or the growth of old ones, what conclusion
> can he draw, except that either the movement is not all that we have
> represented it to be, or that our desire to secure him the best possible
> price for his produce is not as keen as it was?[104]

As it happened in the case of the disputes about the quota allocation and the
remuneration of intermediaries, the Nigerian government was unable to
achieve any change in the policy the Colonial Office thought appropriate for
dealing with the co-operative societies. Again, the Nigerian government blamed
the Colonial Office for being unduly biased towards the interests of the European trading firms to the detriment of Nigerian interests.[105] However, in mid-
1940 the Nigerian government decided that in the circumstances it would be
rather futile to pursue the argument any further, and this laid the issue - at
least for the time being - to rest.[106]

The Determination of the Purchase Price

The least controversial issue of the purchase scheme was the fixing of the
purchase prices in the Gold Coast and Nigeria. In the latter the Ministry of
Food, after consultation with the Colonial Office and the Governor of Nigeria,
fixed the price at £16 10s per ton for grade II cocoa purchased in Lagos. The
better fermented and cleaner grade I cocoa received a premium of 10s and was
thus purchased at £17. These prices formed the basis for those paid at about
100 up-country buying stations, which the local Cocoa Controller determined by
deducting a sum from the Lagos prices, which he thought would cover transport
expenses. Thus grade II cocoa was purchased in Ibadan, about 80 miles north
of Lagos, at £15 10s per ton, whereas in Abeokuta, only about 50 miles away
from Lagos, cocoa of the same grade was sold at £16 per ton in the 1939/40
cocoa season.[107]

The price the Ministry of Food paid in 1939/40 compares favourably with
the prices cocoa farmers had received in the previous season, when the Lagos
price of grade II cocoa had not exceeded on average £14 12s per ton, but
compares unfavourably with the prices farmers had received in the mid-1930s,
when prices had been considerably higher. Thus in the three cocoa seasons
between 1934 and 1937, for example, the firms had paid on average about £23
per ton for grade II cocoa in Lagos, about a third more than the price the
Ministry of Food was prepared to pay in the current season.[108]

Why then was the price fixed at £16 10s per ton? It seems that this was a
compromise between conflicting interests. On the one hand, it was argued that

cocoa production should remain 'reasonably remunerative' to farmers in West Africa and that they should receive a 'fair price'.[109] It was also pointed out that purchase prices should be related to import prices. Since the latter were expected to rise substantially in the near future, purchase prices should be increased over the current level in order to safeguard the real income of cocoa farmers.[110]

On the other hand, it was argued that the purchase price should not be too high so as to discourage consumption in the United Kingdom and the United States in particular, to which sales 'would have to be stimulated as far as possible'[111].

It was also very early clear that the purchase price of cocoa would have to be relatively low in the future in order to reduce the demand for imported merchandise goods on which it was said a large part of the income generated by export crop sales was spent. There is, however, no evidence that this argument played a major role in the determination of the 1939/40 purchase price, probably because in the early months of the war what became later known as the 'war effort' had not assumed such an importance.[112]

However, the price which the Ministry of Food and the Colonial Office fixed in the end was arguably not inspired by concern for the well-being of West African cocoa producers or concern for the state of the British economy, but was largely a result of plain commercial considerations. It was expected that part of the crop would be unsaleable. Thus the purchase price was fixed below the current world free market price in order to accumulate a surplus in the early part of the season which could be used to cushion possible losses in the later part of the season.[113]

From a solely commercial point of view this policy was probably justified, but it opened the door to a much more aggressive pricing policy which the control authorities thought necessary to pursue during and after the war. Once the principle was established that it would be legitimate for statutory bodies to accumulate surpluses from their trading operations, the determination of produce prices became prone to influence, more by the real or imaginative economic exigencies of the day, rather than by considerations about the well-being of cocoa farmers or by considerations about the future development of the cocoa industry.

In the preceding paragraphs of this chapter an attempt was made to describe in some detail the reasoning behind the introduction of the cocoa purchase scheme. Nigerian produce traders, commission buyers and cocoa farmers obviously had different perspectives on the whole affair. Though there had been reports in British newspapers on plans to introduce a cocoa purchase scheme, it seems not unreasonable to assume that most of them only learnt of the scheme by a special edition of the *Nigerian Gazette*, published on the 14th November, 1939. It read:

> The Colonial Office announces that His Majesty's Government have undertaken, as a war measure to purchase the whole 1939-40 crop of B.W.A. cocoa. The price paid to producers will be fixed for the whole season on the basis of ... £16 10s for Nigeria F.A.Q. [grade II] cocoa, ex-scale port of shipment. The crop will be handled by European and other shippers already established in the trade, who will act as agent for Government and will be paid an agreed remuneration for their services... A moratorium on cocoa sale and purchase has been declared in the Gold Coast and Nigeria as from today in order that necessary arrangements may be made by the Colonial Governments. These arrangements will include the setting up of a local control organisation...[114]

The moratorium lasted for ten days. At last, after almost three months of intense discussion between the Ministry of Food, the Colonial Office, the European trading firms, and colonial governments in West Africa, the scheme came into being on the 24th November, 1939.[115] The outcome of these discussions show that the European firms almost invariably won the argument, while colonial governments had relatively little say in the actual design of the scheme. The latter had initially welcomed the scheme, but became increasingly critical of certain aspects of it. This, as we will see in the next chapter, was one of the reasons why the Colonial Office thought it necessary to reorganise the scheme. Here, however, the narrative will be continued with a description of what kind of immediate effects the imposition of control had and how Nigerian produce traders, commission buyers and cocoa farmers and the Nigerian public reacted to it.

Statutory Marketing in Practice: Its Effects and Policies

The short-term impact of the scheme was considerably less dramatic than the Governor had envisaged. For the great majority of cocoa farmers and even smaller produce buyers, especially those who the firms directly employed permanently and, having no capital on their own, received small advances from the firms, very little changed. Produce prices were displayed outside cocoa buying stations as before and business seems to have gone as usual, except that local storekeepers, instead of receiving their daily cable informing them at which maximum purchase price they were allowed to buy produce on that day, now were told that the price prevailing on the 24th November, 1939 would be applicable throughout the season.[116]

For one group of intermediaries, however, the imposition of control proved to be immediately inimical to their interests. These were more independent produce traders and larger commission buyers who with some capital of their own were not so closely tied to the firms. The larger of them had received substantial advances from the firms, but had not yet ventured (and if, only occasionally) into the export market, because it was too risky and their capital basis too small to sustain eventual heavy losses. Anyway, commission buying sometimes offered, as we have seen, large rewards.

It was believed at the time that the total purchases of the class of independent produce traders amounted to about 15,000 tons[117], but this calculation probably underestimates their importance since it is known that just one of them (T.A. Odutola) had a seasonal turnover of 4,000 to 5,000 tons, and there were others in this league, especially Ibadan traders like A.K. Zard and I.B. Ogun[118].

Most of the produce traders and larger commission buyers were now forced to relocate the centre of their businesses away from the buying stations of the European firms, since price differentials in their vicinity were too low to enable them to survive as cocoa traders. Some immediately sustained heavy losses, for they could not recuperate advances they had handed out to their own sub-buyers. Some former independent produce traders were even forced to sell their quota excess tonnage at a loss to the European firms in order to recover at least part of their capital outlay.[119] Many traders - the erstwhile independent produce traders and the larger commission buyers - therefore went out of business, while those who stayed in the trade became tightly controlled by the firms.[120] This development was aided by the firms who at the same time lowered commission rates to about a quarter of their pre-war value and also considerably reduced the amount of money they advanced to their buyers.[121] The Senior District Officer in Ibadan, for example, noted that 'there had been a very marked reduction of credit to Africans by the trading firms since the war started'[122]. It is therefore not surprising that in the early war years many produce traders and commission buyers went out of business.[123]

The elimination of the independent produce traders and larger commission buyers was arguably one of the aims the European firms had in mind when they gave their support to the purchase scheme. The local agent of John Holt & Co. in Lagos reported, for example, almost triumphantly in December 1939 that

> The Syrians are now find themselves driven out of the market, as we wanted them to be...[124]

From an economic point of view the position of the Syrians in the marketing process was not much different from that of their African competitors. It is therefore not unreasonable to assume that when the local agent used the expression 'Syrians' he also meant other independent produce traders.

The firms also hoped to achieve a complete reorganisation of their buying methods. In a circular to all buying stations of the firm in Lagos District the local agent of John Holt & Co. explained what he thought would be the effect of the control scheme:

> The possibilities are that the scheme will result in more producers and small cocoa traders coming direct to the firms' stores where salaried Central and Depot Buyers are employed thus drawing in the full all-in price. It is quite likely that a large number of consolidated commission buyers will disappear altogether ... and or organisation will change from a large number of consolidated commission buyers to a small limited number of Salaried Depot Buyers and a goodly number of small secured credit customers... It is in the realm of possibility that Ventures which today have as many as 60 buyers will in the near future operate with only three well secured large salaried depot buyers as the firms own direct staff, but with all the rest converted into ordinary produce credit customers operating within their security and making for remuneration what they can between the point in the bush where they buy and our scale.[125]

Though the effect of the imposition of the control scheme was not as striking as this agent envisaged, there is some evidence that the firms were indeed able to put their intentions partly into practice.[126]

The immediate reaction of larger produce traders was to try to escape the grip of the firms and apply for export licences and quotas. There were a whole host of traders (S. Agbaje, A.O. Makanjuola, I.B. Ogun and A.K. Zard) for example, who wrote petitions to that effect or went to see the Secretary of the Western Provinces in order to put forward their demands.[127] All these applications were refused on the ground that none of these traders had exported cocoa in the previous three years and was thus not entitled to a quota. Any other decision was categorically ruled out, for allocating a quota to such traders, it was argued, would have meant a violation of the revered 'standstill' principle.[128]

Thus these traders had to reorganise their own firms, if they wanted to stay in business at all. Some ventured into other trades like the foodstuff trade, while others went further afield from the buying stations in order to purchase cocoa at remunerative prices. In this they succeeded since the lower degree of competition in many outlying villages allowed these traders to pay considerably lower purchase prices than were offered at the official buying stations.[129]

Government, it seems, deliberately refrained from controlling such prices in outlying villages. The Cocoa Controller argued that the rigid enforcement of minimum price 'would eliminate large numbers of middlemen and might even lead to trouble. I therefore consider that it would be best to leave things as they are although it is recognised that there are loopholes'[130]. He also made clear that he himself was, when the scheme was put into operation, not too insistent that the loopholes in the scheme were being blocked at once and stated that in his opinion 'the middlemen were let down lightly'[131].

It seems therefore that at least *some* produce traders and commission buyers were far less financially hit by the scheme than either they themselves, the firms and the Nigerian government had expected, though they certainly experienced a reduction in their economic opportunities. They were also helped by a number of factors which mitigated the impact of the scheme and thus ensured their economic survival. Produce traders, who had access to transport facilities or even owned their own lorries, could obtain some profits by transporting cocoa from one buying station to another since official transport rates for various buying stations were very generously fixed.[132]

Moreover, many members of the European supervisory staff in government and private employment left Nigeria in the early months of the war in order to join the armed forces[133], while many Syrians, presumably some of them produce traders, also felt that they should return to their home countries[134], and this very likely opened up new opportunities, including those in the cocoa trade. Finally, some produce traders, especially those the firms were interested in retaining as principal suppliers, were able to extract additional remuneration from the firms[135].

Thus the immediate impact of the scheme was a mixed one. It seemed to have produced considerable hardship for many produce traders and commission buyers, yet some of them were able to use the loopholes in the system to their advantage. Smaller buyers and the majority of cocoa farmers were in 1939/40 only marginally, if at all, aggrieved by the scheme. This was arguably one of the reasons why the introduction of the purchase scheme met comparatively little public reaction as we will see in the next section of this chapter.

Public Reactions

It is a truism to state that the reception of government policies does not depend only on the policies itself, but also on the way these policies are put forward, as well on the circumstances in which these policies are introduced. The establishment of produce control was, in this respect, no exception.

The politically articulate part of the Nigerian populace, as many writers on the period have shown, reacted to the news of the outbreak of war with a genuine and spontaneous show of loyalty to the British government.[136] Though this loyalty was probably partly fuelled by enlightened self-interests, there is enough evidence to show that many Nigerians had very little doubt which side they should support in the war.[137] Since criticism of the government was in those circumstances likely to be seen as unpatriotic, it is reasonable to assume that protest against the introduction of produce control was toned down or even avoided. There were, for example, petitions in the early part of the war in which the writers declared that they would not 'pursue the matter [demands for higher produce prices] in the present state of affairs, but they wish ... to beg to state that the question would be re-opened immediately after the war'[138].

Another factor which may have influenced the way in which the purchase scheme was perceived in Nigeria was the unprecedented amount of information and propaganda the Nigerian government and the Colonial Office disseminated at the beginning of the war. For example, leaflets were printed in the local vernacular of the main ethnic groups in Nigeria (Hausa, Yoruba and Ibo), speeches were broadcast on the wireless, and articles published in all the main Nigerian newspapers and in British papers, which were relatively widely read at the time, such as the weekly journal *West Africa*.[139] Finally, there were public speeches by the Governor, the most important one being at an Emergency Session of the Nigerian Legislative Council on the 4th December, 1939.

The purpose of these activities was to encourage the Nigerian public to contribute voluntarily and freely to the war effort, as well as to prepare the Nigerian populace for further government measures and the hardship the war was expected to bring. The propagation of the necessity and advantages of produce control was part of that exercise. As regards the war effort, the Nigerian populace was told that their main contribution would lie in the mobilisation of financial and natural resources for the prosecution of the war.[140] At the same time Nigerians were warned that the war would bring considerable hardship, i.e. that imports had to be cut down to the barest minimum and that the prices of imported goods would rise in the near future; that government would raise the level of taxation, but would not embark on new development schemes during the war and only complete existing projects.[141] Concerning the imposition of control, the Nigerian government laid strong emphasis on the advantages the scheme would have for cocoa farmers. It painted a very gloomy picture of what would have happened if the Imperial government had not decided to purchase the Nigerian cocoa crop and underlined that the control authorities in London expected that it would be very unlikely that the scheme would generate any profits, while it was almost certain that losses would be eventually incurred.[142]

The presentation of produce control as an integral part of the war effort and, moreover, as an act of extreme generosity, which the Imperial government would afford the West African cocoa producers, contained an element of political whitewash. As early as September 1939 the Secretary of State for the Colonies had given detailed advice as to how the scheme should be presented to the public in order to forestall criticism.[143] This advice was apparently followed since the Governor of Nigeria wrote, after the announcement of the scheme, to the Secretary of State for the Colonies that,

> ...the Cocoa announcement has been worded so as to lay maximum possible stress on the assistance His Majesty's Government's are giving to

producers and I hope that propaganda on these lines will prevent the Union [i.e. the Nigerian Produce Traders Union] from stirring up discontent among producers themselves.[144]

A further measure to inspire confidence in the scheme was an invitation to the Nigerian Produce Traders Union to take part in the set-up of the scheme, as well as a meeting between the Union and the Governor of Nigeria to discuss problems arising from the imposition of produce control. The idea to establish a local committee of African and European firms' representatives to advise the Cocoa Controller in his work came originally from the Secretary of State for the Colonies.[145] Consequently, the Nigerian government began to look out for 'suitable' Africans. Several persons were put forward, but in the end the choice fell on A. Obisesan, the president of the Ibadan Co-operative Marketing Union, and T.A. Odutola, a wealthy Ijebu-Ode produce trader.[146] The former was supposed to represent the interests of co-operative farmers and cocoa farmers in general, while the latter, being a prominent member of the Nigerian Produce Traders Union, as well as of the Nigerian Motor Transport Union, was supposed to represent the interests of the middlemen. However, T.A. Odutola did not become a member of the 'Cocoa Advisory Committee' as it was later called. The Nigerian Produce Traders Union, which had been approached to nominate Odutola, instead put forward its president S. Akinsanya.[147] Thus one of the most vocal critics of the government and of the European firms at the time became an official member of a statutory committee.

Further members of the Cocoa Advisory Committee were the Cocoa Controller G.F.T. Colby, the directors of the Produce Inspection Department E. McL. Watson, the Registrar of Co-operative societies E.F.G. Haig, and one Syrian representative (P.M. Sellers). The committee met twice on the 18th and 23rd November, 1939 in order to fix transport differentials between buying stations and the port of shipment brokerage rates, as well as to agree on the allocation of quotas to small shippers.[148]

Despite the relatively wide responsibilities of the committee, discussions between the members about contentious issues were very brief. The minutes of the committee meetings reveal that the majority of government and firms' representatives seem to have agreed in advance on such vital issues as the size of the "B" Shipper quotas and local brokerage rates.[149] Proposals from S. Akinsanya to discuss higher transport and brokerage rates or higher purchase prices were almost invariably voted down. The committee also declined to examine the position of produce traders and commission buyers in the scheme by arguing that the scheme would not 'interfere with the internal organisation of trade within Nigeria beyond prescribing minimum prices'[150], though this was obviously not the case. In the end, the committee, apart from fixing transport differentials, largely confirmed what had been decided earlier in London.

This treatment caused S. Akinsanya to write a strongly worded protest letter on behalf of the Nigerian Produce Traders' Union to the Chief Secretary of the Government, pointing out that there would be no doubt that 'advantage is being taken of the present War (*sic*) condition to impose unreasonable hardship on a large section of our Community (*sic*)'[151]. In addition, he asked for an interview with the Governor.

This demand was taken up very swiftly, and on the 25th November, 1939 the Governor received a deputation of the Union, consisting of its local representatives T.A. Odutola and J. Aderigbe (Ijebu-Ode), I.B. Ogun and A.O. Johnson (Ibadan), A. Odunsi (Lagos), and its President S. Akinsanya.[152] There are two versions of what was said at that meeting. According to the official version, S. Akinsanya's main criticism was that the Cocoa Control Scheme had been worked out and introduced without any reference to the Nigerians engaged in the cocoa industry and that the functions of the Cocoa Advisory Committee had been too limited. The Governor is reported to have promised the Union to make representations to the Secretary of State for the Colonies that cocoa traders who previously had not shipped cocoa would be deprived of their business by the scheme.[153] According to the version which the Nigerian Produce Traders Union published after the event, the Governor was far more sympathetic to the situation of produce traders and commission buyers. He was reported to have assured them that the cocoa control scheme was purely a wartime measure and that all current restrictions were bound to be removed after the war. It was also reported that the Governor had raised the question of how the Union thought the farmers would benefit if the price was fixed in the United Kingdom, and the local market was left free for competition to which S. Akinsanya had answered that '...there will be competition, and every buying organisation was bound to be making efforts to get as many tons as possible, and in the process price was bound to be raised higher in one place or another to the benefit of the farmers (*sic*)'[154].

When the control scheme was introduced in November 1939 there was thus comparatively intense contact between the Nigerian Produce Traders' Union and the government. Although these contacts did not result in any direct measures to relieve the hardship the scheme was likely to cause, they assisted in mollifying criticism of the purchase scheme. This seems to be the second reason why the introduction of the scheme was such a relatively smooth affair in terms of meeting public discontent.

The government measure which stirred Nigerian cocoa farmers and traders most profoundly at the time was the destruction of some 10,000 tons of cocoa in the later part of the 1939/40 cocoa season.[155] As early as January 1940, barely two months after the scheme was launched, the Nigerian government and the authorities in London, started talks on what should eventually be done with surplus cocoa.[156] As it turned out, previous calculations about prospective sales had been rather optimistic. First, manufacturers in the United Kingdom bought far less cocoa than expected, mainly it seems because they had not received sufficient sugar allocations to turn raw cocoa into chocolate. Moreover, manufacturers at the time had a several months supply of cocoa in stock and were not interested in further deliveries.[157] Secondly, and most likely more importantly, the Ministry of Shipping's allocation of freight space for the transport of cocoa from West Africa to the United Kingdom and the United States turned out to be far too small.

The Ministry argued that other United Kingdom imports such as palm kernels were far more important and would therefore receive shipping priority.[158] Meanwhile more and more traditional outlets of West African cocoa supplies became closed due to the war, including France, the U.S.S.R., the Netherlands, Belgium and the Scandinavian countries, so that by the end of March 1940 it was believed that government would be left at the end of the season with almost 160,000 tons of unsaleable cocoa or a loss of some two million to three million pounds on their hands.[159] Though the situation slightly eased in the following months, the Ministry of Food, after consultations with other Ministries, decided at the end of May 1940 to destroy excess quantities of cocoa.[160]

This decision coincided with the beginning of the harvest of light crop cocoa in Nigeria. The Nigerian government therefore notified the public that from 30th May cocoa would be no longer purchased for export but for destruction and that the purchase price for such cocoa would be lowered by £6 to £10 per ton.[161]

The actual destruction proved to be more difficult than expected. In order to prevent the spread of diseases, excess cocoa had to be dumped into the sea, in inaccessible swamps, into the Niger at Jebba or burnt.[162] The United Africa Company even offered to sell to those West African governments concerned a specially constructed cocoa bean shredder.[163]

However, in the end the amount of cocoa which had to be destroyed turned out to be far less than originally anticipated. Sales to the United States improved, and freight space to the United Kingdom became more readily available. It was thus necessary to destroy all in all "only" some 10,000 tons of Nigerian cocoa, a large part of which was sub-standard.[164] Thus the loss at the end of the season to the United Kingdom Exchequer from the purchase and subsequent resale of West African cocoa amounted to 'only' £208,548, of which some £61,800 probably represented losses sustained in Nigeria.[165]

One political side effect of the destruction of part of the 1939/40 cocoa crop was that it considerably strengthened the position of the Nigerian government in the dispute it had with Nigerian produce traders, commission buyers and cocoa farmers over the purchase scheme. The authorities in London, as well as the Nigerian government, were aware of this factor and tried to get the maximum political benefit out of it. In March 1940, for example, the Colonial Office official responsible for the cocoa scheme, E. Melville, minuted that,

> I think the announcement [of the destruction of cocoa] should be made by the local Governments indicating that the decision to destroy is theirs and explaining the circumstances which made it necessary. This explanation will be valuable in two respects: 1) it will tend to strengthen the American market, and 2) it will provide a practical demonstration to the West Africans that their produce is not indispensable to the war effort: That, on the contrary, there is far too much cocoa being produced and therefore the prices which they are being paid and the guarantee to purchase the whole crop in the first year of the war has been a very generous and expensive gesture by His Majesty's Government.[166]

Consequently, the announcement which informed the public that part of the Nigerian crop would be purchased for destruction was worded in such a way so as to lay maximum stress on the benevolent attitude of the government. It read:

> The public will understand that although His Majesty's Government will purchase the light crop they will be unable to take delivery and dispose of it; in spite of this fact, however, and with the sole object of preventing hardship to West African cocoa producers, His Majesty's Government propose to purchase the whole light crop and spend further money on its destruction. But for their action it can be no doubt that cocoa farmers would have been left with a considerable quantity of unmarketable cocoa on their hands, and the Nigerian government feels sure that the generosity of His Majesty's Government will be fully appreciated by all concerned in the cocoa industry.[167]

There were thus four factors which probably influenced the way the Nigerian public and in particular produce traders, commission buyers and cocoa farmers perceived the imposition of produce control. It was presented as part of the war effort, as well as a project which government would have abandoned if concern for the well-being of West African cocoa farmers had not been stronger. Furthermore, direct contacts between the Nigerian government and the Nigerian Produce Traders' Union helped to smooth the actual introduction of the scheme. Finally, as mentioned in the previous section of this chapter, the immediate effect of the scheme itself was probably only felt by a relatively small number of larger produce traders and commission buyers. This helps to explain why the scheme was, despite its unpalatable features, fairly well received by the Nigerian public and that criticism came only from a small group of middlemen, some cocoa farmers, and their most intimate political allies.[168]

Cocoa farmers in general were probably not too displeased with the scheme. Though it was not intended, the fixing of a seasonal purchase price removed much of the uncertainty which had previously marked the dealings between cocoa farmers and produce traders and commission buyers. The scheme offered security to many cocoa farmers and protected them against the exploitative practices of some produce traders and commission buyers who had previously deliberately misled cocoa farmers about current cocoa prices. The fixing of purchase prices at about 100 buying stations throughout the cocoa growing area thus made it more difficult for produce traders and commission buyers to deceive farmers. Some cocoa farmers were therefore probably initially positively impressed by the scheme.[169]

However, it was ultimately the public destruction of cocoa in Nigeria at the end of the 1939/40 cocoa season, which convinced cocoa farmers, traders and a large part of the public of the supposedly benevolent intentions of the government. The fact that government purchased cocoa and subsequently destroyed it left a deep impression on a wide range of people, including the nationalist movement which in one of its newspapers strongly applauded the 'philantrophic' attitude of the government.[170] But perhaps more important were the reactions from local Chiefs and the populace in general. Thus, for example, the titular political and religious head of all Yoruba Chiefs at the time, the Oni of Ife, was reported to have said that 'nobody is so foolish as not to see the Europeans buying cocoa and burning it without thinking of what might may likely happen [without the purchase scheme]'[171].

Two other quotations illustrate the argument. They are both rather long, but they capture very accurately the sentiment which prevailed at the time. The Senior District Officer, Ibadan Division, wrote in March 1941:

> The predominant spirit that I have encountered was been one of profound gratitude to Government for purchasing the cocoa crop for the second year in succession... When the idea of burning last years' light crop was first mooted someone said to me "The Yoruba will never understand that; he will think it lunacy to pay good money for a thing and then burn it". He was wrong. A few days ago I was discussing the economic situation with a large meeting in Odeomu and the Bale of that town said, that what really impressed them all was the sure proof of government's love for them, in that though much of the cocoa was a dead loss, witness the burning of it, they [Government] were prepared to pay a good market price for it so that "their children" should not suffer. In other words the burning of the light crop was the final and incontrovertible proof of Government's bona fide in native eyes. No disgruntled "bush buyer" could whisper that Government was certainly buying the crop but at a poor price and making a large profit on re-sale elsewhere. The farmer who had been seen with his own eyes the beans for which he had been paid hard cash literally "going up in smoke" was and is proof against the possibility of such propaganda.[172]

And a resolution which the Ibadan Council passed on the 30th September, 1940, part of which was subsequently transmitted to the Secretary of State for the Colonies, reads:

> The appreciative feelings of the entire native population of Ibadan whose economic salvation the purchase scheme makes sure were expressed to you by the Olubadan when amongst other things he said: "You are beloved and affectionate husband: no other man can love us as You and no earthly power can seduce us from You, and even before the death itself can so it will have to struggle a great deal." We must assume that from all we know this generosity of the Government has no equal in any land, and will serve to strengthen our loyal devotion to the God-fearing British Government.[173]

There were other similar resolutions, and again and again the burning of light crop cocoa is cited as an example of the generosity of the government.[174] Given what people were told by the government and even more importantly, what they could see at the time, it is hardly surprising that the attitude of the majority of the Nigerian farmers and traders was one of gratitude and certainly not one of criticism. This may well be the reason why critical voices found no resonance and that there was no common interest between cocoa farmers and traders to protest against the scheme 'as they did at the time of the Cocoa Agreement', as the Governor of Nigeria wrote in February 1940.[175]

The voices of dissent were thus subdued and emerged only infrequently and on special occasions, for example in Legislative Council Debates. On 6th March, 1940 H.S.A. Thomas, the third elected Lagos member of the Legislative Council, argued that there would be 'a general feeling that the trading methods of the European firms leave the African trader or middlemen very little on which to live...'[176]. Such sentiments can also be found in petitions written at the time, for example one by A. Ogden, who wrote that 'opposition is evident against Black people gaining any strength, by being kept down, and poor, by White Control (*sic*)'[177].

Further criticism was directed against low produce prices. In April 1940 the Ibadan Co-operative Marketing Union passed a resolution in which it was stated that the government purchase price was inadequate, especially in view of the fact that prices of imported goods had steeply risen since the beginning of the war. Higher cocoa purchase prices, it was argued, would assist farmers 'to pay their labour bill, taxes, train their children and pay their other legitimate dues'[178].

It appears therefore that insofar as Nigeria was concerned criticism of the scheme in 1939/40 was rather limited and on the whole ineffectual. Politically the scheme had been a great success since no strong opposition emerged, but the Governor was aware that this condition would probably not be permanent. He argued that

> As control progressed the feeling grew locally that, although the Cocoa Control scheme was initiated with a view of protecting the West African cocoa producer, the influence of the exporting firms became so strong in implementing the scheme that the primary object was to some extend obscured, and the interests of the firms became paramount.[179]

Thus one of the minor aims of the imposition of control was not achieved. Though the scheme had probably prevented a rapid fall of cocoa prices in Nigeria at the beginning of the war and thus forestalled political difficulties, the imposition had not succeeded in laying to rest the widespread suspicion of the European firms which already existed before the outbreak of war. This political problem apparently persisted with the added component that in as much as government was responsible for the purchase scheme, criticism directed against the firms automatically became criticism directed against the government. This had important long-term consequences, as we will see in the next chapter, since the anxiety about possible political difficulties was one of the reasons why the purchase scheme was reorganised in 1942.

This section on the immediate reaction to the imposition of produce control concludes with a brief review how the scheme was received by the West African Students' Union in London. Though neither directly connected with the economic interests of cocoa farmers nor produce traders, their view probably accurately reflected the views held in nationalist circles in Nigeria, since these groups to a large extent overlapped.[180]

The West African Students' Union wrote two memoranda during 1939/40, one of which was entirely devoted to the question of price control in Nigeria, while the other dealt more with political questions, but included topics such as the desirability of the provision of credit to African entrepreneurs and the role of the European firms in Nigeria.[181] Both memoranda were published in the weekly journal *West Africa*[182] and caused such a debate that the Colonial Office in one case even decided also to have published its reply to one of the memoranda.[183]

The criticism of the first memorandum, titled 'Price Control and the Standard of Living in West Africa', focused almost exclusively on the question of the price cocoa farmers should receive for their produce. The authors argued that the prices of imported merchandise and, in particular, the price of cotton goods had steeply risen since the beginning of the war and that the purchase prices had been fixed at a comparatively low level. Thus the standard of living of cocoa farmers had considerably declined. This would have many undesirable consequences, such as cuts in social services, increased incidence of crime, as well as severe difficulties in the collection of taxes.[184]

The memorandum also contained a criticism of the way eventual profits of the scheme would be returned to West Africa, which in retrospect was an almost prophetic criticism of future developments. The authors of the memorandum argued that

> It is inequitable to call upon one section of the population, namely the cocoa growers to pay their extra-ordinary war tax on behalf of the rest of the population. It is a tax because the share of the profits on sales which is returned to the colonial administration will not go into the pockets of those to whom it belongs, but will be used to meet the deficit in the public revenue.[185]

Finally, the memorandum criticised the appointment of persons as Cocoa Controllers, respectively as Deputy Cocoa Controller, in the United Kingdom who had a vested interest in the Nigerian cocoa trade. These appointments, it was stated, were not likely to inspire any confidence in the scheme.[186] In this connection it is note-worthy that the Colonial Office strongly defended the impartiality of J. Cadbury and E.C. Tansley. One Colonial Office official even wrote: 'As it often happens with just men, both Cadbury and Tansley have tended to be rather severe upon the established shippers as a whole, and, in particular, upon the firms with which they are connected than strict equity demands.'[187] But, as Peter Bauer has argued, 'even public spirited advisers are likely to be influenced by subconscious considerations of the interests of the firms they represent, which are all too plausibly equated with the general interest...'[188], especially if such advisers are still on the payroll of the firms they are supposed to control, and have to think about their position within the firms once control had been removed.[189]

The second memorandum dealt mainly with political questions, such as adult suffrage, the role of the Native Administration in the future political development of the West African colonies and representation of African interests on the Executive and Legislative Council. However, the second memorandum also commented upon how the West African Students' Union regarded the European trading firms. It stated that:

> ... the members of the West African Student's Union, viewing with deep concern the increase of European and other foreign [i.e. Syrian] combines' stranglehold on the economic life of the inhabitants of West Africa, strongly condemn this commercial malady and humbly call the Government to introduce appropriate legislation to protect the interests of the African traders and farmers.[190]

It is impossible to assess what precise impact these memoranda had, but the wording, as well as the content, suggest that there existed a strong continuity between political thinking expressed during the cocoa crisis of 1938 and the political thinking which now emerged.

It is, in retrospect, somewhat surprising that the most active movement during the cocoa crises in 1938 - the Nigerian Youth Movement - seems not to have exploited the introduction of produce control to make their views more widely known. Though individual members of the Movement, such as A. Awolowo, wrote memoranda at the time which dealt amongst other topics with produce control,[191] the Movement itself was apparently incapable of developing a coherent policy. This was probably due to the internal problems of the Nigerian Youth Movement, which in 1940 were already boiling and culminated one year later in the leadership crisis of 1941, which split the movement and almost completely paralysed it for a large part of the war.[192] Another reason was probably that by 1940 the Nigerian Youth Movement had become a more respectable and less radical organisation. There was, for example, in September 1940 a 'Representative Council' meeting of the Nigerian Youth Movement, which, according to its programme, was addressed by the Governor of Nigeria, Bernard Bourdillon, as well as by the Director of Agriculture, J.R. Mackie.[193] In this meeting the issue of produce control did not, it seems, receive much attention.

Thus political reactions to the imposition of produce control and the way it worked during its first operational season were mixed. There was criticism, but that criticism appears to have been more than balanced by genuine praise for the scheme, most likely because in the eyes of the public there was not much difference between the design of the scheme and how it worked in practice. Though the destruction of cocoa was not envisaged when the scheme was set up, it appeared as part of the same system and thus considerably legitimised it for many observers. However, political reactions to the imposition of produce control and to the way it worked during the 1939/40 cocoa season were not limited to West Africa. Thus, in the last section of this chapter I will briefly discuss, what political effects produce control and its actual working had on the control authorities in London.

Political Repercussions in Britain

The imposition of produce control and the price which the Ministry of Food paid to West African cocoa farmers, as well as the decision to destroy part of the 1939/40 crop, received notable critical attention in the British press[194] and in the House of Commons, especially by members of the Labour Party[195] who even sometimes went to the Colonial Office to have discussions about these issues with the responsible officials in charge of the cocoa scheme.[196]

There were two distinct political questions to which the Ministry of Food and the Colonial Office had to find answers. One was how to avoid in the future parliamentary criticism of the destruction of a foodstuff in West Africa, which at the same time was rationed in the United Kingdom. The other was how to assure the continuation of a scheme which had proved to be a drain on government resources, since the season had closed with an overall loss to the Treasury of £208,548 of which £61,800 was incurred on buying operations in Nigeria.[197] The answer that was found was to establish the West African Cocoa Control Board.

In April and May 1940, when it became clear that part of the 1939/40 cocoa crop would be unmarketable, the Ministry of Food became increasingly uneasy about having the responsibility for the purchase scheme. The Ministry of Food rightly expected criticism in Parliament, as well as from other government departments, on the decision to destroy cocoa.[198] For motives not entirely clear, the Colonial Office decided to help the Ministry of Food by making arrangements so that the decision to destroy cocoa would be announced locally and that the responsibility for organising and supervising destruction would rest with the West African governments.[199] This explains why, although the formal decision to destroy cocoa was taken by the authorities in London on 29th May, 1940, the official announcement published by the West African governments was worded the following day so as to give the impression that the destruction of cocoa was a West African affair.[200]

The crucial interdepartmental meeting on the 29th May, 1940 was not only concerned with the destruction of cocoa. It also discussed the long-term future of the scheme, since it was assumed that the destruction of cocoa would have to be repeated in future seasons as long as supplies vastly exceeded demand and shipping facilities. This problem prompted the Treasury representative at the meeting, G.F. Peaker, to intervene, by asking who would be responsible for the scheme in the next seasons, what in this connection could have only meant the question of who was going to bear the brunt of clearly unpopular political decisions. At this point in the discussion, the representative of the Colonial Office, E. Melville, came up with an outline for a new scheme which he had obviously prepared in advance of the meeting. He argued that there would be no political alternative to continuing the scheme in the 1940/41 season.[201] He then proposed that the Ministry should effectively be divested of its responsibility for the scheme by limiting its role to buying the United Kingdom requirements. The responsibility for foreign sales of West African cocoa should, however, rest with Cocoa Control in London, which would act as an agent for the West African governments. The total estimated receipts on the sales in the United Kingdom and overseas would then be pooled for the purpose of fixing the price to the farmers in West Africa on the basis of the size of the marketable crop. He then made clear in what respect the future scheme would be different from the one in operation. He argued that,

> ... as the financial responsibility would still fall in the last analysis on the United Kingdom Treasury, the scheme outlined was not really fundamentally different from the present scheme of control except in two particulars. In the first place the price paid to growers would not be based on "a fair return" but on the estimated sale value of the estimated crop; in the second place, while the machinery of control would remain broadly as at present, the political responsibility would be shifted from the Ministry of Food.[202]

As we will see in the next chapter the proposal from E. Melville was, apart from minor changes, broadly accepted. Here it is probably sufficient to emphasise that the origin of the institutionalisation of produce control, i.e. the establishment of the West African Produce Control Board in September 1940, had its origins in the political discomfort of the Ministry of Food and that one purpose of the new scheme was to prevent a repetition of the occurrence of further financial losses to His Majesty's Treasury.[203] This was a significant departure from earlier official assurances that the sole purpose of the scheme would be to protect the interests of West African cocoa farmers.

This chapter aims to answer two questions: What were the reasons for the establishment of statutory marketing in 1939 and what were the political repercussions of this policy? It has been shown that the long-term interests of the European trading firms to preserve their dominant position in West African cocoa trade coincided with the short-term interests of the government to prevent a recurrence of political trouble similar to that which occurred in the Gold Coast and Nigeria in 1937 and 1938.[204] In addition, the government was interested in reaping the economic benefits the scheme appeared to offer. Yet, the government was dependent on the firms' help in setting up and running the scheme. This explains why the firms were able to make their interests almost invariably prevail over others in the Nigerian cocoa trade, notably the interests of the keenest competitors in that trade, the Nigerian-based firms. In that respect the imposition of produce control was a remarkable success, since the European firms managed to transform their clandestine buying agreement into an official one with statutory backing. In addition, they were apparently able to inflate their profits on cocoa buying operations in Nigeria. Yet, at the same time the government got a foothold in the trade. This had important long-term consequences, since already at the end of the 1939/40 season the government began to use the marketing system in furtherance of its own political and economic interests. These developments were made possible by the absence of any major popular protest movement in Nigeria or, for that matter, in West Africa. Politically active produce traders could not muster the sort of support they had previously received, partly because only some of them were directly hit by the system and partly because farmers had no obvious reasons for rejecting a system which apparently guaranteed their incomes. In this respect the destruction of part of the 1939/40 cocoa crop proved to be of utmost political importance, although nobody seriously thought that it would become eventually necessary, when the scheme was set up.

Notes

1   There is no comprehensive history of the impact of the Second World War on the Nigerian economy. There also is, for example, no detailed account of the imortant palm produce trade during that period, though admittedly Susan Martin's history of the palm oil industry has covered the latter subject to some extent. See S.M. Martin, Palmoil and Protest: An Economic History of the Ngwa Region, South-Eastern Nigeria, 1800-1980, Cambridge 1988, pp. 169-182.

2   The figure 'one-fifth' represents the percentage of the average combined imports of Germany, Austria and the Netherlands of world imports between 1935 and 1939. See V.D. Wickizer, Coffee, Tea and Cocoa: An Economic and Political Analysis, Stanford 1951, pp. 320 and 485-486.

3   See Report on Cocoa Control in West Africa, 1939-1943; Statement of Future Policy, Cmd.6554 of Sept. 1944, London 1944, p. 2.; Holt Papers, Mss. Afr. s825, file 535(II), Letter from the Administrative Department of John Holt & Co. to DAs Accra and Lagos, 15 Nov. 1939; see also Wickizer, Coffee, Tea and Cocoa, p. 329, and D.K. Fieldhouse, Merchant Capital and Economic Decolonization: The United Africa Company, 1929-1989, Oxford 1994, pp. 229-274.

4   PRO: CO 825, file 256/1, Memorandum 'Cocoa Control', 22 Sept. 1939.

5   PRO: CO 852, file 256/2, Memorandum by J. Caulcutt, Chairman of Barclay's Bank and R.R. Wilson, Chairman of the Bank of British West Africa Limited, 18 Oct. 1939; see also ibid., Memorandum submitted by Secr. of State for the Colonies, 'The Colonial Empire Cocoa Industry in War-time', 13 Oct. 1939. This argument was originally made by A.R.I. Mellor (United Africa Company) in a memorandum he sent to G.L.M. Clauson (Colonial Office) in early September 1939.

6   Holt Papers, Mss. Afr. s825, file 535(II), Letter from the Administrative Department of John Holt & Co. to DAs Lagos and Accra, 15 Nov. 1939, first partially cited in F. Ehler, Handelskonflikte zwischen europäischen Firmen und einheimischen Produzenten in British West Afrika - Die Cocoa "Hold-ups" in der Zwischenkriegszeit, Zürich 1977, p. 403. P. Bauer and many authors on the subject after him have argued that the control scheme was an extension and continuation of the pre-war buying arrangements. On the strength of the quotation from the above letter, one could argue that from the firms' point of view the introduction of the cocoa control scheme was a salvage operation, since without the scheme the firms would have been forced to dissolve the pool. For Bauer's argument, see West African Trade. A Study of Competition, Oligopoly and Monopoly in a Changing Economy, Cambridge 1954, p. 152, see also D. Meredith, The Colonial Office, British Business Interests and the Reform of Cocoa Marketing in West Africa, 1937-1945. In: Journal of African History, XXIX (1988) 2, pp. 297-298.

7   PRO: CO 852, file 256/1, Letter from A.R.I. Mellor to G.L.M. Clauson, 11 Sept. 1939. The memorandum 'Cocoa' is dated 8 Sept. 1939. See also D. K. Fieldhouse, War and the Origins of the Gold Coast Marketing Board, 1939-40, in: M. Twaddle, (ed.), Imperialism, the State and the Third World, London 1992, p. 157.

8   Holt Papers, Mss. Afr. 825, file 535(II), Letter from Administrative Department of John Holt & Co. to DAs Lagos and Accra, 15 Nov. 1939.

9   West Africa, 17 Nov. 1939, p. 1537.

10   See PRO: CO 852, file 318/1, Draft-Memorandum 'Purchase Scheme in British West Africa', 23 Jan. 1940.

11   Ibid.; see also PRO: CO 852, file 317/11, Extract from Official Report (House of Commons), 22 Feb. 1940, Answer by M. MacDonald, Secr. of State for the Colonies, to a question by A. Creech-Jones.

12   Osuntokun, Nigeria in the First World War, pp. 36-40.

13   PRO: CO 852, file 256/2, Memorandum submitted by the Secr. of State for the Colonies, 'The Colonial Empire Cocoa Industry in War-time', 13 Oct. 1939.

14   PRO: CO 852, file 318/2, Memorandum by the Governor of Nigeria, 'Cocoa Control Scheme', n.d. (May 1940); see also G.K. Helleiner, Peasant Agriculture, Government and Economic Growth in Nigeria, Homewood/Illinois 1966, p. 557, table V-E-3.

15   PRO: CO 852, file 256/2, Memorandum submitted by the Secr. of State for the Colonies, 'The Colonial Empire Cocoa Industry in War Time', 13 Oct. 1939; see also West Africa, 20 Jan. 1939, p. 39.

16   See PRO: CO 852, file 256/1, Memorandum 'Cocoa' by A.R.I. Mellor (UAC), 11 Sept. 1939, and PRO: CO 852, file 256/2, Memorandum submitted by the Secr. of State for the Colonies, 'The Colonial Empire Cocoa Industry during War-time', 13 Oct. 1939.

17   See Rhodes House Library, Oxford, Mss. Afr. s823(1), Letter from the Act. Director of Agriculture to all Agricultural Officers, 26 Aug. 1939 (!), PRO: CO 852, file 253/4, Telegram from the Secr. of State for the Colonies to the Governor of Nigeria, 29 Aug. 1939, and NAI: Oyo Prof 2/1, file C 234 Vol.I, Letter from the Secr. Western Provinces to the Resident, Oyo Province, 29 Dec. 1939; see also PRO: CO 852, file 650/14. Memorandum 'British Colonial Exports, 1939-1945' by F.V. Meyer, August 1946, and J. Shuckburgh, Colonial Civil History of the War, unpublished Colonial Office ms. deposited at the Institute of Commonwealth Studies Library, London 1946, p. 110.

18   PRO: CO 852, file 256/1, Colonial Office memorandum 'Cocoa Control', 22 Sept. 1939.

19   See PRO: CO 852, file 256/1, Memorandum 'Cocoa' by A.R.I. Mellor, 22 Sept. 1939.

20   NAI: CSO 26, file 36148 S1 Vol.I, Telegram from the Secr. of State for the Colonies to the Governor of Nigeria, 16 Sept. 1939.

21   PRO: CO 852, file 256/1, Colonial Office memorandum 'Cocoa Control', 22 Sept. 1939; see also NAI: Ib MinAgric, file 17980 Vol.I, Telegram from the Secr. of State for the Colonies to the Governor of Nigeria, 23 Sept. 1939.

22   For a relatively easy accessible account of the Rockwood saga, see the Letter to the Editor by Alexander Singer, Director of Rockwood, in the Manchester Guardian, 14 April 1940.

23   PRO: CO 852, file 256/1, Minutes by E. Melville, 14 Sept. 1939, and O.G.R. Williams, 19 Sept. 1939.

24   For the extension of the cocoa control scheme to other crops, see NAI: CSO 26, file 36148 S 63A, Letter from G.W. Henlen (Secr. to the West African Cocoa Control Board) to G.F.T. Colby (Cocoa Controller, Nigeria), 31 Dec. 1941; see also PRO: CO 852, file 446/6, Letter from S. Caine to the Anti-Slavery and Aborigines Protection Society, 18 Oct. 1941. S. Caine wrote that '...it has been the policy of His Majesty's

Government, primarily in this country but also overseas, to try to prevent increased private profits out of accidental conditions of market scarcity produced by war'. It is, in retrospect, surprising that P. Bauer completely disregarded this aspect of the control scheme; cf. Bauer, West African Trade, pp. 199-201 and 246-249.

25   PRO: MAF 75/31, Ministry of Food memorandum 'Colonial Empire Cocoa: Scheme of Control, 3rd Revise', 16 Feb. 1940, section XVI, Distribution of Profit, p. 7.

26   This aspect of the scheme was later revised. See Report on Cocoa Control in West Africa, 1939-1944, and Statement of Future Policy, Cmd.6554 of September 1944, London 1944, p. 3.

27   This is a summary of the various memoranda which the Colonial Office and the Ministry of Food produced in the early months of the war. This does not, however, mean, that there was much uncertainty about the outcome of these discussions, since as early as on 16th September, 1939 the Governor of Nigeria was informed about the basic structure of the scheme. See NAI: CSO 26, file 36148 S1 Vol.I, Secret Telegram from the Secr. of State for the Colonies to the Governor of Nigeria, 16 Sept. 1939.

28   PRO: CO 852, file 256/1, Telegram from the Secr. of State for the Colonies to the Governor of the Gold Coast and the Governor of Nigeria, 23 Sept. 1939. It is noteworthy that cocoa was not the only colonial commodity for which a purchase scheme was introduced. For marketing schemes of other crops, such as East African sisal and West Indian sugar and bananas, see M.P. Cowen/N.J. Westcott, British Imperial Economic Policy During the War, paper presented at the School of Oriental and African Studies Conference on Africa and the Second World War, London 24th-25th May 1984, p. 20.

29   PRO: CO 852, file 256/1, Ministry of Food, Outline for Scheme for Control of Raw Cocoa, n.d. (2 Sept. 1939); see also Rhodes House Library Oxford, Mss. Brit. Emp. 365 (Fabian Colonial Bureau Papers), file 52/4, Ministry of Food, National Expenditure Paper No. 11, 17 Feb. 1940.

30   PRO: MAF 75, file 31, Control of Raw Cocoa (Official History), Part A, Liaison with the Trade, p. 8.

31   PRO: CO 852, file 256/2, Association of West African Merchants (Cocoa Committee), memorandum 'Cocoa', 3 Nov. 1939.

32   Holt Papers, Mss. Afr. 825, file 535(II), Letter from the Administrative Department of John Holt & Co. to the DAs Lagos and Accra, 15 Nov. 1939.

33   PRO: CO 852, file 256/2, Colonial Empire Cocoa Control. Minutes of a Meeting held at the Ministry of Food, 7 Nov. 1939.

34   Ibid.

35   NAI: CSO 26, file 36148 S39, Advisory Committee on Raw Cocoa, Minutes of Meeting, 5 April 1940. This committee was subsequently divided into an Intermediaries Advisory Committee and a Manufacturers' Advisory Committee. The latter was renamed in April 1942 and was then called the 'Cocoa and Chocolate (War-time) Association'. Under this name it survived well into the 1950s. See PRO: MAF 75, file 31, Control of Cocoa (Official History), part A, p. 8.

36   Ibid.

37   It is noteworthy in this connection, as mentioned in the previous chapter, that J. Cadbury was one of the two members of a sub-committee to which the General (London) Committee of participants in the 1937 Cocoa Buying Agreement had delegated most of its executive functions, while the actual work involved in the administration of the 1937 scheme was mostly done by E.C. Tansley. See Nowell Report, para. 430. The fact, however, that there were many personal continuities

between the 1937 scheme and the war-time control scheme is arguably not sufficient proof for the thesis that the war-time scheme was in theory and practice nothing else but the 1937 scheme in disguise.

38   Meredith, The Colonial Office, p. 294. It is noteworthy that E.C. Tansley was later employed by the West African Cocoa Board.

39   PRO: CO 852, file 256/1. Colonial Office memorandum 'Cocoa Control', 18 Sept. 1939. In retrospect one cannot but admire the subtlety of the argument. The Colonial Office was, in effect, arguing for a government purchase scheme without involvement of government finance since the risks which the memorandum mentions could easily be shifted onto the cocoa producers by fixing relatively low purchase prices, which would cover such risks. Incidentally, the same arguments were also used to justify the nomination of the Association of West African Merchants as the sole agents for the purchase of palm oil, palm kernels and groundnuts. See NAI: Oyo Prof 2/1, file C 234 Vol. I, Letter from the Secr. of State for the Colonies to the Officer Administering the Government of Nigeria, 22 Nov. 1939; see also Bauer, West African Trade, p. 250, and D. Meredith, State Controlled Marketing and Economic 'Development': The Case of West African Produce during the Second World War, in: Economic History Review, XXXIX (1986) 1, p. 78.

40   PRO: CO 852, file 256/1, Telegram from the Secr. of State for the Colonies to the Governor of Nigeria, 23 Sept. 1939.

41   For a different analysis of the origins of the 'quota-system', cf. Bauer, West African Trade, p. 152 and 257, C.E.F. Beer, The Politics of Peasant Groups in Western Nigeria, Ibadan 1976, p. 26, D. Meredith, The Colonial Office, pp. 297-298, and G. Williams, Marketing without and with Marketing Boards: The Origins of State Marketing in Nigeria, in: Review of the African Political Economy, XXXIX (1985) 2, pp. 6-8.

42   This paragraph is based on a telegram the Nigerian government already received from the Secr. of State for the Colonies on 23rd Sept., 1939 in which he outlined the basic structure of the eventuell purchase scheme. See NAI: Ib MinAgric, file 17890 Vol.I, Telegram from the Secr. of State for the Colonies to the Governor of Nigeria, 23 Sept. 1939.

43   RO: CO 852, file 256/1. Colonial Office memorandum 'Cocoa Control', 18 Sept. 1939. The Colonial Office and the Ministry of Food seem to have pursued the same policy as regards the division of the palm kernels, groundnuts, benniseed, cotton crop, and the division of palm oil exports and merchandise imports. For some figures on the distribution of merchandise imports in January 1940, see Holt Papers, Mss. Afr. s825, file 516, Letter from Administrative Department of John Holt & Co. to DA Lagos, 22 Jan. 1940. It is also noteworthy that the position of the Unilever Group (United Africa Company, G.B. Ollivant, and Swiss African Trading Company) in merchandise import was comparable to its position in the export trade. The group's share in the Nigerian war-time merchandise pool, which covered almost all important staple lines, amounted to precisely 57.534 per cent (!). Its share in the Gold Coast merchandise trade was marginally smaller (56.997 per cent).

44   PRO: CO 852, file 256/3, Letter from N.V. Deane (UAC) to E.C. Tansley, 1 Dec. 1939, and to E. Melville, 2 Dec. 1939; see also PRO: CO 852, file 525/4, Colonial Office memorandum 'West African Produce Control Board', Oct. 1943.

45   Holt Papers, Mss. Afr. s825, file 535(II), Letter from Administrative Department of John Holt & Co. to DA Lagos, n.d. (November 1939).

46   See PRO: CO 852, file 318/9 and PRO: CO 852, file 630/4, Memorandum 'British Colonial Exports, 1939-1945' by F.V. Meyer, August 1946, p. 20.

47   Holt Papers, Mss. Afr. s825, file 535(II), Letter from Administrative Department of John Holt & Co. to DA Lagos, n.d. (November 1939).

48   NAI: CSO 26, file 36148 S30, Nigerian Legislative Council: Reply by the Chief Secr. to Question No.44 on 4 March 1940; see chapter two, table 2.

49   Ibid. and NAI: CSO 26, file 36148 S28, Letter from E. Melville to C.C. Wooley, 25 April 1940.

50   The figures in table 5 are the number which officials used in the actual administration of the scheme, for example for the purpose of issuing export licenses. See ibid., Telegram from the Secr. of State for the Colonies to the Governor of Nigeria, 2 Dec. 1939; see also J. Mars, Extra - Territorial Enterprises, in: M. Perham, Economics of a Tropical Dependency, Vol. II, London 1948, p. 56. Note that the Unilever Group (United Africa Company, G.B. Ollivant and Swiss African Trading Company) was thus guaranteed a total market share of about 47 per cent of all Nigerian cocoa exports and and a further 41 per cent of all cocoa exports from the Gold Coast. Since the Gold Coast cocoa crop was about twice the Nigerian crop, the group's West African market share thus amounted to about 43 per cent.

51   PRO: MAF 75/31, Ministry of Food, 'Colonial Empire Cocoa: Scheme of Control, 3rd Revise', 16 Feb. 1940.

52   NAI: NL/FI. Nigerian Legislative Council, Address by Governor B. Bourdillon, 4 Dec. 1939; see also Report on Cocoa Control in West Africa, 1939-1943, and Statement of Future Policy, Cmd. 6554 of Sept. 1944, London 1944, p. 7.

53   Holt Papers, Mss. Afr. s825, file 535(II), Letter from Administrative Department of John Holt & Co. to DA Lagos, 3 Jan. 1940.

54   PRO: CO 852, file 256/1, Colonial Office memorandum 'Cocoa Control', 18 Sept. 1939.

55   See NAI: Oyo Prof 2/1, file C 234, Letter from the Secr. of State for the Colonies to the Officer Administering the Government of Nigeria, 22 Nov. 1939, see also PRO: CO 852, file 630/14, Memorandum 'British Colonial Exports, 1939-1945' by F.V. Meyer, August 1946, p. 20.

56   PRO: MAF 7531, Ministry of Food, 'Colonial Empire Cocoa: Scheme of Control, 3rd Revise', 16 Feb. 1940.

57   NAI: CSO 26, file 36148 S 30, Nigerian Legislative Council, 'Reply by the CS to Question No. 44', 4 March 1940.

58   Bauer, West African Trade, p. 250, and id., Reality and Rhetoric: Studies in the Economics of Development, London 1984, p. 96.

59   PRO: CO 852, file 256/2, Colonial Empire Cocoa Control, Minutes of Meeting, 7 Nov. 1939.

60   D. Meredith, The Colonial Office, p. 298.

61   PRO: CO 852, file 319/3, Minute by G.L.M. Clauson, 11 Sept. 1939. This quotation from G.L.M. Clauson could easily be dismissed as being unrepresentative and historically absurd, were it not for the fact that it reveals a frightening degree of ignorance of a high-ranking Colonial Office official about the social and political dynamics of society in Nigeria, let alone societies of other countries.

62   PRO: CO 852, file 319/3, Minute by O.G.R. Williams, 19 June 1940.

63   Ibid., Minute by E. Melville, 16 June 1940.

64   NAI: Oyo Prof 2/1, file C 234 Vol.I, Telegram from the Secr. of State for the Colonies to the Officer Administering the Government of Nigeria, 22 Nov. 1939.

65 PRO: CO 852, file 256/3, Telegram from the Governor of Nigeria to the Secr. of State for the Colonies, 25 Nov. 1939.

66 NAI: Oyo Prof 2/1, file C 234 Vol.I, Telegram from the Governor of Nigeria to the Secr. of State for the Colonies, 23 Nov. 1939.

67 PRO: CO 852, file 256/3, Telegram from the Governor of Nigeria to the Secr. of State for the Colonies, 28 Nov. 1939.

68 PRO: CO 852, file 256/2, Telegram from the Governor of Nigeria to the Secr. of State for the Colonies, 5 Oct. 1939.

69 PRO: CO 852, file 256/3, Telegram from the Governor of Nigeria to the Secr. of State for the Colonies, 25 Nov. 1939.

70 The demand of the Nigerian Governor for the authority to distribute part of the export licences at his own discretion was only given up in July 1940. See NAI: Ib MinAgric, file 17980 Vol.I, Memorandum by the Governor of Nigeria, 'Cocoa', 30 July 1940. For the discussion itself see PRO: CO 852, file 318/2, Minute by E. Melville, 21 Feb. 1940; see also NAI: CSO 26, file 36148 S 28, Letter from E. Melville to C.C. Wooley, 25 April 1939.

71 NAI: CSO 26, file 36148 S 4 Vol.I, Confidential despatch from the Governor of Nigeria to the Secr. of State for the Colonies, 15 Feb. 1940.

72 For the schedules see PRO: MAF 75/31, Ministry of Food, 'Colonial Empire Cocoa: Scheme of Control, 3rd Revise', 16 Feb. 1940, appendix N1-N4.

73 PRO: CO 852, file 256/2, Colonial Empire Cocoa Control: Minutes of Meeting, 7 Nov. 1939.

74 PRO: CO 852, file 256/2, Colonial Empire Cocoa Control: Minutes of meeting, 7 Nov. 1939, appendix B.3 and B.4. These figures show very clearly why at the end of the 1930s the European firms faced increasing competition from Nigerian-based competitors. As their managerial skills certainly would have improved in the future (and there are examples which indeed show that this was already happening in the 1930s), it seems not unreasonable to assume that in the long term, without the control scheme, some of the European firms would have found it increasingly difficult to stay in the Nigerian cocoa export trade.

75 In a letter from the Managing Director of the United Africa Company, F. Samuel, to E.C. Tansley the former stated that until the 1942/43 season the overall remuneration for the services of his firm had worked out to be around 24s per ton. See PRO: CO 852, file 446/7, Letter from F. Samuel to E.C. Tansley, 15 Sept. 1942; see also PRO: CO 852, file 512/10, Letter from the Cocoa Sub-Committee of the Association of West African Merchants (F. Samuel) to the West African Produce Control Board, 8 Sept. 1943.

76 PRO: MAF 75/31, 'Colonial Empire Cocoa: Scheme of Control, 3rd Revise', 16 Feb. 1940, appendix N1 and N2.

77 PRO: CO 852, file 318/2, Memorandum 'Cocoa Control Scheme' by the Governor of Nigeria, n.d. (May 1940), and PRO: CO 852, file 317/10, Letter from the Chief Secr. to the Secr. of State for the Colonies, 24 April 1940.

78 Bauer, West African Trade, p. 256, and Mars, Extra-territorial Enterprises, p. 92.

79 For the 1937 Agreement schedule, see Holt Papers, Mss. Afr. s825, file 535(I), Letter from Administrative Department of John Holt & Co. to DA Lagos, 2 Nov. 1937; see also Holt Papers, Mss. Afr. s825, file 535(II), Memorandum 'Cocoa' by Administrative Department, n.d. (1945). For the 1939/40 schedule see PRO: MAF 75/31, Ministry of Food, 'Colonial Empire Cocoa: Scheme of Control, 3rd Revise', 16 Feb. 1940. The 1937/38 and 1939/40 schedules are in a strict sense incompatible, since the former

contains certain items which the latter lacks and vice versa. However, in as much as single items in the schedules are concerned, especially the items 'coast establishment charges' and 'remuneration', such a comparison seems to be justified.

80   The figure 5s 1d is taken from an internal memorandum which the Administrative Department of John Holt & Co. had produced in 1945 in order to show the development of the value of the items 'coast establishment charges', 'head office expenses' and 'remuneration' in Nigeria and the Gold Coast during the war. This memorandum used the 1937 Buying Agreement schedule as its point of reference. See also Nowell Report, para. 451. The Commission reported that in the 1937/38 cocoa season the profit margin of the agreement firms on their buying operations in Nigeria had amounted to about 5s per ton.

81   This is probably a conservative estimate, since the actual rate of remuneration on cocoa purchase in Nigeria seems to have increased from 5s 1d per ton to 24s per ton or by 472 per cent (!). For the figure of 24s per ton remuneration see PRO: CO 852, file 446/7, Letter from F. Samuel to E.C. Tansley, 15 Sept. 1942.

82   In 1937/38 the pool firms exported some 97,500 tons of cocoa. In 1939/40 the "A" Shippers purchased about 80,000 tons of cocoa, of which some 10,000 tons were eventually destroyed. Note that the firms received a remuneration of 1 per cent on the purchase price of cocoa, which could not be exported. For figures on total seasonal exports, including exports from "B" Shippers, from Nigeria see Colonial Office, Colonial Annual Reports: Nigeria, no. 1904 for 1938, London 1940, p. 38, and Report on Cocoa Control in West Africa, 1939-1943, and Statement of Future Policy, Cmd. 6554 of Sept. 1944, London 1944, p. 15, appendix II. From these totals one has to subtract the amount of cocoa which was shipped by non-members of the 1937 Cocoa Agreement of about 1,000 tons and the 1939/40 "B" Shipper quota of about 2,000 tons. This calculation does not take into account undisclosed profits which were hidden in some items of the marketing schedule. Note that in the discussion above the term "profit" is always used to describe pre-tax profits. On the exceptionally high rate of taxation levied on trading firms during the war, see Mars, Extra-territorial Enterprises, p.68. Could it be that one reason why the Ministry of Food treated the firms so generously was the knowledge that part of their inflated profits would anyway end up in the Treasury?

83   See Holt Papers, Mss. Afr. s825, file 535(II), Memorandum 'Cocoa' by Administrative Department of John Holt & Co., n.d. (1945).

84   Nigerian Gazette Extra-ordinary, Public Notice No. 73 of 28th November, 1939, 'Cocoa Control (Cocoa prices and Brokerage Rates) Order', 1939; see also NAI: Ib Min Agric I, file 17980 Vol.I, Telegram from the Secr. of State for the Colonies to the Governor of Nigeria, 14 Nov. 1939.

85   PRO: CO 852, file 318/2, Memorandum 'Cocoa Control Scheme' by the Governor of Nigeria, n.d. (May 1940). For a similar argument from the Governor of the Gold Coast, see PRO: CO 852, file 256/4, Telegram from the Governor of the Gold Coast to the Secr. of State for the Colonies, 7 Dec. 1939, and ibid., file 317/11, Telegram from the Governor of the Gold Coast to the Secr. of State for the Colonies, 1 April 1940.

86   NAI: Ib Min Agric I, file 17980 Vol.II, Letter from the Secr. Western Provinces to the CS, 5 Feb. 1940.

87   Holt Papers, Mss. Afr. s825, file 535(II), Circular to all Ventures, Lagos District, John Holt & Co., 23 Nov. 1939.

88   NAI: Ib MinAgric I, file 17980 Vol.II, Letter from the Secr. Western Provinces to the CS, 5 Feb. 1940.

89   NAI: CSO 26, file 36148 S11 Vol.I, Telegram from the Governor of Nigeria to the Secr. of State for the Colonies, 15 Feb. 1939.

90   NAI: CSO 26, file 36148 S11 Vol.I, Letter from the Governor of Nigeria to the Secr. of State for the Colonies, 15 Feb. 1940.

91   PRO: CO 852, file 318/2, Memorandum 'Cocoa Control Scheme' by the Governor of Nigeria, n.d. (May 1940); see also PRO: CO 852, file 256/3, Telegrams from the Governor of Nigeria to the Secr. of State for the Colonies, 25 Nov. 1939, and 12 Dec. 1939.

92   PRO: CO 852, file 256/3, Colonial Empire Cocoa Control: Minutes of Meeting, 15 Nov. 1939.

93   NAI: CSO 26, file 36148 S11 Vol.I, Telegram from the Governor of Nigeria to the Secr. of State for the Colonies, 1 Dec. 1939; see also Kelly Report, para. 25 and para. 26.

94   Obisesan Papers, Report by the Acting RCS (A.G.C. Stainforth) on 'Development and Progress of Cocoa Marketing Societies', n.d. (1943); see also NAI: CSO 26, file 36148 S11 Vol.I, Telegram from the Governor of Nigeria to the Secr. of State for the Colonies, 1 Oct. 1939.

95   PRO: CO 852, file 256/3, Telegrams from the Governor of Nigeria to the Secr. of State for the Colonies, 12 Nov. 1939 and 28 Nov. 1939.

96   PRO: CO 852, file 256/3, Colonial Empire Cocoa Control: Minutes of Meeting, 15 Nov. 1939.

97   NAI: CSO 26, file 36148 S11 Vol.I, Telegram from the Secr. of State for the Colonies to the Governor of Nigeria, 30 Nov. 1939. The influential Agricultural Adviser to the Colonial Office, H. Tempany, was strongly opposed to the idea of rapidly developing co-operative marketing societies. On his advice, it seems, the Colonial Office decided to disallow the allocation of a quota, using the outbreak of war to some extend as a pretext. See PRO: CO 852, file 272/1, Minute by H. Tempany, 13 Dec. 1940.

98   NAI: CSO 26, file 36148 S11 Vol.I, Telegram from the Secr. of State for the Colonies to the Governor of Nigeria, 26 Nov. 1939, and NAI: CSO 26, file 36148 S11 Vol.II. Telegram from the Secr. of State for the Colonies to the Governor of Nigeria, 13 April 1940; see also PRO: CO 852, file 318/6, Letter from G.L.M. Clauson to C.C. Wooley (CS), 13 April 1940.

99   NAI: CSO 26, file 36148 S11 Vol.II, Telegram from the Secr. of State for the Colonies to the Governor of Nigeria, 14 April 1940.

100   In the 1938/39 season co-operative marketing societies had produced some 5,059 tons of cocoa. See Obisesan Papers, Report by the Acting RCS (A.G.C. Stainforth) on 'Development and Progress of Cocoa Marketing Societies', n.d. (1943), and NAI: CSO 26, file 36148 S11 Vol.I, Telegram from the Secr. of State for the Colonies to the Governor of Nigeria, 21 Nov. 1939.

101   The payments of the Association of West African Merchants and the United Africa Company amounted in 1939/40 to £3,161, in 1940/41 to £3,500 and in 1941/42 to £4,000. See NAI: CSO 26, file 36148 S11 Vol.II, Letter by the Acting RCS to the Cocoa Controller, 31 Oct. 1941.

102   NAI: CSO 26, file 36148 S11 Vol.III, Letter from the Cocoa Controller to the RCS, 17 Feb. 1941; see also NAI: CSO 26, file 42125 Vol.III, Letter from RCS to CS, 14 Jan. 1946.

103   NAI: CSO 26, file 36148 S11 Vol.I, Minutes by C.C. Wooley (CS) and B. Bourdillon, 1 Dec. 1939.

104   NAI: CSO 26, file 36148 S11 Vol.I, Letter from the Governor of Nigeria to the Secr.
      of State for the Colonies, 15 Feb. 1940.

105   NAI: Ib MinAgric 1, file 17980 Vol.I, Minute by G.C. Whitely (Acting CS), 18 May
      1940.

106   NAI: CSO 26, 36148 S11 Vol.II, Minute by C.C. Wooley (CS), 3 June 1940.

107   Nigerian Gazette, Public Notice No. 79 of 4th Dec. 1939. Note that these are not road
      mileage figures.

108   Rhodes House Library Oxford, Mss. Afr. s823(I), Memorandum 'War Organisation od
      Agricultural Department' by A.G. Bryce, 4 Aug. 1939.

109   PRO: CO 852, file 256/1, Colonial Office memorandum 'Cocoa Control', 18 Sept. 1939.
      See NAI: CSO 26, file 36148 S10, Minute by A.F.R. Stoddard, 19 April 1939.

110   PRO: CO 852, file 256/1, Colonial Office memorandum 'Cocoa Control', 18 Sept. 1939.

111   PRO: CO 852, file 256/1, Colonial Office memorandum 'Cocoa Control', 18 Sept. 1939.

112   This argument was first put forward in a memorandum by E. Melville, written in
      April 1940. See PRO: CO 852, file 349/1, 'Reply to Memorandum' from the West
      African Students' Union by E. Melville, 10 April 1940.

113   See the calculations in PRO: CO 852, file 256/1, Memorandum submitted by the Secr.
      of State for the Colonies, 'The Colonial Empire Cocoa Industry in War-time', 13 Oct.
      1939.

114   Nigerian Gazette (Extraordinary), No. 68, of 14 Nov. 1939.

115   A more general form of export control had already been established by that date. On
      2nd September, 1939, all prospective exporters, including exporters of cocoa, had to
      apply for special licences. This measure was taken in order to prevent key commodities
      finding their way to the enemy. See Mars, Extra-territorial Enterprises, p.103. Thus
      export licensing preceded produce control. In as much as the legal framework was
      concerned the cocoa control scheme was formally set up on 7th November, 1939.
      Incidentally, statutory control of cocoa exports was abolished in Nigeria almost 50
      years later, on the 30th June, 1986. It was thus one of the most durable colonial
      institutions. See West Africa, 12 May 1986, p. 989.

116   Holt Papers, Mss. Afr. s825, file 535(II), Circular to all Ventures, Lagos District, John
      Holt & Co., 23 Nov. 1939.

117   PRO: CO 852, file 256/3, Telegram from the Governor of Nigeria to the Secr. of State
      for the Colonies, 30 Nov. 1939.

118   NAI: Ib MinAgric 1, file 17980 Vol.II, Letter from the Act. Resident Ijebu Province
      to the Secr. Western Province, 27 Jan. 1940 (T.A. Odutola). The Ibadan trader
      I.B. Ogun, for example, claimed that his seasonal turnover exceeded 3,000 tons. See
      NAI: Ib MinAgric 1, file 17980 Vol.I, Letter from I.B. Ogun to the Secr. Western
      Provinces, 15. Nov. 1939.

119   NAI: Ib MinAgric 1, file 17980 Vol.II, Letter from the Secr. Western Provinces to the
      CS, 5 Feb. 1940; NAI: Ib MinAgric 1, file 17980 Vol.IV, Letter from S. Agbaje to the
      Senior Resident Oyo Province, 5 Oct. 1940; NAI: CSO 26 , file 36148 S26. Minute by
      C.C. Wooley, 18 Jan. 1940.

120   One Kano groundnut trader was cited to have said that 'the United Africa Company
      have this year achieved the aim of many years and made me their slave'. See PRO:
      CO 852, file 253/4, Telegram from the Governor of Nigeria to the Secr. of State for
      the Colonies, 1 Nov. 1939.

121   See PRO: CO 852, file 256/3, Telegram from the Governor of Nigeria to the Secr. of
      State for the Colonies, 25 Nov. 1939.

122   NAI: Oyo Prof 2/3, file C 234 Vol.II, Report by T.A. Shankland, SDO Ibadan, 'Restrictions on the Purchase of Kernels', 12 March 1941.

123   PRO: CO 852, file 318/2, Memorandum 'Cocoa Control Scheme' by the Governor of Nigeria, n.d. (May 1940).

124   Holt Papers, Mss. Afr. s825, file 535(II), Letter from DA Lagos to Administrative Department of John Holt & Co., 15 Dec. 1939.

125   Ibid., Circular to all Ventures, Lagos District, John Holt & Co., 23 Nov. 1939.

126   PRO: CO 852, file 318/2, Memorandum 'Cocoa Control Scheme' by the Governor of Nigeria, n.d. (May 1940).

127   NAI: Ib MinAgric 1, file 17980 vol.II, Letter from A.K. Zard to the Secr. Western Provinces, 15 Nov. 1939, and ibid., Letter from I.B. Ogun to the Secr. Western Provinces, 15 Nov. 1939; see also ibid.; Letter from the Secr. Western Provinces to the CS, 19 Jan. 1940.

128   See, for example, the reply to an application put forward by A.K. Zard in NAI: Ib MinAgric 1, file 17980 Vol.I, Letter from the Secr. Western Provinces to A.K. Zard, 17 Nov. 1939.

129   'Nobody really supposes', reported, for example, the Registrar of Co-operative Societies, 'that the middleman lives on 5/- per ton. His real profit comes from the farmers outside buying stations...' See NAI: CSO 26, file 36148 S11 Vol.II, Letter from the RCS to the CS, 21 May 1940.

130   NAI: CSO 26, file 36148 S10, Minute by G.G.T. Colby, 23 April 1940.

131   Ibid.

132   NAI: Ib MinAgric 1, file 17980 Vol.II, Letter from the Secr. Western Provinces to the CS, 5 Feb. 1940. For a different view see NAI: Ib MinAgric 1, file 17980 Vol.II, Petition by A. Flionis, 8 Dec. 1939, Transport differentials were fixed by the Nigerian government in consultation with the firms and the transport industry. According to a minute by the Acting Secretary of the Western Provinces, H.J. Marshall, the Nigerian government was 'not in possession of the basic principles on which these differentials were fixed'. See NAI: Ib MinAgric 1, file 17980 Vol.IV, Minute by H.J. Marshall, 24 Oct. 1940. For transport rates see Nigerian Gazette, Public Notice No.79 of 4th Dec., 1940.

133   R.D. Pearce, Sir Bernard Bourdillon: The Biography of a Twentieth-Century Colonialist, Oxford 1987, p. 251, and his article 'Morale in the Colonial Service in Nigeria during the Second World War', in: Journal of Imperial and Commonwealth History, XI (1983) 2, p. 179. A similar development seems to have happened in private firms. See Mars, Extra-territorial Enterprises, p. 60; see also Mss. Afr. s1428, Interview with J.B. Davies of U.A.C., 'Service in Nigeria with the United Africa Company from the 1930's'.

134   G.D. Jenkins, Politics in Ibadan, North-Western University Ph.D. thesis, Wisconsin 1965, p. 278 and 311, and A. Harneit-Sievers, Zwischen Depression und Dekolonization: Afrikanische Händler und Politik in Süd-Nigeria, 1935-1954, Saarbrücken-Fort Lauderdale 1991, pp. 198-285.

135   For the payment of additional remuneration to T.A. Odutola, see NAI: Ib MinAgric 1, file 17980 Vol.II, Letter from the Act. Resident Ijebu Province to the Secr. Western Provinces, 27 Jan. 1940; see also Holt Papers, Mss. Afr. s825, file 535(II), Letter from the DA Port Harcourt to the DA Lagos of John Holt & Co., 25 Oct. 1943. T.A. Odutola was the single biggest supplier of cocoa to the firm in Nigeria and his seasonal deliveries amounted to several thousand tons. His additional remuneration throughout a large part of the war amounted to about 5s per ton.

136   See, for example, Olusanya, The Second World War, pp. 40-42, and Pearce, Sir Bernard Bourdillon, p. 253. For a local perspective, see Jenkins, Politics in Ibadan, pp. 271-274 and 283.

137   NAI: CSO 26, file 30055 Vol.I, Resolution by the Nigerian Youth Movement, 25 Sept. 1939; see also O. Awolowo, Path to Nigerian Freedom, London 1947, p. 27. For plans of fascist Germany to acquire colonies in Africa and in particular parts of Nigeria, see H. Stoecker (ed.), German Imperialism in Africa. From the Beginnings until the Second World War, London 1986 (trans. and English edition of Drang nach Afrika, Berlin, 1977), pp. 379-414.

138   NAI: CSO 26, file 36148 S12 Vol.II, Letter from the Agege Planters Union to the CS, 26 Aug. 1939.

139   Pearce, Sir Bernard Bourdillon, pp. 251-256; see, for example, the report on a wireless address by the Secr. of State for the Colonies in West Africa, 21 Oct. 1939, p. 1423.

140   Ibid.

141   NAI: NL/FI, Address by the Governor of Nigeria, 4 Dec. 1939.

142   Ibid.; see also the report on that speech and the comment in West Africa, 6 Jan. 1939, p. 1743 and 1747.

143   PRO: CO 852, file 256/1, Telegram from the Secr. of State for the Colonies to the Governor of Nigeria, 23 Sept. 1939.

144   PRO: CO 852, file 256/4, Telegram from the Governor of Nigeria to the Secr. of State for the Colonies, 12 Dec. 1939.

145   NAI: Ib MinAgric 1, file 17980 Vol.I, Telegram from the Secr. of State for the Colonies to the Governor of Nigeria, 1 Nov. 1939.

146   A. Obisesan was not only chosen because he was the president of the ICCMU, but also, as the Resident Oyo minuted, because 'Mr. Akinpelu (sic) is a man of some personality who is not afraid to speak his mind in the presence of Europeans. He is also a member of the Ibadan Council and would therefore be the natural link with the Native Authority...' See NAI: Ib MinAgric 1, file 17980 Vol.I, Minute by the Resident Oyo Province, 10 Nov. 1939. When A. Obisesan was informed of his appointment he was anxious to assure the Secr. Western Provinces that he would be 'always in readiness to serve wherever His Honour...sends me to serve...' See Ibid., Letter from A. Obisesan to the Secr. Western Provinces, 13 Nov. 1939. After the war A. Obisesan became one of the three African directors of the newly established Nigerian Cocoa Marketing Board.

147   NAI: CSO 26, file 36148 S3, Letter from the Nigerian Produce Traders' Union to the CS, 16 Nov. 1939. This committee was only one of at least three committees on which S. Akinsanya served during the war. In April 1940 he became a member of the Economic and Transport Advisory Board. The other committee on which S. Akinsanya served was the Produce Inspection Advisory Committee (Western Area). See West Africa, p. 100, 1 Feb. 1940.

148   PRO: CO 852, file 318/4, Cocoa Advisory Committee. Minutes of 1st Meeting, 18 Nov. 1939, and ibid., Cocoa Advisory Committee. Minutes of 2nd Meeting, 23 Nov. 1939.

149   Ibid.

150   Ibid., Cocoa Advisory Committee. Minutes of 2nd Meeting, 23 Nov. 1939.

151   NAI: CSO 26, file 36148 S26, Letter from the Nigerian Produce Traders' Union to the CS, 24 Nov. 1939.

152   NAI: CSO 26, file 36148 S15, Report of a Meeting held at Government House on 25th November, 1939 at which his Excellency received a Deputation of the Nigerian Produce Traders' Union, 25 Nov. 1939 (official version). The Chief Secr. C.C. Wooley and the Cocoa Controller G.F.T. Colby were also present at the meeting.

153   Ibid.

154   Ibid., Report of a meeting held at Government House on 25th November, 1939, with a delegation of the Nigerian Produce Traders' Union, 25 Nov. 1939 (unofficial version).

155   NAI: CSO 26, file 36148 S12 Vol.III, Memorandum 'Cocoa Purchases' by Cocoa Controller, 18 Aug. 1942.

156   See, for example, NAI: Ib MinAgric 1, file 17980 Vol.II, Telegram from the Secr. of State for the Colonies to the Governor of Nigeria, 5 Jan. 1940, and PRO: CO 852, file 317/10, Memorandum 'Empire Cocoa Control Scheme' by S.W. Hood (Ministry of Food), 29 Jan. 1940.

157   NAI: CSO 26, file 36148 S33, Notes on Interdepartmental Meeting held at the Ministry of Food, 28 March 1940; see also Wickizer, Coffee, Tea and Cocoa, p. 345.

158   NAI: CSO 26, 36148 S39, Ministry of Food: Meeting to consider 'Cocoa Control', 29 May 1940.

159   NAI: CSO 26, file 36148 S33 Vol.I, Notes on Interdepartmental Meeting held at the Ministry of Food, 28 March 1940.

160   NAI: CSO 26, file 36148 S39, Ministry of Food: Meeting to consider 'Cocoa Control', 29 May 1940.

161   Nigerian Gazette Extra-ordinary, Government Notice No. 557, 30 May 1940. The Cocoa Controller prepared two special marketing cost schedules for the purchase of cocoa for destruction. As in the case of ordinary purchases of Nigerian cocoa, the Cocoa Controller found it necessary to set up one schedule for European firms and one schedule for Nigerian-based firms, although the services they rendered were exactly the same. The difference between the two schedules amounted to 5s 9d per ton.

162   NAI: CSO 26, file 36148 S33 Vol.II, Notes on a Meeting at the Secretariat, 22 May 1940.

163   Ibid., Letter from E. Melville to C.C. Wooley (CS), 25 April 1940.

164   NAI: CSO 26, file 36148 S12 Vol.III, Memorandum 'Cocoa Purchases' by Cocoa Controller, 18 Aug. 1942; see also Wickizer, Coffee, Tea and Cocoa, p. 334; Report on Cocoa Control in West Africa, 1939-1943, and Statement of Future Policy, Cmd.6554 of Sept. 1944, London 1944, p. 3 and 15, appendix II.

165   Report on Cocoa Control in West Africa, 1939-1943, and Statement of Future Policy, Cmd.6554 of Sept. 1944, London 1944, p. 16, appendix V, and NAI: CSO 26, file 36148 S12 Vol.III, Memorandum 'Cocoa Purchases' by Cocoa Controller, 18 Aug. 1942.

166   PRO: CO 852, file 319/II, Minute by E. Melville, 27 April 1940.

167   Nigerian Gazette Extra-ordinary, Government Notice No. 557, 30 May 1940.

168   PRO: CO 852, file 318/2, Memorandum 'Cocoa Control Scheme' by the Governor of Nigeria, n.d. (May 1940).

169   PRO: CO 26, file 36148 S11 Vol.I, Letter from the Governor of Nigeria to the Secr. of State for the Colonies, 15 Feb. 1940; see also Beer, The Politics of Peasant Groups, p. 20, and R. Galletti/K.D.S. Baldwin/I.O. Dina, Nigerian Cocoa Farmers, Oxford 1956, p. 4.

170   West African Pilot, 31 May 1940.

171   NAI: Oyo Prof 2/1, file C 234 Vol.I, Extract from the Minutes of the Ife Native Administration Council Meeting, 8 Aug. 1940.

172   NAI: Oyo Prof 2/3, file C234 Vol.II, Report 'Palm Kernel Survey' by the SDO Ibadan Division T.M. Shankland, 12 March 1941.

173   NAI: CSO 26, file 36148 S12 Vol.II, Letter from the Ibadan Council to the SDO Ibadan, 3 Oct. 1940. This letter contains the resolution from 30th Sept., 1940. The resolution was signed by 11 Ibadan Chiefs, including the Olubadan, and two non-titled councilors, one of whom was the aforementioned A. Obisesan.

174   See, for example, NAI: CSO 26, file 36148 S12 Vol.II, Letter from the Ibadan Co-operative Cocoa Marketing Union to the Governor of Nigeria, 3 Oct. 1940.

175   NAI: CSO 26, file 36148 S11 Vol.I, Letter from the Governor of Nigeria to the Secr. of State for the Colonies, 15 Feb. 1940.

176   Cited in J. Wheare, The Nigerian Legislative Council, London 1950, p. 119.

177   PRO: CO 852, file 317/8, Letter from A. Ogden to the Secr. of State for the Colonies, 18 Jan. 1940.

178   NAI: Ib MinAgric 1, file 17980 Vol.III, Resolution by the Ibadan Co-operative Cocoa Marketing Union, 13 April 1940.

179   PRO: CO 852, file 318/2, Memorandum 'Cocoa Control Scheme' by the Governor of Nigeria, n.d. (May 1940).

180   G.O. Olusanya, The West African Students' Union and the Politics of Decolonisation, 1925-1958, Ibadan 1982, p. 101.

181   PRO: CO 852, file 349/1, Memorandum by the West African Students' Union: Price Control and Living Standards in West Africa, 1 March 1940, and Address Presented to the Secr. of State for the Colonies by the President (L. Solanke) of the West African Students' Union, 29 August 1940, printed in West Africa, 7 Sept. 1940, p. 920.

182   The first memorandum was published in West Africa, 6 April 1940, p. 323.

183   West Africa, 11 May 1940, p. 453, and 18 May 1940, p. 479.

184   PRO: CO 852, file 349/1, Memorandum 'Price Control and Living Standards in West Africa', 1 March 1940.

185   Ibid.

186   Ibid.; See also West African Pilot, 18 March 1940.

187   NAI: CSO 26, file 36148 S57, Letter from E. Melville to E. London, 22 May 1940.

188   Bauer, West African Trade, p. 153.

189   Meredith, The Colonial Office, p. 294.

190   Address presented to the Secretary of State for the Colonies by the President of the West African Student's Union (L. Solanke) on the 29 August 1940, reprinted in: West Africa, 7 Sept. 1940, p. 920.

191   Economic Programme Submitted to the Nigerian Youth Movement, Ibadan Branch, 18 June 1940, by O. Awolowo, cited in: P. Zachernuk, The Economic Programme of the Southern Nigerian Intelligentsia, 1920-1960, paper presented at the Canadian Association of African Studies Annual Meeting, Kingston, Ontario, 11-14 May 1988, pp. 3-4.

192   J.S. Coleman, Nigeria: Background to Nationalism, Berkeley 1958, p. 227, and G.O. Olusanya, The Nationalist Movement in Nigeria, in: O. Ikime (ed.), Groundworks of Nigerian History, Ibadan 1980, p. 559. For the history of the transformation of the Nigerian Youth Movement into the Action Group see F.A. Baptiste, The Relations between the Western Region and the Federal Government of Nigeria: A Study of the 1962 Emergency, University of Manchester M.A. Thesis, Manchester 1965, pp. 20-38.

193   NAI: CSO 26, file 30055 Vol.II, Nigerian Youth Movement, Representative Council Meeting, 6-9 Sept. 1940.
194   See, for example, Manchester Guardian, 13 Dec. 1939.
195   In the House of Commons during 1940 the Secr. of State for the Colonies was asked almost ten times by members of the Labour Party (A. Creech-Jones and S. Sorensen) and a member of the Communist Party, R. Gallacher, about the finer details of the cocoa control scheme.
196   See, for example, the minute by F. Stockdale on a discussion he had with the Labour M.P. A. Haden-Guest: PRO: CO 852, file 256/3, Minute by F. Stockdale, 24 Nov. 1939.
197   See chapter 6, table 7.
198   The Foreign Office, for example, regarded 'the destruction of any food with extreme misgivings...' See NAI: CSO 26, file 36148 S39, Ministry of Food. Minutes of Meeting to consider Cocoa Control', 29 May 1940.
199   NAI: CSO 26, file 36148 S33 Vol.I, Letter from E. Melville to C.C. Wooley, 25 April 1940; see also PRO: CO 852, file 319/11, Minute by E. Melville, 27 April 1940.
200   Nigeria Gazette Extra-ordinary, Government Notice No. 557, 30 May 1940.
201   This was probably a result of strong representations from the Governor of Nigeria. See PRO: CO 852, file 318/2, Memorandum 'Cocoa Control Scheme' by the Governor of Nigeria, n.d. (May 1940).
202   NAI: CSO 26, file 36148 S39, Ministry of Food. Minutes of Meeting to consider Cocoa Control, 29 May 1940.
203   Later, in 1942, it was stated in an internal discussion paper that 'the Ministry of Food were unwilling to continue a commitment which involved them in financial loss and also the political odium of the destruction of foodstuff, for whatever reasons. It was therefore decided to establish the WACCB'. See PRO: CO 852, file 413/2, West African Produce Control Board, Policy Paper No. 7: Sales Prices to the Ministry of Food, 26 Nov. 1942. The whole affair was apparently kept secret from the West African governments. See NAI: CSO 26, file 38300 S4, Minute by G.F.T. Colby, 13 Dec. 1941.
204   For a similar view, see D. K. Fieldhouse, War and the Origins of the Gold Coast Marketing Board, p. 175.

CHAPTER 6

War-time Controls and the Cocoa Economy

The central aim of the war-time economic controls in the colonies was to manipulate the volume, composition and the prices of the goods (raw materials, consumer and capital goods) which the colonies exchanged with the United Kingdom in order to mobilise Imperial resources in support of the latter in her fight against the Axis Powers. As far as trade was concerned, the principal means by which this aim was achieved in the colonies were foreign exchange regulations, import and export controls in the colonies, as well as in the United Kingdom, and shipping regulations.[1]

The way in which all these controls were administered depended on the fortunes of war, allied co-operation and the state of the British economy, particularly its balance of payments position. Thus, for example, the deteriorating balance of payments position of Britain vis-à-vis the United States in the first two years of the war and again immediately after the war led to the application of stringent exchange controls in the colonies, which lasted throughout the war and for a considerable period afterwards. The successive transformation of the British civil economy into a fully fledged war economy led, moreover, to a tightening of import controls in the colonies and export controls in the United Kingdom, which resulted in frequent shortages and sometimes even complete lack of a whole range of goods, in particular consumer goods, in the colonies.[2] As far as the fortunes of war were concerned, the fall of France in 1940, the entry of the United States into the war in late 1941, the Japanese conquest of British colonies in the Far East and South East Asia in early 1942, the Battle of the Atlantic in late 1942 and the North African campaign in 1943 and 1944 proved to be important military events which had a direct bearing on how the war effort was conducted in the African colonies and in Nigeria in particular.

Apart from the continuous shipping shortage between 1940 and early 1943, the loss of the Far Eastern and South East Asian colonies was perhaps the most important single event in the war, since it dramatically increased the importance of many Nigerian raw materials, which those colonies had previously supplied, such as rubber, tin and, above all, vegetable oils and oilseeds.

War-time controls operated well into the post-war period. In the economic field there was little difference between the system which operated during the war and the system which came into being after the war. The imperative to economise on foreign exchange expenditure, to maximise the production and export of raw materials, and to minimise imports from the United Kingdom remained one of the main pillars of colonial economic policy in the immediate post-war years.[3] Exchange controls and restrictions, for example, were only lifted in 1952[4], while import controls from the United States and Japan were only finally scrapped as late as 1958[5].

The Administrative Machinery

Cocoa control was maintained by a host of governmental departments, committees and boards. The allied war effort as regards the foodstuffs trade was co-ordinated from June 1942 onwards by the Combined Food Board. Its main purpose was to allocate foodstuffs supplies between the United Kingdom, the United States and other Allied Nations.[6] However, it was only in 1944 that cocoa became subject to Combined Food Board allocation. After the war the functions of the Combined Food Board were to some extent taken over by International Emergency Food Council under the auspices of the United Nations Relief and Rehabilitation Administration (UNRRA). The international allocation of cocoa was finally disbanded in June 1949.[7] The British side in the negotiations with United States departments was represented from 1941 onwards by Colonial Office officials, specifically by the Colonial Supply Mission in Washington. There were also, if limited, consultations with representatives of the Free French colonial governments in West Africa.

The Colonial Office itself underwent major changes during the war and different departments within the Colonial Office dealt at various times with cocoa marketing. At the beginning of the war, the Economic Department was primarily responsible for all questions regarding cocoa. During the war Colonial Office staff was increased and new departments and committees were set up.[8] Thus in 1942 the Economic Department was split into Production and Supplies Branches. In 1943 the Economic Department was again re-organised into a Economic Division with three sub-branches, a Supplies Branch, a Development Branch and a Production Branch. Within the last named a separate Marketing Department was created which dealt solely with marketing of colonial produce, including cocoa. The former head of the Economic Department, G.H. Creasy, was appointed Under-Secretary of State for the Colonies and put in charge of the Production and Supplies Branches. Apart from S. Caine and probably E.C. Tansley, he was the most influential civil servant within the Colonial Office who dealt with cocoa matters. These arrangements lasted until 1947. During the war a number of new departments within other already existing Government Departments and even new Ministries were set up to administer the war machinery and organise the war effort, including cocoa control: notably the Raw Cocoa Section within the Ministry of Food, and the Ministries of Supply, War Transport and Economic Warfare.

In West Africa and in Nigeria trade matters were initially co-ordinated by the West African Governors Conference. 'Wagon', as it was called, had come into being just before the war as a forum for discussion and initially had no executive functions. However, in 1940 a permanent Secretariat was added under the Chairmanship of the Governor of Nigeria, Sir Bernard Bourdillon, in order to co-ordinate shipping which after the Fall of France had become scarce. One year later, the West African Supply Centre under the direction of the Secretariat was set up in order to regulate the distribution of the supplies of consumer goods between the West African colonies, which at that time were becoming increasingly scarce while at the same time the demand was growing.[9] In early 1942 the Nigerian Supply Board was established in order to administer the food, import, transport, and price controls, and to provide a link with the West African Supply Centre.[10] The Nigerian Supply Board operated until 1946, when its functions were taken over by the newly-established Department of Commerce and Industry.

The 1942 arrangement was not working very successfully. The West African Supply Centre met only once in March 1942 and the military authorities, in particular the British Chief of Staff, were dissatisfied with its performance.[11] Since the Japanese occupation of the Far Eastern and South East Asian colonies had heightened the importance of supplies of raw materials from West Africa, the War Cabinet decided in May 1942 to appoint a civilian Resident Minister for West Africa on lines already established in the Middle East. His main task was to co-ordinate the war effort, especially the production drive in the West African colonies, and to ensure proper liaison between military and civilian authorities in West Africa.[12]

The arrival of Lord Swinton in West Africa (the actual organisation was sited in the Gold Coast) in July 1942 led to a complete overhaul of the system.[13] The Resident Minister presided over the newly-established West African War Council which, apart from Lord Swinton, consisted of the Governors of Nigeria, the Gold Coast, Sierra Leone and the Gambia, and the Commanders of the three Fighting Services in West Africa. The Resident Minister had extraordinary powers and could act without the consent of the Governors or the Military, though in fact he never used these powers.[14] The actual work of the West African War Council was done in three sub-committees, the Service Committee (responsible for military matters), the Production and Supply Committee (responsible for the coordination of supply matters and production programming[15]) and the Civil Members Committee. This last named consisted of the four Governors and the Resident Minister and was the most important committee in which matters, such as the price which cocoa producers were to receive for their produce and the future shape of post-war marketing arrangements, were discussed. The West African Supply Centre was absorbed into the Resident Ministers organisation and was developed into the executive organisation of the West African War Council.[16] After the war the

Civil Members Committee of the West African War Council was replaced by the West African Council. However, this body held only minor importance.

The Policies of the War Effort

One can distinguish between two different types of policies which the Colonial Office and the colonial governments pursued as regards the war effort. One led to the establishment of new forms of regulation, such as the enactment of new legislation, while the other led to the tightening of already existing forms of control.

In the early months of the war, the Nigerian government passed a number of new regulations, including currency regulations and import and export controls, many of which had been prepared well in advance of the outbreak of war.[17] The regulations concerning imports were fairly liberally drafted, whereas export and currency regulations allowed for very tight control.[18] Thus from December 1939 all exports from Nigeria were prohibited except under licence in order to deny supplies to the Axis Powers, while imports of goods from the Sterling Area, with few exceptions, were unrestricted. Imports from the United States, however, were from the beginning of the war subject to licensing and subject to currency regulations. But until mid-1940 it was still possible to obtain goods from the United States or from the area which was later called the Western Hemisphere, i.e. North and South America (excluding Canada) and Liberia. Public announcements at the time, like Governor Bourdillon's address to the Legislative Council in December 1939, were aimed at arousing patriotic feelings, rather than exhortations to do the utmost in the interest of the war effort.[19] This phase came to an end with the occupation of France. In June 1940 the Secretary of the State for the Colonies sent a circular telegram to all colonies, in which he pointed out that

> the deepening gravity of the situation with which the whole Empire is faced today calls for the greatest possible effort from all its people... The development of the German Blitzkrieg has now transformed the perspective in which matters must be regarded... We must now envisage a supreme effort in the next few months, and we must therefore concentrate more exclusively than hitherto on whatever will contribute to our effective war strength in the immediate future... In the economic sphere the general aim of our policy should be to bring to the maximum the positive contribution of the Colonies to the immediate war effort in the ways of supplies; and reduce to the minimum their demands on the resources of men, material and money which are or ought to be made available to this country at home or overseas.[20]

The Secretary of State for the Colonies asked the colonial governments specifically to refrain from making demands for non-essential imports of any kind from Sterling or non-Sterling sources, especially for those imports which involved the use of iron and steel, to increase the production of raw materials for export 'including of course those sold for "hard" currencies', and, finally, to maximise the development of the production of local foodstuffs in order to meet local demand.[21]

Thus in 1940 all the major elements in the war effort were already established: The drive to increase production for export of required raw materials, to decrease consumption of imported goods, and, in particular, to discriminate against all imports from non-Sterling (United States) sources. However, controls, and in particular import controls, were at this time still comparatively liberally handled. This situation lasted until 1941. Prompted by the deteriorating state of the United Kingdom economy and in view of the rapidly decreasing Empire currency reserves, the Secretary of State felt it necessary to send a despatch to all colonial governments in which he addressed the question of what he called 'the right use of resources'[22]. In the despatch he made clear that the war effort and the ensuing austerity which it had imposed on United Kingdom people would be extended to the colonies.[23] One of the main features of the United Kingdom war effort was to limit civilian consumption drastically, thereby freeing resources for military purposes. The same policy was now to be applied in the colonies.[24] Although the Secretary of State made clear that such a policy should be limited to the strata of colonial people who had a similar standard of living as the British people[25], the principal means by which he proposed to limit personal consumption, the curtailment of imports, hardly discriminated between income groups in the colonies. As regards the limitation of imports, he wrote that

> Import licensing should in general be more strictly administered, and imports most drastically curtailed, as this is the most effective means of directly curtailing consumption in Colonial conditions... There are a number of articles of an unessential nature the import of which ought in every Colonial Dependency to be prohibited entirely from all sources, Sterling or non-Sterling. The importation of many, perhaps one should say most, other articles should be cut down to a small percentage of normal imports both from Sterling and non-Sterling sources, especially of course from the latter...[26]

This despatch was a turning point in economic policy in West Africa. Until then, controls had not really bitten. Imports from Sterling sources, for example, were until 1941 still relatively freely available, since merchants were allowed to import goods under General Open Licence. There were shortages of some goods, but these were slight compared with those which were to come. After having received the despatch the Nigerian government considerably tightened all forms of control, but particularly import controls. From 1941 all imports were prohibited except under a specific licence. Apart from the fact that many goods, like, for example, sewing machines, could often not be obtained even with import licences, the more and more restrictive handling of Nigerian import controls after 1941 led to increasing shortages of consumer goods in local markets.[27]

The Secretary of State also indicated what should be done with the excess purchasing power which such a policy of import restrictions would necessarily create. He proposed that purchasing power in the colonies should be reduced by a number of means, such as saving campaigns or by encouraging people to make interest free loans to the government. He also suggested that another way of removing money from circulation would be to increase all forms of taxation. The balances derived by such means were to be invested in United Kingdom securities. They would be repaid after the war and then used for developmental purposes. As the Secretary of State pointed out

> I think that local Governments should regard as a first call upon any surplus which may be realised the building up of reserves adequate to meet any demands which might reasonably expected in the period of post-war reconstruction. It seems to me definitely preferable that Colonial Governments, if they are able to do so, should accumulate surplus balances now which they can use for purposes of reconstruction and development after the war without having recourse to assistance under the Colonial Development and Welfare Act, rather than such balances should be surrendered now and applications for assistance be made at a later date.[28]

Finally, the Secretary of State urged the colonial governments to make plans for the post-war period. Although under current circumstances it was impossible to consider plans under the Colonial Development and Welfare Act, unless they could be carried out solely with local resources and would not interfere with the war effort, colonial governments were advised to make departmental plans for the expansion of social services after the war.[29]

The idea of limiting consumption by increased taxation and using the accumulating balances at a later date for developmental purposes, had a high strategic value for the future (as it will be shown in the next chapter) in the discussion of the origins of post-war marketing schemes. At this point it is enough to emphasise that from mid-1941 onwards import controls in Nigeria began increasingly to stifle the supply of consumer and also capital goods while other controls were also tightened. As Governor Bourdillon told his Nigerian audience in a broadcast in June 1941: 'In brief the Administrative machine is now being converted into a war effort machine.'[30]

The importance of the Nigerian war effort was heightened by the Japanese conquest of early 1942. The United Kingdom was cut off from various vital supplies, most importantly tin, rubber and oilseeds. Since Nigeria produced all three of these products, the Nigerian government was urged to increase their production as quickly as possible. But, this was not a departure from existing policies. The Nigerian government had been urged to maximise its contribution to the war effort by increasing production on a number of previous occasions. However, after 1942 the Nigerian government considerably increased its commitment to this policy.

The Local War Effort

The direct mobilisation of men and materials during the war consisted broadly of four different elements. Import, export and currency controls have been already mentioned. A number of imported merchandise goods, such as petrol, bicycles, cement and gunpowder were allocated to specific areas within Nigeria as an inducement to increase production of particular raw materials. Thus, for example, in the rubber-producing areas in the south gunpowder was relatively freely available, while in other areas gunpowder had completely vanished from the markets. These controls were effected through the Association of West African Merchants.[31] In addition there was a recruitment drive for the army and for military works. It has been estimated that about 100,000 men served for various lengths of time in different capacities in the army during the war.[32] During the early years of the war the military authorities together with the Nigerian government also embarked on a vast service construction programme in order to improve communication lines to North Africa and the Middle East. This involved the building of airfields and military camps, and the improvement of harbour and other facilities, including the building of roads and bridges. Finally, the Nigerian government initiated a whole variety of production programmes for various crops (especially palm products, groundnuts, rubber, cotton, cocoa and timber) and minerals (mainly tin, wolfram and coal) which were partly fulfilled with conscript labour, as in the case of tin production on the Jos Plateau[33] or through the application of compulsory measures, as in the case of palm kernel production in the south-east[34] and groundnut production in the north[35]. So far as agricultural production was concerned, the campaign for increased volumes of exports of palm kernels was probably the most important. Palm kernels had not always been in such demand. When the United Kingdom was receiving adequate supplies from the Eastern colonies and American sources, West African palm kernels were regarded as a surplus commodity. Thus on 24th August, 1940 a 'palm kernel ban' was promulgated which prohibited the harvesting and movement of palm kernels from certain areas in the Western Provinces.[36] The 'palm kernel ban' was extremely unpopular and prompted a number of adverse political reactions, including petitions by the Ibadan Native Authority and local traders' unions,[37] and critical articles in the nationalist press. The ban was effectively removed on 8th May, 1941 and finally withdrawn on 24th July, 1941. The fortunes of war changed this situation. The rapid conquest of the Japanese forces in late 1941 and early 1942 caused the government to initiate a palm kernel production drive in mid-1942, which comprised the employment of special 'palm kernel spotters', the printing of leaflets in local vernaculars, addresses to public meetings by Chiefs and District Officers and radio broadcasts.[38] In 1943 a special officer was appointed to supervise the campaign, whose task it was to set monthly production targets (quotas) for producing areas in southern Nigeria. The Residents of the Provinces within these areas were asked to fulfil these quotas. The production drive for palm kernels lasted well into the late 1940s.[39]

Finally, one development not directly related to the war effort, should be mentioned. The war effort could have not been executed without the employment of a large number of African labourers by, for example, the Public Works Department or the Railway Department. The government considered that 'labour unrest', if possible, had to be avoided during the war and workers had thus a comparatively strong bargaining position in pay negotiations. Demands for better pay emerged in 1941. In 1942 a massive pay rise was granted, which cost the government over £1 million per year.[40] In the following years European civil servants received pay increases each year in the form of higher allowances such as increased separation allowances and increased cost of living allowances (they became universally known as COLA). African government employees, especially manual workers, however did not receive such allowances, let alone increased allowances. This was one of the reasons for the 1945 General Strike, which after 37 days ended with a victory for the workers and their unions.[41] Again massive pay rises were granted.

The increases in pay for African and European workers and employees during the war were not sufficient to compensate for the massive increase in the cost of living during the same period and thus real incomes of manual workers and other government employees certainly declined. However, their treatment was much more favourable than that which other groups received, whose income depended on government decisions. For example, the producers of scheduled crops like cocoa farmers whose incomes declined much faster during the war.[42] In addition, the increases in the nominal pay of government employees added to the inflationary pressures which had been already built up in the Nigerian economy.

The Attempts to Limit the Effects of the War Effort

The simultaneous reduction in imports and the increased military and civilian expenditure led inevitably to severe shortages of certain imported consumer goods.[43] Some articles which before the war had been consumed in large quantities, virtually vanished from the markets, for example stockfish, rice and to some extent certain lines of cotton piece goods. There were also acute shortages of salt, matches and enamel-ware and all forms of more sophisticated consumer goods (like bicycles, sewing machines, corrugated iron sheets and cement) and capital goods (such as cars, lorries and many kinds of spare parts, especially tires and tubes).[44] It was estimated at the time that in 1942 the purchasing power of the African population in West Africa exceeded the value of the maximum volume of goods obtainable by more than a quarter.[45] Another sign of this development was the rapid increase in the Sterling Balances of the West African Currency Board and in the amount of money in circulation in Nigeria itself during the war.[46]

The imbalance between purchasing power and available supplies of imported and locally produced goods necessarily caused prices to rise very rapidly. Here one has to distinguish between the import prices of imported goods and the prices which such goods fetched in the local markets. Import prices increased during the war by a factor of about two to three.[47] Since there was such a large overhang of purchasing power over available goods, local market prices increased much further.[48] Unfortunately, detailed statistics on local market prices of imported goods are not available for this period.[49]

Prices of locally produced goods, especially food, also increased very rapidly. There are some price series for food items, which indicate that their increases were at least as large as the increases in the price of imported goods.[50]

The government undertook various attempts to control inflation and alleviate the shortage of goods. Since these developments themselves were at least partly the result of government policies, this type of government intervention could be seen as some form of 'secondary' war effort. The principal means by which government tried to control inflation and alleviate the shortage of goods, apart from manipulating purchase prices of scheduled crops, were price controls, higher taxation, saving campaigns and subsidisation of some consumer goods.

The savings and loans campaigns lasted throughout the war and on the whole were not particularly successful. By 1946 just over £0.5 million were invested in saving certificates or lent to government free of interest.[51]

Comprehensive price controls were introduced in May 1941 in order to check the developing black market in scarce goods. Government, in collaboration with the large importing firms represented by the Association of West African Merchants, fixed the wholesale prices for a whole range of imported goods like cotton piece goods, matches, tyres and tubes. At the same time, import quotas were fixed for these goods and allocated to the participating firms on the basis of 'past performance'[52]. These controls were not effective and even in Lagos they were more often broken than observed.[53] They certainly did not reduce the scope for profiteering in the growing black market.

Partly in response to the failure to curb the black market and partly in order to reduce the prices of a number of consumer items, in particular food items, in 1941 the government introduced the Pullen Marketing Scheme (Capt. A.P. Pullen was the name of the organising officer). This comprised the bulk purchase of various foodstuffs and the release of a number of imported goods for sale at selected markets in Lagos at or below cost price.[54] Again, this scheme was only partly successful, since foodstuffs marketed through the Pullen Marketing Scheme were sold outside Lagos at considerably higher prices and this naturally widened the scope of the black market rather than containing it. Moreover, Lagos market women did not co-operate with the officer administering the scheme.[55] In 1944 the government also introduced a rationing scheme for some consumer items such as wheat flour, condensed milk and gin (!). These rations were handed out to African consumers based on proof of 'past performance'. European consumers were not subject to such a requirement.[56]

Increased taxation was another means designed to 'mop up surplus money'[57]. Initially, this consisted of increased efforts being put into the collection of taxes. The amount collected in the Western Provinces, for example, increased during the war on the basis of existing legislation by almost a third.[58] Then in 1941 higher income taxes were introduced for companies and the export duty on cocoa was raised from £1 3s 4d to £2 2s per ton.[59] Two years later a whole range of consumer goods (cement, tobacco, cigarettes, matches, perfumery, wines and certain lines of cotton piece goods) became subject to higher import duties. It is interesting to note in this connection that from the financial year 1941/42 Nigerian government revenue continuously exceeded government expenditure despite the large increase in war-related expenditure, presumably in order to build funds for post-war development projects.[60]

Though the proceeding paragraphs are only a rough sketch of the major economic policies the Imperial and the Nigerian government pursued during the war, they provide the background for an evaluation of the specific policies government applied to the cocoa trade. These policies are the subject of the last two sections of this chapter.

U.S. Cocoa Controls

As already mentioned, the international allocation of cocoa supplies was from 1944 until 1948 effected through the Combined Food Board and International

Emergency Food Council. However, between 1941 and 1946 the actual contracts for delivery of West African cocoa to the United States were made between the British control boards (West African Cocoa Control Board and West African Produce Control Board) and the foreign purchasing department of the U.S. Commodity Credit Corporation.[61] (Until 1941 cocoa had been sold directly to U.S. manufacturers and cocoa merchants.[62]) During the larger part of the war the British control boards were thus selling cocoa to one single buyer in the U.S. As will be shown in the next chapter, this considerably influenced the evolution of statutory marketing boards in Britain and West Africa during the war.

After their entry into the war, the U.S. authorities almost immediately imposed a price ceiling (maximum purchase price) of just under £50 per ton c.i.f. on the U.S. American cocoa trade. This ceiling price was removed on 30th June, 1946 while all import controls, including those controls regarding cocoa, were finally abandoned in early 1947.

U.K. Cocoa Controls

In the previous chapter it was shown how in 1939 the Ministry of Food assumed control of the West African and United Kingdom cocoa trade. It was mainly a book-keeping exercise, since the firms were still purchasing cocoa in West Africa and delivering it to their customers in the United Kingdom, the United States and elsewhere. Cocoa control outside Nigeria at that time consisted only of the control of the destination of cocoa exports and of the profits made in the trade. With the establishment of the West African Cocoa Control Board in 1940, the Ministry of Food was divested of its responsibility for the control of overseas sales. At the same time controls in the United Kingdom were enlarged. In August 1940 a ceiling price for West African cocoa beans was imposed in the United Kingdom in order to prevent extreme price rises as a result of shipping difficulties.[63] From October 1940 to October 1941 the Ministry of Food bought the U.K. requirements of West African cocoa from the West African Cocoa Control Board and distributed the supplies between the manufacturers according to their cocoa consumption between July 1938 and July 1939. Sales were at this time also partly effected through cocoa brokers. In 1940/41 cocoa demand from manufacturers outstripped supplies. Since cocoa supplies from countries other than those in West Africa were not controlled and also because the Ministry of Food sold part of the West African crop through cocoa brokers, a black market in cocoa beans soon developed. This prompted the Ministry in 1941 to extend its control over the United Kingdom cocoa market. From 1941 all cocoa imports into the United Kingdom had to be sold to the Ministry of Food. The Ministry also started increasingly to sell cocoa directly to manufacturers and dispensed with the services of the United Kingdom intermediaries. By 1942 the Ministry had assumed complete control of the procurement and distribution of cocoa beans in the United Kingdom, including their purchase and selling prices.[64] The Ministry relinquished its control of the United Kingdom market in November 1950 after the international allocation of cocoa through the International Emergency Food Council had ceased in 1949.[65]

The Ministry of Food Buying Policy

At the beginning of the war, the Ministry of Food fixed a price for United Kingdom purchases which was very close to the commercial free market price of West African cocoa beans at the time. The establishment of the West African Cocoa Control Board did not change that policy and the Ministry of Food purchased its requirements from the Board at the current market prices at the time, which was equivalent to £24 2s 10d per ton f.o.b. Lagos or Accra for grade II cocoa.[66] After a deduction of some minor marketing expenses this price yielded a margin of about £6 per ton to the West African Cocoa Control Board.

The 1940/41 cocoa season ended with an overall profit of over £2 million to the Board. This prompted the Treasury to ask the Board to agree to a lower Ministry of Food purchase price in the approaching 1941/42 season.[67] The Board was able to resist this pressure. However, on the other hand it was unable to extract higher prices from the Ministry of Food although commercial prices, particularly those in the United States had increased since the last season.[68] Accordingly in the 1941/42 season the Ministry paid exactly the same prices as it had paid in the previous season of 1940/1941. Since produce prices in West Africa were increased in 1941/42, the margin of the West African Cocoa Control Board decreased to about £4 per ton. At the same time however, the margin between the sale price to the Ministry of Food and the sales price to customers elsewhere considerably widened. At the end of the season it emerged that the average price of all sales of grade I and grade II cocoa to the Ministry of Food had amounted to only £25 7s whereas other customers of the board had paid £33 5s 8d.

The 1941/42 season ended with a loss to the West African Cocoa Control Board, partly because the Ministry had paid a low price, but also because some cocoa had to be destroyed in West Africa for lack of shipping (see table seven on p. 217). It is noteworthy that if the Ministry of Food had paid the same price like other customers for its purchases, the loss in the 1941/42 season would have turned into a profit.

This fact was also noted by the West African Produce Control Board which argued that 'the present arrangement is open to the criticism that His Majesty's Government, having undertaken to refund a profit, has fixed a price for sale of West African cocoa to the Ministry of Food, which, in the present circumstances, can only result in a deficit, and is consequently open to the charge of bad faith with the producers'[69]. In other words, the initial promise, given in 1939 at the inauguration of produce control, that eventual profits would be returned to the colonies and the cocoa producers, was in effect broken by ensuring that there was were little or no profit to return. However, this internal criticism apparently had very little impact, since the purchase price policy of the Ministry of Food, with backing of the Treasury remained unchanged.

The high differential between the United Kingdom and the United States selling prices became known to the American government. Through the Combined Food Board they proposed that the United States' authorities should, in the approaching 1942/43 cocoa season, not pay higher prices for its cocoa purchases than the relevant United Kingdom authorities on the grounds that this unequal treatment would violate the Mutual Aid Agreement of 1942.[70] A price formula thus had to be worked out which would placate the Americans, as well as satisfy the Treasury. From the 1942/43 season to the 1944/45 season a calculation was applied by which 'the price received by the Board [West African Produce Control Board] from the Ministry in any one season was to be the average price received by the Board in the previous season for all sales, including those to the Ministry of Food'[71]. In effect this formula meant that the price paid by the Ministry would be fixed below the prices other customers of the Board paid, but that, in due time, the margin between these two prices would narrow. Negotiations over the price to be paid by the Ministry of Food for their purchases in the 1942/43 season started in May 1943, when the final results of the 1941/42 season were known. In that season the West African Cocoa Control Board had sold 170,886 tons of cocoa to the Ministry of Food at a price of £25 7s per ton and sold elsewhere 32,126 tons at a price of £33 5s 8d per ton. The average sales price of the West African Cocoa Control Board in the 1941/42 cocoa season was thus £26 12s 2d per ton. This was the price the Ministry of Food was charged in the season of 1942/43.[72] The same method of calculation was applied in the two following seasons.[73]

In the 1945/46 cocoa season the system was again changed. It had become all too apparent that, despite the application of the price formula, the purchase prices paid by the Ministry of Food were too low in comparison with the prices paid by other customers of the Board. Moreover, it was expected that the American price ceiling would soon be either substantially increased or even completely removed.[74] After lengthy negotiations the Ministry agreed that the price paid in 1945/46 would be directly related to the United States ceiling price at the time of purchase.[75]

The United States ceiling price was removed in June 1946 and again negotiations started. Though the Ministry was very reluctant to accept the new solution, it was agreed that the Board's selling price to the Ministry of Food in the 1946/47 cocoa season should be solely based on commercial considerations.[76]

The Ministry of Food Selling Policy

The Ministry of Food was not the ultimate consumer of the cocoa which it purchased from the boards. It resold it to the biscuit and cocoa manufacturers in the United Kingdom. In August 1940 the price at which manufacturers bought cocoa from the Ministry of Food was fixed at £35 per ton.[77] This gave the Ministry of Food a margin between its buying and selling prices of £3 10s per ton which presumably covered United Kingdom handling charges and perhaps allowed for a small profit. At the instigation of the Treasury the Ministry of Food selling price to United Kingdom manufacturers was increased in March 1941 to £45 per ton.[78] Thus the margin between the Ministry of Food's buying and selling prices rose to £13 10s per ton. It was made clear from the beginning that these 'profits' were not to be included in the surplus the marketing boards would eventually hand over to the colonies.

The real, though not publicly declared, purpose of the £10 'levy' (as it was called) was to 'secure by means of revenue from a semi-luxury commodity some offset for the heavy losses which were ... being incurred by the Ministry of Food through subsidisation of the price of certain foodstuffs [bread], which by entering into the cost of living index directly effects the wage rates under wage agreements in a wide range of industries'[79]. This surcharge remained in place until 1946.[80]

A rough calculation shows that between 1941 and 1946 the Ministry of Food made a 'profit' of probably as much as £7.8m on its West African cocoa sales and about £2.4m on the Nigerian cocoa sales to the United Kingdom manufacturers.[81] This latter sum represents about one-quarter of the profits the British government handed over to the Nigerian Cocoa Marketing Board after the war.

The Ministry of Food surcharge attracted a number of critical comments from some Colonial Office officials, as well as criticism from the liberal public. As has been mentioned earlier, the West African Cocoa Control Board made an overall loss in the 1941/42 season. This was partly due to the comparatively low price it had received from the Ministry of Food. But at the same time the Ministry itself had made a profit on its sales. This anomaly prompted, for example, the then Assistant Secretary and Head of the West Africa Department, O.G.R Williams, to minute that 'it is difficult to escape the implication that His Majesty's Government are more concerned about keeping prices down in the United Kingdom than about ensuring that the African producer gets an adequate return for his produce'[82]. Criticism also emerged from outside the Colonial Office. The Anti-Slavery and Aborigines Protection Society[83] and the Fabian Colonial Bureau[84] were particularly active in this question and forced the Colonial Office, despite their own misgivings about the levy, to at least publicly rally behind the Ministry of Food policy.[85] However, this criticism was unable to effect any change in policy.

The Producer Price Policy: An Introduction

The determination of the producer price[86] was in the public eye one of the main responsibilities of the marketing boards (i.e. of the West African Cocoa Control Board and, from 1942, of the West African Produce Control Board). But, since these were in effect Colonial Office executive agencies, the Secretary of State for the Colonies was legally and politically responsible for any decision the boards took. But the Secretary of State for the Colonies himself was not independent in his decision-making. He had to consult the colonial governments concerned and all the other Government Departments and Ministries, who dealt with the allocation, distribution and overseas disposal of cocoa beans, such as the Ministry of Food and the Colonial Supply Mission in Washington. On certain occasions, but not on a regular basis, the Foreign Office, the Board of Trade, the Dominions Office and the Ministry of Supply were also consulted. After 1942 the Resident Minister in West Africa had also an important say in the fixing of the producer price. Finally, because the Board operated with funds provided by the Exchequer, approval also had to be obtained from the Treasury.[87] The actual determination of the producer price in each season was therefore a somewhat lengthy process, at the end of which the responsibility for the decision was a collective one rather than one that could be attributed to a single government department or even an individual.[88] This often tended to obscure where the real responsibility lay for the determination of the producer price.

Secondly, it is noteworthy that the government departments which dealt with the question of producer prices always felt that the government purchase scheme was to some extent a charitable undertaking. It was repeatedly stated that whatever price the cocoa farmers received for their produce it was 'a far better price than he would have been obtained under a free market'[89]. There is, of course, no proof for such an assertion.

Finally, decisions regarding the producer price always entailed an element of speculation, since future developments during the war were particularly unpredictable. This uncertainty revolved mainly around the problem of shipping, at least in the early war years. The major questions were to what extent shipping facilities would be available for cocoa and if it would be possible to profitably dispose of the crop.

The Producer Price Policy

There were two different producer prices to be fixed each season. In August and September the West African Cocoa Control Board (and later the West African Produce Control Board) had to decide which price would be paid in the main season which usually opened on the 1st October each year. In the following April or early May the boards again had to make a decision about the price in the light crop season, which usually started in late May or June.

In the previous chapter it was argued that the price fixed by government in November 1939 (£16 10s per ton for grade II cocoa[90]) was pegged just above the price cocoa producers had received in the early months of the 1939/40 season. It was not a high price, since farmers had been paid considerably higher prices just two seasons before, but it was also not a particularly low price compared with other prices paid in the 1930s. Almost immediately after its introduction the purchase scheme ran into difficulties. Shipping space for cocoa was scarce and only some profitable sales to the United States kept the resulting overall deficit of the season within limits. As a result of the scarcity of shipping during the main harvest, the light crop purchase price was reduced to £10 per ton. All in all some 10,000 tons of cocoa were destroyed in Nigeria during the season, including all light crop cocoa (5,700 tons) and the season ended with a loss to the Treasury of £208,548, of which some £61,800 were due to losses made on Nigerian cocoa sales.

Shipping was very scarce throughout 1940 and thus the outlook for the 1940/41 cocoa season was not a promising one. There was the strong possibility that the Treasury, which had funded the deficit, would disown the scheme.[91] In order to prevent this happening, the Colonial Office, as well as the Nigerian government, presumably with the concurrence with the Gold Coast government, embarked on a new policy. The aim of this was to limit government's liability as far as possible and fix a price which would 'provide the Board with a profit to meet the expected loss of that part on the crop which was then anticipated would not find a market or would be sold at a loss'[92]. The new price had thus to be low, but not so low as to provoke 'social trouble' and high enough to maintain the producers' loyalty to the Allied cause.[93] In addition it was hoped that the new low price would prompt farmers to sell less cocoa to the board, since it was thought that a reduction in the boards' cocoa purchases would reduce the amount of cocoa which had to be destroyed and thus the financial loss which the destruction of cocoa entailed.[94] This was a major departure from the existing policy which aimed at giving the producer an adequate or fair return for his labour, as the participants in the negotiations over the producer price in the 1940/41 cocoa season clearly recognised.[95]

The main crop cocoa price paid to producers was thus lowered to £13 10s per ton. The light crop price, however, remained unchanged at £10 per ton. Comparatively little cocoa had to be destroyed. The season closed with a large surplus to the West African Cocoa Control Board amounting to £2,040,473 of which about £570,100 represented the Nigerian crop. This surplus was largely due to the ingenious selling policy of the West African Produce Control Board which had shipped, before the imposition of the American shipping ban in May 1941, large quantities of cocoa to the United States, without having a firm buyer at the time. It was stored at considerable cost and then, later, resold, when the supplies of cocoa dried up and prices soared.

According to Residents' reports from the Western Provinces of Nigeria, there was no protest from cocoa farmers against the lowering of the price.[96] As has been argued in the previous chapter, this was probably largely due to the public burning of cocoa and intense government propaganda.[97]

The following season of 1941/42 started with a considerable surplus. There was also, at least in the middle of 1941, the prospect that it would be possible to ship almost all of the 1941/42 crop. This strongly influenced the ensuing discussions about the price which producers would receive in the coming season.

Just as the deficit at the beginning of the previous season had prompted the government to change policies, the surplus at the beginning of the new season again forced the government to rethink its position. The basic question apparently was: Should the price be restored to its previous level or not? The discussions which this question prompted had extremely far-reaching consequences.

In Nigeria and West Africa as a whole the supply of consumer goods had become more and more difficult. There were many alarming reports on the scarcity of goods.[98] In the light of these reports and on advice from the governments of the Gold Coast and Nigeria, the decision was taken not to substantially increase the price to be paid to the cocoa farmers in the forthcoming 1941/42 season.[99] It was thought that a large increase in the price to the producers and the ensuing increase in their purchasing power would be 'undesirable in view of the severely restricted range and quantity of imported goods available for purchase by them...'[100] Thus the fixing of the producer price was no longer determined by either the 'fair return' principle nor by the state of the finances of the West African Cocoa Control Board, but by the volume of imports of consumer goods available at the time. Since it was clear that there would be a shortage of consumer goods for the foreseeable future, this policy actually entailed the deliberate creation of a surplus on the cocoa trading account of the West African Cocoa Control Board by lowering producer prices.

The main architect of this policy was S. Caine, the Financial Adviser to the Colonial Office. In a crucial minute from May 1941 he spelled out the origins and main features of the new policy:

> Owing to the offer of an substantially increased quantity of freight for shipment to this country ... it appears possible that practically the whole of this year's crop will be disposed. If this does happen there is little doubt that the financial operations of the West African Cocoa Control Board will show a substantial profit this year which is likely to be considerably more than sufficient to wipe out last year's deficit. We shall therefore have to consider whether the remaining balance should be devoted to increasing the price to the cocoa farmer or how it should be used. For reasons which have been discussed elsewhere there are considerable dangers in putting more money into the hands of West African natives at the moment as it is difficult to find goods which they could buy with that money. It may be therefore that some system by which we would pay the same price in cash as in the present year but would give them a bonus credited to them in a Savings Bank account withdrawable after the war might be the solution.[101]

It was this reasoning which prompted the West African Cocoa Control Board not to substantially increase the producer price. Not all Colonial Officials were satisfied with the decision like the then Chairman of the West African Cocoa Control Board, G.H. Hall,[102] but in the end the views of the colonial governments and of the Financial Adviser to the Colonial Office prevailed. As will be shown in the next chapter, this policy had important long-term effects, since it made it necessary to develop a policy which would define the purpose for which the accumulated profits would eventually be used. After a somewhat lengthy discussion it was decided to increase the Nigerian producer price by only 20s from £13 10s per ton to £14 10s per ton. At the same time the Nigerian export duty on cocoa was increased by 18s 8d from £1 3s 4d per ton to £2 2s per ton.

The seasons' results seemed to have justified a cautious price policy. With the American shipping ban still in place it was impossible to dispose of the crop in the United States (the ban was only lifted in August 1942) and a large proportion of the 1941/42 crop remained unsold. It was this situation which prompted the West African Cocoa Control Board to approach the Ministry of Food at the end of 1941 with the suggestion that cocoa should be bought as an oilseed, since it was cheaper for the Board to sell the crop even at a reduced price to the Ministry than to destroy the crop in West Africa.[103] The Ministry agreed to this proposal, not least because the occupation of the Far Eastern and South East Asian colonies made increased imports of fats and oil from other sources a dire necessity. However, despite these sales, some 17,000 tons of Nigerian main crop cocoa and all light crop cocoa (7,500 tons) had to be destroyed.

In early 1942 the West African Control Board had to decide what price should be paid for light crop cocoa. In the light of shipping difficulties and the knowledge that such cocoa was very likely to have to be destroyed, the price in the light crop season was lowered to £5 per ton. Another reason for this reduction was the desire to encourage the production of palm kernels. It was estimated at the time that this price constituted about half the cost it took to produce a ton of cocoa.[104] The season closed with an overall deficit of £314,051 of which the Nigerian part amounted to about £82,000.

In the 1942/43 season a further constraint against increasing the producer price developed. As already mentioned above the price of light crop cocoa had been reduced to £5 per ton on the reasoning that such a decrease would encourage cocoa farmers to collect more palm kernels in the Western Provinces.[105] Now this argument reemerged with even more force.

The heightened demand for vegetable oils and oilseeds from Nigeria posed the problem of how to achieve maximum production of these commodities without generating so much purchasing power as to create hyper-inflation. As early as December 1941, the Cocoa Controller of Nigeria, G.F.T. Colby argued that increased production of palm kernels and other oilseeds could probably only be achieved by offering relatively higher producer prices than for other commodities. If the prices of other commodities remained as they were, an increase in the price for palm kernels and palm oil would lead to increases in the purchasing power. Since the amount of imported goods was limited, inflationary pressures would become even stronger. Thus the general policy of the Nigerian government, he argued, should be 'to limit the increases in the amount paid for produce to the minimum which is compatible with satisfying the essential produce needs of His Majesty's Government'[106]. The production of cocoa was not regarded as an essential need.

The three main arguments in favour of low prices were as follows: first, it was thought that low produce prices for cocoa would directly stimulate the production of other, more obviously vital crops, notably palm kernels, rubber and local foodstuffs. Second, it was assumed that low prices would help to combat inflation, part of which was caused by increased prices for and larger purchases of other, more crucial, commodities. Finally, it was argued that if the volume of imports was limited, relative produce prices of agricultural commodities would decide which group of the producers, cocoa farmers or the producers of crops which were more in demand by His Majesty's Government, would be able to obtain the limited supplies. Thus even if there was no direct connection between cocoa farming in western Nigeria and palm oil production in eastern Nigeria, the lowering of cocoa prices would assure that more consumer goods would be available to the producers of palm oil.[107]

There were also, however, a number of other arguments which were advanced in favour of low produce prices in general and low cocoa price in particular, such as that increased purchasing power in the hands of producers would not only increase the price level of goods in Nigeria, but also increase the consumption of imported goods. The production of such goods involved manufacturing capacity and labour in the United Kingdom which could be better used for the war effort.[108] Finally, it was also argued that an increase in the cocoa price would lead to an increase in the price of foodstuffs in the urban areas of Lagos and Ibadan which, for political reasons, had to be avoided, or would make employment of labour on the cocoa farms more attractive.[109]

In 1942/43 the arguments concerning the cocoa purchase price therefore seemed to have changed again. Whereas in the previous season, the general combat of inflation in Nigeria had been the main argument, now the stimulation of relative production through the manipulation of the relative prices of crops seemed to have been the most influential reason for fixing the cocoa price at a particular level. The discussion about the price which cocoa farmers would be paid for their produce became interlocked with the discussion of how the Nigerian government could make the most efficient use of Nigerian resources for the prosecution of war. This reasoning, as will be shown, prevailed well into the post-war period.

The determination of the producer price in the 1942/43 season was a prolonged process. There were very heavy stocks at the beginning of the season and the shipping situation was not at all clear. It seems that the Nigerian Secretariat and especially G.F.T. Colby were very much in favour of a reduction of the price to £10 per ton.[110] Such a large decrease was ruled out, not least because the Residents in the producing areas indicated that it would be too harmful to the long-term development of the cocoa industry.[111] The discussion then largely centred on the question of whether the price should be reduced to £12 10s per ton or to £13 10s. The Chief Commissioner of the Western Provinces favoured a reduction to £13 10s per ton while the Secretariat preferred a reduction to £12 10s.[112] In the end the Governor decided to agree with his immediate advisers and recommended a price reduction to £12 10s.[113] This was the price which producers would eventually receive.

Despite large sales to the United States at a considerable profit, it was again necessary to destroy a substantial proportion of the 1942/43 main crop (27,800 tons) and the whole of the 1943 light crop (3,900 tons).[114] The latter was again purchased at a price of £5 per ton. The destruction of cocoa was partly due to shipping difficulties as in previous seasons, but the main problem appears to have been the lack of internal transport. There was a general shortage of lorries, petrol and tyres; it was decided, in order to conserve motor transport for more vital crops for which shipping was almost always available, to destroy considerable quantities of cocoa up-country[115] despite a large increase in storage capacity. The 1942/43 main crop was a very large one compared to previous seasons, though it is noteworthy that light crop purchases fell to about half of their former level. This decline was probably due to the extremely low purchase price in the crop season. The season of 1942/43 ended with a profit of £2,158,379 of which £747,800 represented the Nigerian part.

The war effort reached its peak in 1943. As pointed out above, in early 1943 Nigeria was asked with some urgency to increase the production of a whole range of commodities, including rubber, timber, tin and coal, but above all palm products and groundnuts.[116] At the same time inflation was still on the increase. The situation was perceived as so extremely pressing that Governor Bourdillon felt it necessary to admonish the Director of Agriculture J.R. Mackie with the words: '...remember, we must have immediate results, and that long range considerations must give way to immediate needs.'[117] In this situation any price increase for cocoa was ruled out from the beginning. Instead discussions ensued concerning the advisability or non-advisability of a further reduction in price. The outcome of these discussions was the decision not to reduce the cocoa price on these grounds: that a further reduction would not increase palm kernel production in the Western Provinces; that such a reduction would be probably harmful for 'post-war economics' in that cocoa would be very likely in heavy demand after the war; and that such a reduction would probably also do very little to lower inflation.[118] The Governor of Nigeria was still convinced, however, that 'purchasing power in the hands of cocoa growers must diminish the amount of consumer goods that can be dangled before the nose of the potential palm kernel producer...'[119] The price therefore remained unchanged. Thus the main crop price for cocoa was fixed at £12 10s.

In December 1943 and January 1944 the Marketing Director of the West African Produce Control Board, E.C. Tansley, and the Assistant Under-Secretary of State, G.H. Creasy, visited West Africa and found the cocoa industry in a very critical condition. Diseases were rampant and it was feared that production would seriously decline.[120] After the discussion which they had with the West African War Council, it was agreed that cocoa prices in West Africa should be increased in the forthcoming light crop season to £10 per ton and not fixed at the same price (£5 per ton), which was paid in the 1942/43 light crop season, as originally intended.

The 1943/44 season finished with a surplus of £2,969,190. The profit on Nigerian cocoa sales amounted to about £857,000. There was no need to destroy cocoa. Internal transport, as well as the shipping situation, had considerably improved, which enabled the marketing board to dispose of the crop in the United States and elsewhere very profitably. However, there was a sharp decline in the volume of purchases to about 70,000 tons. This was a very low figure and one not experienced since the early 1930s. The following main crop season of 1944/45 opened with a price of £21 10s per ton. This increase was probably due to the interventions from E.C. Tansley (West African Produce Control Board) and G.H. Creasy (Colonial Office) who after their visit to West Africa in December 1943 and January 1944, had strongly advocated price increases for the following light and main crop seasons.[121] Their demands were supported by the Ministry of Food and the Resident Minister, West Africa.[122]

The main crop price had been negotiated with the new Governor of Nigeria, A. Richards, who had replaced Bourdillon in late 1943. The impact of this change was immediately felt in the price negotiations. While the former Governor had to some extent changed his views on the connection between cocoa prices and the prices of other commodities in mid-1943, the new Governor reaffirmed the old view, that cocoa prices should not or should only be increased marginally on the grounds that such increases would harm the production of palm kernels and foodstuffs and increase inflationary pressures.[123] After some discussion he agreed only reluctantly to a price increase for the main crop season to £17 per ton. This proposal was accepted in February 1944 by the West African War Council,[124] but the Governor of Nigeria changed his view. In May 1944 he suggested a price increase to £21 per ton to the West African War Council. Such an increase would help, he argued, to diffuse criticism of the government which would inevitably emerge after the publication of the 1944 White Paper on cocoa marketing in West Africa, the United Kingdom and the United States. The 1944 White Paper contained detailed information, including figures of the profits so far accumulated by the marketing boards, and it was thought that if the profit became publicly known, the demand for substantial price increases would grow louder. In addition he reasoned that, without such an increase, a large disparity would develop between the price paid in the Gold Coast and that paid in Nigeria which would be very difficult to justify on economic grounds.[125]

The producer prices for 1944/45 were finally fixed at £21 10s per ton for the main crop cocoa and at £18 10s per ton for light crop, which represented an increase of almost 50 per cent. Without political pressure the price would have been much lower. However the price was not much higher because of continuing fears of inflation, the policy of supporting the war effort by manipulating relative produce prices, and the reasoning that higher cocoa prices might lead to higher urban food prices which would in turn increase the cost of living and prompt demands for wage increases. A new argument was also introduced into the discussion. It was suggested that the West African Produce Control Board should build up large financial reserves in order to finance the post-war marketing schemes.[126] This implied that producer prices in the next two or three cocoa seasons should be fixed at a comparatively low level so as to enable the Board to make a sizeable profit on its trading operations.

But the political difficulties mentioned above were not the only reason why the governments of the Gold Coast and Nigeria began to favour increases in the producer price. From as early as 1941 onwards, the Ministry of Food and, in particular, J. Cadbury, the United Kingdom Cocoa Controller, had advocated price rises in order to induce farmers to plant more cocoa.[127] It was thought that an increased acreage of cocoa would be necessary to meet the expected world demand in the post-war period. These pleas were to a large extent unsuccessful. By 1944/45 at least some officials within the Nigerian government and within the Gold Coast government, probably also influenced by the rapid spread of cocoa diseases, recognised the merits of such a policy.[128]

The West African Produce Control Board added some £2,093,328 to its funds after the season closed, of which about £673,000 represented the Nigerian proportion. Despite the higher price offered in the light crop season of 1944/45, actual purchases amounted only to about 700 tons. This was the third consecutive season in which light crop purchases had been much lower than in previous seasons.

The 1945/46 season was almost a replay of the previous season. There was still urgent demand from the United Kingdom authorities to expand the production of oilseeds in Nigeria and again demands for a substantial increase in the purchase price of cocoa were countered by the argument that such an increase would only lead to inflation and divert effort from the production of more vital crops.[129] Initially, the governments of the Gold Coast and Nigeria had planned to pay the same price in the 1945/46 season like in the previous season.[130] but increasing dissatisfaction of cocoa farmers in the Gold Coast, as well as reports from the Gold Coast that the current price would be insufficient to 'encourage the intensified care of farms which would be a necessary part of the measures contemplated to control pests...', prompted the authorities to change their mind.[131] Prices in the Gold Coast were therefore substantially increased. This again necessitated similar price rises in Nigeria and the price for main crop cocoa was thus increased to £26 per ton and for light crop cocoa to £23 per ton.[132] Purchases of light crop cocoa returned to normal. The season of 1945/46 ended with a profit of £1,675,000 (Nigeria's contribution to these profits came to about £717,700).

The 1946/47 season was the last season in which the West African Produce Control Board was responsible for the marketing of Nigerian (West African) cocoa. The fixing of the producer price turned out to be very difficult. It was clear that prices in the international markets would rise very rapidly as soon as the American ceiling price was removed. This was scheduled for June 1946. The main problem proved to be as follows: if local producer prices were fixed at a low level, the likely emergence of an enormous disparity between the international price and the local price would cause acute political embarrassment in the Gold Coast and Nigeria. Thus the actual fixing of the price was delayed until after the removal of the American ceiling price. Again there was a repetition of the 1944 and 1945 events. The Nigerian government was very reluctant to concede any major price increase on the grounds that such an increase would only result in further inflation and disturb the balance of production in the Western Provinces, and again political developments in the Gold Coast and Nigeria made a larger increase than originally intended necessary.[133]

In the Gold Coast it was thought that a higher price in 1946/47 would '...inspire or restore local confidence in controlled marketing and create a favourable atmosphere for the reception of the White Paper scheme, which we want to present as a producers' scheme and must therefore get through the unofficial majority of our Legislative Council with their support'[134]. In Nigeria the problem was rather different. Here the Governor feared that the National Council of Nigeria and the Cameroons, the leading nationalist party at the time, would take up the issue of cocoa producer prices and demand price increases and would initiate a press campaign if the price in Nigeria was fixed far below the price in the Gold Coast.[135] However, the Nigerian government was equally convinced that a very high produce price would also have politically undesirable consequences. It was argued that:

> High cocoa prices will cause food prices to rise ... and thus provide justification for demands for increased COLA [sic] with consequent labour trouble at a time when the situation is causing considerable anxiety.[136]

Thus there were again conflicting interests and the price eventually fixed was very much a compromise between these interests. In Nigeria the price was fixed at £47 10s per ton for main crop cocoa and £45 for light crop cocoa. This was a considerable advance in comparison with the price paid in the previous season (£26 per ton), but it was far below the price which the cocoa would eventually fetch in the international markets. It was also a very low price in real terms compared with the prices farmers had received before the war. The New York spot price for cocoa rose immediately in the 1946/47 season, after the removal of the ceiling on 30th June, 1946, from just under £50 to over £150.[137] There was a similar price rise in the United Kingdom. The season closed therefore with a profit of £16,035,000, of which £5,759,900 was attributable to Nigerian cocoa sales. The profits made in this season alone represented about two thirds of all profits made under statutory control between 1939 and 1947.

Before reviewing the impact of the war effort on the cocoa economy in the final section of this chapter, one further aspect merits attention, since it had extremely important long-term effects for both the Gold Coast and Nigeria. This was the breach of the promise, stated repeatedly by various Secretaries of State for the Colonies, that profits made during the war should only be spent for the direct benefit of cocoa producers.

The background to this decision was as follows: At the beginning of the negotiations over the Gold Coast cocoa price, the Governor of the Gold Coast had suggested that a price of 30s per load (about £56 per ton) should be paid in the forthcoming 1946/47 season. This price was considered too high by the authorities in London. However, the Governor of the Gold Coast was not prepared to accept a lower price, since he thought that a hold-up would immediately ensue if he could not announce a substantial increase in the buying price.[138] The solution eventually found was meant to satisfy all parties, though perhaps not the cocoa farmers. The price to be paid in the forthcoming 1946/47 season would be fixed at 30s per load but only 27s 6d per load would actually be paid over to the cocoa farmer. The remaining 2s d6 per load would be paid into a special fund which would be made available at a later date to the Legislative Council for expenditures on higher education.[139]

It was argued at the time that only a very liberal interpretation of what constituted expenditure for the 'direct' benefit of cocoa farmers could justify this policy.[140] In retrospect, however, it is clear that this decision paved the way for massive expropriation of the cocoa farmers' income by government through statutory marketing control in the following forty years.

Table 7: Cocoa Control Statistics, Nigeria 1939/40 - 1946/47 (in £/s/d and tons)

	1939/40	1940/41	1941/42	1942/43
Main Crop				
price	16 10 0	13 10 0	14 10 0	12 10 0
purchases	76,200	94,000	91,900	107,300
destruction	4,300	1,300	17,100	27,800
Light Crop				
price	10 0 0	10 0 0	5 0 0	5 0 0
purchases	5,700	6,600	7,500	3,900
destruction	5,700	2,300	7,500	3,900
Season				
total purchases	81,900	106,600	99,400	111,200
destruction	10,000	3,600	24,600	31,700
profit/loss (Nigeria)	(-61,800)	570,100	(-82,400)	747,800
profit/loss (West Africa)	(-208,548)	2,040,473	(-314,051)	2,158,379

Table 7 continued

	1943/44	1944/45	1945/46	1946/47
Main Crop				
price	12 10 0	21 10 0	26 0 0	47 10 0
purchases	70,200	84,800	94,700	104,000
destruction	-	-	-	-
Light Crop				
price	10 0 0	18 10 0	23 0 0	45 0 0
purchases	700	700	8,200	5,400
destruction	-	-	-	-
Season				
total purchase	70,900	85,500	102,900	109,400
destruction	-	-	-	-
profit/loss (Nigeria)	857,000	673,000	717,700	5,759,900
profit/loss (West Africa)	2,969,190	2, 093,328	1,675,000	16,035,000

Sources: E. Melville, The Marketing of West African Cocoa, in: Cocoa, Chocolate and Confectionery Alliance Ltd. (ed.), International Cocoa Conference 1948, London 1949, p. 97; Report on Cocoa Control in West Africa, 1939-1943, and Statement of Future Policy, Cmd.6554, London 1944, p. 14; Statement on the Future Marketing of West African Cocoa, Cmd.6950, London 1946, pp. 10-12; PRO: CO 852, file 904/1, Memorandum 'Disposal of Trading Profits from British West African Cocoa', April 1948.

The War Effort and the Cocoa Marketing Scheme: A Summary

The cocoa marketing scheme became slowly incorporated into the war effort. What started as a control scheme for the cocoa trade in 1939 developed in a short period of time into an agency of the war effort, the application of which was to some extent only mitigated by political considerations and fear that diseases might permanently damage the cocoa industry. When these considerations became more important in the immediate post-war years, concessions were made but no fundamental change in the underlying policy occurred.

The war effort concerned mainly the prices at which cocoa was bought and sold. Other aspects of the scheme, such as the distribution of the trade between pre-war participants, remained largely untouched.

It was thought that low cocoa purchase prices during the war would meet three ends.[141] The first was to protect the British taxpayer from paying for the cost of the scheme. The second was to retrain the rise of the monetary income of cocoa farmers in order to limit their demand for imported goods, especially those which involved the expenditure of hard, foreign exchange, and for local foodstuffs, either because these were in short supply or because it was desired that groups other than cocoa farmers in the economy, such as the producers of palm kernels and wage earners[142], should be able consume these goods. The third aim was to induce cocoa farmers and the labourers they employed to switch from cocoa farming to other economic activities which were more desired[143], notably to the production of palm kernels and rubber, or to seek employment in military works[144].

The single most important argument for low cocoa purchase prices during the war was the argument that this would somehow increase the production of palm kernels. It is ironic that precisely this policy failed to achieve its objectives.[145] This was due to the fact that palm kernels are produced by women and especially by older women in Yorubaland, who were not directly involved in cocoa farming. Though the palm fruit was gathered by professional male reapers, the actual cracking of the fruit was almost exclusively done by women. This reflected the then prevailing cultural gender division of labour between men and women in Yoruba agriculture, which apparently proved to be resistant, at least in the short term, to changes in the relative export prices of cocoa and palm produce.[146] As one observer wrote, 'even if he [the cocoa farmer] was willing to crack kernels his womenfolk would most certainly not permit this invasion of their field'[147]. Cocoa farmers usually had no direct financial interests in palm kernel production while conversely cocoa farming was considered by the women as man's work. The idea that government could manipulate production through prices was therefore in the case of cocoa and palm kernels misconceived. This argument was repeatedly put to the authorities in Lagos, but for no apparent reason they chose not to listen.[148]

The Impact of the War Effort on the Cocoa Economy

The first and foremost impact of the war effort was a continuous drain of resources out of the cocoa economy. Between 1939 and 1947 the marketing boards in West Africa accumulated a surplus on their trading operations of £26,448,771 of which £9,420,048 originated from Nigerian cocoa sales.[149] But these figures and the figures on seasonal produce prices are only a poor indicator of what happened to the cocoa farmer during the war.

The Nigerian cocoa farmers experienced a tremendous decline in their real incomes during the war. As table eight indicates, due to price inflation, the real income of cocoa farmers in terms of what amount of imported piece cotton goods they could buy with their money in the second half of the war was only between one third and one fifth of the real income they had enjoyed in the late

1930s. But even these figures are very likely to understate the real loss cocoa farmers had suffered during the war, since they do not take into account the rise in the price of local foodstuffs, some items of which appear to have risen even faster than the price of imported goods, and the increase in production costs, such as the increase in wage rates, cost of farm tools and the cost of transport. The impact of rising food prices was mitigated by the fact that most cocoa farm households also grew food crops which even in small amounts were sold in local markets. However, since many cocoa farm households bought more foodstuffs than they sold food crops in local markets, the rise in local foodstuff prices negatively effected the real income of cocoa farmers.

According to one set of official figures, the price of foodstuffs in Ibadan had risen at least two to three times during the war[150] while agricultural wages probably doubled during the same period (see table nine). Wage labour rates in general increased during the war because of government demand for unskilled labour for civilian and military purposes in the Western Provinces and also because government awarded comparatively high wage increases.[151] These wage increases never exceeded the rate of inflation, but they seem to have caused a shortage of labour in the Western Provinces in the final two war years and cocoa farmers had probably to pay similar wage increases to their labourers.[152] The first reports on the increase of agricultural wage rates appeared by 1942 and then reappeared frequently throughout the war years.[153]

The rise in the prices of locally-grown foodstuffs and the rise in the price of export commodities (other than palm kernels) induced cocoa farmers to divert their labour increasingly to the production of other crops than cocoa, particularly in the second part of the war. They largely moved into the production of rubber and kola, but also to the production of maize, rice, yams, timber and probably cotton.[154]

During the last years of the war farmers thus increasingly reduced the amount of labour they invested in cocoa farming. This meant that they put less effort into the weeding and general maintenance of the farms, and also reduced their efforts to harvest cocoa pods especially in the light crop seasons. According to a report made in early 1945 'approximately 50 percent of the farms ... [were] either completely neglected or improperly cleaned'[155]. Moreover, as has been indicated in chapter 2, the acrage newly planted with cocoa steeply declined during the war, which propably severely constrained the growth of output in the late 1940s and early 1950s. The neglect of cocoa farms as well as the decline in new planting as a result of the low price paid by the marketing board was officially acknowledged as early as 1943, but no major policy shift occurred.[156]

This neglect would probably not have mattered much were it not for the fact that the control of cocoa diseases, in particular black pod, depends to a large extent on the amount of labour spent on the farms and especially on the thorough harvesting of the crop.[157] If diseased pods are left on the tree the infection could spread more easily to other pods with the danger of causing permanent damage to the tree. Diseases had been observed even before the war, but low produce prices paid during the war considerably quickened the spread of disease. This was particularly noticeable in the light crop seasons of 1943 to 1945. Produce prices (£5 per ton) in these seasons were so low that farmers hardly bothered to harvest as the purchase figures of the West African Produce show. Acute observers like the Director of Agriculture attributed the increased incidence of diseases during the following years directly to the fact that a large part of the light season cocoa crop had been left hanging in the trees.[158]

Table 8: Evolution of Real Producer Prices and Real Incomes Derived from Cocoa Sales, 1937/38 - 1947/48

Season	Grade II			Purchases tons	Aprox. incomes	Deflator index	Producer price index	Incomes index
	£	s	d					
1934/35	15	0	0	82,300	1,234,500			
1935/36	17	0	0	93,400	1,587,800			
1936/37	38	0	0	101,700	3,864,600			
Seasonal averages 1934/35- 1936/37	24	0	0		2,229,000	100	100	100
1937/38	17	0	0	98,700	1,677,900	102	69	74
1938/39	14	0	0	113,900	1,594,600	101	58	71
1939/40	16	10	0	81,900	1,351,400	126	55	48
1940/41	13	10	0	100,600	1,358,100	160	35	38
1941/42	14	10	0	99,400	1,441,300	174	35	37
1942/43	12	10	0	111,200	1,390,000	247	21	25
1943/44	12	10	0	70,900	886,250	226	23	18
1944/45	21	10	0	85,500	1,838,300	258	35	32
1945/46	26	0	0	102,900	2,675,400	268	40	45
1946/47	47	10	0	109,400	5,196,500	345	57	68
1947/48	47	10	0	74,000	3,515,000	390	51	40

Sources: As in table 1 and table 7. The deflator index (index of prices of cotton piece goods at landed costs) is taken from P.T. Bauer, West African Trade, p. 421.

Table 9: Agricultural Wage Rates and Food Prices at Moor Plantation (Ibadan), 1934 - 1943

Year	Labour Rates (per diem)	Yams (per cwt.)	Beef (per lb.)	Cocoa (per ton)
1934	2d-10d	2s 6d	7d	£14 11s 10d
1935	3d-1s	2s 6d	7d	£16 9s 7d
1936	3d-1s	2s 6d	7d	£22 17s 8d
1937	4d-9d	2s 6d	4¼d	£22 2s 9d
1938	4d-9d	3s 9d	4¼d	£14 8s 9d
1939	5d-9d	--	--	£13 15s 10d
1940	5d-9d	--	--	£15 2s 10d
1941	5d-10½d	4s 7d	8½d	£14 0s 0d
1942	9d-1s 2d	6s 10½d	9d	£13 6s 3d
1943	1s 2d	10s 3d	9d	£12 6s 3d

Source: NAI: Ib MinAgric 1, file 17980 Vol.VI, Memorandum 'Notes on the Cocoa Industry' by Director of Agriculture, J.R. Mackie, 27 Jan. 1944.
Note: Cocoa prices are annual customs values.

The war effort had therefore very mixed results. Low cocoa purchase prices certainly did not all accomplish what they were supposed to accomplish, as the palm kernel discussion above shows. Produce control was effective as far as it retrained the monetary income of cocoa farmers and thus their demand for foreign exchange, but at the very high price of supporting the spread of the diseases and probably indebtedness among cocoa farmers. It is also clear, that even from the Imperial point of view this policy was rather shortsighted, since it negatively effected the supply of cocoa in the post-war period when hard, foreign currency earnings assumed such an importance. It is one of the ironies of the cocoa marketing scheme that part of the profits made by the West African Produce Control Board were later spent to combat the spread of cocoa diseases partly caused by the incidence of those profits. But it is certainly an exaggeration to conclude - as one observer did at the time - that 'all that five years of produce control has achieved, is to burn the cocoa and to kill the trees'[159].

Notes

1   See A. Hinds, British Imperial Policy and the Development of the Nigerian Economy, University of Dalhousie Ph.D. thesis, Dalhousie 1985, and Sterling and Imperial Policy, 1945 - 1951, in: Journal of Imperial and Commonwealth History, XV (1987) 2, pp. 148-169; see also D. Killingray and R.J.A.R. Rathbone (eds.), Africa and the Second World War, Basingstoke 1986, p. 14, and A. Harneit-Sievers, Zwischen Depression und Dekolonization: Afrikanische Händler und Politik in Süd-Nigeria, 1935-1954, Saarbrücken/Fort Lauderdale 1991, pp. 198-209.

2   PRO: CO 882, file 650/14, Colonial Office memorandum 'British Colonial Exports, 1939-1945' by F.V. Meyer, Aug. 1946, p. 8; see also M. Cowen/N.J. Westcott, British Imperial Economic Policy during the War, in: D. Killingray/R.J.A.R. Rathbone (eds.), Africa and the Second World War, Basingstoke 1986, pp. 20-67.

3   D. J. Morgan, The Official History of Colonial Development, London 1980, vol. II, pp. 4 and 15-16; see also PRO: CO 852, file 1000/3, Address delivered by the Hon. Sir Stafford Cripps to the African Governor's Conference, 12 Nov. 1947.

4   S. Strange, Sterling and British Policy: A Political Study of an International Currency in Decline, London 1971, p. 70.

5   O. Fajana, Import Licensing in Nigeria, in: Development and Change, VIII (1977) 4, p. 516.

6   C. Leubuscher, Bulk-Buying from the Colonies: A Study of the Bulk Purchase of Colonial Commodities by the United Kingdom, London 1956, p. 68; see also H.D. Hall/C.C. Wrigley, Studies of Overseas Supply, London 1956, pp. 299-311.

7   PRO: MAF 75/31, Ministry of Agriculture and Fisheries, Official History: Control of Raw Cocoa, n.d. (1950), pt. I, p. 6.

8   J.M. Lee, 'Forward Thinking' and War. The Colonial Office during the 1940s, in: Journal of Imperial and Commonwealth History, VI (1977) 1, p. 65; Leubuscher, Bulk Buying from the Colonies, p. 69.

9   J. Kent, Regionalism or Territorial Autonomy? The Case of British West African Development, 1939-1949, in: Journal of Imperial and Commonwealth History, XVIII (1990) 1, pp. 62-72.

10   Rhodes House Library Oxford, J.R. Mackie Papers, Mss. Afr. s823 vol.III, p. 20, Circular from the Chief Officer to the Government to all Administrative Officers, M.P. No. 39281, 6 Feb. 1942.

11   J.A. Cross, Lord Swinton, Oxford 1982, p. 233.

12   Ibid.; see also F. Kent, Regionalism, pp. 61-80, and R.D. Pearce, Sir Bernard Bourdillon: The Biography of a Twentieth-Century Colonialist, Oxford 1987, pp. 299-303.

13   For details on Lord Swinton's (his earlier name was Sir Philip Cunliffe-Lister) professional career, see Cross, Lord Swinton, p. 225.

14   J. Shuckburgh, Colonial Civil History of the War, unpublished Colonial Office ms., deposited at the Institute of Commonwealth Studies Library, London 1946, Vol. III, p. 22; see also J.H. Bowden, Development and Control in British Colonial Policy, with Reference to Nigeria and the Gold Coast, 1935-1948, University of Birmingham Ph.D. thesis, Birmingham 1980, p. 143.

15   See PRO: CO 852, file 432/1, Memorandum 'Production Programme' by Resident Minister, 17 July 1942.

16   M. Perham (ed.), The Native Economies of Nigeria, being Vol.I. of Economics of a
      Tropical Dependency, London 1946, p. 13.
17   Shuckburgh, Colonial Civil History, pp. 92-96.
18   J. Mars, Extra-Territorial Enterprises, in: M. Perham, Economics of a Tropical
      Dependency, Vol.II, London 1948, pp. 103-113.
19   NAI: NL/F1. Address by the Governor to the Legislative Council, 4 Dec. 1939; see
      also the wireless address by the Secr. of State for the Colonies, R. MacDonald, to the
      Colonies, reprinted in: West Africa, 21 Oct. 1939, p. 1423.
20   PRO: CO 854, file 117, Circular Telegram from the Secr. of State for the Colonies to
      all Colonies, 5 June 1940.
21   PRO: CO 854, file 117. Circular Telegram from the Secr. of State for the Colonies to
      all Colonies, 5 June 1940.
22   Despatch by the Secretary of State for the Colonies to the Colonial Governments
      regarding certain aspects of Colonial Policy in war-time, Cmd. 6299, London 1941,
      para. 1. The full despatch was reprinted in the monthly journal The West African
      Review, July 1941, pp. 12-15, and in the weekly journal West Africa, 23 Aug. 1941,
      pp. 815-816, and 30 Aug. 1941, p. 839. The new policy was not completely uncritically
      welcomed by the informed press. The journal West Africa, for example, coined the
      memorable phrase that 'Belt-tightening is doubtless a necessity in war-time, but it is
      doubly hard to bear if there are no belts to tighten.' See West Africa, 13 Sept. 1941,
      p. 894.
23   Despatch by the Secretary of State for the Colonies to the Colonial Governments
      regarding certain aspects of Colonial Policy in war-time, Cmd. 6299, London 1941,
      para. 3.
24   Ibid., para. 5.
25   Ibid., para. 3 and para. 12.
26   Ibid., para. 8.
27   PRO: CO 852, file 650/14, Colonial Office memorandum 'British Colonial Exports,
      1939-1945', Appendix A: 'A short note on the Machinery of Import Control in the
      Colonies during the War' by F.V. Meyer, Aug. 1946, p. 48.
28   Despatch of the Secretary of State for the Colonies to the Colonial Governments
      regarding certain aspects of Colonial Policy in war-time, London 1941, para. 8 and
      para. 11.
29   Ibid., para. 13 and para. 18; see also Shuckburgh, Colonial Civil History of the War,
      vol.IV, p. 10. This document has not yet received the merit it deserves in the second-
      ary literature. It was, after all, the origin of the Nigerian ten-years development plan
      of 1946.
30   Cited in: R.D. Pearce, Sir Bernard Bourdillon, p. 204.
31   NAI: CSO 26 38300, file S46, Minute by J.F. Hall, 19 Jan. 1943; see also Shuckburgh,
      Colonial Civil History, p. 222.
32   J.S. Coleman, Nigeria: Background to Nationalism, Berkeley 1958, p. 254.
33   See D. Souter, Labour Policy in Nigeria During the Second World War and Conscrip-
      tion for the Nigerian Tin-Mining Industry, paper presented at the Conference on
      Africa and the Second World War, School of Oriental and African Studies, May 1984.
34   A. Nwabughuogu, Political Change, Social Response and Economic Development:
      The Dynamics of Change in Eastern Nigeria, 1930-1950, Madison/Wis. 1979, p. 253.
35   PRO: CO 852, file 514/1, Telegram from the Governor of Nigeria to the Secr. of State
      for the Colonies, 3 March 1943.

36   Nai: Oyo Prof 2/3, file C234 Vol.II, Report by T.A. Shankland, SDO Ibadan Division, Restrictions on the purchase of kernels, 12 Mar. 1941.

37   NAI: Oyo Prof 2/3, file C 234 Vol.II, Petition signed by the Traders', Scalers' and Women Traders' Union, 4 March 1941; see also O. Awolowo, Awolowo: The Autobiography of Chief Obafemi Awolowo, Cambridge 1960, pp. 125-130; id., Path to Nigerian Freedom, London 1947, p. 74.

38   The history of the war effort in Nigeria also had in its comical side in retrospect. Jenkins reports that during the war Ibadan was divided into thirteen sections with proper wardens and assistant wardens in each of the sections. Each section had its own air-raid post which was supplied with tretchers and a first aid kid. In addition schools were equipped with cutlasses, pickaxes, sand and water buckets. Even special ladders and warning sirens were ordered from the United Kingdom, though Jenkins does not state whether they ever arrived in Ibadan or not. It does not seem very likely that this exercise served any other purpose than providing a moral uplift to the inhabitants of Ibadan. See Jenkins, Politics in Ibadan, North-Western University PH.D. thesis, Madison/Wis. 1965, pp. 274-276.

39   PRO: CO 852, file 525/6, Colonial Office memorandum 'Palm kernel production in Nigeria', 1 July 1943.

40   Enquiry into the Cost of Living and the Control of the Cost of Living in the Colony and Protectorate of Nigeria (Tudor Davies Commission Report), Co. No. 204, Sessional Paper No. 6 of 1945, HMSO, London 1946, p. 12; see also West Africa, 7 Nov. 1942, p. 1081, and 21 Nov. 1942, p. 1131; Pearce, Sir Bernard Bourdillon, pp. 270-71, and W. Ananaba, The Trade Union Movement in Nigeria, Benin 1969, pp. 47-63.

41   Coleman, Nigeria: Background to Nationalism, pp. 255-259.

42   This argument was first implicitly advanced by Coleman, Nigeria, Background to Nationalism, p. 259; see also NAI: CSO 26 40303, file S1, Minutes of the Fifth Meeting of the Supply and Production Committee, 19/20 May 1943.

43   See PRO: CO 882, file 497/1, Despatch by the Secr. of State for the Colonies to the Governors of Nigeria, Gold Coast, Sierra Leone and the Gambia, 15 Aug. 1941. This section of the chapter draws heavily on an article by Meyer Fortes, who was in Nigeria and the Gold Coast during the war. See M. Fortes, The Impact of the War on British West Africa, in: International Affairs, XXI (1945), p. 206-219.

44   For more details, see A. Harneit-Sievers, Zwischen Depression and Dekolonisation: Afrikanische Händler und Politik in Süd-Nigeria, 1935-1954, Universität Hannover Ph.D. thesis, Hannover 1989, pp. 226-257.

45   PRO: CO 852, file 495/1, Note Submitted by the Association of West African Merchants on the Problem of Supplying the British West African Colonies, 24 Nov. 1941.

46   The Sterling balances of the West African currency board were the Sterling equivalent of all British West African currencies in circulation. Between 1939 and 1945 the Sterling balances of the West African Currency Board increased from about £12m to about £29.5m. The amount of money in circulation in Nigeria increased at the same time from £5,856,537 on the 31 March, 1939 to £15,386,109 on the 31 March 1945. See Prest, War Economics of Primary Producing Countries, p. 252, and PRO: CO 657/69, Annual Report for the Year 1948, p. 31; see also W.T. Newlyn and D.C. Rowan, Money and Banking in West Africa, London 1954, pp. 163-164.

47   Rhodes House Library Oxford, A. Creech-Jones Papers, Mss. Brit. Empire s332. Report of the Working Party on Colonial Sterling Balances, 1 Aug. 1946; for details on the import prices and import volume of textile piece goods, see United Africa Company, in: Statistical and Economic Review, 12 (1953), pp. 32-36.

48   P.T. Bauer, West African Trade, Cambridge 1954, p. 410.
49   The reports of the two committees set up during and immediately after the war to inquire into pay and cost of living increases in Nigeria are not very helpful in this respect, since both used import prices as the basis for the calculation of cost of living increases. See Report... to consider the rate of pay of labour and of African government servants and employees in the township of Lagos (H.F.B. Bridges Report), Lagos 1942, p. 8; and Enquiry into the Cost of Living and the Control of the Cost of Living in the Colony and Protectorate of Nigeria, op. cit., p. 87. The Tudor Davies Commission estimated that by October 1945 the cost of living had increased by 175% (!), taking 1939 as the base year.
50   Enquiry into the Cost of Living and the Control of the Cost of Living in the Colony and Protectorate of Nigeria, op. cit., appendix VI, p. 123.
51   Shuckburgh, Colonial Civil History of the War, p. 437.
52   Ibid., p. 143; see also Prest, War Economics of Primary Producing Countries, p. 256, and Fajana, Import licensing in Nigeria, p. 249.
53   Prest, War Economics of Primary Producing Countries, p. 256.
54   W. Oyemakinde, The Pullen Marketing Scheme - A Trial in Food Price Control in Nigeria, 1941 - 1947, in: Journal of the Historical Society of Nigeria, VI (1973) 4, pp. 413-423; see also Prest, War Economics of Primary Producing Countries, p. 257.
55   Oyemakinde, The Pullen Marketing Scheme, pp. 418-420.
56   Shuckburgh, Colonial Civil History of the War, p. 437.
57   This expression can be found in NAI: CSO 26 40303, file S1, Telegram from the Resident Minister to the Secr. of State for the Colonies, 12 Apr. 1943.
58   PRO: CO 657, file 56, Annual Report for the Year 1945 (Western Provinces), 18 June 1946, p. 26.
59   Nigerian Gazette, Government Notice No. 1045, 19 Sept. 1941.
60   Shuckburgh, Colonial Civil History of the War, pp. 310-311.
61   See PRO: CO 852, file 444/1, Reply by His Majesty's Government to Memorandum of the Cocoa Sub-Committee, 22 May 1941.
62   V.D. Wickizer, Coffee, Tea and Cocoa. An Economic and Political Analysis, Stanford 1951, pp. 278, 344 and 449.
63   Statutory Rules and Orders No. 1458 of 1940, The Raw Cocoa (West African)(Maximum Prices) Order, 1940, of 9 Aug. 1940, cited in: PRO: MAF 87/25, Official History of the Ministry of Food (Control of Raw Cocoa), Sept. 1950, p. 2.
64   Statutory Rules and Orders No. 865 of 1941, The Raw Cocoa (Control) Order, 1941, of 18 June 1941, cited in: PRO: MAF 87/25, Official History of the Ministry of Food (Control of Raw Cocoa), Sept. 1950, p. 5.
65   Leubuscher, Bulk Buying from the Colonies, p. 23.
66   PRO: CO 852, file 431/2, West African Produce Control Board memorandum 'Sale Prices to the Ministry of Food', annexure II, 26 Nov. 1942; see also appendix, table A.
67   PRO: CO 852, file 445/1, letter from G.F. Peaker (Treasury) to S. Caine, 11 July 1941.
68   PRO: CO 852, file 444/3, West African Cocoa Control Board, Draft Minutes of Meeting, 8 Sept. 1941; see also PRO: CO 852, file 431/2, Letter from E.C. Tansley to C.Y. Carstairs, 13 Nov. 1942.
69   PRO: CO 852, file 533/8, West African Produce Control Board, Policy Paper No. 7, 26 Nov. 1942.
70   PRO: CO 852, file 529/7, Letter from G.F. Peaker (Treasury) to E.C. Tansley, 27 May 1943.

71   Report on Cocoa Control in West Africa, 1939-1943, and Statement of Future Policy, Cmd. 6554 of Sept. 1944, London 1944, p. 8.

72   PRO: CO 852, file 525/6, West African Produce Control Board, memorandum 'Cocoa', No. 14, 4 June 1943.

73   In 1943/44 the West African Produce Control Board received £30 13s 9d per ton and in 1944/45 £31 8s 9d per ton. All prices quoted in this chapter are Lagos/Accra f.o.b. prices. See PRO: CO 852, file 595/2, Memorandum 'West African Cocoa Prices' by T.A. Noyes and D.H. Sayer (Ministry of Food), 30 Nov. 1945; for a different price series, see P.T. Bauer, West African Trade. A Study of Competition, Oligopoly and Monopoly in a Changing Economy, Cambridge 1954, p. 397.

74   PRO: CO 852, file 595/1, West African Produce Control Board, Minute of 18th Meeting, n.d. (1945).

75   In the negotiations between the board and the Ministry of Food the U.S. ceiling price was always converted at the official exchange rate. Since the fixed Sterling exchange rate against the U.S. Dollar at that time highly overvalued Sterling, this method of calculation ensured that the Ministry purchased cocoa more cheaply than it would have been able to do under a regime of free convertibility. See Bauer, West African Trade, p. 248.

76   Leubuscher, Bulk Buying from the Colonies, p. 23; see also PRO: CO 852, file 569/1. Note on a meeting held at the Treasury, 20 Nov. 1946.

77   PRO: CO 852, file 533/8; West African Produce Control Board, Policy Paper No. 7, 26 Nov. 1942. Prices are quoted c.i.f. excluding United Kingdom import duty.

78   PRO: CO 852, file 444/3, Letter from G.F. Peaker to M.L. Lloyd, 20 Dec. 1940.

79   PRO: CO 852, file 533/8, West African Produce Control Board, Policy Paper No. 7, 26 Nov. 1942; see also PRO: CO 852, file 444/3, Report of the Interdepartmental Committee on Food Prices, 12 Oct. 1940.

80   Leubuscher, Bulk Buying in the Colonies, p. 23.

81   These figures were derived by multiplying the volume of the United Kingdom sales of the marketing boards of Nigerian and Gold Coast cocoa by £10 in the period concerned. For detailed figures of United Kingdom cocoa imports between 1939 and 1947, see E. Melville, The marketing of West African Cocoa, in: Cocoa, Chocolate and Confectionery Alliance, Ltd. International Cocoa Conference 1948, London 1949, pp. 96-97, and PRO: MAF 87/27, Memorandum 'Ministry of Food Debate - Raw Cocoa Beans' by G.W. Henlen, 2 June 1944; see also PRO: CO 852, file 445/5, Letter from C.Y. Carstairs to G.F. Peaker, 14 Apr. 1942.

82   PRO: CO 852, file 446/6, Minute by O.G.R. Williams, 2 Oct 1941; See also PRO: CO 852, file 444/3, Minute by S. Caine, 30 Dec 1940; PRO: CO 852, file 445/1, Minutes of Meeting of the West African Cocoa Control Board, 8 Sept. 1941; PRO: CO 852, file 444/3, Letter from S. Caine to E. Melville, 24 Jan. 1941.

83   PRO: CO 852, file 445/6, Letter by C.W.W. Greenidge, Secr. of the Anti-Slavery and Aborigines Protection Society, to the Under-Secr. of State for the Colonies, 3 July 1941. The Society argued that 'consumers in the United Kingdom are receiving preferential treatment at the expense of the West African cocoa growers by reason of the fact that they are the electors of His Majesty's Government, while the growers of raw cocoa in the Colonies are not receiving due considerations by reason of the fact that they are not enfranchised and are unable to articulate their grievances (!).

84   Manchester Guardian, Letter to the Editor by Rita Hinden, Secr. of the Fabian Colonial Bureau, 25 Sept. 1941 and 1 Oct. 1941.

85 Rhodes House Library Oxford, Fabian Colonial Bureau Papers, Mss. Brit. Empire 365, box 52/4, Letter from S. Caine to the Secr. of the Anti-Slavery and Aborigines Protection Society, 18 Oct. 1941.

86 The 'producer price' was the price which farmers and produce traders received in Lagos naked ex-scale. It was usually the price for grade II cocoa, because most cocoa purchased in Nigeria consisted of that grade. It is important to emphasise that the producer price was not the price farmers received up-country, since even if they were selling cocoa at official buying stations, they were charged with the cost of transport and handling. However, the price the farmer ultimately received depended almost exclusively on the Lagos ex-scale marketing board price. In that restricted sense the use of the word producer price or of phrases like 'the price farmers received' are justified.

87 It is noteworthy that the working capital for the marketing scheme in the early war years was actually supplied by the firms and not by the Treasury. The firms received interests of 1 1/2 per cent over bank rate on the money they lent to the government. For such payments of interest see Report on Cocoa Control in West Africa, 1939-1943 and Statement on Future Policy, Cmd. 6554 of Sept. 1944, p. 16; for the item 'interest' in the marketing schedule, see PRO: MAF 75/31, Ministry of Food memorandum 'Colonial Empire Cocoa: Scheme of Control', 3rd revise, schedule N. 1., 16 Feb. 1940.

88 See for an explicit discussion of this point PRO: CO 852, file 533/7, Notes on Sub-Committee Meeting [of the West African Produce Control Board] to Consider the Scope and Functions of the Board, 1 Apr. 1943.

89 See, for example, PRO: CO 852, file 533/8, West African Produce Control Board, Policy Paper No. 2, 30 May 1942.

90 All figures in this chapter regarding the purchase price of main crop cocoa refer to the Lagos naked ex-scale price for grade II cocoa. The light crop figures, however, refer to the Lagos naked ex-scale price of grade I cocoa, since no other grade was purchased.

91 NAI: Ib MinAgric 1, file 17980 Vol.IV, Memorandum 'Recommendations in connection with the continuation of cocoa control in 1940/41', 30 July 1940; see also PRO: CO 852, file 319/3, Minute by E. Melville, 15 June 1940.

92 Rhodes House Library Oxford, Fabian Colonial Bureau Papers, Mss. Brit. Empire 365, box 52/4, Letter from S. Caine to the Secr. of the Anti-Slavery and Aborigines Protection Society, 18 Oct. 1941.

93 PRO: CO 852, file 346/10, Minutes of an Informal Meeting..., 23 July 1940.

94 PRO: CO 852,file 319/3, Telegram from the Secr. of State for the Colonies to the Governor of Nigeria, 15 Aug. 1940.

95 NAI: CSO 26 36148, file S39, Ministry of Food, Meeting to Consider Cocoa Control, 29 May 1940.

96 NAI: CSO 26 36148, file S70, Telegram from the SWP to the CS, 11 Aug. 1941.

97 See, for example, Nigerian Gazette, Government Press Notice No. 1018 of 26 Sept. 1940.

98 See, for example, PRO: CO 852, file 445/1, Letter from F. Samuel (UAC) to E.C. Tansley, 18 June 1941.

99 PRO: CO 852, file 445/1, Letter from G.F.T. Colby to G.W. Henlen, 12 Aug. 1941. The decision not to increase the producer price was taken in a meeting of the West African Cocoa Control Board on the 14 Oct. 1941. See NAI: CSO 26 36148, file S63A, Draft minutes of a meeting held in the Colonial Office, 14 Oct. 1941.

100 NAI: Ib MinAgric 1, file 17980 Vol.V, Letter from A.F. Stoddard for the CS to the SWP, 6 Sept. 1941.

101 PRO: CO 852, file 445/8, Minute by S. Caine, 15 May 1941. After reading this minute the Assistant Under-Secretary of State for the Colonies, G.L.M. Clauson wrote: 'Seen with interest. The suggestion to bank money for the sellers which would be paid after the war is extraordinarily interesting and may will be of great social advantage to the Gold Coast.' Ibid., Minute by G.L.M. Clauson, 15 May 1941. One day earlier, E. Melville wrote a letter to G.N. Farquhar and G.F.T Colby in which he pointed out that an increase in the producer price '...might well start an inflationary boom in the Gold Coast...' and asked them how they would view '...the fixing of the price paid to the growers at the present level for next year with an additional payment of say 1/- a load to a special reserve account to be liquidated after the war. In other words, a scheme of forced saving on the lines adopted in the 1941 Budget...' See PRO: CO 852, file 445/1, Letter from E. Melville to G.N. Farquhar and G.F.T. Colby, 14 May 1941. This quote suggests that the creation of a surplus fund to be used for some undefined benefit of the producer at some distant date in the future was directly related to the war effort.

102 See NAI: CSO 26 36148, file S63A, Draft-minutes of a meeting of the West African Produce Control held in the Colonial Office, 14 Oct. 1941.

103 PRO: CO 852, file 445/5, Letter from E.C. Tansley to G.W. Henlen, 26 March 1942.

104 NAI: CSO 26 36148, file S84, Letter from the Chief Commissioner Western Provinces to the CS, 23 Sept. 1942.

105 NAI: CSO 26 36148, file S33 Vol.II, Telegram from the Governor of Nigeria to the Secr. of State for the Colonies, 2 May 1942.

106 NAI: CSO 26 36148, file S84, Minute by G.F.T. Colby, 24 Dec. 1941.

107 These arguments are most clearly set out in a long minute by the Cocoa Controller. See NAI: Ib MinAgric 1, file 17980 Vol.VI, Minute by G.F.T. Colby, 20 July 1942; see also PRO: CO 852, file 525/6, Colonial Office memorandum 'Palm Kernel Production in Nigeria', 1 July 1943, and NAI: CSO 26 36148, file S84, Letter from the Governor of Nigeria to the Resident Minister West Africa, 1 May 1943.

108 NAI: CSO 36148, file S84, Minute by G.F.T. Colby, 20 July 1942, and PRO: CO 852, file 650/5, Letter from G.F. Peaker to W.L.B. Monson, 8 March 1945.

109 PRO: CO 852, file 514/1, Extract from Conclusions of the West African War Council, 28 Jan. 1943.

110 NAI: CSO 26 36148, file S84, Minute by G.F.T. Colby, 20 July 1942.

111 NAI: Ib MinAgric 1, file 17980 Vol.VI, Letter from the SWP to the CS, 29 July 1942.

112 See NAI: Ib MinAgric I, file 17980 Vol.VI, Letter from the SWP to the CS 29 July 1942.

113 NAI: CSO 26 36148, file S 84, Minute by G.F.T. Colby, 10 Aug. 1942.

114 The destruction of cocoa became more and more politically unacceptable in Britain. There were even plans to substitute cocoa for tea in British factories. See PRO: CO 852, file 444/1, Minute by C.Y. Carstairs, 30 Nov. 1942. Cocoa as a beverage was however introduced in the collieries in Eastern Nigeria. From January 1943 miners received free cocoa drinks. Considering the number of drinks they consumed (up to September 1943 some 64.000 drinks), cocoa cannot have been very popular. See Holt Papers, Mss. Afr. s825, file 535 (II), Memorandum 'Hot Cocoa Drinks in the Colliery' by G.N. Farquar, 26 Oct. 1943.

115 NAI: CSO 26 36148, file S33, Letter to all Residents, to the Secretary Western Provinces, to the Secretary Eastern Provinces and the Director of Agriculture, 5 Oct. 1942.

116   PRO: CO 852, file 514/1, Telegram from the Secr. of State for the Colonies to the
      Resident Minister West Africa, 3 March 1943; see also ibid., Extract from the Minutes
      of the West African War Council Meeting, 9 Mar. 1943, and NAI: Oyo Prof 2/3, file
      C 234 Vol.III, Letter from the SWP to all Residents, 11 March 1943.
117   Rhodes House Library Oxford, J.R. Mackie Papers, Mss. Afr. s823, file 4, Letter from
      B. Bourdillon to J.R. Mackie, 14 May 1943.
118   PRO: CO 852, file 525/5, West African Produce Control Board, minutes of meeting,
      21 July 1943; see also NAI: CSO 26 36148, file S84, Letter from the Governor of
      Nigeria to the Resident Minister West Africa, 21 June 1943. In this letter Governor
      Bourdillon indicated that he changed his mind about the reciprocal relationship
      between cocoa prices and palm kernel production after having read a report from the
      Palm Kernel Controller R.L.V. Wilkes from early June 1943. This report can be found
      in PRO: CO 852, file 512/8, Report on cocoa and palm kernel prices by R.L.V. Wilkes,
      June 1943.
119   NAI: CSO 26 36148, file S84, Letter from the Governor of Nigeria to the Resident
      Minister West Africa, 1 May 1940.
120   NAI: CSO 26 36148, file S10, Note on a discussion of the West African War Council
      by G.G.T. Colby, 13 Dec 1943.
121   Their demands were first formally raised in a meeting of a West African War Coun-
      cil. See NAI: CSO 26 36148, file S84, West African War Council, Civil Members
      Committee, Memorandum 'Gold Coast Cocoa: Future Price' by E.C. Tansley and G.H.
      Creasy, 12. Jan. 1944.
122   NAI: Ib MinAgric 1, file 17980 Vol.VI, West African War Council, Civil Members
      Committee, Minutes of the 36th Meeting, 14 Jan.1944.
123   NAI: Ib MinAgric 1, file 17980 Vol.IV, Telegram from the Governor of Nigeria to the
      Secr. of State for the Colonies, 14 Feb. 1944. He was supported in this position by his
      advisers G.F.T. Colby and G.N. Farquhar. See PRO: CO 852, file 595/1, Letter from
      A. Richards to G.H. Creasy, 24 April 1944.
124   PRO: CO 852, file 630/7, West African Produce Control Board, Minutes of 18th
      Meeting, 23 Feb. 1944.
125   PRO: CO 852, file 630/7, West African Produce Control Board, Minutes of 20th
      Meeting, 17 May 1944.
126   For a list of arguments which the colonial governments should have considered in
      fixing the producer price, see PRO: CO 852, file 595/1, Telegram from the Secr. of
      State for the Colonies to the Governors of the Gold Coast and Nigeria, 29 Feb. 1944.
127   PRO: CO 852,file 444/4, Memorandum 'Future of Cocoa Supplies' by J. Cadbury, 29
      Nov. 1941; see also NAI: CSO 26, file 39313, Circular Telegram to the Officer Admi-
      nistering the Government of Nigeria, 23 Jan. 1942.
128   NAI: CSO 26 36148, file S84, Minute by G.F.T. Colby, 30 Dec. 1944.
129   PRO: CO 852, file 630/11, West African Produce Control Board, Minutes of Meeting,
      13 June 1945.
130   PRO: CO 852, file 630/11, West African Produce Control Board, Memorandum
      'Cocoa Prices 1945/46 Season', 13 June 1945.
131   PRO: CO 852, file 630/11, Memorandum 'Cocoa Schemes of Control, 1945/46 Buying
      Prices', n.d. (August 1945); see also ibid., West African Produce Control Board,
      Memorandum 'Nigerian Palm Produce', October 1945, and NAI: CSO 26, file 36148
      S73A Vol.I, Minute by F. Beresford-Stooke, Report on a visit to the Gold Coast,
      17 Feb. 1945.

132 PRO: CO 852, file 597/4, Telegram from the Secr. of State for the Colonies to the Governor of Nigeria, 18 Sept. 1945; see also PRO: CO 852, file 630/11, West African Produce Control Board, Minutes of Meeting, 4 Oct. 1945.

133 PRO: CO 852, file 595/3, Letter from the Governors' Deputy to the Secr. of State for the Colonies, 24 Sept. 1946. See also PRO: CO 852, file 596/5. Letter from A. Richards to Sir G. Gater, 1 March 1946.

134 PRO: CO 852, file 595/3, Letter from the Acting Governor of the Gold Coast to E. Melville, 5 Sept. 1946.

135 PRO: CO 852 595/3, Telegram from the Governor's Deputy to the Secr. of State for the Colonies, 24 Sept. 1946.

136 Ibid.

137 Bauer, West African Trade, p. 397.

138 PRO: CO 852, file 596/5, Letter from A. Richards to Sir G. Gater, 1 March 1946.

139 PRO: CO 852, file 595/3, Telegram from the Secr. of State for the Colonies to the Officer Administering the Government of the Gold Coast, 20 Sept. 1946. The money which was made available to the Gold Coast Legislative Council for educational expenditure amounted to £900,000. See PRO: CO 852, file 904/1, Colonial Office memorandum 'Disposal of Trading Profits from British West African Cocoa', Apr. 1948.

140 PRO: CO 852, file 596/5, Letter from S. Caine to G.H. Creasy, 21 Oct. 1946.

141 The reasons for the low purchase price policy of the marketing board were explicitly and extensively discussed in the 1944 White Paper, yet they were not examined in the wider perspective of the war effort. See Report on Cocoa Control in West Africa, 1939-1943, and Statement on Future Policy, Cmd. 6554, London 1944, paras. 25-28.

142 The policy of favouring wage earners was strongly criticised by the Resident Oyo Province T.M. Shankland. See NAI: Ib MinAgric 1, file 17980 Vol.IV, Letter from the Resident Oyo Province to the CS, 8 March 1942.

143 On this aspect of the produce control scheme see, for example, the revealing comment by E. Melville, Control of production as distinct from exports was never contemplated for British West Africa except in so far as this can be brought about by control of price paid to producers..., in: PRO: CO 852, file 444/1, Teleprint message from E. Melville to S. Caine, 11 Feb. 1941.

144 This section of the chapter has much profited from the writings of N. Westcott, for example his contribution 'Stabilising Commodity Prices: State Control of Colonial Commodity Trade, 1930-1950', in: C. Dewey, The State and the Market: Studies in the Economic and Social History of the Third World, New Delhi 1988, pp. 262-287.

145 For purchases of palm kernels in the Western Provinces see Galletti et al., Nigerian Cocoa Farmers, Oxford 1956, appendix table XIII, p. 634. There was no overall increase in the volume of palm kernel production in the Western Provinces during the war and indeed in most areas production declined.

146 See G.I Guyer, Food, Cocoa, and the Division of Labour by Sex in Two West African Societies, in: Comparative Studies in Society and History, XXII (July 1980) 3, pp. 355-373.

147 PRO: CO 852, file 512/8, Report on Cocoa and Palm Kernel prices by R.L.V. Wilkes, Deputy Controller of Palm Kernels, June 1943; see also NAI: CSO 26 36148, file S84, Letter from the Deputy Cocoa Controller to the CS, 11 June 1943.

148 The Deputy Controller put forward the argument about the futility of attempting to change production of palm kernels by lowering cocoa prices as early as June 1942. See NAI: CSO 26 36148, file S84, Letter from the Deputy Cocoa Controller to the CS, 11

June 1942; see also PRO: CO 852, file 630/4, Report by G.H. Creasy and E.C. Tansley to the Secr. of State for the Colonies, 9 Feb. 1943; Annexure VI: Report on a Meeting of the Supply and Production Committee of the West African War Council, held at Lagos on 29 Dec. 1943.
For the ignorance among some government officials regarding basic features of the West African farmers' economy, see, for instance, E. Melville note on the subject of saving habits among Africans: 'The conception of savings has unfortunately been one of slow growth in West Africa and it is fairly certain that, so long as he can do so, the African will spend the cash he gets from his export crop, after paying any Government taxes which he cannot avoid, on a few yards of cloth for his fifth wife or a bottle of gin for his great uncle's funeral...' See PRO: CO 852, file 497/1, Note on West African Produce Prices by E. Melville, April 1941.

149   PRO: CO 852, file 904/1, Colonial Office memorandum 'Disposal of Trading Profits from British West African Cocoa', April 1948.

150   Enquiry into the Cost of Living and the Control of the Cost of Living in the Colony and Protectorate of Nigeria (Chairmen T. Davies), Sessional Paper No. 6 of 1945, London 1946, appendix VI, Memorandum by the Director of Supplies, pp. 121-128.

151   NAI: CSO 26, file 41646, Minute by H.F. Marshall, 8 Oct. 1943.

152   PRO: CO 657/56, Annual Report for the Northern, Western and Eastern Provinces and the Colony for the Year 1944, May 1945, pp. 18-22. This report is very explicit on the relationship between wage rates, cocoa harvesting and the outbreak of diseases. See also ibid., Annual Report on the Western Provinces of Nigeria for the Year 1945, May 1946, p. 28; for a statement to the contrary, see S.S. Berry, Cocoa, Custom and Socio-Economic Change in Rural Western Nigeria, Oxford 1975, p. 144.

153   NAI: Ib MinAgric 1, file 17980 Vol.IV, Letter from the SWP to the CS, 29 July 1942.

154   PRO: CO 852, file 595/1, Letter from the Director of Agriculture to the CS, 12 Aug. 1944; see also NAI: Ib MinAgric 1, file 17980 Vol.VI, Memorandum 'Notes on the Cocoa Industry' by the Director of Agriculture, 27 Jan. 1944.

155   PRO: CO 852, file 597/4, Extract from Minutes of West African Produce Control Board Meeting, 9 March 1945.

156   PRO: CO 631/1, Report to the Secr. of State for the Colonies by G.H. Creasy and E.C. Tansley, 9 Feb. 1944; see also PRO: CO 852, file 595/1, Letter from G.H. Creasyto Sir George Gater, 17 Jan. 1944, and PRO: CO 852, file 595/1, Letter from the Secr. of the West African Produce Control Board to the Secr. of State for the Colonies, 6 Jan. 1944. For a discussion of the problem by the trading firms, see Holt Papers, Mss. Afr. s825, file 535(II), Minutes of the Meeting of the Cocoa Sub-Committee of the Association of West African Merchants, 16 Feb. 1944.

157   Galletti et al., Nigerian Cocoa Farmers, p. 216; see also NAI: Ib MinAgric 1, file 17980 Vol.IV, Letter from the Agricultural Officer Oyo-Ondo Province to the CS, Dec. 1943.

158   NAI: Ib MinAgric 1, file 17980 Vol.VI, Memorandum 'Notes on the Cocoa Industry' by the Director of Agriculture, 27 Jan. 1944; see also Holt Papers, Mss. Afr. s825, file 535(II), Ondo Report, 12 July 1944 and 16 Jan. 1945.

159   Holt Papers, Mss. Afr. s825, file 421B Vol.III, Letter from the Director of John Holt & Co. Ltd., D.L. Rawlings, to J. Mars, 4 Aug. 1944.

CHAPTER 7

The Establishment of the Post-War Marketing Board

Discussions about post-war marketing policy began almost immediately after the establishment of the West African Cocoa Control Board in 1940 and reached an interim conclusion in 1944 with the publication of a White Paper *Report on Cocoa Control in West Africa,1939-1943, and Statement of Future Policy*, Cmd. 6554 of Sept. 1944. Popular reaction to the proposed establishment of the marketing organisations, notably from the merchant firms, cocoa manufacturers and African traders and farmers, delayed the introduction of the scheme for two years and it became necessary to publish another White Paper (*Statement on the Future Marketing of West African Cocoa*, Cmd. 6950 of Nov. 1946). The Nigerian Cocoa Marketing Board finally took over the responsibility for Nigerian cocoa marketing from the West African Produce Control Board in October 1947.

Post-War Planning: Some Basic Features

The institutional origin of the post-war marketing scheme was the West African Cocoa Control Board which the Colonial Office set up in October 1940. It had six members: the Parliamentary Under-Secretary of State for the Colonies *G. H. Hall* (Chairman)[1], the Assistant Secretary and head of the West Africa area department of the Colonial Office *O.G.R. Williams* (Vice-Chairman), the Financial Adviser to the Secretary of State for the Colonies and head of the Economic Department of the Colonial Office *S. Caine* (replaced by *G.H. Creasy* and later by *C.Y. Carstairs*), the Director of Cadbury Brothers Ltd. and Cocoa Controller in the Ministry of Food *J.Cadbury* (in private capacity), the former head of the Cocoa Department of the United Africa Company and designated Marketing Director of the scheme *E.C. Tansley* and the Assistant Cocoa Controller in the Ministry of Food and designated Secretary to the board *E. Melville* (replaced in August 1941 by *G.W. Henlen*). Two additional members were later appointed to the board in 1940 and 1941. The choice fell on *G.H. Findlay*, a former Resident in Southern Nigeria, and Capt. *C.C. Lilley*, who had previously held the post of District Commissioner in the Gold Coast.

The West African Cocoa Control Board was reconstituted in 1942 as the West African Produce Control Board and its membership enlarged to include two commercial representatives and a further Nigerian government representative: *G.B. Spry* of Frank Fehr & Company, *H.B. Balmfourth* of the Co-operative Wholesale Society and *A.J. Findlay*, a former Deputy Director of Agriculture in Nigeria, all of whom had special experience in the oilseeds trade. In addition, a second Secretary, *W.L. Bloomfield*, was appointed to the board.

The definition of a post-war policy largely fell to the permanent official members of the board (in particular on J. Cadbury, S. Caine, G.H. Creasy, C.Y. Carstairs, E.C. Tansley, G.W. Henlen and W.L. Bloomfield). They collaborated with other Colonial Office officials like G.L.M. Clauson and had also to consult other government departments (for example the Treasury), government ministers (in particular the Resident Minister), and the colonial governments in West Africa.

The European firms did not directly participate in the policy making process. This is somewhat surprising, since in 1940 the influence of the firms seemed to have reached its peak. All important decisions regarding the forthcoming 1940/41 season were made in informal meetings between representatives of the Ministry of Food, the Colonial Office and the Cocoa Sub-Committee of the Association of West African Merchants, which included such items as the determination of the producer price, the distribution of the trade between exporters and the fixing of the buying schedule.[2] Since all important issues were discussed with the Association, and also with two leading representatives of the Association in commanding positions in the control scheme (J. Cadbury and E.C. Tansley), the future seemed to be rosy for the firms.

But in many respects the Association lost its influence after the 1940/41 season: the Marketing Director of the West African Cocoa Control Board, E.C. Tansley, was no longer a United Africa Company employee. At the beginning of the 1940/41 season he was directly employed by the West African Cocoa Control Board and, subsequently, seemed to have regarded himself primarily as a public servant. The same appears to be true for J. Cadbury. There is no direct evidence in archival files that Tansley or Cadbury were more predisposed in discussions about the future shape of the marketing scheme towards European firms or the United Africa Company than other colonial officials.

Both E.C. Tansley and J. Cadbury were extremely knowledgeable as regards the cocoa trade in general and the trading practices of the firms in particular, and made this knowledge available to the Colonial Office. The firms therefore lost one of their structural advantages, technical expertise, vis-à-vis the government. Moreover, since the marketing scheme generated a large surplus in the 1940/41 cocoa season, the dependence on the firms' capital declined and increasingly a larger proportion of the working capital of the marketing scheme was provided by the Board itself, rather than borrowed from the firms. Finally, the policies which later became known as the 'war effort' strengthened the role of government in colonial economies.

In the 1930s, colonial governments in West Africa had by and large favoured a 'laissez-faire' attitude towards the economy. But during the war, under the pressure of the war effort, the sphere of government activity became increasingly enlarged, particularly in the field of colonial trade. The partial control of the economy allowed government to become more active and interventionist and opened up the opportunity to initiate policies.

The new approach towards the economy inevitably changed the relationship between the colonial authorities and the European trading firms. This is clearly shown by the fact that European trading firms were no longer regarded as appropriate partners for consultation. They were still involved in the day-to-day running of the war-time control scheme (and were therefore able to successfully promote their own immediate interests), but were largely excluded from the making of post-war marketing policies. This, with the notable exception of J. Cadbury, was even true for the commercial members of the Control Board. When, after three years of internal discussions, the post-war marketing scheme was presented to the public, the European firms were in effect faced with a 'fait accompli'. The development of the post-war marketing policy was thus primarily a government affair.

The participants in the planning process of the future marketing scheme believed that they should address two problems at the same time: one was to solve some of the problems which had emerged in the cocoa trade in the recent past; the other was to solve some of the economic problems which were expected to develop after the war, including those problems which might appear in the cocoa trade or in colonial trade in general. Thus the shape of the future marketing scheme depended to a considerable extent on how those government officials who were engaged in the planning of the scheme viewed the recent past and what kind of post-war world they envisaged.

The Origins of the Discussion about Post-War Control

In the previous chapter it was shown that the 1940/41 cocoa season had ended with a large profit to the West African Cocoa Control Board and that the price in the subsequent season was not restored to its 1939/40 level in order to reduce the consumption of imported goods and to combat inflation. This policy meant that the Board's surplus would inevitably increase over time. This prompted the officials involved in the cocoa marketing scheme to reassess the position and function of the Board and to address the question of what should eventually be done with these profits.

The discussion about post-war implications of the producer price policy was initiated in May 1941.[3] According to a memorandum by E.C. Tansley, the fundamental decision which members of the Board had to make was either to increase the buying price or to increase the reserves of the Board.[4] It was in this connection that on 12th June, 1941 another member of the Board, Cadbury, produced another memorandum in which the functions of the Board and its long-term policy were re-appraised.

In order to avoid repetition, J. Cadbury's arguments will be reviewed later in more detail. At this point it is sufficient to emphasise that his memorandum contained most of the crucial arguments which seemed to have convinced the colonial governments in West Africa and the Colonial Office to adopt the war-time marketing scheme as a post-war development scheme.[5]

After an analysis of the pre-war marketing situation and the war-time operations of the scheme in the Gold Coast and in Nigeria up to the date when the memorandum was written, J. Cadbury came to the conclusion that the scheme had worked extremely satisfactorily and that, if desired, it could be used as the basis for a permanent post-war scheme.[6]

On 5th August, 1941, these two memoranda were sent together with a despatch from the Secretary of State for the Colonies to the colonial governments in West Africa with the request for comment. The despatch informed the colonial governments that major changes in the control scheme were being considered by the Colonial Office and asked them for their views on the questions of the desirability of increased produce prices and of enhanced flexibility in the administration of the quota system. The Secretary of State for the Colonies also indicated that the answers to both questions would have an important impact on post-war policies.[7]

After having received the despatch, the Nigerian Secretariat forwarded the despatch and the accompanying memoranda to the Residents in the cocoa producing areas, to the Registrar of Co-operative Societies and to the Director of Agriculture. There was an almost unanimously positive response to the question of the desirability of the adoption of cocoa control as a permanent scheme, though there was some disagreement about the future pricing policy and the question of introducing some degree of flexibility into the quota system.[8]

The responses of the Residents were reaffirmed in memoranda which the Chief Commissioners of the Western and Eastern Provinces and the Chief Commissioner of the Colony subsequently produced, all of which strongly emphasised the advantages of permanent produce control. With regard to the question of increasing the reserves of the West African Cocoa Control Board or increasing the producer price, however, the Chief Commissioners argued that the profits of the Board should be used for developmental purposes, such as cocoa research and for combatting diseases after the war.[9]

The Nigerian government responded to the despatch from the Secretary of State from 5th October, 1941 only on 13th April, 1942. This delay was probably due to the absence of Governor Bourdillon from Nigeria in early 1942. The responding memorandum was actually written by the 'Officer Administering the

Government of Nigeria' at the time, the Governor of the Gold Coast, Sir Alan Burns.[10]

The memorandum strongly supported the idea of a permanent control scheme buying cocoa at fixed seasonal prices. Here for the first time one finds the proposal that local control boards, under the direction of the colonial governments, should be responsible for the administration of the scheme, and in particular, for the licensing of the agents of the Board and fixing of the producer price. It is noteworthy that these proposals later reappeared in the memorandum which the Acting Governor of the Gold Coast wrote in response to the despatch of 5th August, 1941. This suggests that the Nigerian memorandum was probably not written solely with the Nigerian situation in mind.[11]

However, it is likely that the memorandum of 13th April, 1941 represented the opinion of the majority of the administrative officers in the Nigerian service at the time. Although discussion about the shape of the future marketing scheme continued until the actual establishment of the post-war marketing board in 1947, it appears that the desirability of produce control as such was never seriously questioned after 1941. The discussions revealed a virtual consensus about marketing policy; it can be argued that they represented one of the cornerstones in the development of post-war marketing policy.

The Establishment of the West African Produce Control Board

While the future marketing arrangements were debated, another discussion was held within the Colonial Office about the extension of the war-time cocoa control scheme to other crops, notably palm oil and palm kernels. This discussion was again influenced by short- and long-term considerations, since some Colonial Office officials thought that the decisions resulting from this discussion might prejudice the debate about the future marketing arrangements for cocoa.

The discussion about palm produce control started in late September or early October 1941, well before the entry of the United States into the war and the occupation of British Eastern colonies by the Japanese. Its immediate cause was that the Ministry of Food had allowed the United Africa Company to sell some quantities of palm oil and kernels to the United States and to Spain. The company had made an additional profit of about £80,000 on these sales, since oilseed prices in those countries were much higher than in the United Kingdom - in the case of the United States, prices were in fact more than twice as high.[12] The financial results of these sales were known to the Ministry of Food, but it was apparently only due to an unusual intervention of one of its officials (the Financial Director of the Oils and Fats Division, J.C. Gardiner) that the Colonial Office learnt about these profits.[13]

The Colonial Office reacted swiftly with the proposal to extend the cocoa control system to oilseeds (palm oil and kernels, groundnuts, benniseeds). The Ministry of Food had previously purchased all its oilseeds requirements from the Association of West African Merchants, which shared out the trade between its members. The Colonial Office had little influence over either the level of producer prices or over the terms by which members of the Association bought such produce, for instance the rate of remuneration which the firms received for their services. Contracts for the delivery of certain quantities of oilseeds to the Ministry of Food were negotiated between the Ministry's Oilseeds Controller, J. Knight (a Director of the United Africa Company) and the representatives of the Association of West African Merchants, N.V. Deane and F. Samuel (both Directors of the United Africa Company). This arrangement was in the view of the Colonial Office and the Nigerian government highly questionable, not least because of the apparently incestuous relationship between the negotiators.[14]

The Colonial Office believed that the firms had no right to the extra profits made on outside sales. In addition, it was argued that the deteriorating shipping situation might create a bottleneck in West Africa, in which part of the oilseeds crop would not be bought while very high profits were obtainable on the sale of those quantities for which freight space had been found.[15] These arguments were very similar to those previously advanced in order to justify the introduction of the cocoa control scheme in 1939.

The proposal to extend produce control was thus primarily aimed at controlling the local purchase price of oilseeds and at controlling sales and especially profits on sales in outside markets. But the proposal to extend produce control was also made to control the buying and selling activities of the Association of West African Merchants, in particular those of the United Africa Company, and to gain influence over the terms of the contracts between the Association and the Ministry of Food.[16] The Colonial Office argued that an oilseeds board

> ...being for practical purposes under the control of the Secretary of State, would be able to pursue vis à vis the merchants and the shippers that policy that the Secretary of State desires to follow, without having to attempt this task through the possibly disturbing medium of the Ministry [of Food] with its strong U.A.C. element.[17]

It appears therefore that one aspect of the Colonial Office proposal to extend cocoa control system to other crops was the intention to achieve some measure of control over the activities of Ministry of Food and the United Africa Company.

The Colonial Office approached the Ministry of Food and the Treasury with the proposal to extend the cocoa control system to oilseeds in late October 1941. The Ministry accepted the proposal with considerable reluctance in

December 1941.[18] However, it was only in mid-February 1942 that the Nigerian government was formally notified about the impending creation of the West African Produce Control Board, as the combined cocoa and oilseeds board was called. The Nigerian government strongly welcomed the proposal.[19]

The occupation of the Eastern colonies by Japanese forces had meanwhile drastically changed the supply situation for oilseeds. In addition, consumer goods had become increasingly scarce in West Africa. These developments had an immediate impact on the arguments advanced in favour of oilseeds control. The establishment of a control board was no longer justified merely with the argument that it would be desirable to control outside sales. It was now asserted that an oilseed board would help to alleviate the problem of the shortage of consumer goods in West Africa and that it would provide adequate machinery for the handling of inter-allied supplies. In addition it was maintained that the new board could be instrumental in expanding West African export of oilseeds.[20]

It therefore appears that arguments for an oilseed control board, the future West African Produce Control Board, shifted when the changing war situation made this necessary.[21] It was argued that the establishment of an oilseed board would be necessary for the war effort, but it is clear that this was not the original intention when the discussion about the future oilseeds board started.

The establishment of the West African Produce Control Board was, however, not just an extension of the principles of cocoa control to other crops, since at the same time the system itself was reformed. These changes had important long-term implications. In a crucial memorandum of 20 Nov. 1941 E.C. Tansley argued for reform of the marketing system by asserting that

> The longer the war lasts and the further it spreads the more inconceivable a return to the pre-war form of free trade becomes... If Government decides that complete control is to continue after the war, there are good reasons for making changes in the present scheme...[22]

Thus, the importance of these changes lies in the fact that those Colonial Office officials who were involved in the discussions believed that these changes only made sense if produce control was continued after the war. In other words, the fact that these changes were introduced indicates that as early as 1942 some officials were convinced that produce control had come to stay.

The reform of the trading system largely concerned the position of the merchant firms. In 1939 the firms were employed as agents of the Ministry of Food. They purchased, shipped, and sold cocoa on their own account, but had to hand over any profits made on their sales to the controlling authority which was initially the Ministry of Food and then the West African Cocoa Control Board. In the early war years the firms had also provided a large part of the finance for the scheme. In return they received reimbursement of their costs and a profit margin.

The service which the trading firms provided did not involve much work, because since the beginning of the war the United Kingdom oilseed requirements were exclusively purchased by the Ministry of Food. As far as United Kingdom cocoa sales were concerned, the work of the merchants was also considerably simplified as in 1941 the Ministry of Food became the sole buyer of cocoa in Britain. With the entry of the United States into the war in late 1942, a similar development occurred in the North American market, with only the Commercial Credit Corporation allowed to purchase the United States' main raw material requirements, including cocoa and oilseeds. Thus one of the main functions of the merchants - finding a market for produce - almost vanished, as most of the world's production of cocoa and oilseeds was now sold at fixed prices to only two large buyers. Moreover, the deteriorating shipping situation in 1941 had prompted the authorities to introduce bulk shipment and a central system for the allocation of freight space for all major West African commodities.[23] Thus, in the words of one official, a state of affairs developed in which the merchants were doing 'very little for the money they receive'[24].

It was this situation which prompted the proposal to dispense with their services beyond the port of shipment or f.o.b. point: The firms would continue to purchase produce in West Africa, but the sale and transport of such produce would be exclusively effected through the produce board.[25] It was thought that such a reform could achieve considerable savings in manpower and finance in marketing. The proposal of May 1942 was quickly accepted and put into effect. On 24th June, 1942 the reconstitution of the West African Cocoa Control Board as the West African Produce Control Board was publicly announced.[26] Without much debate the former selling agents of the board were thus reduced to the status of licensed buying agents.[27]

It was assumed that the establishment of the West African Produce Control Board would irreversibly change the pre-war market structure. It was felt that after the war British firms would find it exceedingly difficult to rebuilt their businesses against competition from foreign firms once international trade had returned to normal. Because of this, Colonial Office officials argued that the establishment of the West African Produce Control Board was, indirectly, a decision about the permanency of statutory produce control in the post-war period.[28] The decision to dispense with the services of the trading firms beyond the f.o.b. point further indicates that some consensus had developed in the Colonial Office about the permanence of the control scheme. The establishment of the West African Produce Control Board therefore represents another cornerstone in the development of post-war cocoa marketing policy.

The war therefore strongly influenced post-war marketing policy. But this does not explain why the Colonial Office, as well as the West African governments, were so firmly convinced of the merits of produce control in general and cocoa control in particular. This question will be addressed in the next section of this chapter.

The Argument for Post-War Control

The Colonial Office favoured produce control because it thought that statutory marketing would help to solve problems which had emerged in the pre-war West African cocoa trade or which were expected to develop in the West African cocoa trade in the post-war period. These problems concerned producers and intermediaries alike, but it is noticeable that the difficulties of the latter were considered as more important than those of cocoa farmers.

As regards cocoa farmers, it was argued that certain features of the war-time control system, like the fixed price, the certainty of crop disposal and the more 'orderly' marketing system, would afford producers a form of economic security which they had lacked under the pre-war market system.[29] It was also claimed that war-time control would enable farmers to receive a 'fair price', since produce prices were known in advance.[30]

Another argument put forward was that produce control was necessary in order to protect producers from the 'evil' effects of the predicted post-war boom.[31] The basic idea was that acute shortages of all kinds of goods were likely to occur after the war, not least because the long pent-up demand for raw materials and manufactured goods would be finally unleashed onto the markets. Without produce control, the excess demand over supply would cause prices to rise very rapidly, including the prices of West African raw materials, like cocoa and palm products. The incomes of African farmers would therefore also rise very sharply, if production remained at the same level. But this boom would not last: 'The inevitable nemesis of sharply rising prices is falling prices as soon as the excess demand disappears.'[32]

It was thought that the effects of sharply rising and falling incomes in West Africa were socially, as well as politically, highly undesirable.[33] This idea was supported by reference to events after the previous war. The Colonial Office believed that:

> The consequences [of sharply rising produce prices], so far as most Colonial producers at any rate were concerned, were almost wholly evil. In the first stage they received more money than they knew what to do with; much of it was wasted; and exaggerated ideas of the values of their products and numerous expensive tastes were acquired. The high prices of raw materials led to high prices for the articles manufactured for them, which naturally persisted long after the prices of raw materials had fallen. Thus after a brief period of prosperity, Colonial producers entered the ensuing

slump with exaggerated ideas of the market value of their own products, expensive tastes of various kinds, and high prices still to be paid ... for what they wanted to buy. 9) There can be no doubt that if there was any certainty that the result of preventing prices from rising sharply immediately after the war would be to maintain them in the period after the return to normality at a level higher then might be expected if economic forces were left unchecked, a rigid control of prices during the period immediately after the war would be an unmixed blessing. 10) The situation would of course be greatly eased if the Governments holding stocks of primary products were prepared to set aside any profits gained in the boom and use them to supplement the prices paid to producers in the ensuing slump. Indeed it might be well thought wise for the Government to maintain its control of all sales of Colonial produce ... until normality is restored, by buying all such produce itself and reselling it in the same way that all West African cocoa is now bought and resold by the Government. Some rise of price to the producers would of course have to be allowed in order to compensate them for the higher prices which they would have to pay for their requirements; but if any additional profits were earned it would, at any rate in backward places like West Africa, be better to keep them under control and dole them out in the ensuing slump than to let them get prematurely into the hands of the producers.[34]

The crucial argument put forward by the Nigerian government and Colonial Office regarding the intermediaries was that the war-time history of the marketing scheme had shown that the activities of Syrian, African and European trading firms alike could be successfully controlled. For this reason, produce control should be continued in the immediate post-war period.[35]

Some Colonial Office officials, like, for example, O.R.G. Williams even believed that the produce control scheme should be used to achieve more far-reaching aims.[36] They acknowledged that the trading firms and the produce traders would be essential to the scheme in the immediate post-war period, but they thought that after this period it would be possible to dispense completely with their services. The elimination (as opposed to the control) of the trading firms was suggested by Nigerian officials as early as 1941 and by Colonial Office officials as early as 1942.[37] Though it was never publicly admitted, it appears that the complete removal of the intermediaries from the cocoa trade was at one point considered.[38] The Governor of Nigeria, for example, wrote in November 1944 that with produce control properly set up it would be possible after some time to

> ...gradually eliminate all trading interests and to replace them by co-operative societies thereby securing all profits from the produce trade to the farmers who grows them.[39]

These plans came to nothing, but it is important to realise that they were in the back of some officials' minds while planning the post-war scheme. It shows their determination to find a lasting solution to the problems which in the opinion of these officials had beset West African trade in the 1930s. What then, one might legitimately ask, were the problems which prompted the Nigerian government and the Colonial Office even to consider such a radical policy ?

The Nigerian government and Colonial Office officials were arguably most concerned with problems which were deeply-rooted in the social, economic and political fabric of pre-war West African societies. As regards the social position of the African traders, for example, the Chief Commissioner of the Colony wrote:

> My experience of the African exporter and middlemen may have been unfortunate, but such as it is,it has not encouraged the opinion that the general welfare of the producer is encouraged by their existence. They are often wealthy men but one has yet to hear of any of them using their wealth for the good of the community... A further objection to them is the influence they obtain by this wealth and the hidden, and sometimes subversive, uses to which they can put that influence. It would be unwise to eliminate them suddenly but I do not think anything should be done to encourage their continued existence.[40]

It appears therefore that the establishment of the post-war marketing scheme was to some extent a reaction to the emergence of a new type of politically influential and wealthy local trader. The 1930s cocoa trade had offered commission buyers and a small number of African exporters the opportunity to accumulate and to gain a higher status within their communities, both of which they had used extensively to advance their political and economic interests. The planned marketing scheme now promised to arrest and perhaps even reverse this development and thus contained an element of social engineering by attempting to manipulate the material foundations on which some avenues to wealth and status were based.

The second problem of the late 1930s which the marketing scheme might solve was the hostile commercial relationship between the European firms and the African traders.[41] This idea was based on the analysis that the market system of the 1930s was characterised by the dominance of a small number of large European firms, by violent price fluctuations and intensive competition between African traders and the European firms, as well as competition between the European firms themselves. Price fluctuations and the 'abuses' by African traders had prompted the firms to 'combine' in order to preserve their individual, as well as their shared position in the trade. This in turn had created a general atmosphere of deep distrust and hostility towards the European firms and the government which had most clearly emerged in the 1937/38 cocoa hold-up movement in the Gold Coast and in Nigeria.

The alternative to the creation of a marketing scheme was not seen as the resuscitation of a free market system, but as a return to the 1930s trade system and its political difficulties. The choice was - as the Colonial Office argued:

> ...most probably, not between a board and complete freedom of trading, but between control under Government auspices and private arrangements between the merchants themselves.[42]

Since it was thought that buying agreements between the European firms were likely to attract even more political opposition after the war than they had done before the war, there was

> ...no question after the war of an early reversion to the commercial organisation prevailing in the years preceding it. [Because]... that system [had] led to the serious cocoa hold-up of 1937...[43]

These quotes show that the discussions about the marketing scheme had a strong political aspect. The scheme was later mainly justified by the argument that its aim was to prevent the reappearance of excessive fluctuations in producer prices and 'other undesirable features' in the West African cocoa trade.[44] From the records, however, it is clear that the introduction of the post-war scheme was also meant to prevent the reappearance of political unrest. The planning process thus contained apart from anything else a strong element of political engineering by attempting to manipulate expected fields of conflict.[45]

Another set of arguments in favour of post-war control was related to difficulties which had emerged in the British economy during the war. The context of these discussions was that some problems, like the shortage of oilseeds, would certainly not end with the cessation of hostilities and that, moreover, their importance would increase, rather than diminish after the war.[46] War-time policies would therefore last well into the post-war period. It was felt that a marketing scheme would help to regulate the supply of various raw materials[47] and would help to 'maintain some equilibrium between supply and demand'[48]. It was also believed that a control scheme could be used to reduce inflationary pressures on the prices of manufactured goods in the United Kingdom which were certain to increase rapidly after the war.[49]

A further argument was that a marketing scheme might help British firms to adjust to the post-war world. British manufacturing firms had changed their production lines during the war and it was thus very unlikely that they would be able to respond swiftly and adequately to the expected post-war demand for consumer goods from West Africa and elsewhere. In this situation foreign firms would be able to break into markets which had been habitually supplied by

British firms before the war. A marketing scheme would delay demand for consumer goods until such time as British firms were in a position to supply them.[50] Finally, the Ministry of Food had a strong interest in the continuance of the war-time marketing scheme, since it believed that negotiations of bulk purchase agreements and the administration of control schemes in the United Kingdom would be considerably eased if a West African control scheme was set up after the war.[51] In this context it is noteworthy that the Colonial Office strongly favoured international commodity control schemes. Though no definite plans existed at the time, it was argued that marketing boards in West Africa could be used as a basis for such schemes in the future.[52]

The review of the reasons why the Nigerian government and Colonial Office favoured a cocoa marketing scheme suggests that the future statutory bodies were truly multi-purpose boards. Yet, one important reason why there was such an interest in setting up these boards has not been mentioned: the surplus generating capacity of the Board. From the beginning of the discussion about the shape of the future marketing scheme it was obvious that such a scheme had the potential of raising money for developmental undertakings, even if confined to the cocoa industry.[53] It was also expected that the boards would accumulate large balances in the immediate post-war years which would be invested in government stocks.[54] It was thus possible to make money available for the finance of much desired research on cocoa production and marketing in West Africa and, even more importantly, to provide the large working capital for the future Gold Coast and Nigerian marketing boards themselves.[55] In chapter four it was argued that the Nowell Commission had failed to achieve a reform of the marketing of cocoa largely because neither the Treasury, the Colonial governments nor the representatives of cocoa farmers in the Gold Coast had shown any inclination to come up with the money to finance the Nowell scheme. The availability of the balances of the war-time marketing scheme now made the finance of any future marketing board feasible since the British taxpayer and the Treasury would not have to pay for the establishment of such boards. From this point of view it is quite understandable why Cabinet approval of the post-war marketing scheme was easily obtained. It was obviously one of the quite rare cases in which a development scheme would be able to completely finance itself.[56]

This section of the chapter showed the diversity of reasons why the British and the Nigerian governments favoured a post-war marketing scheme. The main discussions about the post-war scheme were held between 1941 and 1944, and it could be argued that by 1943 a firm consensus between Colonial Office officials and West African governments was reached on the desirability of produce control as a feature of post-war policy.[57] However, it was not clear at the time what precise shape the future marketing organisation would have. The debate turned towards this issue when the publication of a White Paper on cocoa control became politically opportune in 1944.

The Publication of the 1944 White Paper on Cocoa Control

The proposal to publish a White Paper emerged as a result of a visit by E.C. Tansley and G.H. Creasy to West Africa in December 1943 and January 1944.[58] Asked by the Secretary of State for the Colonies to go to Nigeria and the Gold Coast in order to 'clear up misunderstandings regarding the Board's work that may exist'[59], they found that this task was much more difficult than originally expected[60]. It was in this connection that they came up with the idea that the publication of a report on cocoa control would help to allay suspicion surrounding the Board's working in West Africa and the United Kingdom.[61]

The proposal was strongly supported by the governments of the Gold Coast and Nigeria, which on a number of previous occasions had asked the West African Produce Control Board and the Colonial Office, to publish the accounts of the Board.[62] There were also a number of press articles at the time which denounced the secrecy of the Board's financial activities.[63]

Though the draft report was ready in early 1944, it took another six months until the White Paper was presented to the public.[64] There was a long discussion within the Colonial Office and between the Colonial Office and the West African governments and the Resident Minister as to whether the Board's accounts in their present form should be published at all.[65] The Colonial Office argued that it was not advisable to publish the profits of the West African Produce Control Board without giving any indication of what eventually would be done with those profits, because otherwise demands for substantial price increases in the forthcoming 1944/45 cocoa season could only be resisted with great difficulty.[66] It was thought that a detailed statement on future marketing policy was necessary. Thus the issue of the publication of the accounts of the West African Produce Control Board was linked to the question of the precise shape of the future marketing board. For this reason the publication of the *Report on Cocoa Control, 1939-1943* was delayed until a detailed policy was worked out.

The publication of the White Paper was subsequently prompted by two events which had little to do with the White Paper itself. First, a Member of Parliament, John Dugdale (Labour), put forward some detailed questions regarding the scheme and the Colonial Office felt that '...Parliament would [not] willingly accept a temporising reply...'[67] Second, the Governor strongly urged the Colonial Office that a reform of the marketing system in the 1945/46 cocoa season was required.[68] Since it was thought that a reform of the marketing scheme in the Gold Coast could not be made without previous publication of the White Paper, the demand for reform considerably speeded up the proceedings.

There were broadly two questions which had to be decided in mid-1944: which responsibilities, if any, should be taken over by the local West African governments and which role should representatives of producers and traders play in the administration of the future boards?

In 1941 and again in 1943 the governments of the Gold Coast and Nigeria had asked for a transfer to them of part of the responsibility for the administration of the scheme.[69] Both governments were particularly interested in gaining control of the purchasing side of the marketing scheme, which essentially was the power to fix producer prices, quotas and buying schedules for the participants in the trade. There were even demands for a complete transfer of all functions of the West African Produce Control Board to the future local boards.[70]

They justified their demands by arguing that without the transfer of some responsibility from the West African Produce Control Board to the local governments it was unlikely that farmers and traders would co-operate in a future scheme and that local control would avert criticism of the Imperial government. Moreover, it was argued that local control would be able to support the co-operative movement and African traders more effectively than any scheme run by authorities based in the United Kingdom.[71] In addition, the Gold Coast government supported its demand with the argument that the establishment of a local marketing board was necessary in order to prevent a hold-up in the forthcoming 1944/45 cocoa season.[72]

Despite strong opposition from the Resident Minister in West Africa and members of the West African Produce Control Board,[73] the Secretary of State for the Colonies decided that local boards under the control of the Gold Coast and Nigerian governments should assume the responsibility for the purchasing operations of the West African Produce Control Board. The control of selling, however, would remain with an agency whose 'executive staff would be similar or even identical' to the executive staff of the West African Produce Control Board in London.[74]

It is noteworthy that this decision was taken largely for political reasons. In the words of the Permanent Under-Secretary of State, Sir George Gater, the Secretary of State for the Colonies

> ...could not accept any proposal that the responsibility for the marketing arrangements ... should continue to rest in the future with a body in London such as the present Control Board, which is, as it were an organ or projection of the Secretary of State. This would mean simply that the odium and suspicion which have been hitherto attached to the big European firms as buyers of cocoa would be transferred to the Secr. of State and the Colonial Office...[75]

The second question which had to be decided in mid-1944 was to what extent local interests should be represented on future boards. There was a marked difference between the Gold Coast and the Nigerian government policy in this question. The Gold Coast government felt that, for political reasons, it should be 'outwardly' disassociated from the future board and that its governing body should include a substantial number of representatives of farmers and traders in order 'to ensure it a measure of local popularity and forestall criticism'[76]. The Governor of the Gold Coast also suggested that American manufacturing interests should be represented, but subsequently was talked out of that by the Governor of Nigeria and the Resident Minister in West Africa.[77]

The Nigerian government had different ideas. It argued that the cocoa marketing scheme was not a political issue in Nigeria and that thus the establishment of a board separate from government was hardly necessary. Instead, the Nigerian government proposed that the functions of the West African Produce Board could be equally well performed by the Supply Branch of the Nigerian Secretariat or by whatever organisation replacing the Supply Branch after the war.[78]

The Resident Minister in West Africa and the Governors of the Gold Coast and Nigeria were informed of the decision of the Secretary of State on the future marketing scheme on 6th June, 1944.[79] There was a last minute attempt by the Resident Minister to prevent the establishment of local boards in West Africa. On the grounds that a local board with substantial representation of producer and trader interests would be no real reform of the marketing system, but would just give a different set of vested interests the opportunity to influence the policy of the marketing board, the Minister emphatically put forward the idea that instead a 'genuine Producer's Association' on the lines of the 1938 Nowell plan should be set up to take over the functions of the West African Produce Control Board.[80] This idea met heavy opposition from the Governors of Nigeria and the Gold Coast and was finally withdrawn.[81]

The West African Produce Control Board met on 13th September, 1944 to formally endorse the White Paper proposal on the future cocoa control scheme.[82] The White Paper itself (*Report on Cocoa Control in West Africa, 1939-1943, and Statement of Future Policy*, Cmd. 6554) was published later in the month. It contained the proposals already mentioned: cocoa marketing would remain under government control, controls would be administered by local marketing boards in the Gold Coast and Nigeria (financed by the surplus of the war-time marketing scheme), producers' and traders' interests would be directly represented on the Gold Coast board, whereas in Nigeria only an Advisory Committee to the board (without executive functions) would represent such interests. Finally, the boards would come into operation on 1st October, 1945.[83]

It is apparent that the participants in the planning process had very different ideas about the advantages of the future marketing scheme, but could easily agree on the principle that such a scheme was highly desirable. The publication of the 1944 White Paper represents in this restricted sense the end of the consensus building process. But the Colonial Office and the West African governments still had to convince the West African produce traders and cocoa farmers, and the United Kingdom and United States merchant and manufacturing firms, of the advantages of the future control scheme. The last sections of this chapter will discuss to what extent they succeeded in this undertaking.

The Position of the African Intermediaries

Arguably, the reaction of African produce traders and buyers did not count for much. The post-war marketing board was eventually set up in 1947 and their objections or their agreement to the boards bore little influence on the course of events. The reaction to the establishment of the post-war marketing scheme however arguably contained a strategic decision of far-reaching relevance since produce control proved to be one of the most enduring legacies of the colonial period and it was only in 1986 that the Nigerian Cocoa Marketing Board was finally abolished. It is for this reason that a closer look at the reaction of African produce traders and buyers to the announcement of the post-war scheme is justified.

The Nigerian Based 'Exporters'

When the scheme was set up in 1939, nine African and Syrian trading firms were entitled to an export quota, since they could prove that they had exported cocoa in the immediate pre-war years. Two of them did not survive the first year, while another three firms had their export licences revoked in the following year.[84] The demise of these firms was not exclusively due to the operation of the war-time marketing scheme. Some of these firms decided to branch out into other, more lucrative, activities or went bankrupt for reasons which were unconnected with the produce control scheme. However, there is evidence which shows that at least one firm, Flionis Brothers, left the cocoa trade because produce control had made cocoa buying unremunerative.[85]

Thus, by October 1941 there were only four Nigerian-based firms left in the trade. The individual quotas of these firms, however, increased, since the export quotas of the failed firms were distributed among the remaining survivors: S. Thomopulos (940 tons), United Development Trading Company (730 tons), Flionis Brothers (500 tons) and Odutola Brothers (330 tons).[86]

The status of these firms remained unchanged until 1943/44. In the previous season the West African Produce Control Board had dispensed with the services of the European shippers beyond the f.o.b. point and all export quotas automatically became buying quotas. Since there was no longer any need to distinguish between 'A' shippers (the European firms) and 'B' shippers (the Nigerian-based firms), all former exporters were turned into licensed buying agents of the Board. In the 1942/43 cocoa season the Nigerian based firms were paid as if there were still 'B' shippers, but in the 1943/44 season they received, for the first time, the same amount of remuneration for their services as the former 'A' shippers. In the following season of 1944/45, the fixed tonnage quotas were also turned into percentage quotas.[87]

During the war the question as to whether buying quotas should be removed was hotly disputed.[88] However, it was decided to retain them for a variety of reasons: that the system was instrumental in the war effort and that without such a system the firms would not continue to co-operate with the government in the running of the scheme and pre-war 'abuses' would reappear in the trade.[89] The main argument for the retention of the quota system was, however, that the Association of West African Merchants had indicated that if the Colonial Office abandoned the quota system they would immediately resuscitate the pre-war Buying Agreement and use their financial muscle to oust smaller firms from the trade.[90] Such a policy would almost inevitably create political difficulties for the colonial governments since African traders were expected to react very strongly to attempts to exclude them from the cocoa trade. Political difficulties had to be avoided during the sensitive period of the war and thus the quota system and its administration by the war-time control board was kept in place until 1947.[91]

The quota system restricted the growth of the Nigerian-based firms which probably helped to bring about the demise of a number of Nigerian-based firms in the early war years. Yet, the survivors also gained through the system. They no longer faced stiff competition from smaller traders or European firms, and they were thus in a far more secure position than they had been before the war.[92] They also became temporary war-time members of the Nigerian branch of the Association of West African Merchants, which elevated their status.[93] The fact that they received - at least from the 1943/44 cocoa season - the same buying allowance as the European firms was probably even more important. This allowance had considerably increased during the war and as they operated with much lower overhead costs it is likely that their net profits were very high.[94]

Moreover, it appears that a different relationship developed between the European firms and the few African firms still in the trade. The erstwhile keen competitor of the European firms, Odutola Brothers, abandoned its former European selling agent (the London independent broker firm of Daarnhower

& Co. Ltd.) in late 1943 and instead appointed John Holt & Co. Ltd. as its representative for the forthcoming season. Odutola Brothers subsequently became the premier buying agent of John Holt & Co in Nigeria. The new business relationship between the two firms was commented on by Holt's local District Agent (Lagos) with the memorable words:

> I am quite satisfied that handled properly, Odutola can be of immense use to us without jeopardising the interests of our other customers. It has been taken a long time for me to really induce him to develop confidence in us, because for many years, he was imbued with the idea that the big firms were out to smash the African and drive him out of business here, or, if he became too powerful, offer to buy him out first. *He does today realise that for the European firms to be prosperous, the African must be prosperous and that we can help to make him that* [emphasis added].[95]

For the remaining firms the experience of war-time trade controls was thus not a complete disaster. They adapted to the changing economic situation and might even have found the new system far more profitable than they initially expected. The biggest change which they experienced was perhaps that their profits no longer depended on the market, but on the marketing board and that these profits, as argued above, were probably higher in the later part of the war than those they had made in the immediate pre-war years (1937-1939). These firms had therefore something to lose if marketing control was terminated at the end of the war which they had to weigh-up against any advantages such de-control could offer.

The African Cocoa Traders and Commission Buyers

The larger African cocoa traders (and to a lesser extent the commission buyers) were apart from the cocoa farmers perhaps the true 'victims' of the control scheme. Most of the larger independent cocoa traders had not exported cocoa on their own account before the war, but their command of transport facilities and their ability to extract higher commission rates from the firms by selling cocoa to the highest bidder had enabled them to gain a profitable foothold in the trade. The cocoa control system with its fixed buying station prices and low commission rates offered smaller profits than other activities during the war in, for instance, transport and the foodstuffs trade, and there is some evidence that some left the cocoa trade altogether in the early war years, while others reorganised their firms to become large commission buyers.[96]

The main competitors of the African traders and commission buyers were not the few large produce stores which the firms operated in the cocoa belt, but the smaller, far more numerous, depots situated in minor towns and outlying larger markets. These depots were maintained by produce clerks who received, in addition to their salary, a commission for the amount of cocoa they purchased at their depots. They often used the depots' cash reserves alongside the little capital they possessed for trading transactions. They frequently acted as small cocoa buyers and were extremely tightly controlled by the firms.

The competitiveness of the depot clerks increased during the war because of the peculiar method of price fixing which the marketing board employed. Cocoa prices were fixed at buying stations throughout the cocoa belt. These buying station prices *included* the remuneration which commission buyers were supposed to receive from the firms. Commission buyers and farmers therefore received exactly the same cocoa price from the firms and no extra payments were made for whatever services commission buyers might have performed. Commission buyers were therefore forced to recover their remuneration from farmers (or smaller traders). However, this was exceedingly difficult in the vicinity of the firms' buying stations and the firms' depots since farmers would sell their produce to the firms at a higher price, rather than sell it to a commission buyer at a lower price.[97] In addition, the firms massively withdrew the credit from commission buyers which they had so liberally disbursed in the prewar years. It was estimated that by 1943 the total debt owed by produce and merchandise traders to the firms had decreased by about £1 million which, given the relatively small size of the Nigerian economy at the time, was an enormous sum.[98]

Thus many larger commission buyers (and produce traders) were driven out of the market or left the bigger markets and towns and tried to purchase cocoa at more remunerative prices further afield in smaller markets and on farms.[99] At the same time, however, the number of smaller buyers active in the towns seems to have increased. These buyers were attracted to the trade by the security of a guaranteed price and a predictable market.[100] 'It is surprising' wrote one observer, 'how in places like Ibadan one sees more and more sellers (women and youngsters) come in with small headloads of produce which they sell to the depot buyers'[101].

Thus a noticeable change happened in the internal cocoa trade system during the war. Commission buyers and, in particular the larger commission buyers, experienced a sharp cut in their earnings and their credit status. Consequently their numbers decreased while smaller buyers, such as depot clerks, scalemen and itinerant traders seemed to have found their position strengthened and their numbers consequently increased.[102] It is noteworthy that Nigerian government officials believed that this development represented one of the long-term aims of the business policy of the European trading firms.[103]

Yet commission buyers were not completely driven out of the market during the war. This was probably due to the fact that many commission buyers and traders were able to exploit the loop-holes which the system offered, but probably also to the fact that the remuneration system was changed in mid-1943 which assured their subsequent survival.[104] Between the 1939/40 season and the 1942/43 season commission buyers were supposed to receive a commission of 7s 6d from the firms but had to give up part of their remuneration in order to compete with the firms depot clerks. The new system was introduced in the 1943 light crop season and restored and then increased the competitiveness of commission buyers by adding a third pricing schedule to the existing two pricing schedules for graded and ungraded produce.[105] The difference between the latter two schedules amounted to 2s 6d per ton. The new third schedule described the prices which farmers were to receive when they delivered ungraded cocoa to the firms' depot clerk in the same locality. This price was 5s lower than the price farmers received at the firms' main buying stations and the difference was calculated so as to enable commission buyers to earn their 'official' remuneration.

The new system assured the commission buyer a minimum remuneration of 5s per ton since, from the farmers' point of view, it made no difference if they sold ungraded cocoa to a commission buyer or a depot clerk, though they would earn 5s per ton for themselves if they took the trouble to deliver their cocoa to the main buying station. Since most of these buyers graded, bagged and sealed the cocoa which they had bought from the farmers, their total 'official' gross earnings from their commercial activities came to 7s 6d per ton.

In the 1943/44 main crop season the allowance for grading was increased to 4s per ton. A further increase of 2s was granted in the 1946/47 season after the labourers employed in the grading of produce had successfully organised a two day strike in the Western Provinces and in the Colony of Lagos from 18th to 20th November, 1946, and ended with a 100 percent increase in their rates of their pay.[106] Thus the 'official' total gross earnings from cocoa buying came to 11s per ton. When the Nigerian Cocoa Marketing Board was set up in 1947 the remuneration element was increased for the first time since 1939 from 5s per ton to 8s per ton. The grading allowance was also marked up to 9s per ton. The 'official' remuneration of commission buyers in the 1947/48 cocoa season therefore increased to a total of 17s per ton.[107]

Though profit opportunities were severely curtailed, it seems that the post-1943 system offered participants in the trade, in particular commission buyers, a niche in which their further existence was assured. This argument is supported by the fact that cocoa buying became increasingly attractive to smaller buyers, who probably treasured the security which this activity offered. Commission buyers had therefore also something to lose, as well as something to gain, if the cocoa buying system reverted to its pre-war form.

Co-operative Societies and Unions

Co-operative cocoa marketing societies were so badly hit by the introduction of produce control in 1939 that a special subsidy of 10s per ton on co-operative cocoa purchases was introduced in order to secure their survival.[108] This subsidy was paid by the Association of West African Merchants and the United Africa Company and amounted to £3,161 in the 1939/40 season, £3,500 in 1940/41 and £4,000 in 1941/42.[109] It can be safely assumed that the Association of West African Merchants and the United Africa Company made these payments not merely because they were convinced of the advantages of co-operative marketing, but also because they were interested in preventing the co-operatives from applying for an export quota.[110]

In 1942/43 the Association of West African Merchants and the United Africa Company refused to provide further funds. They argued that the subsidy had enabled the co-operative societies to expand the volume of their sales and that a further increase would make cocoa buying unremunerative for firms in Nigeria.[111] However, it is interesting to note that the decision to suspend these payments was taken when it became apparent that government would take over the functions of the merchant firms beyond the f.o.b. point and, consequently, that it was very unlikely that the co-operatives would become real exporters.

The loss of the 10s per ton subsidy again threatened the existence of the co-operative cocoa marketing societies and after much discussion government decided to step in and foot the bill.[112] From 1942/43 to 1946/47 the purchases of co-operative societies were directly subsidised from Nigerian government funds.[113] Thereafter co-operative cocoa purchases were subsidised by the Nigerian Cocoa Marketing Board.

In the 1942/43 season the co-operative societies received a subsidy of about £5,000. It is not known how much the Nigerian government paid in the following season of 1943/44, but from then on the total amount of the subsidy must have steeply declined, since in 1944 the largest two federations of co-operative marketing societies (the Ibadan Co-operative Cocoa Marketing Union and the Ife Co-operative Cocoa Marketing Union) were appointed as licensed buying agents of the West African Produce Control Board and received an 'export' quota of 8,000 tons. Though this quota disqualified the unions from obtaining a subsidy, their new status as licensed buying agents entitled them to the same remuneration and reimbursements of costs as the other agents of the board received and these payments more than equalled the subsidy.

The co-operative quota remained unchanged in the 1945/46 season but two further unions (the Ilesha and Ijebu Co-operative Marketing Unions) became licensed buying agents. With government support, the four 'exporting' co-operative unions subsequently established a combined selling agency, the Association of Nigerian Co-operative Exporters.[114]

In the following season of 1946/47 two more unions, the Ilaro and the Abeokuta Cocoa Marketing Unions, were appointed as licensed buying agents. In the same season the Association of Nigerian Co-operative Exporters was granted, against much opposition from the European firms, an additional quota of 3,500 tons, so that the combined quota of all six marketing unions reached 11,500 tons by then.[115]

After the removal of the quota restrictions in 1947 about 11.5 per cent of the Nigerian cocoa crop, approximately 8,500 tons of cocoa, was marketed through the Association of Nigerian Co-operative Exporters. This was a remarkable achievement. But it could be argued that this position was only achieved because the co-operative cocoa marketing societies and unions received direct financial support from the Nigerian Cocoa Marketing Board.

Apparently, the co-operative societies had very little to gain from a return to the pre-war marketing conditions. The co-operative cocoa marketing societies and unions and the Association of Nigerian Co-operative Exporters received direct financial support from the statutory cocoa marketing board. It could not have been in the interests of its officials and representatives to demand its abolition since the board guaranteed the existence of their institutions.

This brief review of the economic interests of the groups which were likely to support a protest movement against the continuation of war-time controls suggests that opposition to the new marketing board was ambivalent. At the time all groups, with the notable exception of cocoa farmers involved in the marketing of cocoa, had probably as much to lose as to gain from a reversion to its pre-war structure. Arguably, the African intermediaries had become clients of the marketing board during the war and this partly explains why the movement against the introduction of the post-war scheme lacked the kind of support needed to be effective.

Finally, one should mention how remarkably quickly some leading cocoa traders took up the opportunities which the new marketing system offered. After the quota restrictions were removed in 1947, a number of new African and Syrian firms became licensed buying agents of the Nigerian Cocoa Marketing Board. Their owners had survived the war in most cases as commission buyers and were now in a position to qualify as licensed buying agents. The first two African firms appointed by the Nigerian Cocoa Marketing Board were the Ibadan Traders Association Ltd. and Kajola Kawusi Stores. The former was owned by leading Ibadan traders at the time, including S. Agbaje, S.A. Akinfenwa, Chief Y. Adewumi and Alhaji Y. Ladipo, while the latter was allegedly owned by G.A. Babatunde. It is telling that the Ibadan Traders Association was managed by one of the three newly appointed African members of the Nigerian Cocoa Marketing Board, E.A. Sanda, who, moreover, had a small interest in the firm[116], while Kajola Kawusi Stores was owned by another prominent

African member of the Nigerian Cocoa Marketing Board, the Oni of Ife, who had not wished his name to appear publicly in connection with the firm[117].

The Reactions of the African Intermediaries

It took almost three years of produce control before the first opposition against the low price policy and the cocoa marketing scheme emerged. There was some dissatisfaction from commission buyers in 1940 and 1941, but they did not win the support of political groups like the Nigerian Youth Movement and the nationalist press at the time.[118]

The attitude towards produce control changed in 1942 when the marketing board fixed the light crop cocoa price at £5 per ton and the following main crop cocoa price at £12 10s per ton. Cocoa farmers and co-operative cocoa marketing societies considered this far too low. Protest started in May 1942 with a petition signed by the Ibadan, Ife and Ilesha Co-operative Cocoa Marketing Unions and by a number of cocoa sales societies from smaller towns in western Nigeria, like Akure and Ikare.[119] The petitioners asked for a higher cocoa price (£10 per ton) and argued that the current cocoa price of £5 per ton would allow cocoa farmers only to live on 'starvation wages'.[120]

Four months later, on 19th September, 1942, this petition was followed by a mass meeting in Ibadan, which according to an official report, was attended by over four thousand cocoa farmers from Oyo, Ijebu and Abeokuta Provinces. The main speaker was a member of the Ibadan Council and President of the Ibadan Co-operative Cocoa Marketing Union, A. Obisesan.[121] This meeting resolved 'to endorse the Ibadan Co-operative Cocoa Marketing Union to make representations to the Government for an increase in the cocoa price on behalf of co-operative and non-co-operative cocoa producers'[122]. The importance of this meeting lies in that it was the only occasion during the war and in the immediate post-war years when farmers directly articulated their interests. The meeting had no impact on official policy.

The issue of low cocoa prices and the treatment which commission buyers received from the marketing board was taken up by the Nigerian Youth Movement for the first time in November 1942. In that month, the Governor of Nigeria received a delegation which, among other topics, put forward the plight of commission buyers under the control scheme.[123] From then on the Nigerian Youth Movement was firmly committed to the intermediaries' case, demonstrated shortly afterwards by the appearance of critical articles in the nationalist press[124] and by critical questions by the Movement's President, E. Ikoli, in the Legislative Council.[125] Although these articles and questions primarily aimed at obtaining more information about the operation of the marketing board, it is apparent from their wording that they were meant to be the beginning of a longer campaign.

On the occasion of the Secretary of State for the Colonies's visit to Nigeria in September 1943, the Youth Movement published a memorandum, part of which dealt exclusively with trade questions. The memorandum also included two annexes, one of which had been prepared by the Nigerian Association of African Importers and Exporters, while the other was written by the Nigerian Produce Traders' Association.[126] It is noteworthy that the interests of African traders were apparently divided into the interests of potential 'exporters' (in effect the former African 'B' shippers) and those of produce traders (the commission buyers) since both groups found it necessary to state their demands separately. Contrary to apparent unity this suggests that the relationship between these groups of African traders was problematic.

The main memorandum dealt with topics like the importance of the Atlantic Charter for the colonies, 'Racial Co-operation', constitutional reform, education, and industrialisation. In paragraph thirteen, under the heading 'Local Produce Brokers and Middlemen', many of the arguments can be found which were later used against the introduction of the post-war marketing scheme.[127] It appears that the 1944 White Paper proposals on the future marketing scheme only reinforced and accentuated criticism which had been already voiced against the war-time scheme.

The main criticism in the memorandum and in the annexes was that the African traders were squeezed out of the trade by the European firms (or pre-war 'combines') and that the latter were supported in their efforts by the authorities administering the produce control scheme. Moreover, it was argued that the European firms would receive much more favourable treatment in terms of remuneration and quotas from the marketing board than the African firms would. Consequently, the memorandum demanded more protection and support for African traders. As regards the commission buyers, it specifically asked for the curtailment of the activities of the firms' depot clerks and the granting of higher remuneration rates. In respect to the 'B' shippers, the memorandum demanded that the marketing boards should employ more African firms in the purchase of produce in Nigeria and increase the quotas of the African firms which were already established in the trade.

The Nigerian Youth Movement, the Association of African Exporters and Importers and the Nigerian Produce Traders' Association put forward a strong demand to improve the conditions of African traders under the control scheme. It is noteworthy that neither of these groups demanded the immediate abolition of the war-time control scheme. It is also telling that the plight of cocoa farmers was not mentioned at all.

After the preparation of the 1943 memorandum, public interest or the interest of political groupings, like the Nigerian Youth Movement, in cocoa control matters subsided. Instead, attention focused on the role of the European business firms in the Nigerian economy and especially on that of the Association of West African Merchants in the administration of import and export war-time controls. There had been criticism of the firms and their policies throughout the war, but in 1944 the nationalist press started a vigorous campaign aimed at the dissolution of the Association.[128]

In May 1944, for example, three articles were published by the Nigerian Youth Movement in the *Daily Service* under the heading 'The AWAM must Go'[129]. The article extolled the advantages of free trade and accused the Association of manipulating war-time controls with a view to excluding the majority of African firms from the import and export trade. The article justified the demand to disband the Association by arguing that there was not much difference between the activities of the Association and the 1937 'Pool'; since this pool had been dissolved in 1938 the Association should now be dissolved as well.[130] Though this argument had obvious flaws, it is interesting to note that as early as May 1944 a section of the Nigerian Youth Movement favoured a post-war trade regime without controls and, moreover, found it politically opportune to remind the readers of the *Daily Service* of the allegedly successful 1937/38 campaign. There was thus already a press campaign against the European firms under way when the first news appeared in Nigeria about the post-war cocoa marketing plan in October 1944.

The first reaction to the 1944 White Paper proposals in the nationalist press was an article published in the *Daily Service* on 26th October, 1944, informing its readers about the essential features of the post-war marketing scheme. One day later a further article appeared in the same newspaper. It read:

> There is no doubt the sufferings and privations inseparable from war conditions have rendered many people poor, but, at the same time, there are others who have taken advantage of the war to built colossal fortune. To the latter category belong the vested interest in West Africa. European firms occupy today a position no organisation had ever dreamt of before... The control system has placed African traders under the economic dictatorship of European firms. The country can bear this as long as the war lasts but not one minute longer. We do not join Britain in the war against Nazism with a view to strengthening the economic hold of her trading organisations on this country... While the existing control scheme pampers European firms it impoverishes African producers... What are we really fighting for? Is it to make ourselves economic slaves in perpetuity to British and American capitalists? Far from it. We have not said the last word about this intriguing subject.[131]

This is a typical example of many articles published later. Their tone and themes were obviously inspired by the expectation that the end of the war would open up new opportunities in the political and economic field, including in the cocoa trade.[132] High prices in the United States and elsewhere, as well as the disclosure of the profits of the war-time control board, probably induced traders to believe that the cocoa trade would offer very high returns at the time. It is understandable that under these circumstances cocoa control was seen as particularly frustrating and that strong demands for complete de-control or free trade emerged.[133] Such a demand, for example, appeared in an article in the *Daily Service* on 6th December, 1944:

> This is nefarious trading contrary to natural justice, equity and fairplay. Away with control board and quotas! They are the scheme of diabolical brains behind some of the world's greatest enemies - the super-capitalists who formulate schemes and, like the proverbial sugar-coated pills, pass them on to gullible politicians, some of whom are honest enough to dissociate themselves from the profit motive, but others who are not so honest help to force these pills down the African throat.[134]

Both articles show that there was a distinctly political aspect to the criticism of the post-war control scheme. This political criticism was of course part of a much wider political dissatisfaction which was developing at the time. This became most apparent in the nationwide strike and in the campaigns against the introduction of the 'Richards Constitution' in 1946 and the enactment of the so-called four 'obnoxious ordinances'.[135]

Cocoa control was directly linked with wider political questions by the way in which the post-war scheme was introduced, as well as by the way in which the Nigerian government had decided about the disposal of the profits of the war-time marketing board. It was thought that both most clearly showed the paternalistic, if not authoritarian character of the political regime of the time.[136] The main complaint was that nobody in Nigeria was consulted in these matters and that government therefore had no legitimacy to pursue such policies.[137] Given that the Nigerian Government had previously consulted cocoa farmers and traders, this complaint is hardly surprising. This change in policy might be due to the differences in governmental style between Governor Bourdillon and Governor Richards. However, the marked disinclination to consult cocoa farmers and traders probably also demonstrates a general tendency at the end of the Second World War. In this period the Nigerian government displayed an increasing inflexibility towards the nationalist movement and their economic and political demands, probably because the movement's acquiescence in political matters was not any longer thought to be worthwhile to have.

Criticism of the future marketing scheme appeared in the Nigerian press between 1944 and 1947, but reached its peak in 1945 and early 1946. In the same period the opponents of the post-war marketing scheme used two other means to make their view felt. One was to despatch a delegation to London to lobby Parliament and the Secretary of State for the Colonies on behalf of produce traders' interests. The other means consisted in the writing of letters and petitions which, though ambivalent in their actual demands, were worded in the same way as the aforementioned press articles.

As has been mentioned earlier, the Nigerian Produce Traders' Union went into decline in the early war years. In 1941, its function was taken over by the newly-established Nigerian Association of African Exporters and Importers and to some extent by the Ibadan Produce Traders' Union, which was founded in the same year. Its first Secretary was S.A. Akinpelu. In 1943 the Union called itself Ibadan Produce Buyers' and Scalers' Union and was represented by S.A. Akinpelu and the Ibadan Councillor and later member of the Nigerian Cocoa Marketing Board, E.A. Sanda.

In May 1945 the Union (under the name Produce Buyers' Union of Ibadan and the Western Provinces) wrote a long petition to the Governor of Nigeria asking for the complete de-control of the cocoa trade after the war. Yet when it came to positive proposals, it put forward demands which could not be realised under free market conditions, but depended on the very existence of a marketing board. These proposals included the demand for higher commission rates, the demand for increased representation on the future marketing board and, finally, that government should pay higher cocoa prices.[138]

This petition was followed up by a rapid succession of petitions in the second half of 1946, all of which were signed by either S.A. Akinpelu or E.A. Sanda.[139] These showed the same ambivalence. Though the petitioners were highly critical of the post-war marketing board, their actual proposals went no further than demanding higher remuneration for commission buyers, the regulation of the activities of all participants in the trade, and higher cocoa prices.

The other means by which producer traders tried to prevent the establishment of the post-war marketing board was to support a delegation of the so-called 'Farmers' Committee of British West Africa' which stayed in London between September and December 1945.[140] The members of the delegation (A. Nikoi, W.K. Mould and F.O. Blaize) came from the Gold Coast, as well as from Nigeria. They presented the Secretary of State for the Colonies with a memorandum containing a variety of demands, such as for higher cocoa prices (25s per load or just under £47 per ton), for the complete removal of all trade restrictions (including the demand for the dissolution of the West African Produce Control Board) and the demand that all profits of the war-time marketing board should be handed over to producers' organisations in the Gold Coast and Nigeria.[141]

The London delegates failed to achieve their stated objective -to prevent the establishment of the post-war marketing scheme. They were not even granted an interview with the Secretary of State for the Colonies, and were largely ignored on advice from the governments of the Gold Coast and Nigeria.[142] This suggests that the delegation had negligible importance as a political pressure group. Yet the Farmers' Committee received considerable support from various political groups and trade associations in Nigeria. It is for this reason that it is important to review their local background in some detail.

The origins of the Farmers' Committee of British West Africa go back to the Nigerian Farmers' Protection Society and attempts to organise farmers and traders during the war years.[143] The Protection Society was very closely connected with one particular family (Coker) whose farms were located in the Agege area north of Lagos and whose members were prominently involved in the foundation of various farmers' and traders' organisations, such as in the establishment of the Federation of Nigerian Farmers in 1943 (J.M. Coker)[144], and the setting up of the Association of Merchants and Industrialists (J.K. Coker and A.S.O. Coker)[145].

P.T. Coker was the Secretary of the Farmers' Protection Society in 1943. In November of that year he approached the Emir of Zaria twice with the proposal to discuss and probably organise protest against low produce prices.[146] The first letter was headed 'Farmers' Protection Society', yet the second was written on behalf of a commercial firm, the 'Farmers' Committee of British West Africa Ltd.'. One year later the Farmers' Committee of British West Africa and the Association of Merchants and Industrialists became affiliated to the National Council of Nigeria and the Cameroons, the leading nationalist organisation at the time.[147] This suggests that even before its main campaign in 1945 the 'Farmers' Committee of British West Africa' was active either in the form of a business venture or as a political pressure group or both.

According to a report in the *Daily Service* of 19th September, 1945, the Farmers' Committee of British West Africa *Ltd.* was founded in March 1943 in London as a trade association for the four British West African colonies (the Gambia, Sierra Leone, the Gold Coast and Nigeria).[148] It subsequently built up two branches: one in the Gold Coast (the Farmers' Committee of British West Africa, Gold Coast Branch) and one in Nigeria (the Farmers' Committee of British West Africa, Nigeria Branch). The Vice-President of the Farmers' Committee of British West Africa was P.T. Coker, while A.S.O. Coker held the post of Secretary of the Nigerian branch.[149]

The Farmers' Committee became active in Nigeria in the early months of 1945. A. Nikoi[150], W.K. Mould and an 'American representative' (probably K.O. Mbadiwe) visited Nigeria and had talks with Herbert Macaulay, Dr. A. Maya and N. Azikiwe in Lagos, and with S. Agbaje and M. Agbaje in Ibadan, presumably in order to prepare the ground for the following campaign.[151] In August 1945 the Farmers' Committee of British West Africa Ltd. applied for an export quota of 6,000 tons of cocoa to the United Kingdom. This application was rejected on the ground that the Committee had not previously shipped cocoa.[152] One month later, F.O. Blaize, who was at the time in the United Kingdom studying law, was officially appointed to represent the Nigerian branch of the Farmers' Committee in London.[153]

The Farmers' Committee of British West Africa (Nigeria Branch) was a rallying point for many nationalists like D.T. Sasegbon, S.L. Akintola and Dr. A. Maya.[154] Together with A.S.O. Coker they organised various 'mass' meetings in Lagos and Ibadan between September and November 1945. This was done in order to drum up support for the London delegation and included a joint meeting with the Ibadan Produce Traders' Association[155] (16 September 1945) and a joint meeting with the Ibadan Co-operative Cocoa Marketing Union (27 October 1945).[156] In addition, the Farmers' Committee published a special pamphlet and held fund-raising events.[157] The Committee was publicly supported by the Nigerian Youth Movement and the National Council of Nigeria and the Cameroons.[158]

The height of the activities was reached with a meeting of a 'Farmers' Council' in Ibadan on 21st November, 1945, attended by about forty people representing about fifteen farmers' unions from the Western Provinces and from the Colony.[159] The main speakers, apart from D.T. Sasegbon and Dr. A. Maja, were farmers' union members from Shagamu, Ede and Ilepeju.[160] The meeting agreed on a resolution which demanded higher cocoa prices, as well as the official recognition of the London delegation by the Secretary of State for the Colonies.

Despite all their efforts and their, albeit limited, support, the Nigerian branch of the Farmers' Committee seemed to have gained from farmers' organisations, such as the Ibadan Co-operative Marketing Union, the impact of the activities of the local Farmers' Committee on cocoa farmers in general was not very deep. When in October 1945 the London delegation issued an 'order' for the hold-up of cocoa to strengthen its position vis-à-vis the Colonial Office and put pressure behind its demand for an increase in the cocoa price to £50 per ton, almost nobody obeyed, though according to one official report there was a 'go slow' campaign in the early part of the month.[161]

The activities of the Farmers' Committee of British West Africa subsided when it became clear that the Colonial Office would not recognise them as representatives of West African farmers. The Nigerian delegate F.O. Blaize returned to Nigeria in January 1946, and after a meeting in which he gave an account of his work in London, there seem to have been no further public meetings of the Farmers' Committee of British West Africa (Nigeria Branch).[162] Subsequently, and perhaps consequently, criticism of the future marketing scheme seems to have somewhat shifted from the scheme itself to criticism of the its workings.

However, it is noteworthy that the Nigerian Farmers' Union was involved in the activities of the Farmers' Committee of British West Africa. In December

1945 the Nigerian Farmers' Union decided to send another delegate to London.[163] Though some money was collected, it seems that the project was soon abandoned.[164] The delegate supposed to travel to London was O. Akeredolu-Ale, who later became the General Secretary and principal organiser of the Nigerian Farmers' Union.[165]

The press campaigns, the petitions and finally the activities of the Farmers' Committee of British West Africa could not prevent the establishment of the post-war marketing scheme. Yet, the opponents of the post-war marketing scheme were not completely unsuccessful. In the previous chapter it was argued that the West African Produce Control Board raised the producer price from £26 per ton in the 1945/46 cocoa season to £47 10s per ton in the following season, partly in order to make the future marketing scheme more acceptable in the Gold Coast and Nigeria and to appease the widespread dissatisfaction which had emerged. It is probably also not a coincidence, that in January 1946 the Secretary of State for the Colonies strongly argued for increased producer representation on the Nigerian cocoa marketing board. Since this decision was at least partly due to the activities of the opponents of produce control, it appears that the campaign against the post-war control scheme had shown some results, though perhaps not those hoped for.

It might be argued that in any event colonial governments in West Africa at the time hardly responded to demands from political movements, but it seems that the striking immobility of the Nigerian government on this particular occasion was also due to the fact that the introduction of the post-war control scheme enjoyed strong local support and that a large section of the nationalist movement had serious doubts about the advantages of a return to the free trade regime of the 1930s.

Local support was probably forthcoming as a result of government action itself, which included such measures as the printing of pamphlets in the local vernaculars, the publication of articles in nationalist newspapers and public lectures by District Officers in the cocoa producing areas.[166] But it appears that such support also reflected the serious conviction, which was held by some farmer representatives, chiefs and nationalists, that produce control was a favourable option for Nigerian cocoa farmers and traders. Support for the cocoa marketing scheme was, for example, forthcoming from the President of the Ibadan Co-operative Marketing Union, A. Obisesan, and one of the highest ranking Chiefs of Ibadan, I.B. Akinyele.[167] More important, however, was the fact that the nationalist camp was divided over the issue of produce control. O. Awolowo, for example, wrote in the *Daily Service* on 9th January, 1945, that post-war control of the cocoa market would be preferable because 'no one would desire a return to the pre-war vagaries of the cocoa market, if a practical alternative could be provided' and added that 'unrestricted competition in all departments of commerce must be one of the casualties of war'.[168]

There seem to be two main reasons for the striking similarity between the government view and the view held by a section of the nationalist movement. As has been argued above, the return to the pre-war marketing system would not necessarily benefit the economic interests of the groups whom the protest movement was supposed to represent. Though the cocoa control scheme had severely limited the profits which African traders could make in the cocoa trade, a complete return to a free trade regime would threaten the economic niches which the control system had offered. In that sense the marketing board was instrumental in creating a new category of vested interest in the West African cocoa trade. This was arguably the main reason why the demands for a return to the pre-war marketing system lacked widespread support even among African traders and why many newspaper articles, political pamphlets and petitions published at the time showed a marked ambivalence towards the control board.[169]

The other main reason why an important section of the nationalist movement in Nigeria declined to join the anti-control board and free trade movement, was probably due to its more general view that African firms were not served by a free trade regime. On a number of occasions many nationalists had argued that the development of the cocoa trade in the 1930s had offered much evidence for the theory that a free trade system would subject smaller African firms merely to the machinations of the 'combines' of the European firms and stifle their growth.[170]

It is noteworthy that, based on this reasoning, as early as the mid- and late-1930s proposals had emerged to restrict the activities of the European firms by setting up cocoa control boards under the direction of producer and trader organisations.[171] During the war, arguments in favour of government intervention gained more widespread support as the following quote from a memorandum of the Association of African Exporters and Importers from 1943 shows:

> The African Trader is a late arrival in the field of private enterprise, is handicapped by want of financial resources and organisation and if his right to a decent livelihood in his own territory is recognised, he seeks protection against combinations of powerful rivals who can easily oust him out of the field of private enterprise. *It is to the Government that he looks for protection* [emphasis added].[172]

Such reasoning also appeared, though in a less sophisticated manner, in a number of newspaper articles and petitions at the end of the war. In May 1945, for example, a petition of the Produce Buyers' Union of Ibadan and Western Provinces was published in the *Daily Comet* which reads:

> We are respectfully craving that the trade of this country will be allowed to remain free ... [and] that legislation should be introduced to protect the

producer and the small native traders against unfair competition of the capitalist firms.[173]

As argued above, part of the nationalist movement opposed a return to the free trade marketing system of the 1930s. They also severely criticised the way in which the marketing board operated during the war. But they were at the same time convinced that the marketing board system could be adapted to serve the needs of African traders or, as O. Awolowo put it, 'no one would desire a return to the pre-war vagaries of the cocoa market, if a practical *alternative could be provided*' [emphasis added].[174] For this section of the nationalist movement, the main question was thus not whether a statutory marketing scheme should be established after the war, but rather who would be represented on this board and in whose interest it would operate.

Thus, there was a rift within the nationalist movement. One part favoured a free trade system while the other believed that such an option would only help to perpetuate the dominance by European firms. The fact that part of the movement decided to campaign for control of the marketing board, rather than for abolition seems to have great significance in retrospect. It was arguably the moment when part of the nationalist movement made up its mind not only about the future cocoa marketing scheme, but also about the role government and, in the widest sense, the state should play in the economy. So far as trade matters were concerned, this role was perceived as basically interventionist with a view to fostering the growth of indigenous entrepreneurs. From the 1950s, the state interventionist faction within the nationalist movement dominated the regional and federal governments in Nigeria, and it has been argued that this fundamental orientation has had a great impact on the subsequent Nigerian political and economic history.[175]

This section of the chapter reviewed in some detail the reaction of African intermediaries, their trade associations, and of the nationalist movement to the publication of the 1944 White Paper. However, their reaction seems to have only marginally influenced the course of events. In the last part of this chapter it will be shown how other, more influential, pressure groups almost succeeded in preventing the establishment of the post-war marketing scheme.

The Reactions of the European and American Trading Firms and Cocoa Manufacturers

The United Kingdom intermediaries and most of the cocoa manufacturers did not take part in discussions over the post-war marketing scheme and it was only in early September 1944 that they were informed about the basic features of the proposed scheme.[176] Their immediate reaction was one of deep suspicion.

The firms criticised the White Paper as lacking any definition of the future role which the trading firms would play in the proposed scheme and for not spelling out in any detail what powers the new local boards would have.[177] The United Africa Company in particular seems to have been extremely worried by the prospect of sooner or later being driven out of the trade and was concerned that their interests would not be taken into account when the finer details of the scheme were settled.[178] On both issues the Company was officially assured that the Colonial Office had no intention to pursue such policies.[179] These assurances seemed not, however, to have had a major impact, since the European trading firms, led by the United Africa Company, started a powerful campaign against the continuation of the war-time control scheme which included newspaper articles and intensive lobbying of Members of Parliament and the Colonial Office.[180] The opponents of the proposed scheme were organised in two trade associations: the Cocoa Association of London and the British Federation of Commodity and Allied Trade Association. The Colonial Office regarded the latter as a mouthpiece for the United Africa Company.[181] Both associations produced lengthy memoranda on alternative control schemes, whose main feature was to allow the firms the export of cocoa on their own account, while the role of government would be restricted to fixing of minimum prices and stock-piling of cocoa which the firms refused to purchase.[182] After long internal discussions within the Colonial Office and between the Colonial Office and the West African governments, it was decided to reject these proposals.[183]

Despite their generally considerable influence, the trading firms' opposition was relatively easy to overcome. This was probably due to the fact that the firms themselves were divided over the issue. The opposition against the introduction of the future marketing scheme was spearheaded by the United Africa Company and it seems that smaller companies, for example, John Holt & Co. Ltd., only reluctantly supported the campaign. There is even some evidence that the local representatives of John Holt & Co. actually welcomed the scheme.[184] This attitude was probably the result of the re-appearance of competitive practices in the cocoa trade, such as the payment of overriding commissions to African commission buyers.[185] Since 1943 the United Africa Company embarked on an aggressive buying policy and this probably made the smaller European firms aware of the fact that a 'free for all' system would not only drive a number of African firms to the wall, but a number of smaller European firms as well.[186]

Moreover, there is also some evidence which suggests that the trading firms fundamentally differed over their future business strategies. Since 1943, representatives of John Holt & Co., for example, emphatically argued that the European firms should encourage African traders to become active members of the Association of West African Merchants.[187] There is no indication that the United Africa Company shared this view at the time.[188] The distinct lack of cohesion between the trading firms in their approach to African traders and statutory marketing arguably weakened their position vis-à-vis the Colonial Office.

Furthermore, the Association of West African Merchants and its Cocoa Sub-Committee, was sharply divided over the issue of produce control. Its cocoa manufacturing members, especially the firms of Cadbury Brothers Ltd., strongly supported the scheme, which, given that John Cadbury was a member of the West African Produce Control Board, is hardly surprising. The cocoa manufacturers counterweighted to some extent the protest campaign of the trading associations by preparing memoranda and publishing newspaper articles in favour of the proposed scheme.[189] It appears that the long-term interests of cocoa manufacturers were different from those of the trading firms and that, for this reason, the Association of West African Merchants was unable to present a common counter-proposal.[190] The division between cocoa manufacturers and trading firms naturally helped the Colonial Office to defend the scheme against public criticism.

However, the Colonial Office was also faced with strong American criticism.[191] For political and economic reasons it had to be extremely cautious in dealing with American opinion at the time. American criticism of the proposed scheme such as, for example, the criticim which had appeared in a memorandum published by the President of New York cocoa exchange had to be taken very seriously indeed.[192]

American opposition was in the end overcome by postponing the introduction of the scheme for one year, when American opinion was expected to be less vital to British economic interests. It is noteworthy that some American manufacturers had indicated that they would be prepared to accept produce control though they were very critical of various aspects of the proposed scheme.[193]

Finally, one should mention that the influential Fabian Colonial Bureau strongly favoured the idea of produce control.[194] In 1945 the Bureau wrote a letter to the Secretary of State for the Colonies and published a number of articles in support of the scheme, for example, those in the *Manchester Guardian* on 9th and 19th March, 1945.[195]

The Colonial Office Debate

When in September 1944 the Colonial Office presented the outline of the new scheme to the public it was quite surprised by the strength of the opposition aroused. Though some opposition had been expected, the Colonial Office had believed that the firms would reluctantly accept the scheme as in their long-term interest. Thus, for example, the Secretary of State for the Colonies had argued that:

> These proposals have not repeat not as yet been discussed with the firms, as I consider that what is involved at this stage is decision of principle and policy which must be taken by government... Firms cannot be expected to welcome proposals ... [but] I do not expect any serious repercussions partly because some firms, particularly manufacturing interests and smaller shippers are not happy in membership of association with A.W.A.W. and might be expected to co-operate in new arrangements and partly because many of the remainder depends for their profits on merchandise rather than produce and so may be expected to go at considerable length to be allowed to maintain buying stations to attract customers.[196]

The above mentioned principle was, however, soon abandoned. Although the Colonial Office stood solidly behind the 1944 White Paper proposals[197], the Secretary of State decided to retreat from the position, when faced with stiff criticism from the trading firms[198]. On 16th November, 1944, the Secretary of State for the Colonies declared that the 1944 White Paper would not be the last word on the subject and announced in a meeting with representatives of the trading firms that another White Paper would be published in due course which would take into account the criticism the scheme had met from various sides.[199]

In addition, the Colonial Office tried in vain to make the scheme more acceptable to the firms. For example, the firms were repeatedly assured that there was no intention of driving them out of the trade. They were also assured that the board would only allow African traders to become licensed buying agents of the future marketing board on condition that they fulfilled certain minimum requirements. These would guarantee that only a limited number of firms would participate in the trade.[200]

The firms' reaction to these proposals was not encouraging. They continued to press for a change in the marketing system and, consequently, the Secretary of State decided to ask the colonial governments in early February 1945 if they were prepared to reconsider the scheme.[201] He also made clear that he personally would now favour a minimum price scheme on the lines the firms had previously proposed.[202]

The Nigerian government reacted with considerable anger to the news that the Secretary of State was effectively abandoning the 1944 White Paper proposal.[203] This anger seems to have also inspired the official letter which the Governor of Nigeria, A. Richards, wrote in response to the February despatch.[204] The Governor strongly advised the Secretary of State not to deviate from the original proposal. A statement to the same effect was also received from the Governor of the Gold Coast, who added that any retreat on the 1944 proposal would be interpreted as giving in to the demands of the trading firms and might lead to a hold-up of cocoa after the war.[205]

The Secretary of State was thus confronted with strong pressure from the firms to abandon the proposed scheme, while at the same time the colonial governments in West Africa pressed for its retention. Faced with this situation, he decided in February 1945 to follow the advice given by the Governor of Nigeria and postpone the decision on the future marketing scheme until further notice.[206] Meanwhile the West African Produce Control Board would be asked to purchase and sell the West African cocoa crop for another season (i.e. in the 1945/46 cocoa season).

It appears therefore that in February 1945 the Secretary of State for the Colonies might have been abandoned the 1944 White Paper proposals, if the West African Governments had not so forcefully supported the original scheme. It is noteworthy that at the time the campaigns against the introduction of the scheme in West Africa had hardly started. The postponement of the decision about the future marketing scheme was thus not the direct result of political pressure from West African nationalist groups.

The Establishment of the Nigerian Cocoa Marketing Board

The British general election of 1945 brought the Labour Party to power. Among the many changes this brought about was the replacement of the former Secretary of State, Oliver Stanley, by G.H. Hall. His Parliamentary Under-Secretary at the time was Arthur Creech Jones who only one year later was appointed as Secretary of State for the Colonies. Creech Jones had on many occasions publicly expressed his preference for a statutory marketing scheme and as Parliamentary Under-Secretary immediately reaffirmed the government's commitment to the 1944 White Paper proposals.[207]

In October 1945 the colonial governments were informed that the 1944 White Paper proposals would not be changed or amended and that the 1946 White Paper would not contain any surprises.[208] This news was received by the Nigerian government with considerable satisfaction.[209] In the following four months the Colonial Office prepared an outline draft for the White Paper which included negotiations with other government departments and detailed discussions with West African governments.[210] This outline draft was ready by 12th January, 1946.

The draft reaffirmed the 1944 goal of bringing stability to the cocoa industry by establishing marketing boards in the Gold Coast and Nigeria whose purpose was to purchase all cocoa offered at fixed seasonal prices. It also defined the role of the intermediaries. It was stated that, though there was no intention to exclude efficient trading firms, their number and scope would be severely restricted.[211] As regards the future composition of the Nigerian marketing board the draft proposed that

> ...the functions of the Board will be entrusted in the first place to the Department of Commerce and Industry, in association with the Supply Board of the Nigerian Secretariat and assisted by an advisory Committee, representative of the producers and trade interests under the chairmanship of a senior Government official.[212]

As regards the Gold Coast board, the draft just stated that a board would be set up on the lines of the 1944 proposal, which included representation of producer and trader interests on the board itself.

As mentioned above, the decision to establish dissimilar boards in Nigeria and the Gold Coast directly resulted from the different political pressures which African traders and producers had exerted on the respective colonial governments. In May 1944 the Nigerian government had argued that an advisory committee would be sufficient to satisfy local demands for increased influence in the administration of the local boards. Since then, its position had not changed.[213] Meanwhile however, the political situation in the United Kingdom had changed. The new Secretary of State for the Colonies G.H. Hall visited Nigeria in January 1946. In a meeting with the Governor of Nigeria he proposed that the composition of the Nigerian board should also allow the direct representation of producer and trader interests. Governor Richards strongly objected and only after some considerable pressure from the Secretary of State for the Colonies, in the end it was agreed that

> ...the Board would consist of three officials at first and that the remaining two vacancies would be filled by persons representing producers interests as soon as suitable persons could be found.[214]

It seems likely that the Secretary of State for the Colonies' intervention was partly the result of the activities of the Farmers' Committee of British West Africa, whose campaign had just come to an end. However, it is noteworthy that the final version of the 1946 White Paper was less specific on producer representation on the marketing board. It is only stated that the board 'would consist of not less than three nor more than five members to be appointed by the Governor' and that the board 'would be assisted by an Advisory Committee consisting of a Chairman and not more than six members to be appointed by the Governor', whereby the latter would include representatives of producer and commercial interests.[215]

The discussions over the final version of the 1944 White Paper were completed in February 1946. Yet, on the advice of the U.S. State Department it was decided to postpone publication until the United States Congress had concluded its debate about the 1946 British-American loan agreement on the grounds that this debate could be negatively influenced by the publication of a White Paper whose contents was likely to cause strong American criticism.[216] The publication of the 1946 White Paper was therefore delayed until November 1946. It was then, however, too late to introduce the proposed cocoa marketing scheme for the 1946/47 cocoa season, which started in October 1946. The introduction of the scheme was therefore postponed for another season.

The wording of the 1946 White Paper suggests that it was largely written with a view to answering the criticism which the previous 1944 White Paper had attracted from British and American trading firms. Some sections dealt exclusively with the minimum price scheme which the trading firms had put forward as an alternative proposal (paragraphs 2, 8, and 9) as well as a section which tries to address an American audience (paragraph 11). The White Paper also provided an analysis of the cocoa industry and its main problems (paragraphs 4 and 7). However, in substance there is no change between the argument advanced in favour of produce control in the 1944 and the 1946 White Paper. Since these arguments have been already discussed in some detail, it is necessary to highlight only two further points.

The 1946 White Paper defines the activities of intermediaries in very narrow terms (paragraphs 16-20). It makes clear that the future board would only employ a limited number of licensed buying agents whose activities would be moreover tightly controlled. But the White Paper also contains the assurance that the authorities had no intention to exclude any European trading firms or any African trader, from participating in the cocoa trade in the near future. The traders and the firms would be allowed to run their own businesses, instead of becoming merely employees of a marketing board.[217] These paragraphs were probably written in order to allay the trading firms' apprehensions that the marketing board would drive them completely out of the trade in the future.

Finally, the White Paper strongly emphasises that the board was not supposed to make any profit at the expense of the West African cocoa producer (paragraph 23) and explicitly states that any surplus made in the past would be returned in full to the producers (paragraphs 14 and 15) and would be handed over to the future marketing board. This surplus would only be used either to even out price fluctuation or on expenditure from which cocoa producers were likely to directly benefit, such as research on cocoa diseases and cocoa rehabilitation. It also states that any eventual surplus in the future would be exclusively used for similar purposes (paragraph 23). But the White Paper also mentions that a considerable sum of money had been made available to the Gold Coast Legislative Council for expenditure on higher education (paragraph 14), which seems to contradict the statement that there was no question of making a profit at the expense of cocoa farmers.

The publication of the 1946 White Paper was received in Nigeria with far less criticism than the publication of the White Paper of 1944. The main reasons were that the erstwhile opponents of produce control had abandoned their campaign, that other political issues occupied the nationalist groups at the time and that the Nigerian government took great care to inform influential African leaders of opinion about the main contents of the White Paper.[218]

There was also a noticeable shift in the focus of criticism prior to the publication of the White Paper. Whereas in 1945 demands appealed for the complete removal of produce control, in 1946 such demands became increasingly rare as the year progressed. Instead criticism of the future scheme was mainly directed against the working of the scheme. There was considerable apprehension that producer and trader representatives would be excluded from membership of the board and that the future control scheme might prevent African traders from participating in the trade. There was also the fear that the profits of the war-time control board would not be returned to Nigeria.[219] The White Paper assured African traders and producers that their interests would be taken into account in the future administration of the marketing board and that the profits of the war-time control scheme would be returned to the producers. Because of this, public reaction to the publication of the 1946 White Paper was rather subdued.

In 1947, the central political problem for the colonial government in connection with the proposed future marketing scheme was to find 'suitable' persons to represent producer and trader interests on the board. The task to make recommendations fell on the Acting Resident Oyo Province, R.L.V. Wilkes. In May 1947 he held meetings with the Ilesha Native Authority and with the Ibadan Inner Council, in which he asked the councilors and chiefs to make nominations.[220] Both the Ilesha Native Authority and the Ibadan Native Authority came forward with a list of names, which included produce traders, like T.A. Odutola, S. Agbaje, A.O. Makanjuola, J.O. Fadahunsi and E.A. Sanda, as well as local notables like the Oni of Ife, D.T. Sasegbon, A. Obisesan and H.O. Davies, all of whom had been involved in cocoa politics since at least 1937/38.[221]

On the occasion of the meeting with the Ibadan Inner Council the Secretary of the Produce Traders Union, E.A. Sanda, was full of praise for the future marketing scheme. This probably explains why he was subsequently strongly recommended by the Acting Resident as a suitable member for the board.[222] The other nominee was the Oni of Ife.[223] Though the Resident gave no explanation for this particular nomination, it is very likely that he recommended the Oni of Ife because of his important political and religious position in Yorubaland. As regards the future Advisory Committee, the Acting Resident also suggested the leading Ijebu-Ode businessmen T.A. Odutola and, somewhat reluctantly, the President of the Ibadan Co-operative Marketing Union, A.

Obisesan.[224] Alternatively he put forward the names of S. Agbaje (a prominent Ibadan trader) and H.O. Davies (a leading member of the Nigerian Youth Movement) as candidates for either the Marketing Board or the Advisory Committee. The Oni of Ife and E.A. Sanda were chosen by the Nigerian Government to represent African (trading) interests on the Board, whereas T.A. Odutola and J.O. Fadahunsi were invited to become members of the Advisory Committee.

The appointment of prominent African traders to the Board and its Advisory Committee made certain that the future administration and policy of the Board would be strongly influenced by Nigerian commercial interests. It is interesting that this development was precisely what the Governor of Nigeria, Richards, had hoped to prevent when he had tried to resist the establishment of local marketing boards with substantial African representation (see above). He had argued that

> ...to constitute a local Control Board, for membership of which selected individual Africans would be eligible, might only result in replacement of foreign capitalists by local capitalists, thereby perpetuating the system of vested interests...[225]

It might be argued that Richards used this argument only to prevent a development which he resented for other reasons[226] but, as far as the quote above is concerned, his prediction seems to have been by and large correct. In July and August 1947 the Nigerian Cocoa Marketing Board Bill was debated in the newly established Western House of Assembly and in the Legislative Council. On both occasions the Bill received wholesale support from all sides including the Oni of Ife, E.A. Sanda, the Alake of Abeokuta and Chief R. Turton of Ilesha, though some criticism was raised by Chief I.B. Akinyele of Ibadan and T.A. Odutola.[227] On the initiative of Chief Akinyele, the proposed composition of the marketing board was changed in order to increase producer representation. Instead of having only five nominated members as the 1946 White paper had envisaged, the proposed Marketing Board Bill was amended to allow for the appointment of seven members to the Board. These changes were accepted by the Nigerian government and the enabling Bill which established the Nigerian Cocoa Marketing Board as a legal entity was finally published as Sessional Paper No.33 of 6th September, 1947.

The West African Produce Control Board was relieved of the responsibility for the marketing of cocoa in October 1947. As far as the local purchase of cocoa was concerned, its functions were taken over by the Nigerian Cocoa Marketing Board, while the responsibility for cocoa sales in the international markets was taken over by the Nigerian Produce Marketing Company Ltd., a subsidiary of the Board. The new managing director of this company was the former managing director of the West African Produce Control Board, E.C.

Tansley. He held a similar post in the Gold Coast Produce Marketing Company Ltd. which was the selling agency of the Gold Coast Cocoa Marketing Board. This arrangement necessarily meant that the Gold Coast and Nigerian marketing companies acted as one body when it came to selling cocoa in the international markets.

The Nigerian Cocoa Marketing Board began its work on 2nd June, 1947.[228] It was then called 'Shadow Nigerian Cocoa Marketing Board' because the enabling Bill had not yet been enacted by the Nigerian Legislative Council. However, these legal complications did not effect the work of the Board, since all decisions of the shadow board were later accepted as binding decisions by the Nigerian Cocoa Marketing Board, such as the fixing of producer prices for the forthcoming 1947/48 cocoa season and the minimum requirements which buying agents had to fulfil in order to obtain a licence from the board.[229]

The Shadow Nigerian Cocoa Marketing Board consisted initially of three official members (the Financial Secretary, the Director of Agriculture and the Director of the Department of Commerce and Industry) and two unofficial members (E.A. Sanda and the Oni of Ife). The Oni of Ife was also appointed Director of the Nigerian Produce Marketing Company Ltd. The Nigerian Cocoa Marketing Board was subsequently enlarged as a result of a campaign initiated by the *Daily Service* to include a representative for producer interests.[230] The person appointed was A. Obisesan, the President of the Ibadan Co-operative Cocoa Marketing Union.

The Advisory Committee consisted of four official members (the Secretary for Finance and Development, the Deputy Director of Agriculture, the Registrar of Co-operative Societies and the Assistant Director of Agriculture), and eight unofficial members of whom two were appointed to represent European trading and shipping interests (E.D. Lucas of Elder Dempster Lines and A.G. Marshall of the Lagos Chamber of Commerce), another two to represent African trading interests (T.A. Odutola and J.O. Fadahunsi), and one to represent cocoa co-operatives (S.O. Babalola). The remaining three members of the Advisory Committee were political appointees (the Oni of Ife, F.B. Arifalo and Chief I.B. Akinyele).[231]

In the following years the Marketing Board was embroiled in a number of political conflicts, but it appears that these only concerned specific decisions of the Board and not the principle of produce control itself. The fact that the principle of produce control as such was not seriously questioned was arguably due to the policy of the Nigerian Government to appoint only members to the Board who were accepted by farmers and traders as representatives of their interests or because of their distinguished political position in their communities. The introduction of the post-war marketing scheme was in this limited sense a highly successful operation, given the fact that the issue of produce control had raised so much controversy in the past.

The policy of the Nigerian government as regards the composition of the marketing board was described in the 1946 White Paper as an attempt to 'facilitate the association of direct representatives of the producers in the control of marketing'. The subsequent history of the Board raises considerable doubts as to what extent this goal was achieved, since the marketing board heavily taxed cocoa farmers in the years up to independence and beyond.[232]

However, there can be no doubt that African trading interests became fully associated in the control of marketing. A minor aspect of this association was that the first two African firms which the Nigerian Cocoa Marketing Board appointed as licensed buying agents were partly owned by the newly appointed members of the Board, the Oni of Ife and E.A. Sanda. But, more important perhaps was the fact that the interests of all classes of European, Syrian, Nigerian and co-operative traders seem to have been subsequently well served by the Board, as, for example, the remarkable increase in commission rates and buying allowances in the year 1947 shows.

It is even arguable that the European trading firms profited from the continuance of the war-time control scheme, since it removed much of the political odium which was previously attached to them like, for instance, the accusation that they would conclude buying agreements among themselves in order to manipulate produce purchase prices. In addition, the trading and manufacturing firms retained a measure of influence either through their direct membership of the marketing boards in West Africa or through their trade associations in London, particularly through the newly established Consumers' Consultative Committee.[233]

Finally, one should mention that the establishment of the Nigerian Marketing Board was probably also welcomed by Syrian traders. Very little is actually known about the Syrian cocoa traders in Nigeria, but they seem to have kept a very low profile in the whole debate about the future marketing arrangements because their interests were arguably to a large extent identical with those of the larger African traders. It is in any case quite remarkable that six of the nine firms which the Marketing Board newly appointed in the 1947/48 cocoa season were owned by persons of Syrian or Lebanese origin.

The history of the introduction of the Nigerian Cocoa Marketing Board fits well into the political trend at the time. The Colonial Office, for example, argued in 1947 that constitutional development in West Africa should be geared 'to meet the administrative need created by increased business and the expanding sphere of government activity on the one hand and the political need to associate the people of the territory more closely with Government on the other'[234]. The history of the establishment of the Nigerian Cocoa Marketing Board in Nigeria seems to provide a fine example of how this policy worked in practice.

The term 'association with government' should, however, not be confused with the notion of democratic development. The introduction of local marketing boards contained no intention to relinquish the full control of the boards to local interests.[235] It has been already pointed out that one of the main reasons why local marketing boards were set up in the Gold Coast and in Nigeria, as opposed to a central marketing board in London, was that political discontent in West Africa had turned the marketing scheme into a political liability in West Africa, as well as the United Kingdom. It was thought that the incorporation of local interests would help to allay suspicion of the Board and prevent further criticism. Yet, the fact that the Secretary of State for the Colonies was relieved from responsibility for the scheme did not mean that the Colonial Office intended to lose its influence over the administration of the scheme.[236] At the introduction of the scheme in 1947, the Colonial Office considered how to keep an option open in the event of the unofficial majority of the Gold Coast Cocoa Marketing Board taking decisions which it thought would infringe vital British interests. Such decisions could be overturned in the last instance by invoking the special reserve powers of the Governor of the colony concerned.[237]

The use of these powers, as well as the use of formal government direction, was considered as politically extremely inopportune at the time.[238] Instead, the Colonial Office hoped to exercise informal control trough the Chairmen of the marketing boards and the careful handling of its African members, as well as through co-operation between British government departments and the London selling agencies of the Board.[239] Later, such interventions occurred on a number of occasions, but these events belong to a different period in the history of statutory marketing in West Africa.[240]

Notes

1   The ex officio chairman of the board was the Parliamentary Under-Secr. of State for the Colonies. This post was occupied by a rapid succession of various Members of Parliament during the war which probably increased the importance and influence of its official permanent members, notably S. Caine and E.C. Tansley.
2   PRO: CO 852, file 319/7, Minutes of Meeting held at the Colonial Office, 11 Sept. 1940. The first meeting of the West African Produce Control Board was actually held on 1st Nov., 1940; see ibid., Minutes of the 1st Meeting of the West African Cocoa Control Board, 1 Nov. 1940.
3   PRO: CO 852, file 445/1, Letter from E. Melville to G.N. Farquhar, 14 May 1941.
4   NAI: CSO 26, file 36148 S73 Vol.I, West African Cocoa Control Board, 'Memorandum on Scheme of Control for 1941/42...', by E.C. Tansley, 1 June 1941.

5   This account of the origins of the post-war marketing schemes differs significantly from D. K. Fieldhouse, Merchant Capital and Economic Decolonization: The United Africa Company, 1929-1989, Oxford 1994, chapt. 6, pp. 229-280. He argues, that the outline of the schemes emerged only in January 1943. See ibid, p. 244.

6   NAI: CSO 26, file 36148 S73 Vol.I, West African Control Board (*sic*), Memorandum 'Control of West African Cocoa' by J. Cadbury, 12 June 1941.

7   NAI: CSO 26, file 36148 S73 Vol.I, Despatch from the Secr. of State for the Colonies to the Governors of the Gold Coast and Nigeria, 5 Aug. 1941.

8   The whole debate can be found in NAI: CSO 26, file 36148 S73 Vol.I., and NAI: Ib MinAgric 1, file 17980 Vol.V. There are memoranda from the Residents of Oyo, Ondo, Abeokuta, Benin, Ijebu and Ogoja Provinces, from the Chief Commissioners of the Western Provinces, Eastern Provinces and the Colony, from the Director of Agriculture and the Registrar of Co-operative Societies. All these memoranda were written in November and December 1941.

9   NAI: CSO 26, file 36148 S73 Vol.I, Letter from the SWP to the CS, 23 Dec. 1941; Letter from the SEP to the CS, 12 Dec. 1941, and Letter from the Chief Commissioner of the Colony to the CS, 7 Nov. 1941.

10   NAI: CSO 26, file 36148 S73 Vol.I, Letter from the Officer Administering the Government of Nigeria to the Secr. of State for the Colonies, 13 April 1942.

11   NAI: CSO 26, file 36148 S73 Vol.I, Letter from the Acting Governor of the Gold Coast, E. London, to the Secr. of State for the Colonies, 11 May 1941, and ibid. Letter from the Officer Administering the Government of Nigeria, A. Burns, to the Secr. of State for the Colonies, 13 April 1941.

12   NAI: CSO 26, file 36148 S63A, Letter from G.W. Henlen to G.F.T. Colby, 31 Oct. 1941. The same fact is also mentioned by D. Meredith, State Controlled Marketing and Economic 'Development': The Case of West African Produce Control during the Second World War, in: Economic History Review XXXIX (1986) 1, p. 84.

13   PRO: CO 852, file 436/9, Minute by G.W. Henlen, 29 Oct. 1941.

14   Some Colonial Office officials were particularly suspicious of J. Knight, who they said would be 'inclined to view the position [of oilseeds sales] from a commercial attitude, and his policy is to a large extent dictated by his commercial interests'. See PRO: CO 852, file 436/1, Minute by G.W. Henlen, 29 Oct. 1941. For the view of the Nigerian government see NAI: CSO 26, file 38300 S4, Minute by G.F.T. Colby.

15   This argument was made most forcefully in PRO: CO 852, file 436/9, Letter from Secr. of State for the Colonies to the Ministry of Food, 25 Nov. 1941; see also ibid., Letter from the Secr. of State for the Colonies to the Land's Commissioner of His Majesty's Treasury, 27 Nov. 1941, and the minutes by O.G.R. Williams, 5 Nov. 1941 and 27 Feb. 1942. The argument was repeated in: NAI: CSO 26, file 36148 S63A, Letter from G.W. Henlen to G.F.T. Colby, 31 Oct. 1941.

16   PRO: CO 852, file 436/9, Minute by S. Caine, 7 Nov. 1941, and ibid., Minute by G.W. Henlen, 29 Oct. 1941.

17   PRO: CO 852, file 436/9, Minute by G.L.M. Clauson, 7 Nov. 1941.

18   PRO: CO 852, file 436/9, Letter from the Secr. of State for the Colonies to the Ministry of Food, 25 Oct. 1941. In particular J. Knight tried in vain to prevent the establishment of an oilseeds board which he felt was 'utterly unnecessary'. See ibid., Copy of a letter from J. Knight to H. Broadly, 19 Oct. 1941; see also NAI: CSO 26, file 38300 S4, Letter from O.G.R Williams to G.F.T. Colby, 3 Feb. 1942. and Meredith, State Controlled Marketing, p. 84.

19   PRO: CO 852, file 533/1, Telegram from the Officer Administering the Government of Nigeria to the Secr. of State for the Colonies, 5 March 1942.

20   NAI: CSO 26, file 38300 S4, Telegram from the Secr. of State to the Officer Administering the Government of Nigeria and to the West African Governors' Conference Secretariat, 14 Feb. 1942.

21   The Colonial Office had already discussed the question whether it was desirable to have two separate boards (one for cocoa and one for oilseeds) or one multi-commodity board. It was decided, apparently largely for the reason of administrative expenditure, to reconstitute the West African Cocoa Control Board as the West Africa Produce Control Board. See PRO: CO 852, file 436/9, Minute by G.L.M. Clauson, 7 Nov. 1941.

22   PRO: CO 852, file 445/3, West African Cocoa Control Board, Memorandum on Long-Term Policy by E.C. Tansley, 20 Nov. 1941.

23   C. Leubuscher, Bulk Buying from the Colonies: A Study of the Bulk Purchase of Colonial Commodities by the United Kingdom, London 1956, pp. 10-11. The bulk shipment of cocoa was discontinued in February 1944.

24   PRO: CO 852, file 533/1, Minute by G.W. Henlen, 12 June 1942.

25   PRO: CO 852, file 533/8, West African Produce Control Board Policy Paper No.1, annex A, Memorandum 'Possible Form of Control for all West African Produce', by G.W. Henlen, 19 May 1941, and ibid., West African Produce Control Board Policy Paper No. 2 by E.C. Tansley and G.W. Henlen, 30 May 1942; see also PRO: CO 852, file 525/4, Colonial Office Memorandum 'West African Produce Control Board', Oct. 1943.

26   NAI: CSO 26, file 38300 S4, Telegram from the Secr. of State for the Colonies to the Governor of Nigeria, 23 June 1942. The control board actually dispensed with the export services of the firms as from 3rd September, 1942.

27   For a different interpretation of this development, cf. Meredith, The Colonial Office, p. 294.

28   PRO: CO 852, file 445/3, West African Cocoa Control Board, Memorandum on Long-term Policy by E.C. Tansley, 20 Nov. 1941; see also PRO: CO 852, file 533/8, West African Produce Control Board Policy Paper No. 2, Memorandum W.A.P.C.B. by G.W. Henlen and E.C. Tansley, 30 May 1942.

29   PRO: CO 852, file 525/4, Colonial Economic Advisory Council, Colonial Office Memorandum 'West African Produce Control Board', Oct. 1943.

30   Report on Cocoa Control in West Africa, 1939-43, and Statement of Future Policy, Cmd. 6554 of Sept. 1944, London 1944, p. 7; see also Statement on the Future Marketing of West African Cocoa, Cmd. 6950 of November 1946, London 1946, paras. 4-5, and NAI: CSO 26, file 37453, Minute by F. Stoddart, 20 Dec. 1940, and PRO: CO 852, file 533/8, West African Produce Control Board Policy Paper No. 2 by E.C. Tansley and G.W. Henlen, 30 May 1941.

31   This section of the chapter is largely based on: PRO: CAB 117, file 181, War Cabinet: Official Committee on Post-War External Problems, Memorandum 'Colonial Economic Problems', 14 Aug. 1941. This memorandum was actually written in March 1941. For the original version, see PRO: CO 852, file 503/9, Colonial Office Committee on Post-War Problems, Memorandum 'Colonial Economic Policy in the Reconstruction Period' by G.L.M. Clauson, 31 March 1941.

32   PRO: CAB 117, file 181, War Cabinet: Official Committee on Post-War External Problems, Memorandum 'Colonial Economic Problems', 14 Aug. 1941; see also Rhodes House Library Oxford, Arthur Creech Jones Papers, Mss. Brit. Emp. s332, box 45/3.

Ministry of Information, Circular No. 9050, Memorandum 'Colonial Economies: Past, Present and Future', [October?] 1943.

33   See D.M. Williams, West African Marketing Boards, in: African Affairs, LII (1953) 206, pp. 53-54.

34   PRO: CO 852, file 503/9, Colonial Office Committee on Post-war Problems, Memorandum 'Colonial Economic Policy in the Reconstruction Period', by G.L.M. Clauson, 31 March 1941; see also PRO: CAB 117, file 181, War Cabinet: Official Committee on Post-War External Problems, Memorandum 'Colonial Economic Problems', 14 Aug. 1941.

35   The original argument was made by J. Cadbury. See NAI: CSO 26, file 36148 S73 Vol.I, West African Control Board (sic), Memorandum 'Control of West African Cocoa' by J. Cadbury, 12 June 1941. For the view of a Nigerian government official see NAI: CSO 26, file 36143, Minute by the Chief Commissioner Eastern Provinces, 1 Oct. 1941. For the Resident Minister's view see PRO: CO 554, file 132, Colonial Office memorandum 'Economic Policy', Aug. 1943.

36   NAI: CSO 26, file 38300 S4, Letter from O.G.R. Williams to G.F.T. Colby, 3 Feb. 1942.

37   NAI: Ib MinAgric 1, file 17980 Vol.V, Letter from the Act. Secr. Western Provinces to the CS, 12 Dec. 1941, and NAI: CSO 26, file 38300 S4, Letter from O.G.R. Williams to G.F.T. Colby, 3 Feb. 1942; see also NAI: CSO 25, file 36148 S73 Vol.II, Letter from the Resident Minister in West Africa to the Secr. of State for the Colonies, 16 June 1944.

38   See PRO: CO 852, file 596/3, Letter from E.C. Tansley to S. Caine, 21 April 1945.

39   PRO: CO 852, file 596/2, Letter from the Governor of Nigeria, A. Richards, to G.H. Creasy, 21 Nov. 1944.

40   NAI: CSO 26, file 36148 S73 Vol.I, Letter from the Acting Chief Commissioner of the Colony to the CS, 7. Nov. 1941. For a similar view see NAI: CSO 26, file 38300 S53, Minute by G.F.T. Colby, 2 Dec. 1941.

41   This paragraph is based on NAI: CSO 26, file 36148 S73. Vol.I, West African Cocoa Board, Memorandum 'Control of West African Cocoa' by J. Cadbury, 12 June 1941, and PRO: CO 852, file 525/4, Colonial Economic Advisory Council, Colonial Office memorandum 'West African Produce Control Board', Oct. 1943; see also E. Melville, The Marketing of West African Cocoa, in: Cocoa, Chocolate and Confectionery Alliance, Ltd., International Cocoa Conference 1948, London 1949, pp. 72-73.

42   PRO: CO 852, file 525/4, Colonial Economic Advisory Council, Colonial Office memorandum 'West African Produce Control Board', Oct. 1943; see also PRO: CO 852, file 630/6, Minute by E.C. Tansley, 1 Jan. 1946. E.C. Tansley wrote that '...I am convinced that either the Nigerian Government must continue a form of control similar to the existing one, or let the trade gradually go back to its pre-war conditions. There appears to be no half-house. *If Government buying ceases, trade monopoly will come back*' [emphasis added].

43   PRO: CO 852, file 630/4, Letter from Sir George Gater to A. Barlow [Treasury], 7 June 1944; see also PRO: CO 852, file 596/3, Letter from John Cadbury to Creasy, 6 March 1945.

44   Report on Cocoa Control in West Africa, 1939-1943, and Statement of Future Policy, Cmd. 6554 of Sept. 1944, London 1944, para. 34; see also Statement on the Future Marketing of West African Cocoa, Cmd. 6950 of Nov. 1946, London 1946, para. 5, and Statement of the Policy Proposed for the Future Marketing of Nigerian Oils, Oilseeds and Cotton, Lagos 1948, para. 14.

45   For a similar argument, see R.J. Southall, Cadbury on the Gold Coast, 1907-1938: The Dilemma of the 'Model Firm' in a Colonial Economy, University of Birmingham Ph.D. thesis, Birmingham 1975, p. 464, and J. Dunn/A.F. Robertson, Dependence and Opportunity. Political Change in Ahafo, Cambridge 1973, p. 58. It is noteworthy that the same policy was apparently applied in other parts of British colonial Africa at the time. See N.J. Westcott, Stabilising Commodity Prices: State Control of Colonial Commodity Trade, 1930-1950, in: C. Dewey, The State and the Market: Studies in the Economic and Social History of the Third World, p. 275.

46   NAI: CSO 26, file 38143, West African War Council, Minutes of the Fifth Meeting, 18 Dec. 1942.

47   PRO: CAB 117, file 181, Letter from the Secr. of State for the Colonies to A. Greenwood, M.P., 20 Feb. 1942.

48   PRO: CO 594, file 132, Summary of Conclusions of the Seventh Meeting of the Civil Members Committee of the West African War Council, 9 and 10 Dec. 1943.

49   This argument is implicitly made in a discussion paper written by G.L.M. Clauson. See PRO: CO 852, file 504/5, Memorandum (for discussion) 'The Overseas Trade of the British Empire before, during and after the War' by G.L.M. Clauson, 16 Feb. 1942.

50   PRO: CO 852, file 503/9, Colonial Office Committee on Post-war Problems, Memorandum 'Colonial Economic Policy in the Reconstruction Period' by G.L.M. Clauson, 31 March 1941.

51   D.J. Morgan, The Official History of Colonial Development, London 1980, vol. III, p. 145; see also D. K. Fieldhouse, War and the Origins of the Gold Coast Marketing Board, 1939-40, in: M. Twaddle (ed.), Imperialism, the State and the Third World, London 1992, pp. 153-182, and Merchant Capital and Economic Decolonization: The United Africa Company, 1929-1989, Oxford 1994, pp. 229-280.

52   See Report on Cocoa Control in West Africa, 1939-43, and Statement of Future Policy, Cmd.6554 of Sept. 1944, London 1944, para. 38, and Statement on the Future Marketing of West African Cocoa, Cmd.6950 of November 1946, London 1946, para. 22.

53   NAI: CSO 26, file 36148 S73 Vol.I, Letter from the Act. Registrar of Co-operative Societies to the CS, 21 Nov. 1941, and ibid., Letter from the Director of Agriculture to the CS, 30 Dec. 1941.

54   NAI: CSO 26, file 36148 S73 Vol.II, Memorandum 'Cocoa' by E.C. Tansley, 4 Nov. 1944.

55   See Report on Cocoa Control in West Africa, 1939-43, and Statement of Future Policy, Cmd.6554 of Sept. 1944, London 1944, p. 12; see also PRO: CO 852, file 525/4, Letter from G.F. Peaker to C.Y. Carstairs, 13 Oct. 1943.

56   For this argument, see Melville, The Marketing of West African Cocoa, p. 72.

57   For the Colonial Office, see PRO: CO 852, file 525/4, Colonial Economic Advisory Council, Colonial Office memorandum 'West African Produce Control Board', Oct. 1943; for the West African governments, see PRO: CO 852, file 554/132, Extract from the Meeting of the Civil Members' Committee of the West African War Council, 7 June 1943.

58   NAI: CSO 26, file 36148 S84, West African War Council, Minutes of Civil Members' Committee, 24 Jan. 1944. In this meeting the committee discussed a memorandum by E.C. Tansley and G.H. Creasy, titled 'Gold Coast Cocoa'.

59   PRO: CO 852, file 631/1, Report to the Secr. of State for the Colonies by G.H. Creasy and E.C. Tansley on their visit to West Africa, 9 Feb. 1944.

60   See PRO: CO 852, file 631/1, Report to the Secr. of State for the Colonies by G.H. Creasy and E.C. Tansley on their visit to West Africa, annex II, 9 Feb. 1944.

61 PRO: CO 852, file 631/2, West African Produce Control Board, Minutes of Meeting of the Cocoa Sub-committee, 16 Feb. 1944; see also PRO: CO 852, file 630/7, West African Produce Control Board, Minutes of 18th Meeting, 23 Feb. 1943.

62 PRO: CO 852, file 533/11, Telegram from the Governor of Nigeria to the Secr. of State for the Colonies, 17 March 1943, and ibid., Telegram from the Governor of the Gold Coast to the Secr. of State for the Colonies, 9 April 1943.

63 See, for example, West Africa, 11 March 1944, p. 389.

64 PRO: CO 852, file 630/10, West African Produce Control Board, Memorandum 'Draft Report on West African Cocoa Control, 1939-1943', 5 April 1944. The second half of the 1944 White Paper, Statement of Future Policy, was written later in the year. For the long-term planning of the Colonial Office regarding other crops than cocoa, see PRO: CO 852, file 630/4, Memorandum 'Post-war Plans West African Produce Control Board: British West African Production of Cocoa, Oilseeds, Oil and Ginger' by G.L.M. Clauson, 6 April 1944.

65 PRO: CO 852, file 630/10, Note 'Publication of Report on Cocoa Control', 5 April 1944.

66 PRO: CO 852, file 630/4, Letter from Sir George Gater to A. Barlow, 7 June 1944.

67 PRO: CO 852, file 631/2, Minute by C.Y. Carstairs, 19 April 1944.

68 PRO: CO 852, file 630/4, Minute by G.H. Creasy, 9 May 1944; see also ibid., Memorandum 'Proposals for the Establishment of a Joint Gold Coast and Nigerian Cocoa Marketing Board' by the Governor of the Gold Coast, A. Burns, April 1944.

69 NAI: CSO 26, file 36148 S73 Vol.I, Letter from the Acting Governor of the Gold Coast, E. London, to the Secr. of State for the Colonies, 11 May 1941, and ibid., Letter from the Officer Administering the Government of Nigeria, A. Burns, to the Secr. of State for the Colonies, 13 April 1941; for the 1943 debate, see PRO: CO 852, file 530/15, Telegram from the Governor of Nigeria to the Secr. of State for the Colonies, 26 April 1943.

70 PRO: CO 852, file 596/1, Letter from G. Whitely to G.H. Creasy, 31 Oct. 1944.

71 These arguments were already raised in PRO: CO 554/132, West African War Council, Civil Members' Committee, Minutes of Meeting, 9 and 10 March, 1943.

72 PRO: CO 852, file 630/4, Memorandum 'Proposals for the Establishment of a Joint Gold Coast and Nigerian Cocoa Marketing Board' by the Governor of the Gold Coast, A. Burns, April 1944; see also NAI: CSO 26, file 36148 S73 Vol.II, Memorandum on Gold Coast Proposals for an Alteration in the Method of Cocoa Control, n.d. [June 1944).

73 NAI: CSO 26, file 36148 S73 Vol.II, Letter from the Resident Minister in West Africa to the Secr. of State for the Colonies, 16 June 1944; see also NAI: CSO 26, file 36148 S84, West African War Council. Note on a meeting held in the Minister's Office, 14 Jan. 1944.

74 PRO: CO 852, file 630/4, Letter from the Secr. of State for the Colonies to the Resident Minister in West Africa, 6 June 1944; for the quote see ibid., Letter from Sir George Gater to A. Barlow of the Treasury, 7 June 1944.

75 PRO: CO 852, file 630/4, Letter from Sir George Gater to Sir Henry French, 21 July 1944; see also ibid., Letter from Sir George Gater to H. Broadly, 15 Sept. 1944.

76 PRO: CO 852, file 630/4, West African War Council, Extract from Summary of Conclusions of the 6th Meeting of the Civil Members' Committee, 6 and 7 July 1944.

77 Ibid.; see also NAI: CSO 26, 36148 S73A Vol.I, Letter from the Governor of Nigeria to the Secr. of State for the Colonies, 19 Feb. 1946.

78   NAI: CSO 26, file 36148 S73 Vol.II, Minute by the Financial Secretary, 24 April 1944, Minute by A. Richards, 9 Dec. 1944, and Letter from the Governor of Nigeria to the Secr. of State for the Colonies, 13 May 1944; see also PRO: CO 852, file 630/4, West African War Council, Extract from Summary of Conclusions of the 6th Meeting of the Civil Member's Committee, 6 and 7 July 1944.

79   PRO: CO 852, file 630/4, Letter from the Secr. of State to the Resident Minister in West Africa and the Governors of Nigeria and the Gold Coast, 6 June 1944.

80   NAI: CSO 26, file 36148 S73 Vol.II, Letter from the Resident Minister in West Africa to the Secr. of State for the Colonies, 21 June 1944.

81   Ibid., Minute by the Governor of Nigeria, A. Richards, 8 July 1944.

82   PRO: CO 852, file 630/7, West African Produce Control Board, Minutes of the 21st Meeting, 13 Sept. 1944.

83   Report on Cocoa Control in West Africa, 1939-1945, and Statement of Future Policy, Cmd.6554 of Sept. 1944, London 1944, paras. 33-42.

84   Nigerian Produce Farmers' Association and the African Industrial Shipping & Exporting Company went out of business in mid-1940 and Anglo-Nigerian Trade Corporation, W.E. Griffith and C.S. Mandrides in the following year.

85   NAI: CSO 26, file 36148 S71, Letter from the SWP to the CS, 19 Aug. 1941.

86   NAI: CSO 26, file 36148 S58, Letter from the Cocoa Controller to the Comptroller of Customs, 27 Sept. 1941.

87   Holt Papers, Mss. Afr. 825, file 535(II), West African Produce Control Board, Circular L.B. 12 of 5 Oct. 1943 and Circular L.B. 80 of 23 Sept. 1944. The percentage quotas of the former "B" shippers came to: S. Thomopulos/1.00%; United Development and Trading Company/0.78%; Flionis Brothers/0.54%; Odutola Brothers/0.35%. The combined quota of the former "B" shippers amounted to 2.67% of the Nigerian crop. According to this schedule the combined quota of the United Africa Company and the other subsidiaries of Unilever amounted to 47.26% of the Nigerian crop.

88   See NAI: CSO 26, file 36148 S73 Vol.I, Despatch from the Secr. of State for the Colonies to the Governors of Nigeria and the Gold Coast, 5 August 1941; PRO: CO 852, file 533/8, West African Produce Control Board Policy Paper No.1, 19 May 1942, and ibid., West African Produce Control Board Policy Paper No. 2, 30 May 1942; see also Report on Cocoa Control in West Africa, 1939-1943, and Statement of Future Policy, Cmd.6554 of Sept. 1944, London 1944, p. 7.

89   See, for example, PRO: CO 852, file 530/7, Extract from the Minutes of the 5th Meeting of the Supply Committee of the West African War Council, 19 and 20 May 1943, and ibid., Minute by C.Y. Carstairs, 6 May 1943.

90   PRO: CO 852, file 530/7, Letter from R.L.V. Wilkes to the CS, 30 Nov. 1943; see also PRO: CO 852, file 596/3, letter from the Governor of the Gold Coast to the Secr. of State for the Colonies, 21 Aug. 1945. The cost of competition was not paid by the firms themselves. They could make losses on their cocoa buying operations without incurring an overall loss of net profits, since they were liable to Excess Profit Tax during the war. Any loss which would reduce the amount of Excess Profit Tax which they had to pay would therefore not hit the firms, but in the last instance the British taxpayer. For this argument see PRO: CO 852, file 596/1, Letter from the Director of Busi & Stephenson to the Secr. of the West African Produce Control Board, 18 Dec. 1944.

91   The quota system was enforced through a penalty system by which those firms which had bought more cocoa than their share allowed had to hand over their excess tonnage to the firms which were underbought. This system operated between 1942 and 1947 and was administered by the marketing board. It was precisely the same system which the firms had used to enforce the 1937 Buying Agreement. For the system itself, see, for example, Holt Papers, Mss. Afr. s825, file 535 (II), West African Produce Control Board, Circular L.B.I., 8 Oct. 1942; for the formal abolition of the quota system see NAI: CSO 26, file 36148 S201, Minutes of the First Meeting of the Shadow Nigerian Cocoa Marketing Board, 2 June 1947.

92   NAI: Oyo Prof 2, file C81 Vol.V, Letter from the Acting SWP to the Senior Resident Oyo Province, 27 Jan. 1944.

93   NAI: CSO 26, file 38300 S32, Minute by G.F.T. Colby, 24 March 1944.

94   PRO: CO 852, file 530/7, Letter from R.L.V. Wilkes to the CS, 30 Nov. 1943. Between the 1940/41 and 1946/47 seasons the allowance for coast establishment charges, head office expenses and remuneration for services rendered in Africa increased from £1 10s 3d per ton to £2 12s 6d per ton (or 74%).

95   Holt Papers, Mss. Afr. s825, file 535 (II), Letter from the District Agent (Lagos), J.F. Winter, to D.L. Rawlings (John Holt & Co. Ltd.), 30 Nov. 1943.

96   NAI: Oyo Prof 1, file 3909, Letter from the Acting Resident Oyo Province to the SWP, 15 April 1947.

97   NAI: CSO 26, file 38300 S53, Minute by J.E.B. Hall, 20 Nov. 1944.

98   PRO: CO 852, file 497/6, Extract from the Minutes of the 5th Meeting of the Supply Centre Committee, 19 and 20 May 1943.

99   NAI: CSO 26, 38300 S53, Minute by H. Mallinson, 8 Nov. 1944; see also ibid., Petition from the Lagos Produce Buyers Association, 26 Sept. 1944.

100   This fact was observed for Ilesha, Ibadan, and Ife. See J.D.Y. Peel, Ijeshas and Nigerians: The Incorporation of a Yoruba Kingdom, 1890s to 1970s, Cambridge 1983, p. 201; Holt Papers. Mss. Afr. s825, file 535(II), Letter from D.L. Rawlings to A. Wood, 10 Sept. 1943, and NAI: Ib MinAgric 1, file 17980 Vol.VI, Letter from the District Officer of the Ife-Ilesha Division to the SWP, 29 Jan. 1944; see also NAI: Oyo Prof 2/3, file C.107, Minute by R.L.V. Wilkes, 9 May 1947.

101   Holt Papers, Mss. Afr. s825, file 535(II), Letter from D.L. Rawlings to A. Wood, 10 Sept. 1943.

102   NAI: CSO 26, file 38300 S53, Minute by G.F.T. Colby, 2 Dec. 1944.

103   NAI: Oyo Prof 1, file 3909, Letter from the Acting Resident Oyo Province, L.L.V. Wilkes, to the SWP, 15 April 1947. The Resident wrote about commission buyers: 'Their other grievance ... is that at least since 1936 the principal firms have been trying to eliminate the bigger buyers, who can stand up to them, by giving commission agreements ... to more and more smaller buyers whom they can control more strictly.'

104   One of the premier loopholes in the system was that produce traders and commission buyers bought cheap light crop cocoa, stored it and then mixed it with the more expensive main crop cocoa in the following season. See NAI: Ib MinAgric 1, file 17980/2 Vol.II, Letter from the SWP to the CS, 16 June 1942; see also chapter five.

105   Nigerian Gazette Extra-ordinary, Public Notice of 25 May 1943.

106   NAI: CSO 26, file 38300 S122, Letter from the Director of Supplies to the Commissioner of Labour, 21 Nov. 1946.

107   NAI: CSO 26, file 36148 S201, Minutes of the 1st Meeting of the Shadow Nigerian Cocoa Marketing Board, 2 June 1947, and NAI: CSO 26, file 36148 S217 Vol.I, Minutes of the 3rd Meeting of the Nigerian Cocoa Marketing Board, 4 Sept. 1947.

108   For more details on the development of co-operative marketing in Nigeria, see
      C.E.F. Beer, The Politics of Peasant Groups in Western Nigeria, Ibadan 1976, pp. 19-
      40.
109   The 1941/42 subsidy of £4,000 was topped up with an additional government subsidy
      of £346. See University Library Ibadan, Obisesan Papers, Report by the Acting
      Registrar of Co-operative Societies [A.G. Stainforth] on Development and Progress of
      Cocoa Marketing Societies, 4 Aug. 1943.
110   PRO: CO 852, file 445/1, Minutes of Meeting between the West African Cocoa
      Control Board and the Cocoa Committee of the "A" Shippers, 9 Sept. 1941.
111   In 1938/39 co-operative societies had 9,468 members, who produced some 5,059 tons of
      cocoa. By 1943 the number of farmers who had become members in co-operative
      societies had increased to 12,738 producing some 11,738 tons of cocoa. See University
      Library Ibadan, Obisesan Papers, Report by the Acting Registrar of Co-operative
      Societies [A.G. Stainforth] on Development and Progress of Cocoa Marketing
      Societies, 4 August 1943.
112   The President of the Ibadan Co-operative Marketing Union, A. Obisesan, was of the
      opinion that without the subsidy societies would disintegrate and probably loose as
      much as 70 per cent of their members. See NAI: CSO 26, file 42125 Vol.1, Minutes of
      the 1st Meeting of the Committee on Co-operative Societies, 24 May 1943.
113   The whole discussion about the co-operative subsidy is preserved in NAI: CSO 26, file
      42125 Vol.I and Vol.II.
114   The Association of Nigerian Co-operative Exporters was set up in September 1945 in
      order to co-ordinate storage and transport of co-operative cocoa to the ports. The
      Nigerian government supported the establishment of the Association by providing a
      loan of £ 500,000 at an interest rate of 5 percent. See R. Galletti/K.D.S. Baldwin/
      I.O. Dina, Nigerian Cocoa Farmers,   Oxford 1956, p. 47.
115   NAI: CSO 26, file 36148 S116 Vol.II, Letter from the Governor of Nigeria to the Secr.
      of State for the Colonies, 28 Aug. 1946.
116   NAI: Oyo Prof 1, file 4445, Ibadan Traders Association Ltd., First Annual Report, 30
      Sept. 1948. The firm was set up in 1947 with an authorised capital of £25,000, £7,195
      of which were actually paid up in 1948. In its first year of existence the firm had a
      turnover of £74,998, £5,953 of which represented gross profits. Net profits amounted
      to £1,907 in that year £1,439 of which were paid out to the shareholders. On E.A.
      Sanda, see R.L. Sklar, Nigerian Political Parties. Power in an Emergent African
      Nation, Princeton 1963, p. 450, note 29.
117   NAI: Oyo Prof 2/3, file C.107, Letter from the Oni of Ife to the Resident Oyo
      Province, 24 July 1947.
118   The Nigerian Youth Movement, for example, held a large conference in September
      1941 which was attended by the Governor of Nigeria, B. Bourdillon, and other
      Nigerian government officials. None of the 17 separate items discussed touched upon
      the issue of produce control. See NAI: CSO 26, file 30055 Vol.II, Proceedings of the
      Nigerian Youth Movement Representative Council Meeting, 6 to 9 September, 1940.
      For a report on dissatisfaction among commission buyers see NAI: Ib MinAgric 1, file
      17980 Vol.V, Letter from the Resident Ijebu Province to the SWP, 24 Nov. 1941. The
      Ibadan Produce Traders' Union was founded on 1st April, 1941 in order to represent
      the interests of commission buyers vis-à-vis the government. The Union's first secre-
      tary was S.A. Akinpelu who held this post until 1945, or maybe 1946. A leading
      member of this Union was E.A. Sanda, who later became its Secretary. As already
      mentioned, E.A. Sanda was one of the three African members of the newly estab-

lished Nigerian Cocoa Marketing Board. On the foundation of the Union see NAI: Oyo Prof 1, file 3909, Ibadan Produce Traders' Union, booklet 'Rules and Regulations', 1 April 1941.

119   NAI: Ib MinAgric 1, file 17980/2 Vol.II, Petition from the Ibadan Co-operative Marketing Union, 19 May 1942.

120   Ibid. The petitioners argued that farmers would suffer most from the effects of the war and stated that it would be 'easy for the Government to see the plight of the wage earners, but the farmers' case is one which is not easy to be seen, because the Government has not as much direct contact with the farmers as they have with the wage earners'. The petitioners' argument why government treated wage earners and cocoa farmers differently appeared later in a more sophisticated version in: M. Lipton, Why People Stay Poor: A Study of Urban Bias in World Development, London 1977.

121   NAI: Oyo Prof 2/3, file C219, Extract from A.S.P. Letter No.1.C.37/III. 235 of 22 Sept. 1942.

122   NAI: Ib MinAgric 1, file 17980 Vol.VI, Resolution by Ibadan District Farmers, 19 Sept. 1942.

123   NAI: CSO 26, file 30055 Vol.II, Letter from the President of the Nigerian Youth Movement E. Ikoli to the CS, Memorandum covering subjects discussed with the Governor of Nigeria, [?] December 1942.

124   See Daily Service, 6 Feb. 1943.

125   NAI: CSO 26, file 36148 S30, Question No. 92 by the Hon. E. Ikoli, 3rd Lagos Member of the Nigerian Legislative Council, 14 March 1943.

126   PRO: CO 583, file 263, Memorandum submitted by the Nigerian Youth Movement to the Rt. Hon. Colonel Stanley on the occasion of his visit to Nigeria in September, 1943; for details on the Nigerian Association of African Importers and Exporters, see A. Harneit-Sievers, African Business, 'Economic Nationalism', and British Colonial Policy: Southern Nigeria, 1935-1954, paper presented to the African Studies Association Meeting, Toronto, 3-6 November 1994.

127   This is of some importance since this criticism influenced the planning of the post-war scheme, whose features - as I have argued above - were partly designed in order to forestall political difficulties.

128   For an example from 1939 see PRO: CO 657, file 47, Administrative Reports. Annual Report of the Western Provinces, 1939, p. 78, and ibid., Administrative Reports, Annual Report of the Eastern Provinces, 1939, p. 67.

129   Daily Service, 11, 12 and 15 May, 1944.

130   This theme later reappeared in a speech which E. Ikoli held at the meeting of the Nigerian Legislative Council on the 8th March, 1945. See NAI: CSO 26, file 36148 S73A Vol.I, Copy of a speech in the Nigerian Legislative Council by the Hon. E. Ikoli, 8 March 1945.

131   Daily Service, Post-War Cocoa Control, 27 Oct. 1944.

132   The hope that the end of the war might bring changes in the narrow field of cocoa control was part of the general expectation that great political and material changes would occur immediately after the war, such as a general improvement in the standard of living, greater welfare and constitutional reform. On such post-war expectations, see PRO: CO 657, file 56, Administrative Reports, Annual Report for the Northern, Western, Eastern Provinces and the Colony 1945, p. 15.

133   See the articles in the Daily Service from the 27 Oct. 1944, 6 Dec. 1944, 7 Aug. 1945 and 20 Sept. 1945; see also West African Pilot, 16 Aug. 1946 and 12 Sept. 1946; see also A. Harneit-Sievers, Zwischen Depression und Dekolonization: Afrikanische Händler

und Politik in Süd-Nigeria, 1935-1954, Saarbrücken/Fort Lauderdale 1991, and A. Olo-runfemi, Effects of War-Time Trade Controls on Nigerian Cocoa Traders and Producers, 1939-45: A Case Study of the Hazards of a Dependent Economy, in: International Journal of African Historical Studies, XIII (1980) 4, p. 686.

134   Daily Service, Cocoa Jigsaw Puzzle, 6 Dec. 1944.

135   R.L. Sklar, Nigerian Political Parties, Princeton-New York 1963, pp. 58-60; see also J.S. Coleman, Nigeria: Background to Nationalism, Berkeley-Los Angeles 1958, pp. 271-284.

136   For an example of how political demands were directly tight up with cocoa control matters, see NAI: CSO 26, file 36148 S73A Vol.I, Copy of a speech in the Nigerian Legislative Council by the Hon. E. Ikoli, 8 March 1945.

137   NAI: CSO 26, file 36148 S73A Vol.I, Copy of a speech in the Nigerian Legislative Council by the Hon. E. Ikoli, 8 March 1945; see also the quote from a speech by E. Ikoli in the Legislative Council Meeting on the 22nd March, 1945, in: J. Wheare, The Nigerian Legislative Council, London 1949), p. 70; see also O. Awolowo, Path to Nigerian Freedom, London 1947, p. 125. The fact that there were no consultations between the government and cocoa farmers, African traders or politicians was even lamented by the weekly journal West Africa, 3 Feb. 1945, p. 121. It is noteworthy that the Nigerian government replied the demands from the the Secr. of State for the Colonies to consult producers on the White Paper proposal that nothing 'would be gained by consultation with producers at this stage' and that anyway 'it would be difficult to find ... the proper person to consult'. See NAI: CSO 26, file 36148 S 73A Vol. I, Letter from the Governor of Nigeria to the Secr. of State for the Colonies, 22 Nov. 1945.

138   I have not found a trace of this petition in the Nigerian archive, but it was fully reproduced in the Daily Comet: Petition to His Excellency, the Governor, by the Produce Buyers' Union of Ibadan and the Western Provinces, 2 , 3 and 4 May 1945.

139   NAI: Oyo Prof 1, file 3909, Petition by the Nigerian Produce Buyers' Union, 3 Sept. 1946; ibid., Petition by the Nigerian Produce Buyers' Union, 4 Nov. 1946 (both petitions were signed by S.A. Akinpelu); NAI: CSO 26, file 38300 S122, Letter from the Nigerian Produce Buyers' Union, 3 Dec. 1946 (this letter was signed by E.A. Sanda).

140   It is not completely clear, when the delegation actually went to the United Kingdom. The first report on the delegation appeared in the Nigerian press on the 12th September, 1945. See Daily Service, 12 Sept. 1945. This section of the chapter owes much to C.E.F. Beer, The Politics of Peasant Groups in Western Nigeria, Ibadan 1976, appendix II, pp. 233-237.

141   Rhodes House Library Oxford, Fabian Colonial Bureau Papers, Mss. Brit. Emp. s365, box 52/4, Memorandum of Protest by the Farmers' Committee of British West Africa, Sept. 1945. For a reprint of the memorandum, see Daily Service, 11 Oct. 1945.

142   C.E.F. Beer, The Politics of Peasant Groups in Western Nigeria, Ibadan 1976, pp. 234-236.

143   The Farmers' Protection Society started to protest against low cocoa prices as early as October 1941. See NAI: CSO 26, file 36148 S12 Vol.II, Petition from the Farmers' Protection Society to the Secr. of State for the Colonies, 13 Oct. 1941. The petition was signed by P.T. Coker.

144   C.E.F. Beer, The Politics of Peasant Groups in Western Nigeria, Ibadan 1976, pp. 42-43. C.E.F. Beer reports that since 1942 A. Obisesan and the Ibadan Co-operative Cocoa Marketing Union were affiliated to the Federation of Nigeria Farmers through the Federal Union of Nigerian Farmers Western Provinces. He seems to mix up two

different events, since the Federal Union of Nigerian Farmers Western Provinces, of which A. Obisesan was President, was only established in October 1943 after a 'big meeting of farmers' representatives' in Ibadan. See NAI: CSO 26, file 36148 S116 Vol.I, Letter from the Registrar of Co-operative Societies to the CS, 21 Oct. 1943.

145 C.E.F. Beer, op.cit., p. 42, note 8, and p. 43, note 14; see also NAI: CSO 26, file 36148 S167, Minute by A.Y. Cann, Aug. 1945.

146 NAI: CSO 26, file 40734, Letters from P.T. Coker to the Emir of Zaria, 8 Nov. 1943 and 19 Nov. 1943.

147 Anonymous, Two Nigerian Lists (Trade Unions, National Council), In: A f r i c a n Affairs, XXXXIV (1945) 174, p. 165. The National Council of Nigeria and the Cameroons was founded in mid-1944.Its first president was the owner of the West African Pilot, N. Azikiwe.

148 Daily Service, 19 Sept. 1945. The article is paraphrasing a speech by A.S.O. Coker on a 'mass' meeting in Ibadan on 17th September, 1945.

149 The Farmers' Committee of British West Africa (Gold Coast branch) consisted of two organisations. One was the West African Cocoa Producers' Agency Ltd, headed by J.B. Danquah and the second was 'an organisation comprising of all constitutional elected Farmer Chiefs (Akuafohenfo)' in the Gold Coast. The latter was lead by J.K. Ayew. The quotation is taken from NAI: CSO 26, file 36148 S167, Letter from the Governor of the Gold Coast to the Secr. of State for the Colonies, 15 Oct. 1945.

150 The Gold Coast delegates in London, A. Nikoi and J.B. Danquah, later became not only leading figures in the United Gold Coast Convention Party and the Conventions' People's Party, but also members of the Gold Coast Cocoa Marketing Board. See B. Beckman, Organizing the Farmers. Cocoa Politics and National Development in Ghana, Uppsala 1976, p. 53.

151 Daily Service, 19 Sept. 1945. The Committee's first public statement opposing the introduction of the post-war control scheme appeared in the West African Pilot, 8 March 1945.

152 NAI: CSO 26, file 36148 S167, Letter from the Farmers' Committee of British West Africa to the Director of Supplies, 7 Aug. 1945.

153 See ibid. F.O. Blaize held the power of attorney of the Association of Merchants and Industrialists, the Farmers' Committee of British West Africa (Nigeria Branch) and of the Farmers' Committee of British West Africa Ltd. See NAI: CSO 26, file 36148 S167, Letter from A.S.O. Coker to the Secr. of State for the Colonies, 20 Sept. 1945.

154 According to newspaper reports, Dr. A. Maya was the recipient of the telegrams, as well as letters which the London delegation sent to Nigeria. It was reported that he had joined the Farmers' Committee while he was in London. See Daily Times, 19 Sept. 1945.

155 Daily Service, 18 Sept. 1945. The principal speakers on this meeting were A.S.O. Coker, S.A. Akinfenwa and E.A. Sanda.

156 Daily Service, 31 Oct. 1945. The principal speakers on this meeting were, apart from the President of the Ibadan Co-operative Marketing Union, A.Obisesan, Comrade (*sic*) Dr. M. Agbaje, Comrade (*sic*) Dr. A. Maya and Comrade (*sic*) S.L. Akintola. Other meetings were held in Lagos on 19th September, 1945 (Daily Service, 20 Sept. 1945), 11th October, 1945 (Daily Service, 13 Oct. 1945), and in Abeokuta on 22nd October, 1945 (Daily Service, 23 Oct. 1945).

157 Holt Papers, Mss. Afr. S825, file 535 (III), The AWAM or the British Government by Cocoa Control Delegation Committee (Nigeria Branch), 6 Nov. 1945. A support fund for the London delegation was set up in October 1945. Subscription was paid by

various well known nationalist activists and companies, such as Dr. A. Maja, the Ikorodu Trading Company (respectively S.O. Gbadamosi), A.S.O. Coker, D.T. Sasegbon, J.K. Ladipo, E.A. Pearce, the National Bank of Nigeria Ltd., W.A. Balogun, R. Williams, S.L. Akintola, and L. Solanke. See Daily Times, 13 Oct. 1945.

158   Daily Service, 4 Oct. 1945.

159   NAI: CSO 26, file 36148 S167 Vol.I, Letter from the Act. Secr. Western Provinces to the CS, 20 Dec. 1945.

160   Daily Service, 27, 28 and 29 Nov. 1945.

161   For the 'order', see Daily Service, 9 and 16 Oct. 1945, and West African Pilot, 9 Oct. 1945. For the report on the 'go slow campaign' see NAI: CSO 26, file 36148 S167 Vol.1, Letter from the Act. Secr. of the Western Provinces to the CS, 20 Dec. 1945.

162   West African Pilot, 21 Jan. 1946. There was some further activity in the Gold Coast. See PRO: CO 852, file 903/2, Cable telegram from the Farmers' Committee of West Africa, Oman Chambers, 17 Sept. 1947.

163   West African Pilot, 20 Dec. 1945. The origins of the Nigerian Farmers' Union are obscure. The Union was mentioned for the first time in October 1944 in an article in the Daily Service, 31 Oct. 1944. There it was announced that a 'mass meeting' to discuss the future cocoa marketing scheme was to be held on 27th January, 1945 under the auspices of the Union.

164   West African Pilot, 7 Feb. 1946.

165   O. Akeredolu-Ale was a prominent member of the Nigerian Youth Movement, of the Egbe Omo Oduduwa and later of the Action Group. In 1952 he became member of the Nigerian Cocoa Marketing Board. On the activities and the career of O. Akeredolu-Ale, see Beer, The Politics of Peasant Groups, pp. 42-43; see also PRO: CO 852, file 904/4, Extract from Nigerian Political Summary, 47272/3c/48, n.d. [1948].

166   The 1946 White Paper on Cocoa Control was distributed well in advance of the actual publication in order to 'exercise influence on the formation of public opinion'. See NAI: CSO 26, file 36313, List of Persons to whom Distribution of the White Paper is Suggested, n.d. [March 1946?]. For an example of very effective presentation of the government's point of view, see Nigerian Daily Times, Regulation of Cocoa Trade after the War' by the Director of Supplies, 30 Nov. 1944. This article was also published in the West African Pilot (29 Nov. 1944) and in the Daily Service (30 Nov. 1944). For an example of the local activities of District Officers, see NAI: Oyo Prof 2/3, file C.107, Minutes of the Ibadan Native Authority Special Inner Council Meeting, 8 May 1947. On the subject of war-time propaganda and its political ramifications in general, see C. Thomas, Colonial Government Propaganda, Public Relations and the Administration in Nigeria, 1939-1951, University of Cambridge Ph.D. thesis, Cambridge 1986.

167   NAI: Oyo Prof 1, file 3905, Report on Visit to Ede by A. Obisesan, [?] November 1944. For the support from A. Obisesan and the Ibadan Chief I.B. Akinyele see Williams, J. Akinpelu Obisesan, loc. cit.

168   Daily Service, 9 Jan. 1945, Post-war Cocoa Control by Comrade O. Awolowo (Now Studying Law and Commerce in England)(sic). On the contacts between the Fabian Colonial Bureau and leading West African nationalists see also P. Zachernuk, 'The Economic Programme of the Southern Nigerian Intelligentsia, 1920-1960, paper presented at the Canadian Association of African Studies Annual Meeting, Kingston, Ontario 11-14 May 1988, p. 4.

169   For a typical example of that sort of ambivalence, see the reprint of an article by H.O. Davies in West African Review, April 1945, pp. 49-51. According to the West African Review, the article had previously appeared in W.A.S.U. Magazine, XII (1945) 1; see also the article by the same author in the Daily Service, 25 Sept. 1945, Cocoa Control in West Africa: An Evil Gesture, and the report of a meeting between the Nigerian Youth Movement and the Financial Secretary, A.W.L. Savage, on 3rd Sept., 1946, in: Nigerian Daily Times, 12 Sept. 1946.

170   See, for example, the Youth Charter of the Nigerian Youth Movement, in: NAI: CSO 26, file 30055, Vol.I, Letter from H.O. Davies to the Governor of Nigeria, 4 May 1938.

171   See R.J. Southall, Polarisation and Dependence in the Gold Coast Cocoa Trade, 1890-1938, in: Transactions of the Historical Society of Ghana, XVI (1976) 1, p.109; see also H.O. Davies' article, Why I joined the Anti-Pool Movement, in: Nigerian Daily Times, 2 April 1938.

172   PRO: CO 583, file 263, Memorandum Submitted by the Nigerian Youth Movement to the Rt. Hon. Colonel Stanley on the Occasion of his Visit to Nigeria in September 1943, Appendix I, Memorandum Presented by the Nigerian Association of African Importers and Exporters, Sept. 1943.

173   Daily Comet, Petition to His Excellency, the Governor, by the Produce Buyers' Union of Ibadan and the Western Provinces, 2, 3 and 4 May 1945. For a similar argument see West African Pilot, 29 April 1946.

174   Daily Service, 9 Jan. 1945, Post-war Cocoa Control by Comrade O. Awolowo; see also ibid., 26 Jan. 1946.

175   For this idea, see also A.G. Hopkins, An Economic History of West Africa, London 1973, p. 271. There is no space to even touch the question what kind of results this policy later had. A treatment of the subject can, however, be found in W.D. Graf, The Nigerian State: Political Economy, State Class and   Political System in the Post-Colonial Era, London 1988.

176   See Holt Papers, Mss. Afr. s825, file 535(II), Note by R.L. Rawlings, 31 March 1944.

177   NAI: CSO 26, file 36148 S73 Vol.II, Note on a meeting held in the Secretary of State for the Colonies' room, 16 Nov. 1946.

178   PRO: CO 852, file 630/4, Minute by G.H. Creasy, 26 Sept. 1944. In this minute G.H. Creasy records a telephone conversation with F. Samuel of the United Africa Company from the same day.

179   See also PRO: CO 852, file 596/1, Minute by G.H. Creasy, 2 Nov. 1944.

180   See, for example, the articles in The Economist, 24 March 1945, The Times, 11 Nov. 1945, and the Manchester Guardian, 13 March 1945.

181   NAI: CSO 26, file 36148 S73A Vol.I, Letter from G.H. Creasy to A. Richards, 14 May 1945.

182   PRO: CO 852, file 596/2, Memorandum by the Cocoa Association of London Ltd., 7 Jan. 1945, and NAI: CSO 26, 36148 S73A Vol.I, Letter from the British Federation of Commodity and Allied Trade Association Ltd. to the Secr. of State for the Colonies, 18 Jan. 1946. A reprint of the memorandum of the Cocoa Association of London was reprinted in: West African Review, January 1945, pp. 19-24.

183   Statement on the Future Marketing of West African Cocoa, Cmd. 6950 of November 1946, London 1946, para. 9.

184   Holt Papers, Mss. Afr. s825, file 535(II), Letter from District Agent Lagos to D.L. Rawlings, 28 Oct. 1944; see also ibid., Mss. Afr. s825 232(II), Quarterly Report of Ibadan Venture, 18 Sept. 1944.

185   Holt Papers, Mss. Afr. s825, file 535(II), Memorandum 'Gold Coast: 1943/44 Cocoa Season' by D.L. Rawlings, 14 June 1944; see also PRO: CO 852, file 595/4, Minutes of Meeting of the Gold Coast "A" Shipper members of A.W.A.M., 31 May 1944, and Holt Papers, Mss. Afr. s825, file 232, Quarterly Report of Ibadan Venture, 18 Sept, 1944. The Ibadan representative of John Holt & Co. wrote that the United Africa Company 'appears to be getting organized for the big drive after the war'. The Association of West African Merchants tried in vain to prevent the reappearance of competition practices in the cocoa trade. See NAI: CSO 26, file 38300 S32, Telegrams from the Association of West African Merchants (Liverpool) to L.C. Booth (A.W.A.M. Lagos), 1 March 1944 and 25 March 1944.
       It is noteworthy that at this point the erstwhile members of the 1937/38 Buying Agreement decided that the 'Agreement terminated on the date in 1939 on which the Ministry of Food assumed control'. This suggests that the 1937/38 Buying Agreement was actually dissolved in 1944, but probably for legal reasons the date was made effective from 1939.

186   See Southall, Cadbury on the Gold Coast, p. 465. This point was also made, though in a different context, by representatives of the United Africa Company in a meeting with a Nigerian government official. See PRO: CO 852, file 530/7, Letter from R.L.V. Wilkes to the CS, 30 Nov. 1943.

187   Holt Papers, Mss. Afr. s825, file 421 B VII, Letter from J.F. Winter to D.L. Rawlings, 6 Sept. 1943. This policy was probably much inspired by enlightened self-interest since in another letter J.F. Winter argued that '...if Europeans want to continue to exert an influence on economic policy, they will have to do it with the aid of the Africans...' See ibid., Mss. Afr. s825, file 232, Letter from J.F. Winter to D.L. Rawlings, 24 Aug. 1943.

188   The view that co-operation with African traders and politicians was necessary in order to safe-guard their long-term interests was adopted by all the European trading firms not before the late 1940s. See Hopkins, An Economic History of West Africa, London 1973, p. 278.

189   The Economist, Letter from W.M. Hood (Cadbury Brothers Ltd.), 6 Oct. 1945; see also the reports on the address which J. Cadbury delivered at the 64th Annual General Meeting of Cadbury Brothers Ltd. in April 1945, in: Manchester Guardian, 17 April 1945 and The Times, 17 April 1945; for the supporting memoranda, see NAI: CSO 26, file 36148 S73A Vol.I, Letter from the Cocoa and Chocolate (War-time) Association Ltd. to the Secr. of State for the Colonies, 24 Jan. 1946.

190   See CSO 26, file 36148 S73 Vol.I, West African Control Board, Memorandum 'Control of West African Cocoa' by John Cadbury, 12 June, 1941; for further detail, see the exchange of letters between J. Cadbury and E. Melville, in: PRO: CO 852, file 903/2, Letter from J. Cadbury to E. Melville, 13 Feb. 1947, and ibid., Letter from E. Melville to J. Cadbury, 19 Feb. 1947. Futhermore, the debate about plans of British Cocoa Mills Ltd. to set up a cocoa manufacturing plant in Nigeria can be found in: PRO: CO 852, file 444/1, Letter from J. Cadbury to C.Y. Carstairs, 13 March 1942. In this connection it is perhaps allowed to record that the honour to have actually manufactured cocoa in Nigeria for the first time has to be attributed to J.K. Ladipo of Lisabi Mills (Nigeria) Ltd. In 1943 he bought 5 cwt. of cocoa in order to make 'drinking cocoa' and even perhaps chocolate. He seems to have abandoned his plans to set up a cocoa manufacturing company very soon. See NAI: CSO 26, file 36148 S12 Vol.III, Letter from J.K. Ladipo to the Deputy Director of Supplies, 17 May 1943.

191 For details on the American positions see V.D. Wickizer, Coffee, Tea and Cocoa, Stanford 1951, pp. 258-259.

192 The memorandum was reprinted in: The West African Review, Dec. 1944, p. 14, 'Open Letter by Mr. I. Witkin, President of the New York Cocoa Exchange'; see also D. Scott, Production for Trade, in: M. Perham (ed.), Economics of a Tropical Dependency, Vol.I, London 1946, p. 269.

193 Pro: CO 852, file 596/5, Minute by E.C. Tansley, 12 July 1945, and PRO: CO 852, file 596/4, Letter from J. Clevenger (President of the Cocoa Trading Corporation), to E.C. Tansley, 22 Jan. 1946.

194 The Fabian Colonial Bureau was a powerful pressure group with strong links to the Labour Party. Already in 1943 the Fabian Colonial Bureau had submitted a memorandum to the Cabinet, which envisaged the permanency of the war-time control scheme. See PRO: CAB 117, file 181, Memorandum 'Social Welfare in World Commodity Control Schemes' by Arthur Creech Jones, n.d. [1943]. On the subject of the support for a post-war control scheme through the Bureau see also J.H. Bowden, Development and Control in British Colonial Policy, with Reference to Nigeria and the Gold Coast, 1935-1948, University of Birmingham Ph.D. thesis, Birmingham 1980, p. 140.

195 See Rhodes House Library Oxford, Fabian Colonial Bureau Papers, Mss. Brit. Emp. 365, box 52/4, Letter from the Secretary of the Fabian Colonial Bureau to the Secr. of State for the Colonies, 28 Feb. 1945, and the letters to the editors by the Secretary of the Bureau, Rita Hinden, which were published in the Manchester Guardian, 9 and 19 March 1945; see also the letter to the editor from C.W. Greenidge, the Secr. of the Anti-Slavery and Aborigines Protection Society, in: Manchester Guardian, 15 March 1945.

196 NAI: CSO 26, file 36148 S73 Vol.II, Letter from the Secr. of State for the Colonies to the Resident Minister West Africa, 24 June 1944; see also ibid., West African War Council, Civil Members Committee, Extract from Conclusions of the 6th Meeting, 6 and 7 July 1944.

197 NAI: CSO 26, file 36148 S73 Vol.II, Note on a discussion in Mr. Creasy's room, 7 Nov. 1944.

198 Ibid., Note of a meeting held in the Secr. of State for the Colonies' room, 16 Nov. 1944.

199 Ibid. The Secr. of State specifically confirmed his retreat in a letter to F. Samuel of the United Africa Company. See ibid., Letter from O. Stanley to F. Samuel, 24 Nov. 1944.

200 PRO: CO 852, file 596/2, Note on a meeting with the Cocoa Sub-Committee of the Association of West African Merchants, 28 Nov. 1944.

201 The West African governments officially were informed about the change in policy on 2nd February, 1945. However, first news that the Secretary of State was about to abandon the scheme reached the Nigerian government already in early December 1944. See NAI: CSO 26, file 36148 S73 Vol.II, Letter from G.H. Creasy to A. Richards, 7 Dec. 1944.

202 NAI: CSO 26, file 36148 S73A Vol.I, Letter from Secr. of State for the Colonies to the Governor of Nigeria, 5 Feb. 1945.

203 See NAI: CSO 26, file 36148 S73 Vol.II, Minute by T.M. Shankland, 19 Dec. 1944.

204 Richards accused the Secretary of State of abandoning the principles of 'good' colonial administration. He argued that the decision to retreat from the 1944 White Paper meant to allow the powerful vested interests of commercial firms to outweigh

the interests of West African cocoa farmers which would have serious repercussions on African opinion. See PRO: CO 852, file 596/2, Letter from the Governor of Nigeria to the Secr. of State for the Colonies, 15. Feb. 1945.

205   PRO: CO 852, file 596/2, Letter from the Governor of the Gold Coast to the Secr. of State for the Colonies, 11 Feb. 1945. For the letter of the Governor of Nigeria see, NAI: CSO 26, file 36148 S73A Vol.I, Letter from the Governor of Nigeria to the Secr. of State for the Colonies, 15 Feb. 1945. A copy of this letter can be found in PRO: CO 852, file 596/2.

206   NAI: CSO 26, file 38148 S73A Vol.I, Letter from the Secr. of State for the Colonies to the Governor of Nigeria, 27 Feb. 1945.

207   PRO: CO 852, file 596/4, Minute by S. Caine, 8 Sept. 1945; see also Office International du Cacao et du Chocolat, International Cocoa Conference 1946: Proceedings, Speech by Parliamentary Under-Secretary of State for the Colonies, A. Creech-Jones, n.d. (Bruxelles 1946), p. 16-21. There he said: 'All the money which does accumulate from the trading of the Board is not profit which goes to individuals, but is social money, which will be used for social ends, for the well being of the people engaged in the production of the commodity.' He also made clear that he considered it would become 'of vital interest to a colony, that it should be able to sustain a sufficient revenue in order to meet the rising standards, which the communities now demand'.

208   NAI: CSO 26, file 36148 S73A Vol.I, Letter from G.H. Creasy to A. Richards, 24 Oct. 1945.

209   Ibid., Letter from A. Richards to G.H. Creasy, 3 Nov. 1945.

210   The first version of the outline draft was accepted by the Nigerian government as early as 4th December 1945. See PRO: CO 852, file 596/4, Letter from the Governor of Nigeria to the Secr. of State for the Colonies. For the crucial meeting between representatives of the Treasury, the Colonial Office, the Ministry of Food, the Board of Trade and the Foreign Office, see PRO: CO 852, file 596/5, Note on a meeting held in the Colonial Office to consider the final draft of the White Paper, 10 Jan. 1946.

211   NAI: Oyo Prof 2/3 C219, Outline of the Proposed Marketing Policy for Cocoa, 12 Jan. 1946, paras. 13 and 18.

212   Ibid., para. 8.

213   NAI: CSO 26, file 38148 S73 Vol.II, Letter from the Government of Nigeria to the Secr. of State for the Colonies, 13 April 1944; see also ibid., Minute by A. Richards, 9 Dec. 1945.

214   NAI: CSO 26, file 36148 S73A Vol.I, Minutes of meeting at Government House, 25 Jan. 1946.

215   Statement on the Future Marketing of West African Cocoa, Cmd. 6950, of November 1946, London 1946, para. 12.

216   See PRO: CO 852, file 596/5, Letter from E. Melville to K.G. Bradley, 22 Oct. 1946, and PRO: CPP(46) 85, Memorandum by the Secretary of State for the Colonies to the Cabinet, 23 Feb. 1946; see also Bowden, Development and Control, p. 323.

217   D. K. Fieldhouse, War and the Origins of the Gold Coast Marketing Board, p. 178.

218   See for example, NAI: CSO 26, file 36313, List of Persons to whom Distribution of the White Paper is Suggested, [March 1946?].

219   Daily Service, 12 Sept. 1946, Report on the Meeting of the Nigerian Youth Movement with the Financial Secretary, 3 Sept. 1946; see also NAI: CSO 26, file 38300 S12, Notes on a Meeting with representatives of the Nigerian Association of African Importers and Exporters, 6 June 1946.

220 Nai: Oyo Prof 1, file 4363 Vol.I, Minutes of the Ilesha Native Authority Meeting with R.L.V. Wilkes, 7 May 1947, and NAI: Oyo Prof 2/3, file C.107, Minutes of the Ibadan Native Authority Special Inner Council Meeting, 8 May 1947.

221 Ibid.

222 Ibid., Letter from the Acting Resident Oyo Province to the CS, 9 May 1947. The Acting Resident wrote that Sanda '...had done more than anyone else in the Province to explain the purpose and merits of the [Marketing Board] Bill to the people and to enlist their support of it... It should be noted that when he was elected a member of the Ibadan Native Authority three years ago he was the leader of a large group whose members were highly critical and even hostile to both the Government and the Native Administration.'

223 The Oni of Ife (A. Aderemi) was born in 1889. He joined the Nigerian Railway Department in 1909, but left in 1919 and started a later successful produce trading firm. Supported by the DO Ward-Price he became Oni in 1930. See NAI: Oyo Prof 2/1, file 472, Life History by Mr. Adesoji Aderemi, n.d. [July 1930]. For more details on the Oni of Ife's biography see P. Ogunshakin, The End of an Epoch: Sir Adesoji Aderemi I, KBE., KCMG., Oni of Ife (1930-1980), (Lagos 1981).

224 The Acting Resident had the following unkind things to say about A. Obisesan: 'The Honourable Mr. A. Obisesan is a nominated member of the Western House of Assembly and elected Member of the Legislative Council. Although he is the acknowledged head of the Co-operative Cocoa Farmers (*sic*), he really knows very little about cocoa or the cocoa trade and his verbosity would be a continuous nuisance to the Board.' See NAI: Oyo Prof 2/3 C.107, Letter from the Acting Resident Oyo Province to the CS, 9 May 1947.

225 NAI: CSO 26, file 36148 S73 Vol.II, Letter from the Governor of Nigeria to the Secr. of State for the Colonies, 13 May 1944.

226 Richards was known to be particularly conservative. See H. Foot, A Start in Freedom, London 1964, p. 103, where Foot stated that Richards '...often allowed his intelligence to overcome his delight in pretending to be a cynical reactionary'. H. Foot became Governor of Nigeria just before Independence in 1960.

227 See the reports on the meetings in Daily Service, 19 July 1947 and 30 Aug. 1947. A copy of the draft bill had been previously sent to a number of African leaders of opinion, including A. Obisesan, E.A. Sanda and Chief I.B. Akinyele. The debate in the newly established Western House of Assembly and in the Legislative Council had thus only declamatory value. For the distribution of the draft bill, see NAI: Oyo Prof 2/3 C.107, Telegram from the Resident Ibadan Province to the CS, 24 April 1947.

228 NAI: CSO 26, file 36148 S201, Minutes of the 1st Meeting of the Shadow Nigeria Cocoa Marketing Board, 2 June 1947.

229 Both were highly contentious issues at the time. In retrospect it is surprising that the Oni of Ife and E.A. Sanda accepted without any discussion most of the proposals and memoranda which the Chairman of the meeting put forward. See NAI: CSO 26, file 36148 S201, Minutes of the First Meeting of the Shadow Nigeria Cocoa Marketing Board, 2 June 1947. It is noteworthy that they also showed the same attitude in subsequent meetings of the Board.

230 See, for example, the article in: Daily Service, 2 Aug. 1947.

231 NAI: CSO 26, file 36148 S201, Minutes of the 1st Meeting of the Shadow Nigerian Cocoa Marketing Board, 2 June 1947.

232 See G.K. Helleiner, Peasant Agriculture, Government and Economic Growth in Nigeria, Homewood/Illinois 1966, table V-F-1.

233   See NAI: CSO 26, file 36148 S201, Minutes of the First Meeting of the Shadow
       Nigeria Cocoa Marketing Board, 2 June 1947. For a discussion of the problem
       between the Colonial Office and the firms see PRO: CO 852, file 596/2, Note on a
       meeting with the Cocoa Sub-Committee of the Association of West African Mer-
       chants, 28 Nov. 1944; see also Southall, Cadbury on the Gold Coast, pp. 479-80, and
       Holt Papers, Mss. Afr. s1428, Interview with J.B. Davies of U.A.C., Service in Nigeria
       with the United Africa Company from the 1930's, Oxford, 9 March 1971.

234   PRO: CO 852, file 904/3, Report of the Committee on the Conference of African
       Governors, 16 July 1947, p. 5; see also J.W. Cell, On the Eve of Decolonization: The
       Colonial Office's Plans for the Transfer of Power in Africa, 1947, in: Journal of
       Imperial and Commonwealth History, VIII (May 1980) 3, pp. 235-257, and D. Killing-
       ray/R.J.A.R. Rathbone, Africa and the Second World War, Basingstoke 1986.

235   See, for example, PRO: 852, file 630/4, Letter from Sir George Gater to Sir Henry
       French, 21 July 1944, and PRO: CO 852, file 596/2, Note on a discussion held at Mr.
       Creasy's Room, 7 Nov. 1945.

236   PRO: CO 852, file 903/3, Minute by E. Melville, 13 May 1947.

237   This possibility was explicitly mentioned in a discussion between representatives of the
       Colonial Office, the Ministry of Food and members of the Cocoa and Chocolate
       (War-time) Association in July 1947. See PRO: CO 852, file 903/4, Notes on a Meet-
       ing held in the Colonial Office, 31 July 1947.

238   PRO: CO 852, file 903/2, Letter from E. Melville to A. Beresford-Stooke, 8 March
       1948.

239   PRO: CO 852, file 903/2, Letter from E. Melville to G. Leach, 15 May 1947. It is
       evident that this policy depended on the co-operation of the local Chairman of the
       Board. Such co-operation was not always forthcoming. See PRO: CO 852, file 903/2,
       Minute by E. Melville, 24 Sept. 1947. For how the Nigerian and the Gold Coast
       Produce Marketing Companies co-operated with the Treasury and the Board of Trade
       to increase the United Kingdom Dollar earnings in the period between 1947 and 1949,
       see PRO: CO 852, file 902/7, Extract from Working Party on Raw Material Prices,
       appendix I, Supply Position and Prices, para. 6, July 1949; see also PRO: MAF 87/25,
       Official History of the Ministry of Food, Control of Raw Cocoa, Sept. 1950, part C,
       p. 1.

240   See, for example, PRO: CO 852, file 904/3, Extract of the Minutes of a Meeting
       between Gold Coast Officials and the Secretary of State for the Colonies, D. Rees-
       Williams, 22 Aug. 1948, and PRO: CO 852, file 904/6, Letter from the Governor of
       Nigeria to the Secr. of State for the Colonies, 20 Sept. 1949.

CHAPTER 8

Conclusion

This book analyses the evolution of an important aspect of Nigeria's recent political and economic history: The involvement of government agencies in the export trade of agricultural commodities. Before the Second World War, the Nigerian export trade was conducted by European trading firms and a small number of African and Syrian traders and the period was marked by severe political conflict between the trading firms and their African buying agents. In the 1950s, however, all major agricultural export commodities were marketed by statutory government agencies and political conflicts in the internal and external trade of those commodities were conspicuous by their absence.

Based on evidence from Nigerian and British government, as well as private, archives it appears that the establishment of the post-war cocoa marketing board was a reaction to two separate developments: The evolution of the relationship between European trading firms and African traders in the 1930s and the repercussions of the British war effort.

The relationship between European trading firms and African traders became increasingly strained in the 1930s. This was due to the increasing ability of the African traders to successfully challenge the dominant position of the European trading firms in the cocoa trade. The outward sign of this development was increasing competition amongst the European firms for the services of African traders by offering them higher commission rates and better credit terms.

Competition in the 1936/37 cocoa season was particularly fierce. When the cocoa price fell in the latter part of the season, the firms suffered from heavy financial losses which had been partly caused by the activities of their African buying agents. In September 1937, the European trading firms, with the notable exception of one smaller firm, the English and Scottish Co-operative Wholesale Society, concluded a buying agreement which severely restricted competition between the firms. One of the primary objectives of the agreement was to regain control over the African buying agents and, as a local representative of one of the European firms put it, to 'educate' African buyers in business methods.

The introduction of the buying agreements occurred alongside a severe fall in the cocoa price in the international markets. In this particular situation, Nigerian traders and nationalist groupings, like the Nigerian Youth Movement, were able to organise a powerful protest movement against the firms which comprised of the farmers' organisations (Ibadan Co-operative Cocoa Marketing Union), trade associations (Nigerian Produce Traders' Union) and the emerging nationalist press. A similar development occurred in the Gold Coast, where the protest movement even included many of the southern Gold Coast Chiefs.

The climax of the West African anti-agreement movement was a hold-up of cocoa and a boycott of imported goods in the Gold Coast, which lasted from November 1937 to April 1938. A corresponding move in Nigeria, however, failed due to the lack of public and especially farmers' support.

At this point the West African colonial governments as well as the Colonial Office became involved in the dispute. The cocoa hold-up in the Gold Coast had precipitated a political and economic crisis of the first order, since the protest movement threatened to cut off the mainstay of the Gold Coast economy - cocoa exports. Moreover, the protest movement sharply criticised the colonial authorities for their stance in the dispute, especially for their refusal to protect the interests of African traders and cocoa farmers against the machinations of the European trading firms.

In order to pacify the protest movement, the Colonial Office appointed a commission of inquiry under the chairmanship of W. Nowell. In April 1938, a truce was concluded between the protest movement and the European firms. The firms promised to suspend the agreement until the publication of the Report of the commission of enquiry on the condition that the Gold Coast and the Nigerian governments introduced legislation which would prevent the reappearance of competitive practices in the trade. The leaders of the protest movement in turn promised to lift the ban on cocoa sales to the European firms and the boycott of imported goods. Cocoa sales subsequently returned to normal.

The Report of the Commission was published after the beginning of the 1938/39 cocoa season. Its recommendations failed to receive support from the West African governments, farmers' organisations and from the Colonial Office. Meanwhile the firms continued to purchase cocoa as if the buying agreement had been only suspended until the beginning of the 1938/39 cocoa season. It was then apparently reactivated.

The outbreak of the Second World War thus caught the European firms unprepared. The 1937/38 buying agreement contained no provisions for the sudden loss of a major market and the firms were faced with the unappealing prospect of buying substantial stocks of cocoa for which there were no customers. They consequently approached the Colonial Office to bail them out and suggested that the British government should purchase the entire West African cocoa crop and employ the trading firms as its buying agents.

The Colonial Office readily adopted this plan for its own reasons: It believed that without government intervention there was a danger of a repetition of the 1937/38 events and that, moreover, the firms would profit unduly from the wartime trade situation. However, lack of finance and expertise forced the British government to seek the co-operation from the firms, which was readily forthcoming, albeit at a price. The firms were virtually given *carte blanche* as regards the determination of the finer details of the scheme, while the relevant government authority responsible for the scheme, the Ministry of Food, restricted itself to the fixing of the producer price. The marketing system which came into being in November 1939 was thus a government purchase scheme whose salient features effectively reinforced the 1937/38 buying agreement with statutory powers.

Despite its objectionable features, Nigerian farmers and even traders, as well as political organisations, approved of the establishment of a government purchase scheme. There was some criticism of the scheme but such criticism was quickly silenced by the public burning of cocoa, which convinced the Nigerian public that statutory marketing would serve the interests of Nigerian cocoa farmers. This conviction was so strong that it was not until the latter part of the war that widespread criticism of the marketing scheme emerged.

In 1940, the responsibility for the scheme was transferred from the Ministry of Food to the newly established West African Cocoa Control Board (later West African Produce Control Board) under the direction of the Colonial Office. At the same time, the marketing scheme was turned into an instrument for the prosecution of the British war effort, which in practical terms meant exceedingly low cocoa purchase prices. Cocoa farmers experienced a serious de-cline in their incomes from cocoa sales and consequently either left or neglected their farms. This had almost ruinous consequences for the cocoa industry. Meanwhile, however, the statutory marketing board made a substantial profit on its cocoa buying operations.

The execution of the war effort changed the relationship between the European trading firms and the colonial authorities. Statutory control of the cocoa trade had motivated the Colonial Office and the West African colonial governments to prepare definite plans for the post-war period as well as enabled the authorities to acquire the means to finance post-war schemes. The outward sign of the new relationship between the colonial authorities and the trading firms was that the latter were not consulted about the shape of the future marketing scheme.

From as early as 1941 discussions were held about the post-war marketing arrangements. The Colonial Office and the West African governments soon came to the conclusion that a return to the pre-war free trade regime with its inevitable conflicts was undesirable and that, for political reasons, the responsibility for the future marketing scheme should rest with local marketing boards administered by the West African colonial governments. In addition, it was believed that statutory marketing had an important role to play in the post-war recovery of the British economy. The acquisition of the control of the oilseeds trade from the Ministry of Food and subsequent establishment of the West

African Produce Control Board in 1942 proved to be the decisive step towards the continuation of produce control after the war.

The 1944 White Paper proposal to establish marketing boards in the Gold Coast and Nigeria was initially met with severe criticism from all sides. The anti-marketing board alliance included such unlikely partners as British and American trading firms, African traders and farmers' organisations and parts of the nationalist movements in the Gold Coast and Nigeria.

In the following three years, this formidable opposition was partly overcome by adjusting the proposed scheme to the criticism it had met. The composition of the future marketing board, for instance, was changed to allow for the representation of farmers' and traders' interests as well as for the representation of local political interests. The realisation of the 1944 plan was considerably helped by the distinct lack of cohesion within each section of the opposition movement. This was particularly noticeable within the nationalist camp, an important part of which had actually declined to join the opposition movement against the proposed post-war marketing scheme on the grounds that the only alternative, the return to the pre-war free trade regime would merely help to perpetuate the hegemony of the European firms in the cocoa trade. It appears that African traders had learnt the lessons of the 1930s, though perhaps not those which the European trading firms had hoped for. When the Nigerian Cocoa Marketing Board was finally set up in October 1947, it met widespread approval.

The main conclusion of this study is that the decision to establish the Nigerian Cocoa Marketing Board was largely taken because the Colonial Office and the West African governments believed that statutory marketing provided a convenient administrative solution for the recurrent political conflicts in the 1930s cocoa trade. The establishment of the marketing boards was arguably a preemptive strategy which aimed at the subtle manipulation of expected fields of conflict. The success of this strategy depended to some extent on local support for the scheme, which due to the incorporation of local political leaders as well as of representatives of local economic interest groups was eventually forthcoming. In retrospect it thus appears that the establishment of the Nigerian Cocoa Marketing Board was an important part of the multifaceted process which led to independence and the end of colonial rule in Nigeria.

But it should not be forgotten that the price for the political pacification of the cocoa trade was paid by the cocoa farmers. Statutory marketing had allowed the colonial authorities to appropriate a substantial part of the farmers' income through the accumulation of marketing board surpluses. These profits were initially solely used to finance the post-war marketing scheme and a number of smaller developmental undertakings, but this policy opened the door for the massive exploitation of cocoa farmers by statutory marketing boards in subsequent years.

Annex

Tables

Table A: Producer and Government Share in the Price Paid by United Kingdom Manufacturers for Cocoa in 1940/41

	£	s	d	£	s	d	in %
Producer price				13	1	4	23
Marketing expenses:							
Charges to f.o.b.	2	19	6				
Charges from f.o.b. to c.i.f.	7	7	2				
Charges by Ministry of Food	3	10	0				
	13	16	8	13	16	8	24
Government receipts:							
Gold Coast export tax	2	2	0				
Marketing Board profit	6	0	0				
United Kingdom import duty	11	13	4				
Ministry of Food surcharge	10	0	0				
	29	15	4	29	15	4	53
Price to manufacturers				56	13	4	100

Source: PRO: CO 852, file 431/2. West African Produce Control Board memorandum 'Sale Prices to the Ministry of Food', annexure II, 26, Nov. 1942

Table B: The Licensed Buying Agents of the Nigerian Cocoa Marketing Board and their Purchases in the 1947/48 Cocoa Season (in percent)

European:

Compagnie Française de l'Afrique Occidentale, Lagos	(4.45%)
Co-operative Wholesale Society Limited, Lagos	(0.85%)
John Holt & Company (Liverpool) Limited, Lagos	(10.26%)
G.B. Ollivant Limited, Lagos	(7.67%)
Paterson Zochonis & Company Limited., Lagos	(6.77%)
Rowntree-Fry-Cadbury (Nigeria) Limited, Lagos	(13.79%)
Société Commerciale de l'Ouest Africain, Lagos	(3.96%)
Union Trading Company, Lagos	(3.05%)
United Africa Company, Lagos	(24.54%)
C. Zard & Company, Lagos	(5.48%)
London Africa & Overseas Limited, Lagos	(1.55%)
Witt § Busch, Lagos	(0.48%)
	(82.85%)

"Syrian":

Flionis Brothers, Ondo	(0.64%)
S. Thomopulos & Company Limited, Lagos	(0.47%)
A.G. Leventis & Company Limited, Lagos	(0.31%)
Mandilas & Karaberis, Lagos	(0.95%)
Cristos S. Mandrides, Benin City	(0.06%)
A. K. Zard, Ibadan	(0.50%)
N. K. Zard, Ibadan	(0.77%)
N. Abizakhem, Ibadan	(0.64%)
	(4.34%)

African:

Ass. of Nigerian Co-operative Exporters, Ibadan	(11.43%)
United Development Trading Company, Ibadan	(0.23%)
Odutola Brothers, Ijebu-Ode	(0.11%)
Ibadan Traders Association Limited, Ibadan	(0.74%)
Kajola Kawusi Stores, Ife	(0.30%)
	(12.81%)

Source: NAI: CSO 26, file 36148 S 217 Vol.I. Minutes of the Sixth Meeting of the Nigerian Cocoa Marketing Board, 16 Aug. 1948, appendix XXXIV, p. 3.

Note: The firms which are emphasised were newly appointed by the Nigerian Cocoa Marketing Board in September 1947.

Table C: Agricultural Wage Rates and Food Prices at Moor Plantation (Ibadan), 1919 - 1943

Year	Labour rates (per diem)	Yams (per ctw.)	Beef (per lb.)	Cocoa (per ton)
1919	1s	30s	1s 9d	£47 12s 0d
1920	6d - 1s	8s	1s 3d	£47 9s 4d
1921	6d - 1s	15s	1s 6d	£15 8s 7d
1922	6d - 1s	18s	1s 3d	£20 3s 2d
1923	6d - 1s	35s	2s 6d	£18 13s 10d
1924	6d - 1s	25s	1s	£19 3s 9d
1925	6d - 1s	5s	2s	£25 13s 1d
1926	6d - 9d	6s	1s 10½d	£33 9s 1d
1927	7½d - 1s 10d	7s 3d	2s 1½d	£55 8s 9d
1928	7½d 1s 10d	10s	1s 1½d	£44 1s 1d
1929	5d - 11d	10s	1s 1½d	£33 5s 0d
1930	5d - 11d	8s 6d	1s ½d	£24 8s 10d
1931	9½d	8s 6d	1s ½d	£14 1s 8d
1932	6½d	3s	1s ½d	£15 1s 2d
1933	6¼d	2s 2d	9d	£14 4s 11d
1934	2d - 10d	2s 6d	7d	£14 11s 10d
1935	3d - 1s	2s 6d	7d	£16 9s 7d
1936	3d - 1s	2s 6d	7d	£22 17s 8d
1937	4d - 9d	2s 6d	4¼d	£22 2s 9d
1938	4d - 9d	3s 9d	4¼d	£14 8s 9d
1939	5d-9d	--	--	£13 15s 10d
1940	5d - 9d	--	--	£15 2s 10d
1941	5d - 10½d	4s 7d	8½ d	£14 0s 0d
1942	9d - 1s 2d	6s 10½d	9d	£13 6s 3d
1943	1s - 2d	10s 3d	9d	£12 6s 3d

Source: NAI: IB MinAgric 1, file 17980 Vol.VI, Memorandum 'Notes on the Cocoa Industry' by Director of Agriculture, J. R. Mackie, 27 Jan 1944.

Note: Cocoa prices are annual customs values and therefore differ widely from seasonal values listed in tables 1, 3, 6, and 7.

Table D: Approximate Nigerian Government Revenue and Marketing Board Surplus in Relation to Producer Incomes, 1936/37 - 1946/47 (in £ '000)

	Producer Income (A)	Export Duty (B)	Import Duty (C)	Marketing Surplus (D)	Government Appropriation (B+C+D)	(B+C+D/A)
1936/37	3,864	119	645	-	764	20%
1937/38	1,677	115	357	-	472	28%
1938/39	1,594	133	336	-	469	29%
1939/40	1,351	96	297	(61)	332	25%
1940/41	1,358	117	276	570	963	71%
1941/42	1,441	209	210	(82)	337	23%
1942/43	1,390	234	350	747	1,331	96%
1943/44	886	149	311	857	1,317	149%
1944/45	1,838	180	460	673	1,313	71%
1945/46	2,675	216	828	717	1,761	66%
1946/47	5,196	230	1,713	5,759	7,702	148%

Source: G.K. Helleiner, Peasant Agriculture, Government and Economic Growth, Homewood/Illinois 1966, tables IV-A-1, IV-A-7, V-E-4; E. Melville, The Marketing of West African Cocoa, in: Cocoa, Chocolate and Confectionery Alliance Ltd. (ed.), International Cocoa Conference 1948, London 1949, p. 76.

Note: The import duty which cocoa farmers paid on their purchases of imported goods is actually unknown. In the calculation above, it was therefore assumed that in the same period the relation between cocoa export and total exports was approximately equal to the relation between the import duty paid by cocoa farmers and the total amount of import duty collected by the Nigerian government. In October 1941 export duty on cocoa was increased from £1 3s 4d to £2 2s per ton. United Kingdom import duties and the levies imposed on cocoa sales by the Ministry of Food during the war were not taken into account.

Sources and Selected Bibliography

Primary Sources

a) *Archival Material*

Classes of files used:

I) National Archive Ibadan (NAI)

CSO 26 (Chief Secretary's Office)
Ib MinAgric (Department of Agriculture)
Oyo Prof (Oyo Provincial Records)
Ondo Prof (Ondo Provincial Records)
Iba Prof (Ibadan Divisional Records)
DCI (Department of Commerce and Industry Records)

II) Public Record Office/London (PRO)

CO 537 (Secret Correspondence)
CO 554 (Original Correspondence "West Africa")
CO 583 (Original Correspondence "Nigeria")
CO 657 (Nigerian Sessional Papers)
CO 847 (Original Correspondence "Africa")
CO 852 (Economic Department/Colonial Office)
CO 879 (Confidential Print "Africa")
CAB (Cabinet Papers)
MAF (Ministry of Agriculture and Fisheries)

III) Rhodes House Library/Oxford

Mss. Afr. s604 (Cocoa Inquiry Commission)
Mss. Afr. s823 (J.R. Mackie Papers)
Mss. Afr. s825 (John Holt & Co. Ltd. Papers)
Mss. Afr. s913 (Cocoa in British West Africa, 1930-49)
Mss. Afr. s1428 (Interview with J.B. Davies of U.A.C., Service in Nigeria
     with the United Africa Company from the 1930's', Oxford, 9 March 1971)
Mss. Brit. Emp. s332 (Arthur Creech-Jones Papers)
Mss. Brit. Emp. s365 (Fabian Colonial Bureau Papers)

IV) University of Ibadan Library

Obisesan Papers

V) University of Birmingham Library

Cadbury Papers

VI) Cadbury Ltd. (Birmingham)

Minutes and Reports 1934-1939

b) *Government Publications*

Final Report of the Committee on Commercial and Industrial Policy after the War, Cmd. 9035, London 1918.
Committee on Trade and Taxation for British West Africa, Cmd. 1600, London 1922.
Private Enterprise in British Tropical Enterprise, Cmd. 2016, London 1924.
Memorandum on the Creation of a Fund for Improving the Quality and Marketing of Cocoa, Nigerian Sessional Paper no. 18 of 1930-31, Lagos 1931.
Report on the Introduction of Co-operative Societies into Nigeria (C.F. Strickland), Lagos 1933.
Report on Land Tenure in the Yoruba Provinces (H.L. Ward-Price), Lagos 1933.
Report on the Introduction of Co-operative Societies into Nigeria (C.F. Strickland), Lagos 1933.
Report on Agricultural Marketing Schemes for the Year 1938, Cmd.5734, London 1938.
Report of the Commission of Inquiry on the Marketing of West African Cocoa (Chairman: W. Nowell), Cmd.5845 of September 1938, London 1938.
Memorandum on the Future Political Development of Nigeria (B.H. Bourdillon), Lagos 1939.
Report of a Committee Appointed in Nigeria to Examine Recommendations Made by the Commission on the Marketing of West African Cocoa (Chairman: E.J.C. Kelly), Nigerian Sessional Paper No. 20 of 1939, Lagos 1939.
Despatch from the Secretary of State for the Colonies to the Colonial Governments Regarding Certain Aspects of Colonial Policy in War-Time, 5th June, 1941, Cmd.6299, London 1941.
A further Memorandum on the Future Political Development of Nigeria (B.H. Bourdillon), Lagos 1942.
Memorandum on Organization and Control of War-time Trade and Production, Lagos 1943.
Report on Cocoa Control in West Africa, 1939-1943, and Statement of Future Policy, Cmd. 6554 of Sept. 1944, London 1944.
Preliminary Statement on Development Planning in Nigeria, Nigerian Sessional Paper no.6 of 1945, Lagos 1945.
A Ten Years Plan of Development and Welfare for Nigeria 1946, Nigerian Sessional Paper no. 24 of 1945, Lagos 1946.
Enquiry into the Cost of Living and the Control of the Cost of Living in the Colony and Protectorate of Nigeria (Chairman: T. Davies), Nigerian Sessional Paper no.6 of 1945, London 1946.
Statement on the Future Marketing of West African Cocoa, Cmd. 6950 of November 1946, London 1946.
An Ordinance to Establish a Cocoa Marketing Board for Nigeria, Nigerian Sessional Paper no. 33 of 1947, Lagos 1947.
Statement of the Policy Proposed for the Future Marketing of Nigerian Oils, Oil seeds and Cotton, Lagos 1948.
Report of the Commission of Enquiry into Conditional Sales (Chairman: H. Adsheat), Lagos 1948.

Nigerian Cocoa Marketing Report. Annual Report 1947/48.
Nigerian Produce Marketing Company. Annual Report 1947/48.
Report on Financial and Physical Problems of Development in the Gold Coast (D. Seers and C.R. Ross), Accra 1952.
Report by the Advisory Committee on Aids to African Businessmen (Chairman: H.O. Davies), Lagos 1959.
Report of the Commission of Enquiry into the Affairs of Certain Statutory Corporations in Western Nigeria (Chairman: A.S.O. Coker), Lagos 1962.

c) *Newspapers and Magazines (for selected periods only)*

West Africa
West African Review
West African Pilot
Nigerian Daily Service
Nigerian Daily Times
The Economist
The Times
The Manchester Guardian

Secondary Sources

a) *Books*

Abbot, J.C.: Agricultural Marketing Boards. Their Establishment and Operation. FAO Marketing Guide, No. 5, Rome 1974.
Adebayo, A.: White Man in Black Skin, Ibadan 1981.
Adebo, Chief S.E.: Our Unforgettable Years, Lagos/Ibadan 1984.
Adelabu, A.: Africa in Ebullition. A Handbook of Freedom for Nigerian Nationalists, Ibadan 1952.
Ajayi, A.F.A./I. Espie (eds.): A Thousand Years in West African History. A Handbook for Teachers and Students, Ibadan 1965.
Ajayi, J.F.A./M. Crowder (eds.): History of West Africa, Vol.II, London 1974.
Akeredolu-Ale, E.O.: The Underdevelopment of Indigenous Entrepreneurship in Nigeria, Ibadan 1975.
Akinjogbin, I.A./S. Osoba (eds.): Topics on Nigerian Economic and Social History, Ile-Ife 1980.
Aladeyana, A.: The Marketing Board System. A Bibliography, Ibadan 1971.
Albertini, R. von: Dekolonisation. Die Diskussion über Verwaltung und Zukunft der Kolonien, 1919-1960, Köln 1966.
Allen, C./R.W. Johnson (eds.): African Perspectives. Papers in the History, Politics and Economics of Africa Presented to T. Hodgkin, Cambridge 1970.
Ananaba, W.: The Trade Union Movement in Nigeria, Benin 1969.
Are, L.A./D.R.G. Gwynne-Jones (eds.): Cocoa in West Africa, Ibadan 1974.

Arhin, K.: West African Traders in Ghana in the Nineteenth and Twentieth Centuries, London 1979.

Arhin, K./P. Hesp/L. van der Laan (eds.): Marketing Boards in Tropical Africa, London 1985.

Aronson, D.R.: The City is Our Farm. Seven Migrant Ijebu Yoruba Families, Boston 1978.

Asiwaju, A.I.: Western Yorubaland under European Rule, 1889-1945. A Comparative Analysis of French and British Colonialism, London 1976.

Atanda, J.A.: The New Oyo Empire: Indirect Rule and Change in Western Nigeria, 1894-1934, London 1973.

Austen, R.: African Economic History. Internal Development and External Dependency, London 1987.

Awolowo, O.: Path to Nigerian Freedom, London 1947.

Awolowo, O.: Awo: The Autobiography of Chief Obafemi Awolowo, (Cambridge 1960).

Awolowo, O.: My Early Life, Lagos 1968.

Ayandele, E.A.: The Educated Elite in the Nigerian Society, Ibadan 1974.

Ayandele, E.A.: Nigerian Historical Studies, London 1979.

Baldwin, K.D.S.: The Marketing of Cocoa in Western Nigeria, London 1954.

Baldwin, K.D.S.: The Niger Agricultural Project. An Experiment in African Development, Oxford 1957.

Bangura, Y.M.: Britain and Commonwealth Africa: The Politics of Economic Relations, 1951-75, Manchester 1983.

Bareau, P.: The Sterling Area. What it is and how it Works, London 1948.

Barker, J. (ed.): The Politics of Agriculture in Tropical Africa, Beverly Hills 1984.

Bates, R.H./M.F. Lofchie (eds.): Agricultural Development in Africa, New York 1980.

Bates, R.H.: Essays on the Political Economy of Rural Africa, Cambridge 1983.

Bates, R.H.: Markets and States in Tropical Africa. The Political Basis of Agricultural Policies, Berkeley 1981.

Bauer, P.T.: West African Trade. A Study of Competition, Oligopoly and Monopoly in a Changing Economy, Cambridge 1954.

Bauer, P.T.: Nigerian Development Experience. Aspects and Implications, Ile-Ife 1974.

Bauer, P.T.: Reality and Rhetoric: Studies in the Economics of Development, London 1984.

Bayart, J.-F.: The State in Africa: The Politics of the Belly, Harlow 1993.

Beckman, B.: Organizing the Farmers. Cocoa Politics and National Development in Ghana, Uppsala 1976.

Beer, C.E.F.: The Politics of Peasant Groups in Western Nigeria, Ibadan 1976.

Belasco, B.I.: The Entrepreneur as Culture Hero: Pre-adaptations in Nigerian Economic Development, New York 1980.

Berry, S.S.: Cocoa, Custom and Socio-Economic Change in Rural Western Nigeria, Oxford 1975.

Berry, S.S.: Fathers Work for Their Sons: Accumulation, Mobility and Class Formation in an Extended Yoruba Community, Berkeley 1985.

Bienen, H./V.R. Diejomah (eds.): Inequality and Development in Nigeria, New York-London 1981.

Biersteker, T.J.: Multinationals, the State, and Control of the Nigerian Economy, Princeton/N.Y. 1987.

Bonin, H.: C.F.A.O.: Cent Ans de Compétition, Paris 1987.

Boone, C.: Merchant Capital and the Roots of State Power in Senegal, 1830-1985, Cambridge 1992.

Breuilly, J.: Nationalism and the State, Manchester 1982.

Brown, C.V.: Government and Banking in Western Nigeria, Ibadan/Lagos 1964.

Brown, C.V.: The Nigerian Banking System, London 1966.

Brown, I.: The Economics of Africa and Asia in the Inter-War Depression, London 1989.

Bunker, S.G.: Peasants against the State: The Politics of Market Control in Bugisu Uganda, 1900-1983, London 1987.

Burns, A.C.M.: Colonial Civil Servant, London 1949.

Button, R.F.: Wanderings in West Africa, London 1943.

Cairncross, A.: Years of Recovery: British Economic Policy, 1945-51, London 1985.

Carney, D.E.: Government and Economy in British West Africa. A Study of the Role of Public Agencies in the Economic Development of British West Africa, 1947-1955, New York 1961.

Cocoa, Chocolate and Confectionery Alliance Ltd. (ed.): International Cocoa Conference 1947, London 1948.

Cocoa, Chocolate and Confectionery Alliance Ltd. (ed.): International Cocoa Conference 1948, London 1949.

Coleman, J.S.: Nigeria: Background to Nationalism, Berkeley 1958.

Cox-George, N.A.: Studies in Finance and Development. The Gold Coast (Ghana) Experience 1914-1950, London 1973.

Cross, J.A.: Lord Swinton, Oxford 1982.

Crowder, M. (ed.): West Africa under Colonial Rule, London 1968.

Crowder, M. (ed.): Colonial West Africa. Collected Essays, London 1978.

Crowder, M. (ed.): The Cambridge History of Africa, Vol. VIII, c.1840-1975, Cambridge 1984.

Cruise O'Brien, D./J. Dunn/R. Rathbone (eds.): Contemporary West African States, Cambridge 1989.

Dand, R.: The International Cocoa Trade, Cambridge 1993.

Darwin, J.: The End of the British Empire: The Historical Debate, Oxford 1991.

Davies, P.N.: The Trade Makers: Elder Dempster in West Africa, 1852-1972, London 1973.

Davies, P.N.: Trading in West Africa, 1840-1920, London 1976.

Dewey, C./A.G. Hopkins (eds.): The Imperial Impact: Studies in the Economic History of Africa and India, London 1978.

Dewey, C. (ed.): The State and the Market. Studies in the Economic and Social History of the Third World, New Delhi 1988.

Drummond, I.M.: Imperial Economic Policy, 1917-1939, London 1974.

Duignan, P./L.H. Gann (eds.): Colonialism in Africa 1870-1960, Vol.I: The History and Politics of Colonialism 1870-1914, Cambridge 1969.

Duignan, P./L.H. Gann (eds.): Colonialism in Africa 1870-1960, Vol. IV: The Economics of Colonialism, Cambridge 1975.

Dumont, R.: False Start in Africa, London 1966.

Dunn, J./A.F. Robertson: Dependence and Opportunity. Political Change in Ahafo, Cambridge 1973.

Dunn, J. (ed.): West African States: Failure and Promise. A Study in Comparative Politics, Cambridge 1978.

Eades, J.S.: The Yoruba Today, Cambridge 1980.

Ehler, F.: Handelskonflikte zwischen europäischen Firmen und einheimischen Produzenten in British West Afrika - Die Cocoa "Hold-ups" in der Zwischenkriegszeit, Zürich 1977.

Eicher, C.K./C. Liedholm (eds.): Growth and Development of the Nigerian Economy, East Lansing/Michigan 1970.

Ekundare, R.O.: An Economic History of Nigeria, 1860-1960, London 1973.

Fadipe, N.A.: The Sociology of the Yoruba, ed. by F.O. Okediji and O.O. Okediji, Ibadan 1970.

Falola, T. (ed.): Britain and Nigeria: Exploitation or Development?, London 1987.

Famoriyo, S.: Land Tenure and Agricultural Development in Nigeria, Ibadan 1979.

Fieldhouse, D.K.: Economics and Empire, 1930-1914, London 1973.

Fieldhouse, D.K.: Unilever Overseas: The History of a Multinational, 1895-1965, London 1978.

Fieldhouse, D.K.: Black Africa 1945-1980. Economic Decolonization and Arrested Development, London 1986.

Fieldhouse, D.K.: Merchant Capital and Economic Decolonization: The United Africa Company, 1929-1989, Oxford 1994.

Fitch, B./M. Oppenheimer: Ghana: End of an Illusion, New York 1966.

Flint, J.E.: Sir George Goldie and the Making of Nigeria, London 1960.

Foot, H.: A Start in Freedom, London 1964.

Forrest, T.: Politics and Economic Development in Nigeria, Boulder/Colorado 1993.

Forrest, T.: The Advance of African Capital, Edinburgh 1994.

Freund, B.: Capital and Labour in the Nigerian Tin Mines, Harlow 1981.

Fry, R.H.: Bankers in West Africa. The Story of the Bank of British West Africa Ltd., London 1972.

Gallagher, J.A.: The Decline, Revival and Fall of the British Empire, Cambridge 1982.

Galletti, R./K.D.J Baldwin/I.O. Dina: Nigerian Cocoa Farmers, Oxford 1956.

Gann, L.H./P. Duignan (eds.): African Proconsuls: European Governors in Africa, New York 1978.

Gardner, R.N.: Sterling-Dollar Diplomacy in Current Perspective, New York 1980.

Garlick, P.C.: African Traders and Economic Development in Ghana, Oxford 1971.

Geis, H.-G.: Die Geld- und Banksysteme der Staaten Westafrikas, München 1967.

Geiss, I.: Pan-Afrikanismus. Zur Geschichte der Dekolonisation, Frankfurt/M. 1968.

Gifford, P./W.R.R. Louis: Transfer of Power in Africa: Decolonization, 1940-1960, New Haven 1982.

Goldsworthy, D.: Colonial Issues in British Politics, 1945-1961, Oxford 1971.

Graf, W.D.: The Nigerian State: Political Economy, State Class and Political System in the Post-Colonial Era, London 1988.

Gunnarson, C.: The Gold Coast Cocoa Industry, 1900-1939. Production, Prices and Structural Change, Lund 1978.

Gupta, P.S.: Imperialism and the British Labour Movement, New York 1975.

Gutkind, P.C.W./P. Waterman (eds.): African Social Studies, London 1977.

Gutkind, P.C.W./I. Wallerstein: The Political Economy of Contemporary Africa, Beverly Hills 1985.

Guyer, J.I.: Representation without Taxation: An Essay on Democracy in Rural Nigeria, Centre for Advanced Social Science, Occasional Monographs No. 3, Lagos 1994.

Hailey, M.: Native Administration and Political Development in British Tropical Africa, Report, 1940-42, unpublished report London 1944 (reprinted Liechtenstein 1979).

Hailey, M.: Native Administration in the British African Territories, London 1951.

Hall, H.D./C.C. Wrigley: Studies of Overseas Supply, London 1956.

Hancock, W.K.: Survey of British Commonwealth Affairs, Vol.II: Problems of Economic Policy, 1918-1939, London 1940.

Hancock, W.K./M.M. Gowing: British War Economy, London 1975, 2nd ed.

Hanisch, R./C. Jakobeit (eds.): Der Kakaoweltmarkt. Weltmarktintegrierte Entwicklung und nationale Steuerungspolitik der Produzentenländer, Vol. II: Afrika, Hamburg 1991

Hargreaves, J.D.: Decolonization in Africa, London 1988.
Harneit-Sievers, A.: Zwischen Depression und Dekolonization: Afrikanische Händler und Politik in Süd-Nigeria, 1935-1954, Saarbrücken-Fort Lauderdale 1991.
Hart, K.: The Political Economy of West African Agriculture, Cambridge 1982.
Hawkins, E.K.: Road Transport in Nigeria: A Study of African Enterprise, London 1958.
Helleiner, G.K.: Peasant Agriculture, Government and Economic Growth in Nigeria, Homewood/Illinois 1966.
Herskovitz, M.J./M. Harwitz (eds.): Economic Transition in Africa, London 1964.
Heyer, J./P. Roberts/G. Williams (eds.): Rural Development in Tropical Africa, London 1981.
Hieke, E./G.L. Gaiser: Hamburg - West Afrika, Hamburg 1949.
Hill, P.: The Migrant Cocoa-Farmers of Southern Ghana. A Study in Rural Capitalism, Cambridge 1963.
Hodder, B.W./U.I. Ukwu: Markets in West Africa. Studies of Markets and Trade among the Yoruba and Ibo, Ibadan 1969.
Hodgkin, T.: Nationalism in Colonial Africa, London 1956.
Hodgkin, T. (ed.): Nigerian Perspectives: An Historical Anthology, Oxford 1960.
Hogendorn, J.S.: Nigerian Groundnut Exports: Origins and Early Development, Ibadan 1978.
Holland, R.F.: European Decolonization 1918-1981: An Introductory Survey, Basingstoke 1985.
Hoos, S. (ed.): Agricultural Marketing Boards in International Perspective, Cambridge/Mass. 1979.
Hopkins, A.G.: An Economic History of West Africa, London 1973.
Hourani, A./N. Shehadi: (eds.): The Lebanese in the World, London 1992.
Howard, R.: Colonialism and Underdevelopment in Ghana, London 1978.
Hurstfield, J.: The Control of Raw Materials, London 1953.
Ikime, O. (ed.): Groundworks of Nigerian History, Ibadan 1980.
Iliffe, J.: The Emergence of African Capitalism, London 1983.
Ingham, B.: Tropical Exports and Economic Development. New Perspectives on Producer Response in Three Low-Income Countries, London 1981.
International Bank for Reconstruction and Development, Report of a Mission Organized by the International Bank for Reconstruction and Development at the Request of the Governments of Nigeria and the United Kingdom, 'The Economic Development of Nigeria', Baltimore 1955.
International Cocoa Research Conference, Ibadan 1975, Conference Proceedings, London 1975.
Isichei, M.A.: A History of Nigeria, London 1983.
Jones, A.C.: New Fabian Colonial Essays, London 1959.
Joseph, R.: Democracy and Prebendal Politics in Nigeria: The Rise and Fall of the Second Republic, Cambridge 1987.
Kay, G.B. (ed.): The Political Economy of Colonialism in Ghana. A Collection of Documents and Statistics, 1900-1960, Cambridge 1972.
Kayode, M.O./Y.B. Usman (eds.): Nigeria since Independence: The First 25 Years, Vol.II: The Economy, Ibadan 1989.
Kennedy, P.T.: Ghanaian Businessmen. From Artisan to Capitalist Entrepreneur in a Dependent Economy, München 1980.
Kennedy, P.: African Capitalism. The Struggle for Ascendency, Cambridge 1988.
Kilby, P.: Industrialization in an Open Economy: Nigeria 1945-1966, Cambridge 1969.

Killick, T.: Development Economics in Action. A Study of Economic Policies in Ghana, London 1978.

Killingray, D./R.J.A.R. Rathbone (eds.): Africa and the Second World War, Basingstoke 1986.

Knapp, A.W.: The Cocoa and Chocolate Industry, London/New York 1930, 2nd revised ed..

Kohnert, D.: Klassenbildung im Ländlichen Nigeria. Das Beispiel der Savannenbauern in Nupeland, Hamburg 1982.

Konings, P.: The State and Rural Class Formation in Ghana: A Comparative Analysis, London 1986.

Kotey, R.A./C. Okali/B.E. Rourke: The Economics of Cocoa Production and Marketing. Proceedings of Cocoa Economics Research Conference, Legon, 1973, Legon 1974.

Kriesel, H.C.: Cocoa Marketing in Nigeria, East Lansing 1969.

Kwamena-Poh, M./J.Tosh/R. Waller/M. Tidy: African History in Maps, Harlow 1982.

Kwem, M.C.: Der Weltmarkt für Kakao unter besonderer Berücksichtigung der Position Nigerias, Frankfurt/M. 1985.

Laboratoire Connaisance du Tiers-Monde (ed.): Entreprises et entrepreneur en Afrique, 2 Vols., Paris 1982.

Langley, J.A.: Pan-Africanism and Nationalism in West Africa, 1900-1945. A Study in Ideology and Social Classes, Oxford 1973.

Lee, J.M.: Colonial Development and Good Government, Oxford 1967.

Leith-Ross, S.: Stepping-Stone. Memoirs of Colonial Nigeria, 1907-1960, London 1983.

Leubuscher, C.: Bulk Buying from the Colonies: A Study of the Bulk Purchase of Colonial Commodities by the United Kingdom, London 1956.

Leubuscher, C.: The West African Shipping Trade, 1909-1959, Leyden 1963.

Lipton, M.: Why People Stay Poor: A Study of Urban Bias in World Development, London 1977.

Lister, P. Cunliffe: I Remember, n.d. [London 1949].

Lloyd, P.C.: Yoruba Land Law, London 1962.

Lloyd, P.C. (ed.): The New Elites of Tropical Africa. Studies Presented and Discussed at the 6th International African Seminar, 1964, London 1966.

Lloyd, P.C.: Africa in Social Change. Changing Traditional Societies in the Modern World, Harmondsworth 1967.

Lloyd, P.C./A.L. Mabogunje/B. Awe (eds.): The City of Ibadan, Cambridge 1967.

Lloyd, P.C.: Power and Independence. Urban Africans' Perception of Social Inequality, London 1974.

Longe, O.: A Rare Breed: The Story of Chief Timothy Adeola Odutola, Ogbeni Oja Ijebu-Ode, Lagos 1981.

Louis, W.R.: Imperialism at Bay, 1941-1945. The United States and the Decolonization of the British Empire, Oxford 1977.

Loynes, J.B. de: The West African Currency Board, 1912-1962, London 1962.

Lubeck, P.M. (ed.): The African Bourgeoisie: Capitalist Development in Nigeria, Kenya and the Ivory Coast, Boulder/Colorado 1987.

Macmillan, A.: The Redbook of West Africa, London 1920.

MacPhee, A.: The Economic Revolution in British West Africa, London 1926.

Mansergh, P.S.: Survey of British Commonwealth Affairs. Problems of Wartime Cooperation and Post-War Change, 1938-1952, London 1958.

Martin, S.M.: Palm Oil and Protest: An Economic History of the Ngwa Region, South-Eastern Nigeria, 1800-1980, Cambridge 1988.

Meillassoux, C. (ed.): The Development of Indigenous Trade and Markets in West Africa, London 1971.

Milburn, J.F.: British Business and Ghanaian Independence, London 1977.

Gerth, H.H./C.W. Mills (eds.): From Max Weber: Essays in Sociology, London 1948.

Milward, A.S., War, Economy and Society 1939-1945, London 1987^2.

Morgan, D.J.: The Official History of Colonial Development, London 1980.

Morris-Jones, W.H./G. Fischer (eds.): Decolonisation and After: The British and French Experience, London 1980.

Muffett, D.: Empire Builder Extraordinary: Sir George Goldie, Isle of Man 1978.

Munro, J.F.: Britain in Tropical Africa, 1880-1960: Economic Relationships and Impact, London 1984.

Nafzinger, E.W.: African Capitalism. A Case Study in Nigerian Entrepreneurship, Stanford 1977.

Newlyn, W.T.: Money and Banking in British Colonial Africa: A Study of the Monetary and Banking Systems of Eight British African Territories, London 1954.

Nicolson, I.F.: The Administration of Nigeria, 1900-60: Men, Methods and Myths, Oxford 1969.

Nigerian Daily Times, Who's Who in Nigeria. A Bibliographical Dictionary, Lagos 1956.

Niven, Sir R.: Nigerian Kaleidoscope: Memoirs of a Colonial Servant, London 1982.

North, D.C.: Structure and Change in Economic History, New York 1981.

Nwabughuogu, A.: Political Change, Social Response and Economic Development: The Dynamics of Change in Eastern Nigeria, 1930-1950, Madison/Wis. 1979

Nwabueze, B.O.: A Constitutional History of Nigeria, London 1982.

Obichere, B.I. (ed.): Studies in Southern Nigerian History, London 1982.

Office International du Cacao et du Chocolat, International Cocoa Conference 1946: Proceedings, n.d. [Bruxelles 1946].

Ofonagoro, W.I.: Trade and Imperialism in Southern Nigeria, 1881-1929, New York 1979.

Ogunshakin, P.: The End of an Epoch: Sir Adesoji Aderemi I, KBE., KCMG., Oni of Ife, (1930-1980), Lagos 1981.

Olatunbosun, D.: Nigeria's Neglected Rural Majority, Ibadan 1975.

Oliver, R./A. Atmore: Africa Since 1800, 3rd ed. Cambridge 1981.

Olusanya, G.O.: The Second World War and Politics in Nigeria, 1935-1953, Lagos 1973.

Olusanya, G.O.: The West African Students' Union and the Politics of Decolonisation, 1925-1958, Ibadan 1982.

Olusanya, G.O.: Fifty Years of National Bank of Nigeria Limited, Festschrift: A Golden Jubilee Souvenir, Lagos n.d. [1983].

Oluwasanmi, H.A.: Agriculture and Nigerian Economic Development, Ibadan 1966.

Onimode, B.: Imperialism and Underdevelopment in Nigeria, London 1982.

Onitiri, H.M.A./D. Olatunbosun (eds.): The Marketing Board System. Proceedings of an International Conference, Ibadan 1974.

Orewa, G.O.: Taxation in Western and Mid-Western Nigeria, Ibadan 1979^2.

Osuntokun, A.: Nigeria in the First World War, London 1979.

Otite, O. (ed.): Themes in African Social and Political Thought, Enugu 1978.

Padmore, G.: Africa: Britain's Third Empire, London 1949.

Pearce, R.D.: The Turning Point in Africa. British Colonial Policy 1938-48, London 1982.

Pearce, R.D.: Sir Bernard Bourdillon: The Biography of a Twentieth-Century Colonialist, Oxford 1987.

Pedler, Sir F.J.: The Lion and the Unicorn in Africa. A History of the Origins of the United Africa Company, 1787-1931, London 1974.

Peel, J.D.Y.: Ijeshas and Nigerians: The Incorporation of a Yoruba Kingdom, 1890s-1970s, Cambridge 1983.

Perham, M. (ed.): The Native Economies of Nigeria, being Vol.I. of Economics of a Tropical Dependency, London 1946.

Perham, M. (ed.): Mining, Commerce and Finance in Nigeria, being Vol.II. of Economics of a Tropical Dependency, London 1948.

Petter, M./J.M. Lee, The Colonial Office, War and Development Policy. Organisation and the Planning of a Metropolitan Initiative, 1939-1945, London 1982.

Phillips, A.: The Enigma of Colonialism: British Policy in West Africa, London 1989.

Porter, A.N./A.J. Stockwell (eds.): British Imperial Policy and Decolonization, 1938-1964, 2 vols., London 1987/1989.

Post, K.W.J./G.D. Jenkins: The Price of Liberty. Personality and Politics in Colonial Nigeria, Cambridge 1973.

Prest, A.R.: War Economies of Primary Producing Countries, Cambridge 1948.

Price, H.L.: Dark Subjects, London 1939.

Ranger, T.O./O. Vaughan (eds.): Legitimacy and the State in Twentieth Century Africa: Essays in Honour of A.H.M. Kirk-Greene, London 1993.

Rothchild, D./N. Chazan (eds.):, The Precarious Balance: State and Society in Africa, Boulder/Colorado 1988.

Rothermund, D.: Die Peripherie in der Weltwirtschaftskrise. Afrika, Asien und Lateinamerika, 1929-39, Paderborn 1983.

Schärer, T.: Das Nigerian Youth Movement, Bern 1986.

Schatz, S.P. (ed.): South of the Sahara: Development in African Economies, London 1972.

Schatz, S.P.: Nigerian Capitalism, Berkeley 1977.

Schönwälder, H.-G.: Die Kakao-Wirtschaft in West-Afrika, Hamburg 1969.

Seers, D. (ed.): Dependency Theory: A Critical Assessment, London 1981.

Shenton, R.W.: The Development of Capitalism in Northern Nigeria, London 1986.

Shonfield, A.: British Economic Policy since the War, Harmondsworth 1959.

Sieberg, H.: Colonial Development: Die Grundlegung moderner Entwicklungspolitk durch Großbritannien, 1919-1949, Stuttgart 1985.

Sklar, R.L.: Nigerian Political Parties. Power in an Emergent African Nation , Princeton 1963.

Smith, B.S.: But Always as Friends: Northern Nigeria and the Cameroons, 1921-1957, London 1969.

Spinnler, K.: Außenhandel und Zahlungsbilanz Nigerias in der Nachkriegszeit, Basel 1964.

Stahl, K.M.: The Metropolitan Organisation of British Colonial Trade. Four Regional Studies, London 1951.

Stoecker, H. (ed.): German Imperialism in Africa. From the Beginnings until the Second World War, London 1986 (English edition of Drang nach Afrika, Berlin 1977).

Stolper, W.P.: Planning without Facts. Lessons in Resource Allocation from Nigeria's Development, Cambridge/Mass. 1966.

Strange, S.: Sterling and British Policy: A Political Study of an International Currency in Decline, London 1971.

Swinton, Lord: I Remember, London 1948.

Tamuno, T.N.: Nigeria and Elective Representation, 1923-1947, London 1966.

Tomlinson, B.R.: The Political Economy of the Raj, 1914-1947. The Economics of Decolonization in India, London 1979.

Twaddle, M. (ed.): Imperialism, the State and the Third World, London 1992.

Usoro, E.J.: The Nigerian Palm Oil Industry. Government Policy and Export Production, 1906-1965, Ibadan 1974.

Walker, G.J.: Traffic and Transport in Nigeria. The Example of an Underdeveloped Tropical Territory, London 1959.

Warren, B.: Imperialism: Pioneer of Capitalism, London 1980.

Watts, M.: Silent Violence. Food, Famine and Peasantry in Northern Nigeria, Berkeley 1983.

Watts, M.: State, Oil, and Agriculture in Nigeria, Berkeley 1987.

Wheare, J.: The Nigerian Legislative Council, London 1950.

Whetham, E.H./J.I. Currie (eds.): Readings in the Applied Economics of Africa, Vol.I., Micro-Economics, Cambridge 1967.

Whetham, E.H./J.I. Currie (eds.): Readings in the Applied Economicsof Africa, Vol.II, Macro-Economics, Cambridge 1967.

Wickizer, V.D.: Coffee, Tea and Cocoa. An Economic and Political Analysis, Stanford 1951.

Williams, G. (ed.): Nigeria - Economy and Society, London 1976.

Wilson, C.H., History of Unilever, London 1954.

Wood, G.A.R.: Cocoa, London 1975, 3rd. ed.

Woolton, Earl of: The Memoirs of the Rt. Hon. the Earl of Woolton C.H., P.C., D.L., LL.D., London 1959.

Wyn, D. (ed.): Catalogue of the Cadbury Papers, Birmingham 1973.

Zdunnek, G.: Marktfrauen in Nigeria. Ökonomie und Politik im Leben der Yoruba-Händlerinnen, Hamburg 1987.

Zeleza, T.: A Modern Economic History of Africa., Vol.I: The Nineteenth Century, Dakar-Oxford 1993.

b) *Articles and Chapters in Books*

Abbott, J.C.: The Efficiency of Marketing Board Operations, in: Onitiri, H.M.A./D. Olatunbosun (eds.), The Marketing Board System. Proceedings of an International Conference, Ibadan 1974, pp. 229-240.

Adamu, S.O.: On the Stabilization Policy of Marketing Boards in Nigeria, in: Nigerian Journal of Economic and Social Studies, XII (1970) 3, pp. 323-340.

Ady, P.: Fluctuations in Incomes of Primary Producers. A Comment, in: Economic Journal, LXIII (1953) 251, pp. 594-607.

Akeredolu-Ale, E.O.: Values, Motivations and History in the Development of Private Entrepreneurship: Lessons from Nigeria's Experience, 1946-1966, in: The Nigerian Journal of Economic and Social Studies, XIII (1971) 2, pp. 195-219.

Akeredolu-Ale, E.O.: A Sociohistorical Study of the Development of Entrepreneurship Among the Ijebu of Western Nigeria, in: African Studies Review, XVI (1973) 3, pp. 347-364.

Albertini, R. von: Das Ende des Empire. Bemerkungen zur britischen Dekolonisation, in: Historische Zeitschrift, CCXXXXIX (Dec. 1989) 3, pp. 583-617.

Alence, R.: The 1937-38 Gold Coast Cocoa Crises: The Political Economy of Commercial Stalemate, in: African Economic History, XIX (1990-91), pp. 77-104

Aluko, O.: Politics of Decolonisation in British West Africa, 1945-1960, in: Ajayi, J.F.A./ M. Crowder, History of West Africa, Vol.II, London 1974, pp. 622-663.

Anonymous: Two Nigerian Lists (Trade Unions, National Council), in: African Affairs, XXXXIV (1945) 174, pp. 164-165.

August, T.: Locating the Age of Imperialism, in: Itinerario, X (1986) 2, pp. 85-97.

Austin, G.: The Emergence of Capitalist Relations in South Asante Cocoa Farming, c.1916-33, in: Journal of African History, XXVIII (1987) 2, pp. 259-279.

Austin, G.: Capitalists and Chiefs in the Cocoa Hold-Ups in South Asante, 1927-1938', in: International Journal of African Historical Studies, XXI (1988) 1, pp. 63-95.

Awe, B.: Militarism and Economic Development in Nineteenth Century Yoruba Country: The Ibadan Example, in: Journal of African History, XIV (1973) 1, pp. 65-77.

Ayandele, E.A.: The Ideological Ferment in Ijebuland, 1892-1943, in: id., Nigerian Historical Studies, London 1979, pp. 270-294.

Bates, R.H.: The Commercialization of Agriculture and the Rise of Rural Political Protest, in: Bates, R.H., Essays on the Political Economy of Africa, Cambridge 1983, pp. 92-104.

Bauer, P.T.: Origins of the Statutory Export Monopolies of British West Africa, in: Business History Review, XXVIII (1954) 3, pp. 197-213.

Bauer, P.T.: The Economic Development of Nigeria, in: Journal of Political Economy, LXIII (1955), pp. 398-411.

Bauer, P.T.: British Colonial Africa: Economic Retrospect and Aftermath, in: Duignan, P./ L.H. Gann (eds.), Colonialism in Africa 1870-1960, Vol.IV: The Economics of Colonialism, Cambridge 1975, pp. 632-654.

Bauer, P.T.: Black Africa: The Living Legacy of Dying Colonialism, in: Bauer, P.T., Reality and Rhetoric: Studies in the Economics of Development, London 1984, pp. 90-105.

Beer, C.E.F./G. Williams: The Politics of the Ibadan Peasantry, in: Williams, G. (ed.), Nigeria. Economy and Society, London 1976, pp. 135-158.

Berg, E.J.: Real Income Trends in West Africa, 1939-1960, in: Herskowitz M.J./M. Harvitz (eds.), Economic Transition in Africa, London 1964, pp. 199-238.

Berg, E.J.: Urban Real Wages and the Nigerian Trade Union Movement, 1939-60: A Comment, in: Economic Development and Cultural Change, XVII (1968-69) 4, pp. 604-617.

Berry, S.S.: Christianity and the Rise of Cocoa-Growing in Ibadan and Ondo, in: Journal of the Historical Society of Nigeria, IV (Dec. 1968) 3, pp. 439-451.

Berry, S.S.: Cocoa and Economic Development in Western Nigeria, in: Eicher, C.K./ C. Liedholm (eds.), The Growth and Development of the Nigerian Economy, East Lansing/Michigan 1970, pp. 16-29.

Berry, S.S.: The Concept of Innovation and the History of Cocoa Farming in Western Nigeria, in: Journal of African History, XV (1974) 1, pp. 83-95.

Berry, S.S.: Supply Response Reconsidered: Cocoa in Western Nigeria 1909-44, in: Journal of Development Studies, XIII (1976) 1, pp. 4-17.

Berry, S.S.: Rural Class Formation in West Africa, in: Bates, R.H./M.F. Lofchie (eds.), Agricultural Development in Africa. Issues of Public Policy, New York 1980, pp. 401-424.

Berry, S.S.: Oil and the Disappearing Peasantry: Accumulation, Differentiation, and Underdevelopment in Western Nigeria, in: Watts, M. (ed.), State, Oil, and Agriculture in Nigeria, Berkeley 1987, pp. 202-222.

Bourdillon, B.: Nigeria's War Effort, in: Journal of the Royal African Society, XXXIX (1940) 155, pp. 115-122.

Brown, C.V.: Price Stabilization of Nigeria's Export Crops, in: Nigerian Journal of Economic and Social Studies, I (1962) 4, pp. 40-50.

Caine, S.: Instability of Primary Product Prices: A Protest and a Proposal, in: Economic Journal, LXIV (1954) 255, pp. 610-614.

Callaghy, T.M.: The State and the Development of Capitalism in Africa: Theoretical, Historical and Comparative Reflections, in: Rothchild, D./N. Chazan (eds.), The Precarious Balance: State and Society in Africa, Boulder/Colorado 1988, pp. 45-79.

Cell, J.W.: On the Eve of Decolonization: The Colonial Office's Plans for the Transfer of Power in Africa, 1947, in: Journal of Imperial and Commonwealth History, VIII (May 1980) 3, pp. 235-257.

Clarke, J.: Households and the Political Economy of Small-Scale Cash Crop Production in South-Western Nigeria, in: Africa, LI (1981) 4, pp. 807-823.

Coleman, J.S.: Nationalism in Tropical Africa, in: American Political Science Review, XXLVIII (1954) 2, pp. 404-426.

Cooper, F.: Africa and the World Economy, in: African Studies Review, XXIV (1981) 2/3, pp. 186.

Cooper, F.: Peasants, Capitalists, and Historians: A Review Article, in: Journal of Southern African Studies, VII (1981) 2, pp. 284-314

Coquery-Vidrovitch, C.: L'impact des Interests Coloniaux: S.C.O.A. et C.F.A.O. dans l'Ouest Africain, 1910-1965, in: Journal of African History, XVI (1975) 4, pp. 595-621.

Cowen, M.P.: Early Years of the Colonial Development Corporation: British State Enterprise Overseas During Late Colonialism, in: African Affairs, LXXXIII (1984) 330, pp. 63-75.

Cowen, M./N.J. Westcott: British Imperial Economic Policy during the War, in: Killingray, D./R.J.A.R. Rathbone (eds.), Africa and the Second World War, Basingstoke 1986), pp. 20-67.

Crowder, M.: The 1939-45 War and West Africa, in: Ajayi, J.F.A./M. Crowder (eds.), History of West Africa, Vol.II, London 1974, pp. 596-621.

Crowder, M./O. Ikime: West African Chiefs, in: Crowder, M. (ed.), Colonial West Africa. Collected Essays, London 1978, pp. 209-230.

Crowder, M.: The Second World War: Prelude to Decolonisation in Africa, in: id. (ed.), The Cambridge History of Africa, Vol.VIII, from c.1940 to c.1975, Cambridge 1984, pp. 8-51.

Darwin, J.: British Decolonization since 1945: A Pattern or a Puzzle?, in: Journal of Imperial and Commonwealth History, XII (June 1984) 2, pp. 187-209.

Deutsch, J.G.: Nigeria, in: Hanisch, R./C. Jakobeit (eds.), Der Kakaoweltmarkt. Weltmarktintegrierte Entwicklung und nationale Steuerungspolitik der Produzentenländer, Vol. II: Afrika, Hamburg 1991, pp. 167-341.

Driessen, H. van den: Patterns of Land Holding and Land Distribution in the Ife Division of Western Nigeria, in: Africa, XXXXI (1971) 1, pp. 42-53.

Dudley, B.J.: The Political Theory of Awolowo and Azikiwe, in: Otite, O. (ed.), Themes in African Social and Political Thought, Enugu 1978, pp. 199-216.

Duffield, I.: The Business Activities of Dusé Mohammed Ali: An Example of the Economic Dimension of Pan-Africanism, 1912-1945, in: Journal of the Historical Society of Nigeria, IV (June 1969) 4, pp. 571-600.

Duffield, I.: Pan-Africanism, Rational and Irrational. Review Article, in: Journal of African History, XVIII (1977) 4, pp. 597-620.

Dumett, R.: Africa's Strategic Minerals during the Second World War, in: Journal of African History, XXVI (1985) 4, pp. 381-408.

Ehrlich, C.: Building and Caretaking: Economic Reality in British Tropical Africa, 1890-1960, in: Economic History Review, XXVI (1973) 4, pp. 649-667.

Ekechi, F.K.: Aspects of Palm Oil Trade at Oguta (Eastern Nigeria), 1900-1950, in: African Economic History, X (1981), pp. 35-65.

Ekundare, R.O.: The Political Economy of Private Investment in Nigeria, in: Journal of Modern African Studies, X (1972) 1, pp. 37-56.

Essang, S.M.: Impact of the Marketing Board on the Distribution of Cocoa Income in Western Nigeria, in: Nigerian Geographical Journal, XV (1972) 1, pp. 35-47.

Essang, S.M.: Investment Pattern of Licensed Buying Agents in Nigeria: A Study of Enterprise Diversification and Entrepreneurship in an Underdeveloped Economy, in: Nigerian Journal of Economic and Social Studies, XVI (Nov.1974) 3, pp. 403-417.

Evans, H.: Studies in War-time Organisation, in: African Affairs, XXXXIII (1944) 173, pp. 152-158.

Fajana, O.: Import Licensing in Nigeria, in: Development and Change, VIII (Oct.1977) 4, pp. 509-522.

Falola, T.: The Yoruba Toll System: Its Operation and Abolition, in: Journal of African History, XXX (1989) 1, pp. 69-88.

Falola, T.: Lebanese Traders in Southwestern Nigeria, in: African Affairs, LXXXIX (1990) 357, pp. 523-553.

Falola, T.: 'My Friend the Skylock': Moneylenders and their Clients in South-Western Nigeria, in: Journal of African History, XXXIV (1993) 3, pp. 403-423.

Fieldhouse, D.K.: Can Humpty-Dumpty Be Put Together Again? Imperial History in the 1980s, in: Journal of Imperial and Commonwealth History, XII (Jan.1984) 2, pp. 9-23.

Fieldhouse, D.K.: Anglophone West Africa: Ghana and Nigeria, in: Fieldhouse, D.K., Black Africa 1945-1980. Economic Decolonization and Arrested Development, London 1986, pp. 139-162.

Fieldhouse, D.K.: War and the Origins of the Gold Coast Marketing Board, 1939-40, in: M. Twaddle (ed.), Imperialism, the State and the Third World, London 1992, pp. 153-182.

Flint, J.E.: Economic Change in West Africa in the Nineteenth Century, in: Ajayi, J.F.A./ M. Crowder (eds.), History of West Africa, Vol.II, London 1974, pp. 380-401.

Flint, J.: Planned Decolonization and Its Failure in British Africa, in: African Affairs, LXXXII (1983) 328, pp. 389-411.

Forde, D.: The Rural Economies, in: Perham, M. (ed.), Economics of a Tropical Dependency, Vol.I, London 1946, pp. 29-212.

Forrest, T.: Agricultural Policies in Nigeria 1900-78, in: Heyer, J. et.al., Rural Development in Tropical Africa, London 1981, pp. 222-258.

Fortes, M.: The Impact of the War on British West Africa, in: International Affairs, XXI (1945), pp. 206-219.

Freund, W.M./R.W. Shenton, 'Vent for Surplus' Theory and the Economic History of West Africa, in: Savanna, VI (1977) 2, pp. 191-199.

Garlick, P.C.: African Traders in Kumasi, in: African Business Series, No.1, University College of Ghana, Legon 1959.

Garlick, P.C.: The Development of Kwahu Business Enterprise in Ghana since 1874 - an Essay in Recent Oral Traditions, in: Journal of African History, VIII (1967) 3, pp. 463-486.

Gertzel, C.: Relations Between African and European Traders in the Niger Delta 1880-1896, in: Journal of African History, III (1962) 2, pp. 361-366.

Geschiere, P./P. Konings (eds.): Itinéraires d'accumulation au Cameroun, Leiden 1993.

Gill & Duffus Ltd.: Cocoa Statistics, London, April 1981.

Goldsworthy, D.: Keeping Change Within Bounds: Aspects of Colonial Policy during the Churchill and Eden Governments, 1951-57, in: Journal of Imperial and Commonwealth History, XIII (1990) 1, pp. 81-108.

Green, R.H.: Multi-Purpose Economic Institutions in Africa, in: Journal of Modern African Studies, I (June 1963) 2, pp. 163-184.

Green, R.H./S.H. Hymer: Cocoa in the Gold Coast: A Study in the Relations between African Farmers and Agricultural Experts, in: Journal of Economic History, XXVI (1966) 3, pp. 299-319.

Greenstreet, D.K.: Public Administration: Development and Welfare in the British Territories of West Africa during the Forties, in: Economic Bulletin of Ghana, I (1971) 2, pp. 3-23.

Grier, B.: Underdevelopment, Modes of Production, and the State in Colonial Ghana, in: African Studies Review, XXIV (1981) 1, pp. 21-47.

Gutkind, P.C.W.: The View from below: Political Consciousness of the Urban Poor in Ibadan, in: Cahier d'Etudes Africaines, XV (1975) 57, pp. 5-35.

Guyer, J.I.: Food, Cocoa, and the Division of Labour by Sex in Two West African Societies, in: Comparative Studies in Society and History, XXII (July 1980) 3, pp. 355-373.

Hanisch, R.: Confrontation between Primary Commodity Producers and Consumers: The Cocoa Hold-up of 1964/65, in: Journal of Commonwealth History and Comparative Politics, XIII (Nov. 1975), pp. 242-260.

Hanna, M.I.: The Lebanese in West Africa, Part I, in: West Africa, 19 April 1958, p. 361; Part II, in: West Africa, 26 April 1958, p. 393.

Harris, J.R.: On the Concept of Entrepreneurship, with an Application to Nigeria, in: Schatz, S.P. (ed.), South of the Sahara: Development in African Economies, London 1972, pp. 5-27.

Hawkins, E.K.: Marketing Boards and Economic Development in Nigeria and Ghana, in: Review of Economic Studies, XXVI (Oct.1958) 69, pp. 51-62.

Helleiner, G.K.: The Fiscal Role of the Marketing Boards in Nigerian Economic Development 1947-61, in: The Economic Journal, LXXIV (Sept.1964) 3, pp. 583-610.

Helleiner, G.K.: The Marketing Board System and Alternative Arrangements for Commodity Marketing in Nigeria, in: Onitiri, H.M.A./T. Olatunbosun (eds.), The Marketing Board System. Proceedings of an International Conference, Ibadan 1974, pp. 57-70.

Hill, P.: Markets in Africa, in: Journal of Modern African Studies, I (1963) 4, pp. 441-453.

Hill, P.: Landlords and Brokers: A West African Trading System (With a Note on Kumasi Butchers), in: Cahier d'Etudes Africaine, VI (1966) 3, pp. 349-366.

Hill, P.: The Myth of the Amorphous Peasantry: A Northern Nigerian Case Study, in: Nigerian Journal of Economic and Social Studies, X (1968) 2, pp. 239-260.

Hinds, A.: Sterling and Imperial Policy, 1945-1951, in: Journal of Imperial and Commonwealth History, XV (1987) 2, pp. 148-169.

Holbrock, W.P.: British Propaganda and the Mobilization of the Gold Coast War Effort, 1939-45, in: Journal of African History, XXVI (1985) 4, pp. 347-361.

Holland, R.F.: The Imperial Factor in British Strategies from Attlee to Macmillan, 1945-1963, in: Journal of Imperial Commonwealth History, XII (Jan.1984) 2, pp. 165-186.

Hood, W.M.: Cocoa in West Africa, in: Bournville Works Magazine, XLIII (1946) 2, p. 19-32.

Hopkins, A.G.: The Lagos Chamber of Commerce 1888-1903, in: Journal of the Historical Society of Nigeria, III (1964-67), pp. 241-248.

Hopkins, A.G.: Economic Aspects of Political Movements in Nigeria and in the Gold Coast 1918-1939, in: Journal of African History, VII (1966) 2, pp. 133-152.

Hopkins, A.G.: Imperial Business in Africa, Part I: Sources, in: Journal of African History, XVII (1976) 1, pp. 29-48.

Hopkins, A.G.: Imperial Business in Africa, Part II: Interpretations, in: Journal of African History, XVII (1976) 2, pp. 267-290.

Hopkins, A.G.: Innovation in a Colonial Context: African Origins of the Nigerian Cocoa-Farming Industry, 1880-1920, in: Dewey, C./A.G. Hopkins (eds.), The Imperial Impact: Studies in the Economic History of Africa and India, London 1978, pp. 83-96.

Hopkins, A.G.: Big Business in African Studies, in: Journal of African History, XXVIII (1987) 1, pp. 119-140.

Hopkins, A.G.: African Entrepreneurship: An Essay on the Relevance of History to Development Economics, in: Genève - Afrique, XXVI (1988) 2, pp. 7-28.

Howard, R.: Differential Class Participation in an African Protest Movement: The Ghana Cocoa Boycott of 1937-38, in: Canadian Journal of African Studies, X (1976) 3, pp. 469-480.

Idachaba, F.S.: Commodity Boards in Nigeria. A Crisis of Identity, in: Arhin, K./P. Hesp/ L. van der Laan (eds.), Marketing Boards in Tropical Africa, London 1985, pp. 149-168.

Jenkins, G.: Government and Politics in Ibadan, in: Lloyd, P.C./A.C. Mabogunje/B. Awe (eds.), The City of Ibadan, Cambridge 1967, pp. 213-233.

Kent, F.: Regionalism or Territorial Autonomy? The Case of British West African Development, 1939-49, in: Journal of Imperial and Commonwealth History, XVIII (1990) 1, pp. 61-80.

Khuri, F.I.: Kinship, Emigration, and Trade Partnership among the Lebanese of West Africa, in: Africa, XXXV (1965) 4, pp. 385-395.

Kilson, M.: Nationalism and Social Classes in British West Africa, in: Journal of Politics, XX (May 1958) 2, pp. 368-387.

Kilson, M.: The Emergent Elites of Black Africa, 1900 to 1960, in: Duignan, P./L.H. Gann (eds.), Colonialism in Africa 1870-1960, Vol.II, The History and Politics of Colonialism 1914-1960, Cambridge 1970, pp. 351-398.

Kilson, M.: The National Congress of British West Africa, 1918-1935, in: Mazrui, A./R. Rotberg (eds.), Protest and Power in Black Africa, Oxford 1970, pp. 571-588.

Kirk-Green, A.H.M.: The Thin White Line: The Size of the British Colonial Service in Africa, in: African Affairs, LXXIX (1980) 314, pp. 15-44.

Kubicek, R.V.: The Colonial Steamer and the Occupation of West Africa by the Victorian State, 1840-1900, in: Journal of Imperial and Commonwealth History, XVIII (1990) 1, pp. 9-32.

Lass, R.A./N.E. Egbe: Cocoa in Nigeria, in: Cocoa Growers Bulletin, XVIII (1972), pp. 6-13.

Lee, J.M.: 'Forward Thinking' and War: The Colonial Office during the 1940s, in: Journal of Imperial and Commonwealth History, VI (1977) 1, pp. 64-79.

Leubuscher, C.: Marketing Schemes for Native-Grown Produce in African Territories, in: Africa, XII (1939) 2, pp. 163-187.

Lloyd, P.C.: The Integration of the New Economic Classes into Local Government in Western Nigeria, in: African Affairs, LII (1953) 206, pp. 327-334.

Lloyd, P.C.: Cocoa, Politics and the Yoruba Middle Class, in: West Africa, 17 Jan. 1953, p. 39.

Lonsdale, J.: States and Social Processes in Africa: A Historiographical Survey, in: African Studies Review, XXIV (1981) 2/3, pp. 139-225.

Lynn, M.: From Sail to Steam: The Impact of the Steamship Services on the British Palm Oil Trade with West Africa, 1850-1890, in: Journal of African History, XXX (1989) 2, pp. 227-245.

Mars, J.: Extra - Territorial Enterprises, in: Perham, M., Economics of a Tropical Dependency, Vol.II, London 1948, pp. 43-135.

Martin, S.M.: The Long Depression: West African Export Producers and the World Economy, 1914-45, in: I. Brown, The Economies of Africa and Asia in the Inter-War Depression, London 1989, pp. 74-94.

Melville, E.: The Marketing of West African Cocoa, in: Cocoa, Chocolate and Confectionery Alliance Ltd. (ed.), International Cocoa Conference 1948, London 1949, pp. 70-76.

Meredith, D.: The British Government and Colonial Economic Policy, 1919-1939, in: Economic History Review, XXVIII (1975) 3, pp. 484-499.

Meredith, D.: Government and the Decline of the Nigerian Oil-Palm Export Industry, 1919-1939, in: Journal of African History, XXV (1984) 3, pp. 311-329.

Meredith, D.: State Controlled Marketing and Economic 'Development': The Case of West African Produce during the Second World War, in: Economic History Review, XXXIX (1986) 1, pp. 77-91.

Meredith, D.: Imperial Images: The Empire Marketing Board, 1926-32, in: History Today, XXXVII (Jan.1987), pp. 30-36.

Meredith, D.: The Colonial Office, British Business Interests and the Reform of Cocoa Marketing in West Africa, 1937-1945, in: Journal of African History, XXIX (1988) 2, pp. 285-300.

Milburn, J.: The 1938 Gold Coast Cocoa Crisis: British Business and the Colonial Office, in: The International Journal of African Historical Studies, III (1970) 1, pp. 57-74.

Miles, J.: Rural Protest in the Gold Coast: The Cocoa Hold-Ups, 1908-1938, in: Dewey, C./ A.G. Hopkins (eds.), The Imperial Impact: Studies in the Economic History of Africa and India, London 1978, pp. 152-170 and 353-357.

Milewski, J.J.: The Great Depression of the Early 1930's in a Colonial Country: A Case Study of Nigeria, in: African Bulletin, (1975) 23, pp. 7-45.

Milewski, J.J.: Capitalism in Nigeria and Problems of Dependence: Some Historical Comments, in: Seers, D. (ed.), Dependency Theory: A Critical Reassessment, London 1981, pp. 109-118.

Milverton, Lord: Nigeria, in: African Affairs, XXXXVII (1948) 186, pp. 80-89.

Newbury, C.: Credit in Early Nineteenth Century West African Trade, in: Journal of African History, XIII (1972) 1, pp. 81-95.

Newbury, C.: Trade and Technology in West Africa: The Case of the Niger Company, 1900-1920, in: Journal of African History, XIX (1978) 4, pp. 551-575.

Newton, C.C.S.: The Sterling Crisis of 1947 and the British Response to the Marshall Plan, in: Economic History Review, XXXVII (1984), pp. 391-408.

Nixon, C.R.: The Role of the Marketing Boards in the Political Evolution of Nigeria, in: Eicher, C./C. Liedholm (eds.), Growth and Development of the Nigerian Economy, East Lansing/Michigan 1970, pp. 156-161.

Njoku, O.N.: Evolution of Produce Inspection in Nigeria up to 1936, in: ODU: A Journal of West African Studies, (Jan./July 1979) 19, pp. 43-57.

Njoku, O.N.: Trading with the Metropolis: An Unequal Exchange, in: Falola, T. (ed.), Britain and Nigeria: Exploitation or Development?, London 1987, pp. 124-141.

Njoku, O.N.: Contributions to War Efforts, in: Falola, T. (ed.), Britain and Nigeria: Exploitation or Development?, London 1987, pp. 164-185.

Noah, M.E.: Inland Ports and European Trading Firms in South-Eastern Nigeria, in: African Affairs, LXXXVIII (1989) 350, pp. 25-40.

Nordman, C.R.: The Decision to Admit Unofficials to the Executive Councils of British West Africa, in: Journal of Imperial and Commonwealth History, IV (1976) 2, pp. 194-205.

Nwabughuogu, A.I.: From Wealthy Entrepreneurs to Petty Traders: The Decline of the African Middlemen in Eastern Nigeria, 1900-1950, in: Journal of African History, XXIII (1982) 3, pp. 365-379.

Nwaka, G.I.: Trade in Oguta, Nigeria, 1885-1945, in: Bulletin de l' I.F.A.N., IXL (1979) 4, pp. 773-786.

Nwosu, E.J.: The Role of Government in the Development of the Co-operative Movement in Nigeria, in: Vierteljahresberichte, (1976) 64, pp. 143-158.

Ogunremi, G.O.: The Nigerian Motor Transport Union Strike of 1937, in: Journal of the Historical Society of Nigeria, IX (1977-79), pp. 127-144.

Ogunsheye, A.: Marketing Boards and the Stabilisation of Producer Prices and Incomes in Nigeria, in: Nigerian Journal of Economic and Social Studies, VII (July 1965) 2, pp. 131-143.

Ojemakinde, W.: The Pullen Marketing Scheme: A Trial in Food Price Control in Nigeria, 1941-1947, in: Journal of the Historical Society of Nigeria, VI (1973) 4, pp. 413-423.

Ojemakinde, W./R.J. Garwin: Economic Development in Nigeria, in: Ikime, O. (ed.), Groundworks of Nigerian History, Ibadan 1980, pp. 482-517.

Olatunbosun, D.: Pricing Policy and Supply Response in Cocoa Production: The Nigerian Case, in: Kotey,R.A./C. Okali/B.E. Rourke, The Economics of Cocoa Production and Marketing. Proceedings of Cocoa Economics Research Conference, Legon 1973, pp. 236-250.

Olatunbosun, D./S.O. Olayide: Effects of the Marketing Boards on the Output and Income of Primary Producers, in: Onitiri, H.M.A./D. Olatunbosun (eds.), The Marketing Board System. Proceedings of an International Conference, Ibadan 1974, pp. 1-46.

Olayemi, J.K./S.A. Oni: Asymmetry in Price Response: A Case Study of Western Nigerian Cocoa Farmers, in: Nigerian Journal of Economic and Social Studies, XIV (Nov.1972) 3, pp. 347-355.

Olorunfemi, A.: Background to the Establishment of the Nigerian Cocoa Marketing Board 1947/48, in: ODU: A Journal of West African Studies, (Jan./July 1979) 19, pp. 58-77.

Olorunfemi, A.: Effects of War-Time Trade Controls on Nigerian Cocoa Traders and Producers, 1939-45: A Case Study of the Hazards of a Dependent Economy, in: International Journal of African Historical Studies, XIII (1980) 4, pp. 672-687.

Olusanya, G.O.: The Nationalist Movement in Nigeria, in: Ikime, O. (ed.), Groundworks of Nigerian History, Ibadan 1980, pp. 545-569.

Olusanya, G.O.: The Nigerian Civil Service in the Colonial Era: A Study of Imperial Reactions to Changing Circumstances, in: Obichere, B.I. (ed.), Studies in Southern Nigerian History, London 1982, pp. 134-159.

Osoba, S.: The Nigerian Power Elite, 1952-65, in: Gutkind, P.C.W./P. Waterman, African Social Studies, London 1977, pp. 368-382.

Osuntogun, A.: Co-operative Marketing of Cocoa in Western Nigeria, 1922-1973, in: International Cocoa Research Conference, Ibadan 1975, Conference Proceedings, London 1975, pp. 598-607.

Osuntokun, J.: Post-First World War Economic and Administrative Problems in Nigeria and the Response of the Clifford Administration, in: Journal of the Historical Society of Nigeria, VII (Dec.1973) 1, pp. 35-48.

Otobo, D.: Bureaucratic Elites and Public-Sector Wage Bargaining in Nigeria, in: Journal of Modern African Studies, XXIV (1986) 1, pp. 101-126.

Oyediran, O.: The Position of the Ooni in the Changing Political System of Ile-Ife, in: Journal of the Historical Society of Nigeria, VI (June 1973) 4, pp. 373-386.

Peace, A.: The Politics of Transporting, in: Africa, LVIII (1988) 1, pp. 14-27.

Pearce, R.D.: Governors, Nationalists and Constitutions in Nigeria, 1935-51, in: Journal of Imperial and Commonwealth History, IX (1981) 3, pp. 289-307.

Pearce, R.D.: The Colonial Office in 1947 and the Transfer of Power in Africa: An Addendum to John Cell, in: Journal of Imperial and Commonwealth History, X (1982) 2, pp. 211-215.

Pearce, R.D.: Morale in the Colonial Service in Nigeria during the Second World War, in: Journal of Imperial and Commonwealth History, XI (1983) 2, pp. 175-196.

Pearce, R.D.: The Colonial Office and Planned Decolonization in Africa, in: African Affairs, LXXXIII (Jan.1984) 330, pp. 77-93.

Pedler, Sir F.: British Planning and Private Enterprise in Colonial Africa, in: Duignan, P./L.H. Gann (eds.), Colonialism in Africa 1870-1960, Vol.IV: The Economics of Colonialism, Cambridge 1975, pp. 95-126.

Peel, J.D.Y.: Inequality and Action: The Forms of Ijesha Social Conflict, in: Canadian Journal of African Studies, XIV (1980) 3, pp. 473-502.

Peel, J.D.Y.: Social and Cultural Change, in: Crowder, M. (ed.), The Cambridge History of Africa, Vol.VIII, from c.1840-c.1975, Cambridge 1984, pp. 142-191.

Post, K.W.J.: Nationalism and Politics in Nigeria: A Marxist Approach, in: Nigerian Journal of Economic and Social Studies, VI (1964) 2, pp. 167-176.

Post, K.W.J.: British Policy and Representative Government in West Africa, 1920-1951, in: Duignan, P./L.H. Gann (eds.), Colonialism in Africa 1870-1960, Vol.II, The History and Politics of Colonialism 1914-1960, Cambridge 1970, pp. 31-57.

Post, K.W.J.: Peasantization and Rural Political Movements in Western Africa, in: Archives Européennes de Sociologie, XIII (1972) 2, pp. 223-254.

Rathbone, R.J.A.R.: The Government of the Gold Coast after the Second World War, in: African Affairs, LXVII (1968), pp. 209-218.

Rathbone, R.J.A.R.: Businessmen in Politics: Party Struggle in Ghana, 1949-57, in: Journal of Development Studies, IX (1973) 3, pp. 391-401.

Rathbone, R.J.A.R.: World War I and Africa: Introduction, in: Journal of African History, XIX (1978) 1, pp. 1-9.

Rhodie, S.: The Gold Coast Cocoa Hold-up of 1930-31, in: Transaction of Historical Society of Ghana, IX (1968), pp. 105-118.

Rimmer, D.: The Abstraction from Politics: A Critique of Economic Theory and Design with Reference to West Africa, in: Journal of Development Studies, V (April 1969) 3, pp. 190-204.

Rimmer, D.: Development in Nigeria: An Overview, in: Bienen, H./V.R. Diejomah (eds.), Inequality and Development in Nigeria, New York/London 1981, pp. 17-75.

Robertson, A.F.: Abusa: The Structural History of an Economic Contract, in: Journal of Development Studies, XVIII (1982) 4, pp. 447-478.

Robinson, R.: Andrew Cohen and the Transfer of Power in Tropical Africa, 1940-1951, in: Morris-Jones, W.H./G. Fischer (eds.), Decolonisation and After: The British and French Experience, London 1980, pp. 50-72.

Robinson, R.: Imperial Theory and the Question of Imperialism after Empire, in: Journal of Imperial and Commonwealth History, XII (Jan.1984) 2, pp. 42-54.

Samuel, F.: The East African Groundnut Scheme, in: African Affairs, 46 (1947) 182, pp. 135-145.

Scott, D.: Production for Trade, in: Perham, M. (ed.), Economics of a Tropical Dependency, Vol.I, London 1946, pp. 217-293.

Shenton, R.: Nigerian Agriculture in Historical Perspective: Development and Crisis, 1900-60, in: Watts, M. (ed.), State, Oil, and Agriculture in Nigeria, Berkeley 1987, pp. 34-57.

Simensen, J.: Rural Mass Action in the Context of Anti-Colonial Protest: The Asafo Movement of Akim Abuakwa, Ghana, in: Canadian Journal of African Studies, VIII (1974) 1, pp. 25-41.

Smyth, R.: Britain's African Colonies and British Propaganda during the Second World War, in: Journal of Imperial and Commonwealth History, XIV (1985) 1, pp. 65-82.

Southall, R.J.: Polarisation and Dependence in the Gold Coast Cocoa Trade, 1890-1938, in: Transactions of the Historical Society of Ghana, XVI (1976) 1, pp. 93-115.

Southall, R.J.: Farmers, Traders and Brokers in the Gold Coast Economy, in: Canadian Journal of African Studies, XII (1978) 2, pp. 185-211.

Tawney, R.H.: The Abolition of Economic Control, 1918-1921, in: Economic History Review, XIII (1943) 1/2, pp. 1-30.

Tomlinson, B.R.: The Contraction of England: National Decline and Loss of Empire', Journal of Imperial and Commonwealth History, XI (1982) 1, pp. 58-72.

Tamuno, T.N.: Unofficial Representation on Nigeria's Executive Council, 1886-1943, in: ODU: A Journal of West African Studies, (1970) 4, pp. 46-66.

Udo, R.R.: British Policy and the Development of Export Crops in Nigeria, in: Nigerian Journal of Economic and Social Studies, IX (Nov.1967) 3, pp. 300-314.

United Africa Company: Some Financial Aspects of Trading in West Africa, in: Statistical and Economic Review, IV (1949), pp. 50-58.

Usoro, E.J.: Colonial Economic Development Strategy in Nigeria 1919-1939: An Appraisal, in: Nigerian Journal of Economic and Social Studies, XIX (1977) 1, pp. 121-141.

Van der Laan, L.: The European Trading Companies in West Africa: Their Withdrawal from Up-Country, 1945-80, in: Laboratoire Connaisance du Tiers-Monde (ed.), Entreprises et entrepreneur en Afrique, Vol.II, Paris 1982, pp. 369-384.

Van der Laan, L.: Modern Inland Transport and the European Trading Firms in Colonial West Africa, in: Cahiers d'Etudes Africaines, XXI (1984) 4, pp. 547-575.

Van der Laan, L.: Marketing West Africa's Export Crops: Modern Boards and Colonial Trading Companies, in: Journal of Modern African Studies, XXV (1987) 1, pp. 1-24.

Van der Laan, L.: Selling Tropical Africa's Export Crops: The Experience of the Inter War Years, in: Dewey, C. (ed.), The State and the Market: Studies in the Economic and Social History of the Third World, New Dehli 1988, pp. 238-261.

Vaughan, O.: Dekolonization and Legitimation in Nigeria, in: Ranger, T.O./O. Vaughan (eds.), Legitimacy and the State in Twentieth Century Africa: Essays in Honour of A.H.M. Kirk-Greene, London 1993, pp. 135-161.

Wassermann, G.: The Politics of Consensual Decolonization, in: The African Review, V (1975) 1, pp. 1-15.

Watts, M./R. Shenton: State and Agrarian Transformation in Nigeria, in: Barker, J. (ed.), The Politics of Agriculture in Tropical Africa, Beverly Hills 1984, pp. 173-203.

Watts, M./T.J. Bassett: Crisis and Change in African Agriculture: A Comparative Study of the Ivory Coast and Nigeria, in: African Studies Review, XXVIII (Dec.1985) 4, pp. 3-27.

Weber, M.: Class, Status, Party, in: Gerth, H.H./C.W. Mills (eds.), From Max Weber: Essays in Sociology, London 1948, pp. 180-195.

Webster, J.B.: The Bible and the Plough, in: Journal of the Historical Society of Nigeria, (1960-63) 2, pp. 418-434.

Westcott, N.J.: The East African Sisal Industry, 1929-1949: The Marketing of a Colonial Commodity during Depression and War, in: Journal of African History, XXV (1984) 4, pp. 445-461.

Westcott, N.J.: The Impact of the Second World War on Tanganyika, 1939-49, in: Killingray, D./R.J.A.R. Rathbone (eds.), Africa in the Second World War, Basingstoke 1986, pp. 143-159.

Westcott, N.J.: Stabilising Commodity Prices: State Control of Colonial Commodity Trade, 1930-1950, in: Dewey, C. (ed.), The State and the Market: Studies in the Economic and Social History of the Third World, New Delhi 1988, pp. 262-287.

Williams, D.M.: West African Marketing Boards, in: African Affairs, LII (1953) 206, pp. 45-54.

Williams, G.: The Social Stratification of a Neo-Colonial Economy: Western Nigeria, in: Allen, C./R.W. Johnson (eds.), African Perspectives. Papers in the History, Politics and Economics of Africa Presented to T. Hodgkin, Cambridge, 1970, pp. 225-250.

Williams, G.: Marketing Without and with Marketing Boards: The Origins of State Marketing Boards in Nigeria, in: Review of the African Political Economy, XXXIV (1985) 2, pp. 4-15.
Williams, G.: Why there is no Agrarican Capitalism in Nigeria, in: Journal of Historical Sociology, I (1988) 4, pp. 345-398.
Williams, G.: Garveyism, Akinpelu Obisesan and His Contemporaries: Ibadan 1920-1922, in: Ranger, T.O./O. Vaughan (eds.), Legitimacy and the State in Twentieth Century Africa: Essays in Honour of A.H.M. Kirk-Greene, London 1993, pp. 112-132.
Winder, R.B.: The Lebanese in West Africa, in: Comparative Studies in Society and History, IV (1961), pp. 296-333.
Wrigley, C.C.: The Colonial Phase in British West Africa: Economic and Social Developments, in: Ajayi, A.F.A./I. Espie (eds.), A Thousand Years in West African History. A Handbook for Teachers and Students, Ibadan 1965, pp. 423-439.
Wrigley, C.C.: Aspects of Economic History, in: Roberts, A.D. (ed.), The Cambridge History of Africa, Vol.II, from 1905-1940, Cambridge 1986, pp. 77-139.

C) *Seminarpapers, Theses and Unpublished Manuscripts*

Adeleke, A.R.: Labour Use in the Development of Nigerian Peasant Cocoa Production, paper presented at the Nigerian Institute of Social and Economic Research, Ibadan, 1981.
Adeyeye, S.O.: The Western Nigerian Cooperative Movement, 1935-1964, University of Ibadan M.A. thesis, Ibadan 1967.
Austin, G.: Class Struggle and Rural Capitalism in Asante History, School of Oriental and African Studies, African History Seminar, London 19 Oct. 1988.
Baptiste, F.A.: The Relations between the Western Region and the Federal Government of Nigeria: A Study of the 1962 Emergency, University of Manchester M.A. thesis, Manchester 1965.
Bowden, J.H.: Development and Control in British Colonial Policy, with Reference to Nigeria and the Gold Coast, 1935-1948, University of Birmingham Ph.D. thesis, Birmingham 1980.
Chikelu, G.P.O.: The Operations of Nigerian Marketing Boards, with Special Reference to their Effects on Economic Development, London School of Economics M.Sc. thesis, London 1963.
Clarke, R.J.M.: Agricultural Production in a Rural Yoruba Community, University of London Ph.D. thesis, London 1979.
Cowen, M.P./N.J. Westcott: British Imperial Economic Policy During the War, paper presented at the School of Oriental and African Studies Conference on Africa and the Second World War, London 24th-25th May 1984.
Davies, P.N.: British Shipping and the Growth of the West African Economy, 1910-50, University of Liverpool D.Phil., Liverpool 1968.
Deutsch, J.G.: Cocoa Marketing in Nigeria: 1936-1986, paper presented at the Nigerian Research Workshop, St. Peter's College, Oxford 29-31 March, 1989.
Deutsch, J.G.: Educating the Middlemen: A Political and Economic History of Statutory Cocoa Marketing in Nigeria, 1936 - 1947, University of London Ph.D. thesis, London 1990.
Deutsch, J.G.: The Relevance of the Historical Study of Marketing Boards in Africa, paper presented at the School of Oriental and African Studies, African History Seminar, 13 March 1991.

Deutsch, J.G.: Cocoa versus Palm Products in Nigeria, 1939-45: The Impact of Price Levels on the Production Decisions, International Conference on Cocoa Production and Economic Development in the 19th and 20th Centuries, London, 15-17 September 1993.

Drummond Thompson, P.H.: The Development of Motor-Transport in South-Western and Northern Nigeria, 1907-1937, School of Oriental and African Studies Ph.D. thesis, London 1987.

Duffield, I.: Dusé Mohammed Ali and the Development of Pan-Africanism, 1866-1945, University of Edinburgh Ph.D. thesis, Edinburgh 1972.

Edwards, N.: Cadbury on the Gold Coast, Cadbury Ltd., ms. 1955.

Ehrlich, C.: Marketing Boards in Retrospective - Myth and Reality, in: Edinburgh University Centre of African Studies, African Public Sector Economies. Proceedings of a Seminar, Edinburgh 1971.

Essang, S.M.: The Distribution of Earnings in the Cocoa Economy of Western Nigeria: Implications for Development, Michigan State University Ph.D. thesis, Michigan 1970.

Falola, T.: Lebanese Traders in South-Western Nigeria, 1900-1960, paper presented at the School of Oriental and African Studies, African History Seminar, 31 May 1989.

Fieldhouse: D.K., War and the Origins of the Gold Coast Cocoa Marketing Board, 1939-40, unpublished draft paper, July 1989.

Füllberg-Stolberg, K.: Nordnigeria während der Weltwirtschaftkrise 1929-1939, University of Hannover Ph.D. thesis, Hannover 1988.

Garlick, P.C.: African and Levantine Trading Firms in Ghana, paper presented at the Nigerian Institute of Social and Economic Research Conference, Ibadan, December 1960, pp.119-131.

Gertzel, C.J.: John Holt: A British Merchant in West Africa in the Age of "Imperialism", University of Oxford D.Phil thesis, Oxford 1960.

Goddall, M.: French Marketing in the Ivory Coast: A Historical Survey, paper presented at the African Studies Centre, International Seminar on Marketing Boards in Tropical Africa, Leiden, 19-23 Sept.1983.

Goldsworthy, D.: Contemplating Decolonization: Some Policy Dilemmas of the Churchill and Eden Governments, 1951-7, paper presented at the School of Oriental and African Studies African History Seminar, 26 Oct. 1988.

Gordon-Walker, S.: British Firms and Officials, and the Debate over the Nowell Commission Report on the Marketing of Cocoa in Nigeria and the Gold Coast, School of Oriental and African Studies M.A. thesis, London 1983.

Graham, R.W.: American Imperial Interests in West Africa During the Second World War, paper presented at the School of Oriental and African Studies Conference on Africa and the Second World War, London May 1984.

Graham, R.W.: American Perspectives on Decolonisation: The Case of Nigeria 1941-1960, paper presented at the University of Maiduguri, History Department, Maiduguri 1984.

Hanna, M.I.: Lebanese Emigrants in West Africa: Their Effect on Lebanon and West Africa, University of Oxford D.Phil. thesis, Oxford 1959.

Harneit-Sievers, A.: African Business, "Economic Nationalism", and British Colonial Policy: Southern Nigeria, 1935-1954, paper presented to the African Studies Association Meeting, Toronto 3-6 November, 1994

Harneit-Sievers, A.: African Traders, European Firms, and "Nationalism" in Nigeria in the Period of the Second World War, paper presented at Deutscher Historikertag, Trier, October 1986.

Harneit-Sievers, A.: Dependent Cocoa Buying in the Early 1950s - The Case of UAC Credit Produce Buyers in Nigeria, unpublished ms. deposited at the University of Hannover, History Department Library, Hannover 1987.

Harneit-Sievers, A.: A "Turning Point" between "Production Drive" and "Short Supply"? Remarks on the Political Economy of Nigeria During World War II, University of Hannover, History Department, Research Paper No.2, Sept.1987.

Harneit-Sievers, A.: Zwischen Depression und Dekolonisation: Afrikanische Händler und Politik in Süd-Nigeria, 1935-1954, Universität Hannover Ph.D. thesis, Hannover 1989.

Hesse, G.F.: Die West-afrikanischen Marketing Boards und ihre Bedeutung für die Entwicklungspolitik, Universität Hamburg Ph.D. thesis, Hamburg 1968.

Hinds, A.E.: Colonial Policy and the Processing of Groundnuts in Nigeria 1950-1952: The Case of Mr. Georges Calil, paper presented at the University of Dalhousie, History Department, 1986.

Hinds, A.: British Imperial Policy and the Development of the Nigerian Economy, University of Dalhousie Ph.D. thesis, Dalhousie 1985.

Hinds, A.: Imperial Policy and the Colonial Sterling Balances 1943- 1956, paper presented at the Institute of Commonwealth Studies seminar on Commonwealth History/Decolonization, London 22 Feb. 1990.

Holmes, A.B.: Economic and Political Organisations in the Gold Coast 1920-1945, University of Chicago Ph.D. thesis, Chicago 1972.

Hood, W.M.: Raw Cocoa Marketing in British West Africa, paper presented at the International Cocoa Conference, London 2 Oct. 1946, ms. deposited at the International Development Centre Library Oxford.

Hopkins, A.G.: An Economic History of Lagos, 1880-1914, University of London Ph.D. thesis, London 1964.

Horn, F.: Die Geschichte der Royal Niger Company von 1886-1900, Humboldt Universität zu Berlin Ph.D. thesis, Berlin 1986.

Idachaba, F.S.: Commodity Boards in Nigeria: A Crisis of Identity, paper presented at the African Studies Centre, International Seminar on Marketing Boards in Tropical Africa, Leiden, 19-23 Sept. 1983.

Jenkins, G.D.: Politics in Ibadan, North Western University Ph.D. thesis, Wisconsin 1965.

Jones, P.A., The United Africa Company in the Gold Coast/Ghana, 1920-1965, School of Oriental and African Studies Ph.D. thesis, London 1983.

Kent, J.: The International Dimensions of British West African Policy, 1939-49, University of Aberdeen Ph.D. thesis, Aberdeen 1985.

Kuiper, F.: Some Aspects of the Operations of Marketing Boards, Nigerian Institute of Social and Economic Research, Conference Proceedings, Ibadan, December 1958.

Lloyd, P.C.: The Impact of Local Government in the Yoruba Towns of Western Nigeria: An Analysis of the Parts Played Today by the Obas and Chiefs and by the New Groups of Traders and Literates, University of Oxford D.Phil. thesis, Oxford 1958.

Marshall, G.A.: Women, Trade and the Yoruba Family, University of Columbia Ph.D. thesis, Columbia 1963/64.

Martin, S.M.: The History of the Palm Oil Industry in South-Eastern Nigeria: The Case of the Ngwa Region, 1891-1929, University of Birmingham Ph.D. thesis, Birmingham 1984.

Mengersen, O. von: Lohnarbeit und Gewerkschaftsentwicklung in Nigeria in der Zwischenkriegszeit, University of Heidelberg, occasional papers, no.4, Heidelberg July 1989.

Meredith, D.G.: The British Government and Colonial Economic Development, with Particular Reference to British West Africa, 1919-1939, University of Exeter Ph.D. thesis, Exeter 1976.

Miles, J.: Cocoa Marketing in the Gold Coast and the African Producer, 1919-39. With Special Reference to the Hold-up Movements, University of London Ph.D. thesis, London 1978.

Misra, D.M.: The Lebanese in Nigeria, 1890-1960, University of Calabar Ph.D. thesis, Calabar 1985.

Misra, D.M.: Public Reaction to the Lebanese Presence in Nigeria during the Colonial Period, paper presented to the Conference on Lebanese Emigration, 11-13 September 1989.

Muhammad, K.: The Working of Nigerian Marketing Boards as a Means to Economic Development, paper presented at the Institute of Social Studies, Le Hague June 1965.

Nordman, C.R.: Prelude to Decolonisation in West Africa: The Development of British Colonial Policy 1938-1947, University of Oxford D.Phil. thesis, Oxford 1976.

Ojowu, J.O.: Technological Transformation in Nigerian Agriculture: An Analysis of the Nigerian Agricultural Development Policies, Including the Role of the Marketing Boards, University of Connecticut, Ph.D. thesis, Connecticut 1980.

Olayemi, J.K.: Peasant Cocoa Industry in Western Nigeria: An Economic Analysis, McGill University Ph.D. thesis, Montreal 1970.

Olomola, G.O.: Nigeria's Involvement in the Second World War, 1939-1946, University of Ife, History Department M.A. thesis, Ife 1972.

Oni, O.: An Economic Analysis of the Provincial and Aggregate Supply Response among Western Nigerian Cocoa Farmers, University of Ibadan Ph.D. thesis, Ibadan 1971.

Pearce, R.D.: The Evolution of British Colonial Policy towards Tropical Africa, 1938-48, University of Oxford D.Phil. thesis, Oxford 1978.

Rathbone, R.J.A.R.: The Transfer of Power in Ghana, 1945-57, University of London Ph.D. thesis, London 1968.

Richards, P.: Ideas, Environment and Agricultural Change: A Case Study from Western Nigeria, University of London Ph.D. thesis, London 1977.

Rimmer, D.: Markets and Marketing in West Africa: Proceedings of a Seminar, University of Edinburgh, Centre of African Studies, 1966.

Rimmer, D.: The Public Sector in West Africa, proceedings of a seminar on African Public Sector Economies at the University of Edinburgh, Centre of African Studies, 27th and 28th Nov., 1970.

Shuckburgh, J.: Colonial Civil History of the War, unpublished Colonial Office ms. deposited at the Institute of Commonwealth Studies Library, London 1946.

Souter, D.: Labour Policy in Nigeria during the Second World War and Conscription for the Nigerian Tin-Mining Industry, paper presented at the Conference on Africa and the Second World War, School of Oriental and African Studies, London May 1984.

Souter, D.: Colonial Labour Policy and Labour Conditions in Nigeria, 1939-1945, University of Oxford D.Phil thesis, Oxford 1980.

Southall, R.J.: Cadbury on the Gold Coast, 1907-1938: The Dilemma of the "Model Firm" in a Colonial Economy, University of Birmingham Ph.D. thesis, Birmingham 1975.

Stockwell, S.: British Business, Politics, and Decolonization in the Gold Coast, c.1945-1960, University of Oxford D. Phil. thesis, Oxford 1993.

Thomas, C.C.M.: Colonial Government Propaganda and Public Relations and the Administration in Nigeria, 1939-1951, University of Cambridge D.Phil. thesis, Cambridge 1986.

Twaddle, M.: Decolonisation: A New Historiographical Debate, paper presented at the Institute of Commonwealth Studies seminar, London 17 Jan. 1985.
Uchegbu, B.O.: The Routine of Colonial Anti-Nationalist Propaganda in British West Africa, University of New York Ph.D. thesis, New York 1978.
Van Hear, N.: Northern Labour and the Development of Capitalist Agriculture in Ghana University of Birmingham Ph.D. thesis, Birmingham 1982.
Westcott, N.J.: The Impact of the Second World War on Tanganyika, 1939-50, University of Cambridge D.Phil. thesis, Cambridge 1982.
Westcott, N.J.: Sterling and Empire: The British Imperial Economy, 1939-1951, paper presented at the Institute of Commonwealth Studies seminar on Decolonization in the 20th Century, London 20 Jan. 1983.
Westcott, N.J.: The Slippery Slope: Economic Control in Africa During the Second World War, paper presented at the Third World Economic History Group Workshop, London, 4 Jan.1990.
Williams, G.: The Political Sociology of Western Nigeria, 1939-1965, University of Oxford B.Phil thesis, Oxford 1967.
Williams, G.: Inequalities in Rural Nigeria, occasional paper, University of East Anglia, School of Development Studies, Norwich 1981.
Williams, G.: Garveyism, Akinpelu Obisesan and his Contemporaries: Ibadan 1920-22, paper presented at St. Peter's College, Nigerian Research Seminar, Oxford 10 Oct. 1988.
Williams, G.: J. Akinpelu Obisesan: A Biographical Essay, paper presented at St. Peter's College seminar, Oxford Nov.1988.
Zachernuk, P.: Nigerian Socialism. Olafemi Awolowo's Economic Thought in Historical Perspective, paper presented at the University of Alberta Canadian Association of African Studies Annual Conference, Alberta 7th-9th May 1987.
Zachernuk, P.: The Economic Programme of the Southern Nigerian Intelligentsia, 1920-1960, paper presented at the Canadian Association of African Studies Annual Meeting, Kingston, Ontario 11-14 May 1988.
Zachernuk, P.: Intellectuel Life in a Colonial Context: The Nigerian Intelligentsia, 1860-1960, University of Toronto Ph. D. thesis, Toronto 1991.

FORSCHUNGSSCHWERPUNKT MODERNER ORIENT

ARBEITSHEFTE

Nr. 1 ANNEMARIE HAFNER/ JOACHIM HEIDRICH/ PETRA HEIDRICH:

Indien: Identität, Konflikt und soziale Bewegung

Nr. 2 HEIKE LIEBAU:

Die Quellen der Dänisch-Halleschen Mission in Tranquebar in deutschen Archiven. Ihre Bedeutung für die Indienforschung

Nr. 3 JÜRGEN HERZOG:

Kolonialismus und Ökologie im Kontext der Geschichte Tansanias - Plädoyer für eine historische Umweltforschung (herausgegeben von Achim von Oppen)

Nr. 4 GERHARD HÖPP:

Arabische und islamische Periodika in Berlin und Brandenburg, 1915 - 1945. Geschichtlicher Abriß und Bibliographie

Nr. 5 DIETRICH REETZ:

Hijrat: The Flight of the Faithful. A British file on the Exodus of Muslim Peasants from North India to Afghanistan in 1920

Nr. 6 HENNER FÜRTIG:

Demokratie in Saudi-Arabien? Die Āl Saʿūd und die Folgen des zweiten Golfkrieges

Nr. 7 THOMAS SCHEFFLER:

Die SPD und der Algerienkrieg (1954-1962)

Nr. 8 ANNEMARIE HAFNER (Hg.):

Essays on South Asian Society, Culture and Politics

Nr. 10 UTE LUIG/ ACHIM VON OPPEN (Hg.):

Naturaneignung in Afrika als sozialer und symbolischer Prozeß